Mass Culture and Italian Society
from Fascism to the Cold War

Mass Culture and Italian Society from Fascism to the Cold War

David Forgacs and Stephen Gundle

Indiana University Press
BLOOMINGTON AND INDIANAPOLIS

This book is a publication of

Indiana University Press
601 North Morton Street
Bloomington, IN 47404-3797 USA

http://iupress.indiana.edu

Telephone orders   800-842-6796
Fax orders   812-855-7931
Orders by e-mail   iuporder@indiana.edu

The paper used in this publication meets the minimum
requirements of American National Standard for Information Sciences—Permanence of Paper for Printed Library
Materials, ANSI Z39.48-1984.

Manufactured in the United States of America

Library of Congress Cataloging-in-Publication Data

Forgacs, David.
    Mass culture and italian society from fascism to the
cold war / David Forgacs and Stephen Gundle.
        p.   cm.
    Includes bibliographical references and index.
    ISBN-13: 978-0-253-34981-1 (cloth : alk. paper)
    ISBN-13: 978-0-253-21948-0 (pbk. : alk. paper) 1. Mass
media—Italy—History—20th century. 2. Mass media—
Political aspects—Italy—History—20th century. I. Gundle,
Stephen, 1956- II. Title.
    P92.I8F67 2007
    302.230945′09044—dc22
                                           2007026933

1 2 3 4 5 12 11 10 09 08 07

CONTENTS

PREFACE AND ACKNOWLEDGMENTS

Fulvio M., born in 1927 in Borgata Gordiani, Rome, begins his life story like this:

If I have to talk about my life, say something about my family, yes, my father died in 1936 and left my mother with four small children and she made lots and lots of sacrifices and then she died too, after the bombing of San Lorenzo and the effects it had. She had been trapped under a building and her heart started beating badly and then I lost her too. There were four of us small children, the eldest was eleven, my elder brother. And he had to make lots of sacrifices because there was a regime that didn't pay any welfare, so there we were in this *borgata* [new housing district], because they sent all poor people to these *borgate,* workers from the city center, because they had demolished all the poor people's houses to make wide roads, things like that, and they exiled everyone to these conglomerations. Then gradually as we started growing up our culture was that of reading a lot of books that we passed around among us. The same book may have been read by as many as ten or fifteen people to save money. Because there was no television. Then . . . we started working . . . and we had a little bit of money to go and have fun on Saturday or Sunday, so we went dancing. We came back . . . on foot from a long way away because we had no money left so we didn't even take the tram. Then it was bad at work, because of the bosses . . . . The workers were not protected by a union, but then the workers started to win victories, things that raised our standard of living a bit, and we began buying a newspaper and doing cultural activities, sport.

The story continues for an hour of recording, forty pages of transcription. It is one of 117 life narratives that we collected from different people in various parts of Italy to find out about their cultural consumption from the late 1930s to the early 1950s. During the first stage of each interview, we began with a short explanation of our research. Then we asked all the interviewees to tell us about their life generally in these years. Some of them, like Fulvio M., produced a narrative that flowed almost imperceptibly into stories about cultural consumption and recreation. Others said less about these things, but their life stories gave us an outline that helped us, in a second stage of the interview, to intervene with more focused questions from a list we had prepared. People told us their memories of filmgoing—how often they went to the cinema, what they saw, where they sat, which actors they remembered. They recalled when and where they first heard a radio and what they listened to. Those who read books or magazines talked about what they read and how they read: on their own, silently, or with someone reading out loud. Women told us where they got their ideas about fashion, when they first wore new styles or put on makeup, and how their families reacted. Men and women both talked about how people behaved in dance halls. The stories we collected were very varied. Some interviewees gave detailed accounts of their consumption of a whole range of cultural products. Others were more reticent or they submerged their accounts of these things within the stories that they preferred to tell: of being evacuated during the war, deaths of parents or children, political activism, work or hardship.

The oral history interviews were part of a research project called "Cultural Industries, Governments, and the Public in Italy, 1938–1954," from which this book ultimately derives, and which has also yielded several interim publications. The project also involved interviews with individuals who had worked in publishing or the record business and visits to archives in Italy and the United States.

The history of this project goes back a long way. The original research was funded in 1991–94 by a grant from the United Kingdom's Economic and Social Research Council (ESRC) to the University of Cambridge, where David Forgacs was then based. Stephen Gundle (then at University College, Oxford) was an equal partner in the project, and Dr. Marcella Filippa (University of Turin) coordinated the oral history interviews. After the end of the project's grant period, we analyzed the interviews closely and did further research to fill in gaps.

The original project's aims were to examine the relations between cultural production, consumption, and political power during the period from the late 1930s through the early 1950s; to collect a substantial body of new information about mass culture and Italian society in those years; and to use oral history to elicit evidence about cultural consumption. We deliberately chose a period that cut across the change of regime from Fascism to the Republic in order to test a hypothesis about continuity. It is generally agreed that the events of 1940–48—World War II, occupation and resistance, liberation, and the Constituent Assembly—split our period into two separate eras in political terms. Yet we wondered whether the operations of cultural firms—the types of products they sold, their approach to markets, their relations with governments—as well as popular cultural consumption might not be shown to have had substantial continuities over the whole period. We also wanted to understand the extent of continuity in the state and in the voluntary associations in civil society, including parish organizations and political parties, in their relations with mass culture. Our intention was not to adhere rigidly to the continuity hypothesis but to use it as a frame for inquiry and to remain open to evidence that might contradict or falsify it.

We chose a start date in the late 1930s (we later moved it back to 1936 to encompass the creation of the Ministry of Popular Culture in 1937) because this was a time when the Fascist regime began to intervene in culture in a more directive way. It was also when modern cultural forms—glossy magazines, talking pictures, mass radio broadcasts—were starting to develop. We decided to set an end point in 1954, not only because this took us well into the Republic and the Cold War (it was when Alcide De Gasperi, political leader of the postwar period, died) but also because it was the year when a regular television service started and after which a new phase of mass culture, and of the Italian media system, began. The start and end dates, in other words, were significant both politically and in the history of mass culture.

One of the things that drew us to this research was dissatisfaction with existing work on the subject. Most of it described the period and its culture with concepts and paradigms that seemed to us inaccurate or simplistic and, when put together, did not fit to make a coherent picture. On the one hand Fascism was presented as a "mass society," with popular culture harnessed to the "organization of consent"; on the other hand, Italy in the 1930s and 40s was described as having "artisanal" culture industries, and Italian society in the 1950s was seen as living under a benighted clerico-conservative regime that retarded its cultural modernization. Many of these descriptions of mass culture and Italian society were made by historians whose main interests were in other areas, such as the political system or the economy, and who looked only casually and incidentally at culture. Those who did specialize in cultural history tended to focus largely on high culture and on intellectuals and to deal summarily with popular and mass culture—that is, with the cultural forms with which the majority of the population came into contact.

We believed not only that these descriptions were reductive but that they were often based on careless generalizations and a lack of good evidence. What, after all, was actually known about "mass culture" at the level of individual cultural firms? What was known about the operations of different parts of the state in relation to mass culture: not just regarding censorship and propaganda but also in giving support to cultural industries, helping them export, protecting them from foreign competition? Above all, what was known about consumers, popular taste, and everyday patterns of consumption? Had anyone actually asked people what music they listened to, what films they saw, and what had stuck in their memory? We set out to address these questions and set up a project that would help us answer them.

This project, as we said, goes back a long way. Fulvio M.'s life story was recorded on October 29, 1991, and the book was sent to the publisher in 2006. Fifteen years from the start of a project to publication of its findings is a long time, even by the standards of academic research. There are several reasons why it has taken so long. The main ones are that the project generated a very large amount of material, particularly in the form of interviews (over 200 hours of recordings, nearly 4,000 pages of transcripts), which required much time and patience to process; that the two authors had demanding university jobs and personal lives; and that we sometimes allowed other, shorter-term research commitments to jump ahead of this one. Both of us are used to working fairly quickly, and the longevity of this project has been a source of frustration for us as well as of humor and ironic, reciprocal banter. Clearly, there have been negative effects. A quarter of our interviewees were already over seventy-five years old when we recorded them, and many have since died. We greatly regret that we cannot show them how we have used their testimonies and thank them again directly for their help. Hearing these recordings or rereading the transcripts now has a particular poignancy for us. It at once evokes the memory of the live interview and resonates uncannily, like hearing the voice of a dead person left on an answering machine. And yet by leaving the interviews sealed up and publishing them only now, we found that we had unwittingly preserved their freshness. We hope that the passages we have quoted from the interviews will convey something of this quality to the reader and give them a sense of the living speaker. At the same time, the gap between initial research and publication has had a number of positive effects. Our judgments of the period, of the material we collected, and of our own earlier assumptions and methods have changed and matured over the years. We have benefited from reading work published by others, as well as from rereading, criticizing, and rethinking our own earlier drafts. In all these respects, the book we offer here has benefited from its long gestation.

The book is divided, after the introduction, into three parts. Part 1, "Cultural Consumption and Everyday Life," draws extensively on our oral history project, as well as on other sources, and attempts to tell the story of mass culture in the period "from below." Part 2, "Cultural Industries and Markets," draws, by contrast, mainly on the research we carried out on cultural firms, using archival and published sources, and it shows how the main cultural industries operated in relation both to markets and political forces over the period as a whole. Part 3, "Politics and Mass Culture," looks at the world of mass culture from the point of view of the state and of forces in civil society, and in the latter case (chapter 8) incorporates again some of the oral testimonies. The three parts represent three different perspectives on the same reality: the increasing diffusion of mass culture in a society in transition to economic, political, and bureaucratic modernity.

The writing of the book has been very much a shared task. We designed the overall structure together and each of us read and commented at every stage on the other's drafts and revisions. Chapters 2, 6, 7, and the conclusion were written by both authors. However, the introduction and chapters 1 and 3 were primarily the work of David Forgacs and chapters 4, 5, and 8 were written mainly by Stephen Gundle. Most of the material in the book is previously unpublished, with the exception of the section on Disney and Mondadori in chapter 3, which originally appeared in a longer version as part of David Forgacs, "Uomini e topi: la connessione Disney-Mondadori nella ricostruzione," in *Hollywood in Europa. Industria, politica, pubblico del cinema 1945–1960*, ed. David W. Ellwood and Gian Piero Brunetta (Florence: Ponte alle Grazie, 1991), 172–85; and parts of chapter 5, which have appeared in Stephen Gundle, "Film Stars and Society in Fascist Italy," in *Re-viewing Fascism: Italian Cinema 1922–43*, ed. Piero Garofalo and Jacqueline Reich (Bloomington: Indiana University Press, 2002), 315–39. Some of the general findings of Parts 2 and 3 of the book were summarized in David Forgacs, "Industria culturale, politica e pubblico in Italia, 1936–1954," in *Polis: Ricerche e Studi su Società e Politica in Italia* 14, no. 2 (August 2000): 213–34; and his "How Exceptional Were Culture-State Relations in Twentieth-Century Italy?" in *Culture, Censorship and the State in Twentieth-Century Italy*, ed. Guido Bonsaver and Robert S. C. Gordon (Oxford: Legenda, 2005). Other publications by David Forgacs arising from the original research project are "Americanization: The Italian Case, 1938–1954," in *Americanization and the Transformation of World Cultures*, ed. P. H. Melling and D. J. Roper (London: Edward Mellen, 1996), 81–96; "Postwar Italian Culture: Renewal or Legacy of the Past?" in *Reconstructing the Past: Representations of the Fascist Era in Post-War European Culture*, ed. Graham Bartram, Maurice Slawinski, and David Steel (Keele, UK: Keele University Press, 1996), 49–63; and "The Mass Media and the Question of a National Community in Italy," in *The Politics of Italian National Identity*, ed. Gino Bedani and Bruce Haddock (Cardiff: University of Wales Press, 2000), 142–62. Some of the data in the tables were previously collected and elaborated by David Forgacs in his essay and statistical survey "Spettacolo: teatro e cinema," in *Guida all'Italia contemporanea, 1861–1997*, Vol. 4, *Comportamenti sociali e cultura*, ed. Massimo Firpo, Pier Giorgio Zunino, and Nicola Tranfaglia (Milan: Garzanti, 1998), 203–94. Other publications by Stephen Gundle arising in part from the original project are "Feminine Beauty, National Identity and Political

Conflict in Postwar Italy, 1945–54," *Contemporary European History* 8, no. 3 (1999): 359–78; "L'età d'oro dello star system," in *Storia del cinema mondiale* 2, *tome* 1, *Gli Stati Uniti*, ed. Gian Piero Brunetta (Turin: Einaudi, 1999), 695–744; "Memory and Identity: Popular Culture in Postwar Italy," in *Italy Since 1945*, ed. Patrick McCarthy (Oxford: Oxford University Press, 2000), 183–96; "Visions of Prosperity: Consumerism and Popular Culture in Italy from the 1920s to the 1950s," in *Three Postwar Eras in Comparison: Western Europe 1918–1945–1989*, ed. Carl Levy and Mark Roseman (London: Palgrave, 2001), 151–72; also in an Italian version: "Immagini della prosperità," in *Il Pci nell'Italia repubblicana*, ed. Roberto Gualtieri (Rome: Carocci, 2002), 253–84.

We are grateful to the institutions that helped fund and support the research: the ESRC for the major grant that supported the fieldwork and the other initial work in Italy and the United States, the University of Cambridge for giving a further two terms' leave to David Forgacs, and University College, Oxford, for providing funding for Stephen Gundle to visit the Harry Ransom Humanities Research Center at the University of Texas in Austin, Texas in 1993. Stephen Gundle also wishes to express his gratitude to the British Academy for a small personal research award on "Cinema and Society in Italy, 1930–1960," which allowed him to undertake supplementary library and archival work in Italy between 1997 and 2000.

In a project as long and complex as this one we have accumulated many debts of thanks to individuals. First of all, we want to recognize the fundamental contribution of Marcella Filippa, who not only coordinated the oral history interviews and helped us devise the questionnaire but also conducted thirty-nine of the interviews herself, organized the work of transcription, and produced the first analysis of the findings. Marcella's professionalism, experience in oral history, and constructive suggestions and criticisms were invaluable assets at this stage of the research. Her presentation of the oral history project is included in the appendices at the end of this book. Marcella also carried out the initial research on the radio, music, and record industries and her thoughtful reflections on the oral testimonies influenced some of our observations in the introduction and in chapters 1 and 2. We are also very grateful to Paola Pallavicini, who carried out with great commitment and skill a further fifty-three interviews, including all the ones in Calabria, Sardinia, and Trentino and some of those in Piedmont and Valle d'Aosta. We want to thank all those who gave us advice and critical feedback on the oral history project, or who acted as mediators to put us in touch with people to interview: Anna Anfossi, Manlio Brigaglia, Rosalba Dondeynaz, Mirella Grenzi, Paolo Jedlowski, Diego Leoni, Lucio Levrini, Albina Malerba, Luisa Mulas, Peppino Ortoleva, Giangiacomo Ortu, Luisa Passerini, Lidia Piccioni, Katia

Pizzi, Armando Pomatto, Alessandro Portelli, Renate Siebert, Fausto Viccaro, Gianni Vizio, Camillo Zadra, Katia Zumpano, and Antonella Zuncheddu. Lidia Sinchetto and Giuseppina Pertusio did the invaluable work of transcribing the interviews.

The following helped us with access to archival material: Gianluigi Mariani, Franco Caldara, and Daniele Sironi at the Fondazione Arnoldo e Alberto Mondadori (Milan); Luisa Gandolfi at the historical archive of Bompiani (Milan); Angela Pecchio at the Archivio Einaudi (Turin); Vito Laterza and Tonina Sollecito at the Archivio Storico Laterza (Bari); Gabriella Di Cagno for the commercial records of Vallecchi (Calenzano); Gloria Manghetti and Margherita Ghilardi at the Archivio Contemporaneo Gabinetto Vieusseux (Florence); Marina Giannetto at the Archivio Centrale dello Stato (Rome); Maria Liberatrice Vicentini at the Archivio Storico Diplomatico of the Ministero degli Affari Esteri (Rome); Charles Bell at the Harry Ransom Humanities Research Center at the University of Texas (Austin); Ned Comstock at the Cinema and Television Library of the University of Southern California (Los Angeles); and Kristine Krueger at the National Film Information Service at the American Academy of Motion Picture Arts and Sciences (Los Angeles). Gian Piero Brunetta, Barbara Corsi, David Ellwood, Alberto Farassino, Paul Ginsborg, Franco Minganti, Paul Swann, and Albertina Vittoria all offered helpful advice during the operational phase of this project. Denis Mack Smith kindly loaned Stephen Gundle many books from his personal library relating to the themes of the project. For help in locating photographic illustrations we should like to thank Lucio Levrini, Roberto Palmas, and Father Antonio Toso. We are grateful to Mauro Bianchi at the SIAE and to Gian Luca Corradi at the Biblioteca Nazionale Centrale in Florence for their help in supplying data for some of the tables.

Various individuals, some of whom, sadly, like those in our oral history project, are no longer alive, kindly gave us valuable interviews at the start of the project on their personal recollections of working for or in collaboration with various cultural firms in our period: Orlando Bernardi (Mondadori), Valentino Bompiani (Mondadori and Bompiani), Piero Bigongiari, Maria Luigia Guaita, Mario Luzi, Geno Pampaloni (Vallecchi), Giulio Bollati and Roberto Cerati (Einaudi), Roberto Bonchio (Editori Riuniti), Franco Crepax (VCM), and Alessandro Ferraù (*Cinespettacolo*). Stefano Guidi and Gilberto Tinacci Mannelli helped arrange the interviews on the history of Vallecchi. Franco Fortini, who died in 1994, and Giulio Einaudi, who died in 1999, were both invaluable mediators for the interviews at Einaudi.

In the preparation of the book for publication we are grateful to the two anonymous readers for Indiana University Press who reviewed the manuscript and offered support and constructive suggestions for revision; to our editors at the Press, Michael Lundell and Jane Behnken; to our copy editor, Karen Kodner; and to Eleanor Chiari for her help with revision and checking of bibliographical references. David Forgacs would like to thank Rachele Tardi for her valuable help in the last stages of preparation of the text for publication.

Lastly, we want to record our special thanks to all the people who agreed to be interviewed for the oral history project. We remember them all with affection and gratitude for the time they gave us and the memories they shared with us. This book would not have been possible without them.

LIST OF ABBREVIATIONS

AA	Artisti Associati
AC	Azione Cattolica
ACLI	Associazioni Cristiane Lavoratori Italiani
AFHQ	Allied Force Headquarters
ANICA	Associazione Nazionale Industrie Cinematografiche e Affini
API	Anonima Periodici Mondadori
ATAC	Azienda Tranvie Comune di Roma
BBC	British Broadcasting Corporation (originally British Broadcasting Company)
BMM	Biblioteca Moderna Mondadori
BNCF	Biblioteca Nazionale Centrale Firenze
BUR	Biblioteca Universale Rizzoli
CBS	Columbia Broadcasting System
CCC	Centro Cattolico Cinematografico
CGIL	Confederazione Generale Italiana del Lavoro
CLN	Comitato di Liberazione Nazionale
COLIP	Cooperativa del Libro Popolare
CONI	Comitato Olimpico Nazionale Italiano
CSC	Centro Sperimentale di Cinematografia
DC	Democrazia Cristiana
DGG	Deutsche Grammophon Gesellschaft
DGPS	Direzione Generale di Pubblica Sicurezza
DLL	Decreto Legge Luogotenenziale
EIAR	Ente Italiana Audizioni Radiofoniche
EMI	Electric and Musical Industries
ENAL	Ente Nazionale Assistenza Lavoratori
ENEL	Ente Nazionale per l'Energia Elettrica
ENIC	Ente Nazionale Industrie Cinematografiche
ENIT	Ente Nazionale Italiano per il Turismo
EPT	Ente Provinciale per il Turismo
ERR	Ente Radio Rurale

FNFIS	Federazione Nazionale Fascista degli Industriali dello Spettacolo
GATT	General Agreement on Tariffs and Trade
GIAC	Gioventù Italiana di Azione Cattolica
GUF	Gruppi Universitari Fascisti
IFE	Italian Film Export
IMF	International Monetary Fund
IRCE	Istituto nazionale per le Relazioni Culturali con l'Estero
IRI	Istituto per la Ricostruzione Industriale
Istat	Istituto Nazionale di Statistica
MCP	Ministero della Cultura Popolare
MGM	Metro-Goldwyn-Mayer
MPAA	Motion Picture Association of America
MPEA	Motion Picture Export Association
MPPDA	Motion Picture Producers and Distributors of America
NBC	National Broadcasting Company
OGAM	Officine Grafiche Arnoldo Mondadori
ONB	Opera Nazionale Balilla
ONC	Opera Nazionale Combattenti
OND	Opera Nazionale Dopolavoro
PCA	Production Code Administration
PCI	Partito Comunista Italiano
PNF	Partito Nazionale Fascista
PSIUP	Partito Socialista Italiano di Unita Proletaria
PWB	Psychological Warfare Branch
RAI	Radio Audizioni Italia
RAM	Roach And Mussolini
RCA	Radio Corporation of America
RSI	Repubblica Sociale Italiana
SIAE	Società Italiana Autori e Editori
SIP	Società Idroelettrica Piemontese
SIPRA	Società Italiana Pubblicità Radiofonica e Affini
UA	United Artists
UISP	Unione Italiana Sport Per tutti
UNESCO	United Nations Educational, Scientific, and Cultural Organization
URI	Unione Radiofonica Italiana
UTET	Unione Tipografico-Editrice Torinese
VCM	La Voce del Padrone-Columbia-Marconiphone

**Mass Culture and Italian Society
from Fascism to the Cold War**

Introduction

CULTURE, PLACE, AND NATION

This book is a study of a relatively early phase in the development of modern mass culture and cultural consumption in Italy, from the mid 1930s to the mid 1950s. It has two main aims. The first is to show that this period, often seen both by historians and in popular representations as a sort of primitive forerunner of the era of mass culture that would erupt in the 1960s, was in fact itself a decisive stage in the slow gestation of that era. The second aim is to describe the relationships in this period between mass culture, political power, and collective behavior and to propose a different account of them from those that have prevailed up to now. The most common way of expressing these relationships has been functionalist or instrumental. Mass culture and the media have been seen primarily as tools to shape public opinion and promote consent, first in the Fascist regime, then under the Christian Democrat governments of the Cold War, while mass leisure has been seen as serving in the long run to integrate people into a more consumerist way of life. This view has had a strong grip on both popular and elite attitudes to the media in Italy, not only because of the well-known involvement of successive governments, parties, and individual politicians in the press and broadcasting but also because of an established tradition of media studies that has given prominence to such political interferences. The recent intertwining of political power, media ownership, and control in the election campaigns and governments led by Silvio Berlusconi in 1994 and 2001–2006 has led some commentators to interpret this as simply the latest and most extreme phase of a process rooted way back in the past. There is also a widely shared view, sometimes stated overtly, sometimes just implied, that with the development of mass culture and high levels of consumption, as living standards rose and class antagonisms were attenuated, people became more complacent and passive.

In contrast with these views, we show in this book that mass culture had other social functions and effects than those of political integration from above or the encouragement of apathy and passivity. In particular, mass culture set in motion two processes that worked in opposing directions during the period under analysis. First, certain media and media products—radio programs, recorded music, cinema newsreels, magazine photographs—helped make Italian society more visible and audible to its own members. This process was accompanied by a wider public perception of national politics and an increased participation in national occasions such as sporting events or song festivals. Second, the media and mass culture put in circulation words, sounds, and images from other societies and these fueled private aspirations and desires, changed perceptions of what were deemed acceptable sexual behavior and gender roles, and drove a wedge between generations, helping to create new social demarcations. In other words, mass culture functioned "disintegratively" as well as "integratively." This limited its efficacy as an instrument of political consensus-formation and also meant that its social function was not always conservative.

As we argue, this has significant implications for our understanding both of this period of Italian history and of the way modern mass culture interacts with political power more generally. For one thing it means that a view that has recently enjoyed a resurgence among some historians should be treated with caution: according to this view, the Fascist regime effectively shaped the mentality of the Italian people, or at the very least bound them into a transient emotional complicity, by creating a "lay religion" or, in its mass rallies, a "rite of communion."[1] Even in its most interventionist and repressive phase (examined in chapter 7 on the state), which lasted from the setting up of the Ministry of Popular Culture in 1937 to Mussolini's expulsion from office in July 1943, Fascist cultural policy always operated in an arena where other powerful forces were in play. These included, in the first place, the cultural industries—book and magazine publishing, film production and distribution, radio, the music business—and the commercial groups involved in them; and, in the second place, consumers themselves, who exercised their choices of cultural goods and activities increasingly through the market. Sometimes the interests of these groups converged with those of the Fascist elites, at other times they conflicted. The result was a complex web of negotiations, concessions, and compromises, as well as various, often tacit, forms of opposition, noncompliance, and resistance. The same applies to the postwar years, when the Christian Democrats, after their decisive electoral victory of April 1948, controlled all government posts and, from the early 1950s, began to extend their capillary influence in society. Here too the attempts by a political elite to impose a clear moral and political direction on cultural activities such as the cinema and the periodical press had to accommodate and eventually succumb to the power of the cultural industries and the rapidly evolving tastes of consumers, not to mention the political pragmatism of some of the Christian Democrat leaders themselves. As for people's attitudes to mass cultural products and collective rituals in this period, one should be wary of generalizing about them without first examining the available evidence. This evidence is by no means easy to collect and, once collected, to interpret. In particular one needs to avoid the methodological fallacy, particularly common in work on totalitarian and authoritarian states, of reading off the assumed effects of a ritual from the intentions of its organizers. We discuss this fallacy and the arguments against it in chapter 7.

What applies to governments and the state applies also to forces in civil society. The period covered by this book was one in which strong collective movements sought to direct the activities of large numbers of people outside the home and the workplace. The three most significant of these, in size and range of operations, were the mass-membership organizations of the Fascist Party, those of the Catholic movement, and, from the end of the war, those of the Italian Communist Party. The Catholic and Communist organizations both had their high points in terms of numbers of members in the 1950s. Yet, as we show in chapter 8, the forms of collective cultural activity, known in Italian as *associazionismo*, promoted by all these movements operated in a situation where the market was coming increasingly to deliver cultural goods and recreational services. The social movements too therefore had to organize themselves in relation to commercial mass culture and, in some cases, to compromise or modify their goals accordingly. The same general point may be made, therefore, about the Fascist regime, the postwar governments of the Christian Democrats, and the organized social and political movements, namely that their attempts to manage cultural life, to give it a national shape, a moral dimension, or a collective ethos, did have an impact, and this impact was sometimes significant, but it could also be cushioned or even counteracted by the workings of mass culture itself. An Italian popular culture did develop, as we demonstrate, but by and large it was the product not of autarkic protectionism, pastoral nurturing, or grassroots political activism but of a series of flows and exchanges of cultural goods between regions of Italy and between Italy and other countries.

It follows from this that certain conventional periodizations need to be reassessed. In the first place, the division that political historians of Italy normally make of the twentieth century into three distinct phases, marked by the prevailing type of state—Liberal up to 1922, Fascist to 1943 and (after the transitional period of the war years), Republic from 1946—does not really work for cultural history, and certainly not for the history of mass and popular culture. This is not only because there were significant continuities in the ownership, structure, and personnel of key cultural industries (see chapters 3–6) and in the forms of state regulation (chapter 7), from censorship to the broadcasting monopoly and the government subsidy of theater and cinema, but also because patterns of consumer behavior carried over from one political phase to the next (chapter 1). We do not seek to minimize the important differences that did exist between these phases, and we give them due weight in the discussion. In particular we stress that the political events that bisect our period—the collapse and defeat of Fascism, World War II, and the Resistance—brought some decisive cultural changes and, in particular, led to greater pluralism in the forms of commercial mass culture. However, we argue that, on balance, the continuities were more significant than the changes.

In the second place, as we stated at the beginning, we want to modify the commonly held view that the economic miracle (1958–1963) was a unique "great transformation" that served to divide an old, "traditional" or peasant society of low consumption from a "modern" society of mass consumption. When one examines consumption patterns more closely this view can be seen to distort the facts in two opposing directions. On the one hand it exaggerates the extent of the changes that took place in the miracle period itself, generalizing to society as a whole levels and patterns of consumption that before the 1970s were limited to particular social groups and regions; on the other, it represents Italian rural society up to the late 1950s as too uniformly "backward" and static and underestimates the extent to which cultural modernization had already begun to affect people outside the main cities. In the light of these objections, the period from 1936 to 1954 needs to be seen afresh as part of a longer wave of cultural modernization. We develop this point in more detail in chapter 1.

Mobility and Sense of Place

One way in which cultural impacts may be expressed is in terms of a changing geography of consumption. This involves movements both of cultural products to consumers and of consumers from one place to another, where they encounter new cultural products and associated forms of behavior. The way the movement of products affects consumption is fairly easy to demonstrate, and cinema may be used as an example for which readily available statistics allow a rough map to be drawn. The cinema was the most popular site of mass entertainment throughout our period. We know, according to the data collected by the Società Italiana Autori e Editori (SIAE), that sales of cinema tickets accounted in 1936 for 65 percent of total expenditure in Italy on paid entertainments. The proportion rose in the war years to a range of 74 to 76 percent and remained at around 70 percent in the early 1950s (Table 0.1). The SIAE's figures also give us a geographical profile of the audience. In 1951, 76 percent of tickets were sold in the North and Center and 24 percent in the mainland South and Islands (Sicily and Sardinia).[2] Up to the late 1940s around two-thirds of spectators were in cities and larger provincial towns and only a third were in small towns or villages, whereas after the war these proportions began to change (see Table 1.2, chapter 1). From the end of the 1950s to the early 1980s, as television took off in the cities, there were more film spectators outside main towns than in them. From other sources we know that foreign films made up the majority of those screened throughout our period (see Table 4.1, chapter 4). Most of the films released in Italy up till 1939, when the Monopoly Law (discussed in chapters 5 and 7) came into force, and again after 1945, when it was rescinded, were American, and in between these dates, although many more Italian films were made and released, French and British films, as well as German, Austrian, and Hungarian films were partially substituted for the absent American imports (Table 4.2, chapter 4). Put together, these sets of data allow us to plot, somewhat crudely, the flow of imported films into Italy and the size of the audience in different areas; and they serve as a baseline, but no more than that, for a subsequent analysis of the reactions of critics and audiences.

As for the movement of people, the way this involves changes in cultural consumption is less obvious and requires a more detailed explanation. Movement, in cultural terms, involves both increased mobility in physical space and, to use Joshua Meyrowitz's expression, changes in one's imagined "sense of place," that is, one's perception of where one is located socially in relation

Table o.1. Expenditure by public on commercial entertainments 1936–1954 in billions of lire (adjusted to 1985 prices).

	Theatre and Music		Cinema		Spectator Sports		Various*		Radio†		Total
	Amount	%	Amount	%	Amount	%	Amount	%	Amount	%	
1936	76.00	13.50	363.41	64.56	21.60	3.84	57.56	10.22	44.34	7.88	562.91
1937	74.26	12.10	396.85	64.66	23.44	3.82	70.75	11.53	48.43	7.89	613.73
1938	71.93	11.34	411.81	64.61	25.72	4.03	73.55	11.54	54.39	8.53	637.40
1939	80.73	12.69	401.29	63.08	27.60	4.34	65.58	10.31	60.93	9.58	636.13
1940	66.34	11.45	390.47	67.41	24.02	4.15	37.02	6.39	61.41	10.60	579.26
1941	60.31	9.96	449.87	74.27	18.39	3.04	13.72	2.26	63.44	10.47	605.73
1942	74.40	10.31	544.97	75.48	23.07	3.20	18.13	2.51	61.39	8.50	721.96
1943	40.81	9.79	318.19	76.37	12.00	2.88	9.95	2.39	35.71	8.57	416.66
1944	22.83	14.89	106.89	69.72	3.99	2.60	12.29	8.02	7.31	4.77	153.31
1945	34.12	12.84	192.78	72.55	11.87	4.47	19.28	7.25	7.67	2.89	265.72
1946	49.15	10.10	350.10	71.92	32.86	6.75	35.67	7.33	19.02	3.91	486.80
1947	55.27	8.53	450.99	69.62	48.66	7.51	62.47	9.64	30.42	4.70	647.81
1948	72.45	7.79	625.56	67.26	69.00	7.42	84.23	9.06	78.80	8.47	930.04
1949	82.15	7.26	783.21	69.25	78.87	6.97	96.49	8.53	90.38	7.99	1,131.10
1950	106.13	7.85	927.87	68.62	86.30	6.38	120.16	8.89	111.82	8.27	1,352.28
1951	101.18	7.23	976.42	69.74	86.49	6.18	116.20	8.30	119.71	8.55	1,400.00
1952	109.45	7.20	1,070.59	70.38	84.33	5.54	124.81	8.21	131.87	8.67	1,521.05
1953	115.72	6.91	1,186.07	70.82	92.49	5.52	133.49	7.97	146.94	8.78	1,674.71
1954	114.60	6.33	1,285.41	71.06	96.69	5.34	142.99	7.91	169.21	9.36	1,808.90

* Includes dance halls, fairs, amusement parks, circuses, exhibitions, and open-air events.

† Radio license fees. The figure for 1954 includes, for the first time, television licenses as well as radio. The dramatic fall in expenditure during the war years is largely accounted for by the difficulty of collecting the fees and does not imply a fall in radio listening.

Source: elaborated from *Lo spettacolo in Italia nel 1994* (Rome: SIAE, 1995), 8–9.

to others—family members, other generations and genders, members of other social groups, even whole societies elsewhere.[3] Migration provides us with a good example of how movement in these two senses affects the cultural consumption both of the migrants and of the communities of origin to which they sometimes returned. The great flows of migration out of poor rural areas of Italy, which began in the 1880s, both to other parts of the country and abroad, brought some striking new forms of cultural exchange. The "Americans" in Luigi Capuana's *Gli americani di Ràbbato* (1912), a book written for children, were emigrants and returnees from the United States who settled back in their Sicilian community of origin with their accumulated savings, gold teeth, and tales first of fabulous prosperity and then also of hostility and maltreatment, for instance in labor gangs. Emigration and return had changed irrevocably their perceptions of themselves and others around them. Although migration abroad was slowed down considerably during the Fascist period, internal migrations continued and even increased, despite the existence of penal sanctions against those who changed their place of residence without permission.[4] There were also flows of skilled labor, particularly of public employees and the professions, toward major centers of tertiary employment like Rome. For many of those who did not move permanently, there was an enhanced possibility of temporary movements to and from home because of the development of public and private transport, and an opening up to other parts of society through such "virtual windows" as the magazine photograph, the radio, and the cinema screen, which, taken together, produced a great increase in what John B. Thompson has called "mediated visibility."[5] All these movements, both physical and virtual, brought increased cultural exchange between different parts of Italy and with other countries beyond its borders and a partial erosion of cultural differences between regions and between localities. The single most significant index of this internal cultural exchange over the long term was the decline in the use of dialects and the development of varieties of spoken Italian as a language of everyday use. Similarly, the absorption of loan words into Italian, mainly from English and French, provided a record of cultural flows from outside Italy's borders.

These exchanges, and the changes in a perceived sense of place that they helped bring about, were to be highly significant. They served, for many people, particularly working-class people and peasants whose physical mobility was often limited, to redefine their sense of community by breaking down boundaries and enlarging their purviews in both a physical and a mental sense. The traditional boundaries of the local community were, for city dwellers, those between districts (*quartieri*) and, for the inhabitants of smaller towns and villages, the edges of the town or village: the latter were sometimes physically marked out by perimeter walls or by being located on a hilltop. For many people these boundaries functioned as real physical barriers, particularly in the prewar years, not only because poverty effectively limited their movement beyond them but also because to step outside them was to go into territory where they were not known and might not be accepted. The war itself both hardened and relaxed these boundaries: freedom to move was restricted in cities by curfews and, after September 1943, by military occupations and tighter policing; on the other hand, as a result of bombings and the severe economic crisis there were movements of people both out of cities as evacuees and into them in search of work. As a result, the war features in many urban life stories as a watershed between a less mobile and a more mobile world.

Arnaldo B., born in 1928, was one of the 117 people we interviewed in researching the first part of this book in order to help reconstruct a picture of cultural consumption in Italy in the period 1936–1954. He grew up in San Lorenzo, a district of about three square kilometers just outside the ancient city walls of Rome, which had first been developed and settled in the late 1870s, and which is conventionally described as physically enclosed on three of its four sides: the Labican walls (part of the old Roman walls built under the Emperor Aurelian); the railway line and rail yard (*scalo merci*) of Roma Termini (the main link between San Lorenzo and the Esquilino district on the other side of the railway lines was and is the tunnel under them known as the *arco di Santa Bibiana*); and the Cimitero del Verano.[6] The northwest boundary was more indeterminate, but for inhabitants of the district it either coincided with the Via Tiburtina or extended no more than a few blocks beyond it. In her book on San Lorenzo in the Fascist period, historian Lidia Piccioni claims that its quadrilateral shape "on the one hand physically isolates the district from the rest of the city, making it a veritable village [*paese*] within Rome, and on the other defines the environment in which the residents will conduct their economic activity."[7] Most of the inhabitants were locally employed: Arnaldo B. eventually took over his father's trade as a barber; many other people worked in the goods yard or in the artisan trades, such as stonecutting or carving, linked to the cemetery. One of the centers of social life in the *quartiere* was a few yards from Arnaldo's home: the Cinema Palazzo in Piazza dei Sanniti, a third-run (*terza visione*) movie theater with *avanspettacolo* (a live stage show between screenings), which had opened in 1929. Beyond the Santa Bibiana tunnel were other cinemas and theaters: the Ambra Jovinelli, the Politeama Margherita, and the Brancaccio, but Arnaldo never went to these. As a boy he and his friends played a game in the street where they marked imaginary cities on the ground with chalk and pretended to race from one to the other, "like they do in the Giro d'Italia [bicycle race]." However, "if we went beyond the Santa Bibiana tunnel it was an adventure because it seemed to be a different city from the one we were used to in San Lorenzo"

(19: 2–3).[8] "I once tried to cross beyond the Santa Bibiana tunnel, I got as far as Piazza Vittorio [about a kilometer away]; when I got there I had to stop a Fascist patrol and get them to bring me home because I had got lost" (19: 17). He did not go to the city center, about three kilometers away, until after the war.

I only saw Rome afterwards. It was an adventure; it was impossible to go there because who would bring you home again? . . . I once got on the number 10 [tram], which went down Via Tiburtina. I took this tram, I did the whole route because they told me this tram did a round trip and came back to the same place. I got on, paid the fare and did the whole route: Piazza Indipendenza, I saw the station, which seemed like a big adventure, as if I was dreaming America. . . . I did this trip and when I couldn't tell where the tram was going and couldn't remember where I had got on. I started to get worried and said to myself, "Now who's going to take me home?" (19: 17–18)

The testimony of Clorinda is equally striking. Born in 1923 in Providence, Rhode Island—her father was an emigrant worker and an antifascist—she returned from America with her family when she was six, got married in 1942, and settled in San Lorenzo. In the Allied bombing of July 19, 1943 her house was destroyed and her husband was killed. She remained with a newborn baby. She described her life then and subsequently as being bounded within the *quartiere:* "Even today when I go to the city center I ask the bus driver. 'I have to go to San Silvestro: can you tell me when I need to get off?' You can just imagine what it was like then" (66: 6). The first time she went to the center was after the war:

I went to the center to Via Veneto and it made me so angry to go there, I'm telling you the truth, because I saw all those bars, with all those tables outside, with all these people without a care in the world smoking, drinking, and all that, and there I was wearing clogs because I didn't have anything, no house, nothing, and like I said I was walking there, I was still very young, nineteen or just over, and I saw all these carefree people at the bar, whereas we had a load of worries inside us. (66: 7)

These descriptions may have become somewhat exaggerated in memory and in the retelling, and the perceived boundaries may consequently be over-dramatized. We know, for instance, that San Lorenzo during the Fascist period took in new residents from outside—white-collar workers on fixed incomes and migrant workers from the South—so the community was modified by contact with others.[9] Even so, the way people represent these boundaries in their retrospective accounts shows how large they loom in their subjectivity as symbolic markers of the difference between "then" and "now." It is the difference that recurs most frequently in all the life stories we collected: it emerges, unbidden, again and again when people recount their lives in terms of cultural activities involving "going out" (*uscire*) and "having fun" (*divertirsi*). One of the principal ways in which many people represent the *temporal* difference between then and now is in terms of this difference in *spatial* mobility and movement: then there was a world that was much less physically mobile; now space is more permeable; people are more mobile. This difference, moreover, repeatedly becomes correlated with others: between, on the one hand, a world where, particularly for girls and young women, one was much more under the surveillance of one's parents, where certain places were out of bounds, where certain activities, like dancing, were only permitted if one was chaperoned; and, on the other hand, a world where there is a lot of freedom (frequently expressed in old people's testimonies as "too much freedom"), more familiarity, more conflict between generations, less respect for old people.

Other sources present a similar picture. Vasco Pratolini's novel, *Il Quartiere*, written in 1943 and first published in 1945, is set in the Santa Croce district of Florence, where the author was born and grew up in a working-class family. The novel follows a group of neighborhood friends through their adolescence from 1932 to 1936 and is particularly attentive both to the symbolic meanings of place and to the way the characters' perceptions of place change over time. It starts by mapping out the limits of the district, which coincide with boundaries of class. The district extends east from the edge of the historic city center to Via Aretina, "the first middle-class houses and the villas," where the suburbs begin; south to the Arno; and north toward Piazza San Marco and the University: "But over here it was already a place for the rich people . . . deserted by the common people." The inhabitants of Santa Croce have a clear sense of their separateness not only from the center of Florence and the bourgeois districts and suburbs but also from the other working-class areas:

The city was on the other side of our republic, for us it was both like an archaeological site and an Eldorado: in order to take part in it we had to have a shave and wear our best clothes. We were divided from the other working-class districts by an imprecise but vivid sense of rivalry and emulation; as soon as we got together we split up again, fighting, by the Arno in the summer, football games on Sundays, the stage of the Giro d'Italia.[10]

Toward the end of the book, however, the young people's mobility beyond the district increases (some of them are called up to fight in the Abyssinian War; others move away) and some of the old boundaries and landmarks are broken up by a demolition and rebuilding program (*risanamento*).

If boundaries within cities became more permeable after World War II, the same is true for boundaries in rural areas, though the timing and the rate of change differed from place to place, depending on such variables as when public roads were asphalted, when a bus service began, how much contact there was with neighboring towns. In all cases, the "isolation" of a village was never absolute; it varied according to the amount of contact that the village, and different individuals within it, had with a wider world. The village of Burcei in Sardinia, for example, is on a hilltop 680 meters above sea level and thirty-eight kilometers from the coastal city and regional capital, Cagliari. Before mass motorization in the 1960s there were various ways in which one could get from Burcei to Cagliari and back: on foot, by bicycle (44: 25), on horseback (43: 16), by oxcart (*carro buoi*), by pony trap (*carretto col cavallino*), or by bus (*corriera*), which cost 10 lire, the equivalent of a day's agricultural wages. For some villagers Cagliari was, and still is, "another world." Desiderio P., born in 1926, described his first visit to Cagliari by bus:

I must have been about seven or eight, I had never been on a bus before, so for me this . . . was wonderful. I hoped the bus would never stop so that I could see the view, see all these things. I almost didn't get off, I didn't want to get off, arrive, it was like discovering another world. Perhaps for me it was like when the astronauts arrived on the moon. (42: 8)

Despite this perceived distance, there were various forms of contact and exchange both between Burcei and Cagliari and with nearby villages, such as Quartu. The teachers in the village school came from the city, rented houses, and resided in Burcei for nine months of the year; they are remembered as having introduced the villagers to Italian dances (*balli all'italiana*) where previously they had known only the Sardinian ones. During the war, evacuees (*sfollati*) from Cagliari became temporary residents and they too brought "city ways." In the 1960s, finally, major changes were effected by emigration. As Igino Q. put it:

We were still closed in this circle; then the villagers started to leave in the 1960s when there was the building boom in Milan, in northern Italy, and there was a total evacuation again. . . . In the 60s I got married and eventually I decided to leave too. I had a brother who lived in Italy [*in continente*, that is, on the Italian mainland] and who is still there and he was always saying to me: "Come here where it's different." Then, after the 60s, in the 70s there was the building boom in Cagliari, the tourist boom, and people left, but then they came back again. (43: 13)

As with the inhabitants of San Lorenzo in Rome and Santa Croce in Florence, we can establish a correlation from many of these testimonies between on the one hand increased mobility and exchanges with the world outside and on the other cultural changes within the community itself. As in other villages, the possibilities and patterns of movement inside Burcei were strongly sex-differentiated. On Sundays, for instance, girls would stand in the doorways of their houses; when they walked "out" it was to go to the morning and evening services in the church; boys and men could move around from door to door to court the girls (44: 5). For dances, girls and women dressed in traditional costume: a pleated and brocaded skirt, blouse, and shawl. It was not permitted for them to ask boys directly to dance: this had to be done through a brother or a male cousin (44: 6). Adelia Q. (born 1924) remembers the cultural differences in the small town of Rossano, in the province of Cosenza in Calabria, when she moved there from Naples as a child with her mother, her elder sister, and her two brothers in the 1930s. Her father, who had been born in Trento in the North , had taken a job as an accountant in Rossano with the Meridionale electric company and after a year he had persuaded his wife, who was reluctant to move, to join him there with the children.

At first we really suffered from the mentality there, because although Naples may be a southern city it is still a city. This was a small village, in those days it had less than 20,000 inhabitants, so you had all the prejudices of Calabria: "You don't do this, you don't say that, you can't go out with open shoes because you look like a dancing girl, you can't go to the bar because it's shameful." Nowadays it seems absurd because Calabria has developed, but in those days it was like that, so we had a very hard time, me in particular since I was always a very free spirit and because I worked hard at school. I was someone who liked schoolwork, because in a village where there was nothing it was the only entertainment, the only occupation. (57: 2–3)

All these rules began to be modified after the war, in Rossano, Burcei, and elsewhere: girls could go out in a *passeggiata* (the walk, formerly restricted to men, in public spaces); they could go to bars; they could initiate conversation with boys rather than wait to be addressed. A research project based on 400 interviews carried out by three sociologists in 1957 in the Sicilian town of Ragusa found the older generation repeatedly reporting and evaluating similar changes and in some cases linking them in part to the influence of mass culture:

Moralistic expressions are commonly used in judging the present situation: the inhabitants often remark that Ragusa has become, as far as free time is concerned, an immoral and corrupt town: "people have more vices," "young people have more vices," "there is immorality and corruption," "there is more freedom and corruption in the way young people enjoy themselves." By contrast, "customs were more rigid in the past," "women and young people did not have so much freedom."

According to a priest, however, one notices a greater "openness," rather than "corruption," particularly in young people. At the same time, he considers school to be a negative influence, because of the "mixing of the sexes it permits," as well as the free time activities of cinema and reading. However, the Church can do little, he said, to "heal" the situation, since it is unable to draw young people to its organizations with attractive free time sporting and cultural activities.

A housewife admitted that there had been a change in customs among students: "now they address each other as 'tu' [that is, in the intimate form] and stop and talk if they meet."[11]

One of the main vehicles for the enhancement of individual mobility in our period was the bicycle, which saw its apotheosis, both as a form of mass transport and as the object of the most popular summer spectator sport, in the late 1940s and early 1950s. When it was first introduced in Italy in the late nineteenth century, the bicycle had been a bourgeois status symbol. The first Italian manufacturer, Bianchi, was founded in Milan in 1885. In 1897 the Touring Club Ciclistico Italiano (founded, also in Milan, in 1894) campaigned successfully for a reduction of the tax on bicycles brought in by a government that had dismissed them as toys for the rich.[12] A contemporary journalist, Paolo Mantegazza, described the bicycle as the "triumph of human thought over material inertia. Two wheels that hardly touch the ground and can seem like wings ... a miracle of balance, simplicity, lightness. A maximum of power and a minimum of friction, a prodigy of speed and elegance."[13] The club dropped the term "Ciclistico" in 1900 to become the Touring Club Italiano, perhaps because the bicycle was coming to be outstripped as a symbol of modernity by the automobile, famously celebrated by Marinetti in the founding text of Futurism in 1909.[14] It was at the turn of the century, too, that the bicycle began to be taken up by the Catholic and socialist movements, both of which founded cycling clubs that hired out bicycles to their working-class members. Thus the bicycle developed, through a social trickle-down process, into a mass means of transportation.[15] The car, on the other hand, remained restricted to the rich until the 1950s. The seventh edition of Panzini's *Dizionario moderno,* published in 1942, recorded "macchina" as a standard antonomasia for bicycle; it was not till the 1960s that the term became widely used for the automobile. By 1947 there were 3.5 million bicycles on the roads, compared to 184,000 cars.[16] A new bicycle cost upward of 20,000 lire, though there was also a vast secondhand market, whereas the cheapest car, the Fiat Topolino 500B, launched in 1948, when the average wage was 139,000 lire, cost 650,000.[17] Bruno Roghi, cycling correspondent of the *Gazzetta dello Sport,* described the bicycle in 1946 as "the inseparable com-

Figure 1. A group of friends gather to organize a Sunday bicycle outing in the village of Canolo, near Correggio (Reggio Emilia), early 1950s. Photo by permission of Egeo Ferretti.

panion of the peasant, the worker, the professional, the clerk, the student, the housewife and our rosy-cheeked girls . . . the ambassador of Italian labour, in the streets, regions, cities, small towns, mountains and valleys."[18]

The bicycle was never quite as ubiquitous as this suggests. In poor rural areas, bicycles were still a relative rarity until the economic miracle and were then rapidly superseded by mopeds (*motorini*), scooters, and small cars. In Burcei, Michele Z., born in 1922, married in 1952, was one of the few inhabitants to own a bicycle in the early 1950s. It was useful for his work as an itinerant laborer but also fashionable and a local status symbol:

I took my wife around by bicycle. We were pretty much unique as a couple with a bicycle, because there weren't any others. We were in Burcei before and at that time I even made some money with the bicycle. How? By teaching friends to balance on the bicycle because they didn't know how. (45: 15)

In the cities, however, bicycles had become affordable and commonplace long before. The cohort of male interviewees in Maurizio Gribaudi's research into working-class communities in Turin recollected that in 1924, when they were fifteen and sixteen, they all had bicycles. They would meet during their lunch hour, play a scratch game of football in Piazza Marmolada, then, when the siren went off at ten minutes to two o'clock, they would rush off on their bicycles to their different places of work.[19]

Among the most potent sets of images relating to the bicycle during our period is the sequence in the 1948 film *Ladri di biciclette* (*The Bicycle Thief*), directed by Vittorio De Sica, where Antonio Ricci (Lamberto Maggiorani) and his son Bruno (Enzo Staiola), helped by Ricci's Communist friend, scour the market in Piazza Vittorio in Rome looking for Ricci's stolen bicycle, which they suspect may have been broken up or repainted. Row upon row of bicycles are on sale, as well as endless spare parts—frames, handlebars, sprockets, chains, brake levers and cables, bells—but none of them is the right one. Bicycles are everywhere but Ricci cannot have any of them. This image of lack in the midst of plenty is repeated at the end of the film outside the Stadio Flaminio where a football match is taking place between Roma and Modena. Again there is a mass of bicycles, both those belonging to the spectators inside the stadium and those of the racing cyclists who flash past Ricci as he sits with his face in his hands on the pavement, and again he is not allowed to have. Various meanings are condensed together into the bicycle as the object of Ricci's quest and desire: utility (a necessary tool of the trade for his job as a billposter), recreation and pleasure (he gives his wife a ride home from the pawnbroker's on the crossbar), and sporting prowess; it is also, and fundamentally, the index of a minimum of well-being, a sign that one has paid employment, and a guarantee of food on the table: the Riccis have pawned their sheets to pay for the bicycle.

During cycling's peak as a spectator sport—the Giro d'Italia was first run in 1909 and was held annually thereafter apart from the war years (the Tour de France had started in 1903)—it seems likely that its popularity was connected to its appearance of democratic accessibility and the simplicity of its technology. Unlike motor racing, a sport associated with technical complexity, money, and glamour, cycling depended almost exclusively on physical fitness, stamina, and gritty determination. The majority of riders were of working-class or peasant origin.[20] Anyone, potentially, could join in. This was the main running gag of *Totò al Giro d'Italia* (Mario Mattoli, 1949), in which the Neapolitan comic actor Totò (Antonio De Curtis), playing an ordinary citizen, barges onto the starting line alongside Gino Bartali and Fausto Coppi. As the sports journalist Franco Cordelli put it:

For us cycling fans there is nobody greater than a racer, whether a champion or a supporting rider. Cyclists are all simple, all God's creatures, even the cleverest of them. We [journalists] may joke or digress; sometimes we get annoyed because "nothing is happening" and there's no contest and we wax nostalgic over the past. But let's not ever forget the profoundly humble nature of the cyclist.[21]

Cycling has remained popular as a spectator sport in Italy, as in other European countries, in a way that it has never been in Britain or North America, and the mass media have continued to be the essential vehicles and windows for this popularity. However, the social meaning of cycling has shifted since the 1950s as the bicycle has declined from the primary means of utilitarian transport for working-class Italians into a secondary means, used mainly for leisure, or, from the early 1980s, used by middle-class commuters as a green alternative to an overly motorized society. This decline may be correlated with the rise of the motor scooter, first introduced in 1946; the "popular car," the Fiat 600 and 500, introduced respectively in 1955 and 1957; and the *motorino* (moped), which was developed in the same period. These developments in transport also correlated with the generalized rise in living standards that accompanied them. By the late 1960s the mass use of the bicycle had become associated with the past and with a lower standard of living. The period covered in this book is one in which the bicycle could still possess great material and symbolic value for a working-class family but in which it was also starting to be eclipsed by mechanized means of personal transport associated with higher standards of living and with modernity.

Community, Modernization, Identity

The various forms of flow and mobility we have described all have to do with the redefining of place and therefore of the communities that are associated with particular places. Developments such as the repeated exposure to media images, films, fashion items, or radio broadcasts; the physical movement back and forth across boundaries; and the increased use of means of transport, from the train to the bicycle and the scooter, are linked because they all allow for modifications in people's sense of place, and hence their perceptions of community. In the period we are examining the increases in physical mobility and in "mediated visibility" changed people's sense of community in important ways and these changes were part of the wider process of modernization.

We seek to demonstrate that a stronger sense of a national community, what one might call a popular Italian national identity, did develop in our period. This was partly a result of internal political forces and events—Fascist nationalism, wars, occupation, the Resistance, conflicts between different groups in the Republic over the definition of the nation—and partly an effect of the media creating a sense of national belonging. At the same time, we maintain that this sense of national community developed through processes of repeated comparison and conflict with others within and beyond Italy's borders; that is, it was the product of continual cultural exchange, defensive reaction, and mediation, and the mass media played an important part in this process. We argue, then, that the media and mass culture functioned over the long term in Italy in different ways in relation to the consolidation of national identity. On the one hand they assisted the process of national aggregation; on the other, they brought about a turning toward other cultures. In fact, we identify three distinct processes, each of which may be related to the notions of community and place, and in turn to the concept of modernization.

First, the mass media, by creating national markets and networks—including national readerships for illustrated magazines, a nationwide radio network with a synchronized program schedule, and a national distribution circuit for cinema newsreels and recorded music—and by circulating images of national events as well of Italy's different regions and localities, helped create at a mass level, in the course of the twentieth century, "Italian society" as a felt place community, whereas in the nineteenth century that community had remained largely circumscribed to political and cultural elites. The media were not the only agents in this process. Others included the Italian language, which gradually became adopted at a mass level in the course of the century; national sporting events; flows of internal migration; conscription and military service; and the state education system, with its national curriculum and the development of national statistics.[22] However, the media and mass culture played a central role and in some cases interacted with these other agents. As Tullio De Mauro argued in 1963, radio and sound film, and more recently television, had been major channels in bringing about the recognition and use of Italian at a mass level. Film and television in particular had contributed to the development of what De Mauro and other linguists called "italiano popolare," that is, the varieties of colloquial spoken Italian for informal everyday use that were gradually supplanting the use of dialects in different parts of the country.[23]

Second, and at the same time, the media put in circulation products and images from other countries, opening windows onto a wider world. This was partly because the national media themselves carried these images, in the form of foreign news reports and features, and partly because the cultural products to which people were exposed in Italy were never only national but were also imported. Foreign films, music, comic strips, and popular fiction, as we discuss in chapters 3 through 6, brought other cultures into Italy and often exerted a strong fascination. In this way, the media and mass culture drew Italian citizens inexorably into international circuits of images, consumer goods, and lifestyles. The efforts of cultural protectionists to stem the flow of products from outside Italy's borders were, with a few partial and temporary exceptions, which we discuss, frustrated because the appeal of the imported products was so strong and because the protectionists in most cases lacked the means to back up their efforts with effective coercion.

Third, the media created not only standardized national markets but also particular markets for different subterritories—regions and localities, and in some cases also emigrant communities abroad—and for different social subgroups: men and women, older and younger generations, children, middle- and working-class people, political and religious subcultures. In this way they both reinforced and redefined the internal fragmentation and stratifications of Italian society.

On the face of it these three tendencies might appear to be in conflict with one another because they push in different directions: respectively toward national aggregation, internationalization, and the formation of subnational communities. However, it is probably more accurate to see all three as interrelated and interdependent. Just as the sense of a national community was continually fashioned and refined by comparison with other communities outside the nation-state, so it was defined and redefined by interaction with the various subnational communities within the nation—regions, localities, social subgroups—and the latter defined themselves against the nation-state and various supranational communities.

The latter process may be illustrated with the example of locality. Local cultures are often thought of as forms of "primary community," or what Ferdinand Tönnies caled *Gemeinschaft,* which gradually get absorbed and eroded by incorporation into the national society. However, locality may more accurately be represented as a form of community that is itself produced and reproduced by the consolidation of the nation-state and later by the enhanced role of the "regions," those supralocal administrative units that came into being after unification and whose political role was strengthened after World War II, and of a supranational political entity, the European Union. People, of course, lived in small-scale, territorially circumscribed communities—towns and villages—long before the age of nation-states, regions, and a federal Europe, but the very notion of these communities as "local," and the particular modern meanings that came to be attached to locality (small, traditional, close-knit, and so on), in contradistinction to other kinds of community, only emerged when those communities came to be seen as peripheries to a center, subordinate units of a superordinate polity, and their long-term survival as distinct communities was felt to be threatened. The anthropologist Paola Filippucci, in a study of the town of Bassano in the Veneto, has stressed that it was the elites there who invented the idea of locality in the late nineteenth century when they sought legitimation from the nascent nation-state. The same elites, in this and other contexts, also imagined and constructed locality and local identity culturally, for instance, through forms of institutionalized remembering, such as the museum, local monument, war memorial, or commemorative plaque, or by promoting civic rituals such as the carnival, the local village festival (*sagra*), and the patron saint's day (*festa del santo patrono*).[24]

Each of the three processes we have described here may be linked to a wider one, that of modernization, which is, we argue, closely bound up with the rise of mass communications. In invoking the concept of modernization we are not referring to the controversial work of W. W. Rostow and his followers, which represented modernization as a set of "stages of growth" from "traditional" to "modern" society, in which the fifth and final stage was that of mass consumption.[25] Rostow (who later became a policy adviser to Presidents Kennedy and Johnson and a staunch supporter of sustained military engagement in Vietnam) identified these "stages" with the American model and presented the latter as desirable for all societies in order to draw them into a virtuous path of capitalist growth and away from communism. His thesis triggered extensive criticism from dependency theorists and historians and is now widely discredited.[26] Likewise, the concept of "traditional society" used by Rostow has been challenged by both social and economic historians. As Gareth Stedman Jones put it: "The historian should refrain from calling the history he does not know 'traditional society.' This bad habit, it seems to me, has been one of the many unfortunate spin-offs from sociological theories of modernization."[27]

The term "modernization," as we use it here, is intended, rather, as a much more general and value-neutral designation of some aspects of the development of European societies since the late fifteenth century. The core elements of the modernization thesis in this form are drawn from the work of Marx and Weber. It is normally seen as consisting of three interrelated developments. In the economy, it means the transition from feudalism to capitalism, the rise of the wage contract, industrialization, and the growth of market economies. In politics, it means the transition from absolutist states to nation-states, accompanied by national armies and police forces that acquire a monopoly on the legitimate use of force (Weber's *Gewalt*, sometimes translated as "violence") in their own territories and normally, though not necessarily, by liberal-parliamentary forms of democracy. In administration it means the growth of modern centralized bureaucracies and the managerial rationalization of private firms.

Neither Marx nor Weber nor later theorists of modernization gave much emphasis to culture or communications media; at most they tended to see the core politico-economic processes as having cultural spinoffs, such as the formation of national education systems or national media markets. However, other scholars have argued that the media and cultural processes are intrinsic to modernization and indeed that the latter is unthinkable without them. Jürgen Habermas, in his influential account, first published in German in 1962, of the rise and fall of the bourgeois public sphere in Europe, gave particular prominence to the early periodical press as an arena of critical debate emerging in the interstices between the state and civil society. He argued that the rise of merchant capitalism and changing forms of political power from the sixteenth century had produced not only the modern separation between the state (a realm juridically distinct from the Church and royal courts) and civil society (a sphere of private relations separate from public authority) but also a new type of public arena intermediate between them and independent from both, which functioned as a sphere of rational criticism, deliberation and debate. In Habermas's account, this new bourgeois public sphere consisted of critical journals, such as Defoe's *Review* and Swift's *Examiner* in England, and places of sociability such as clubs and coffeehouses, and it had an important role as a critical voice independent of parliament that obliged the latter to become more transparent and responsive to criticism.[28] In other words, Habermas saw the nascent communications media of modern society as central to the modernization of political institutions and to the formation of a modern notion of independent public opinion. Benedict Anderson, writing some twenty years later, linked the development of the nation-state to what he called the rise of "print-capitalism" and the formation of national language communities, with the vernaculars being fixed in print and becoming official state languages.[29] He argued that the expansion of print, and the development of the newspaper, was bound up with the consolidation of nations as "horizontal-secular, transverse-time" communities, as opposed to the "vertical," hierarchical, script-based communities that rested upon notions of divine right and in which a modern separation between cosmology and history, sacred time and secular human time, had not yet been instituted.

Both these accounts argue that cultural processes, and the development of the media, were closely enmeshed with other aspects of modernization. Just as, for Habermas, the periodical press was central to the development of modern bourgeois society and to the ethos of rational critical debate that enabled a mature parliamentary state system to come into being, so, for Anderson, the promotion in print of a national vernacular language and a periodical and newspaper press were essential in forging the modern sense of an imagined national community. The arguments of both Habermas and Anderson have been partially adopted, but also criticized, by John B. Thompson, for whom the cultural sphere and the media are central to the modernization process. Thompson dissents from Habermas's emphasis on the eighteenth-century bourgeois public sphere at the expense of the subsequent formation of a sphere of radical working-class culture in the labor movement, which in its turn opposed the bourgeois sphere, and also from his pessimistic account of the decline of the bourgeois public sphere in the face of the rise of the modern mass media. Habermas, influenced by the negative and totalizing view of the Frankfurt school theorists Adorno and Horkheimer, saw the growth of commercial mass media and advertising since the late nineteenth century as stifling critical debate and reestablishing the power of the state by endowing the political sphere with the unchallengeable aura and prestige it had previously enjoyed in the feudal era.[30] Thompson argues, by contrast, that

the development of communication media has created new forms of interaction, new kinds of visibility and new networks of information diffusion in the modern world, all of which have altered the symbolic character of social life so profoundly that any comparison between mediated politics today and the theatrical practices of feudal courts is superficial at best.[31]

As for Anderson, although Thompson finds his link between the formation of national communities and the development of new systems of communication in a common language persuasive, he notes that he is vague when it comes to explaining how this connection actually worked. It remains "loose and tentative."[32] Above all, Anderson

does not examine the ways in which media products were used by individuals, the changing forms of action and interaction made possible by new media of communication and the ways in which the development of communication media gradually altered the nature of tradition and individuals' relation to it.[33]

We would extract from these various accounts the following propositions. First, the formation of the nation-state was part of a wider process of modernization and this, in turn, was bound up with the development of communications media. The media, as they developed, increasingly shaped for the citizens of each country a sense of their national belonging. Second, the media tended to retain a role separate both from that of the state and from that of the characteristic elements of civil society—economic relations, the family, and private or semipublic associations like the school. Third, the media created new forms of social interaction and enabled individuals to take a distance from traditional attitudes and beliefs. In all these ways the media played an important role in the reshaping of national identity and of citizens' sense of their place in a wider world.

Italy has often been described as having a "weak" national identity combined with strong traditions of "localism" and "familism." This is variously attributed to the early development of the peninsula as a collection of separate city-states, the relatively late formation of an Italian nation-state (unification in 1859–1861, and then the subsequent additions and subtractions of territories up to 1954), the persistence of low literacy levels and relatively limited geographical mobility well into the twentieth century, and the simultaneous persistence of family ties, evidenced for example by the strong role played by family firms in the national economy. The cultural anthropologist Carlo Tullio-Altan argued in the 1980s that Italy's "socio-cultural backwardness" derived from the traditions of proto-capitalist individualism and familism, which, he claimed, with an eye to Weber, survived through the nineteenth and twentieth centuries because of the lack of a Protestant Reformation that elsewhere had effected the change in mentality by which individualism and collective responsibility were conjoined. However these judgments have been widely challenged. It has been argued that Italy does not really constitute so exceptional a case, that in all modern nations there are tensions between local, regional, and national interests, that despite Italy's relatively late formation as a nation-state (though no later than that of Germany or Japan or many other non-European nations) it succeeded quite rapidly in creating national symbols and a sense of national cohesion, that local and family traditions managed to integrate their interests fairly successfully with the national state and economy, that Italy experienced, with Fascism, a strong movement toward national self-assertion, that the Resistance against German occupation and Fascism demonstrated the powerful cohesion that could be created in defense of the nation, and that Italy emerged after World War II with a state that had a strong degree of mass legitimation, demonstrated, among other things, by the high turnouts in successive general elections and referendums as well as by various mass demonstrations in defense of the Republic, for instance in 1960 over the Tambroni affair (when the Christian Democrats proposed to form a government with the support of the neofascist party, the Movimento Sociale Italiano) and 1978 over the murder of Aldo Moro (president of the Christian Democrat party and former prime minister) by the Red Brigades. On balance, we do not find the thesis of a pathologically weak national identity convincing.

There was intense concern with nationhood not just in the Fascist regime but equally in the postwar state that succeeded it. The nation was the central term in the transition from Fascism to the Republic: during the civil war of 1943–1945 the antifascist parties and the last-ditch defenders of Fascism both laid claim to the *patria* and sought to be the legitimate advocates of the deepest interests of the nation, drawing upon Risorgimento names and traditions. If it is true, as Silvio Lanaro has suggested, that at the end of the war there was also a widespread "conviction that the name and very idea of Italy had been irreparably sabotaged by Fascism" and that this tended to produce an emphasis both in public speeches and policy on a rejection of Italy's imme-

diate imperialist past and a turning outward to membership of a larger transnational community,[34] it is also true that the nation remained the key counter
in political and cultural debate. It was the nation whose interests were articulated and fought over in the campaign for the 1948 election, the first election to parliament under the new Constitution of the Republic. It was the nation whose culture political leaders and cultural activists officially sought to
remake, whether by giving a new democratic identity to the institutions and
media inherited from Fascism, or by creating new organs or by promoting
the idea of an enlarged, people's nation, as the Communist Party did, adapting Gramsci's slogan of the "national-popular." The autonomist and region-
alist programs of various parties were accommodated and neutralized by a
new, centralized national political system that made limited concessions to
administrative devolution. Postwar Italy, under the premierships of De Gasperi, sought a new role in a federal peacetime Europe, but it did so as a nation
whose identity would henceforth be linked to collective European interests.

The main claims we have made in this introduction, and shall substan-
tiate and elaborate further in the course of this book, are that commercial
mass culture and the spread of forms of cultural consumption associated with
it—a spread that was assisted by greater physical mobility between places and
a greater permeability of formerly bounded places—played a very important role in Italy's modernization but that this role was not a simple one, nor
did it have a univocal relationship to the formation of national identity. On
the one hand, by creating national cultural markets, symbols, and identifications (such as through sport or music), mass culture helped people construct
a sense of national belonging. On the other hand, mass culture opened out the
experience of consumers to international flows and circuits of communication and to comparisons with communities abroad and worked against a narrow and limited sense of national identity. One of the reasons why this was
possible was that the cultural industries and consumer tastes were not subjugated to effective political controls. The regulatory policies of successive regimes were, on balance, failures. Voluntary associations that sought to direct
people's leisure sometimes pushed against the tendency toward a modernized
familial and individualist consumption and sometimes worked with it.

Part 1.

Cultural Consumption and Everyday Life

1 Patterns of Consumption

The prevailing historical view of cultural consumption in Italy from the mid-1930s to the mid-1950s is that it was still to a large extent "traditional" and that the modification of most people's daily repertoires by mass culture would not begin until later. According to this view, the 1960s was the era of the "great transformation," a term used by Silvio Lanaro in 1993 as the title of part of his history of postwar Italy starting with the economic miracle years 1958–1963.[1] We do not dispute that the period dating from the end of the 1950s was a time of particularly rapid change, but this retrospective account misrepresents the way the changes actually took place. The impression of a "great transformation" compressed into a decade or so is, we maintain, largely illusory, the result of looking at the end product and creating a kind of average out of many different individual and collective cultural repertoires, which contained many contradictory processes. In reality, the changes were often slow and took several generations to work through. Above all, one needs to distinguish occasional contact with mass culture from regular exposure to it and habitual use. Much of the evidence we have seen suggests that many people had some experience of mass cultural products long before the communities they lived in were habitually and permanently exposed to them, even when they had little money and time to permit regular access to them. Among our own interviewees it was very difficult to find anyone who was not in some way in contact with, and aware of the existence of, modern mass culture in the period we were investigating, no matter how "remote" an area they lived in, how poor they were, and how much of their waking time was taken up by productive labor. Yet very often these people had little or no leisure or recreational time, or at any rate they had no consciousness that parts of their time belonged to these categories.

There are some exceptions to this rule, limit cases of people who had negligible or minimal contact with mass culture or indeed with any form of recreation. However, these are rare enough to suggest that their circumstances were unusual. Editta L., born in Turin in 1913, was a Jewish woman who worked first as a teacher in a nursery school and then later as a head teacher. She told a life story that was so full of privations and personal sufferings—her mother's chronic illness, her father's and brother's suicides, forced changes of residence, racial persecution—that she was unable, or did not allow herself, to recall any enjoyments or moments of distraction or relaxation. When we asked her about these she did then mention the occasional visit to the theater, and some excursions to the mountains, but she had not volunteered these recollections. Editta L.'s testimony shows, in this way, the important role played by subjectivity in accepting or rejecting a narrative agenda centered on recreation and leisure. In her case she resisted this agenda. This was not the life story she wanted to tell. She wanted to recount it as a sequence of hard experiences. Another, different kind of limit case was that of interviewees whose working lives did not leave time for anything except rest and sleep between work. Natalia, born in 1922, whom we interviewed in Turin, said that her husband used to work a twelve-hour shift at the Pirelli factory six days a week and an eight-hour shift (6 A.M. to 2 P.M.) on Sundays (4: 34, 41). However, for most people we interviewed there were moments of rest or respite: Sundays or Saturday evenings at least.

In order to build up a picture of the particular forms and types of cultural consumption in our period, we shall start this chapter with a brief survey of two of the regions in which we carried out our interviews, situated at different extremes of the peninsula: Calabria in the South and Piedmont in the North-West. Then, in the remainder of the chapter, we shall broaden out to other regions and examine, in turn, different types of cultural consumption: reading, cinemagoing, listening to the radio, and listening and dancing to live and re-corded music.

Calabria and Piedmont

The life stories we collected in Celico show the sporadic way that mass cul-ture and communications permeated an upland rural community in Cala-bria in the 1930s and 1940s. Celico, whose population at that time was about 2,500, had a social structure that one of the interviewees, Arturo M., born in 1917, described as between fifteen to twenty families of "americani" (re-turned emigrants) at the top, the service class (*impiegati*) in the middle, and the various categories of workers at the bottom. The latter were all badly off ("stavano tutti male") but there was a hierarchy within this category ranging from the artisans—cobbler, tailor, cooper—down to the poor peasants (74: 18, 28). There was no cinema in Celico until 1955; when it did open, as one resi-dent recalled, "nobody went and it shut down, it went bust." There was, how-ever, the Cinema Scrivano in nearby Spezzano. "They put up the first cinema in Spezzano in 1938 or 1939. But very few women went" (71/72: 16). "Since there was only one cinema you went to see what they showed. And I was lucky because when I was young I worked and scraped together some money. Not everyone could go to the cinema because they couldn't afford it" (71/72: 26). Rita L., born in 1916, used to walk the four kilometers from Celico to Spez-zano to go to the cinema and she remembered how the films were publicized in 1949–1951: "They shouted through loudspeakers: 'Tomorrow at the Cinema Scrivano *Domani è troppo tardi*' [*Tomorrow Is Too Late* (Léonide Moguy, 1950)]; 'At the Cinema Scrivano *I figli di nessuno* [*Nobody's Children* (Raffaello Matarazzo, 1951], *Catene* [*Chains* (Raffaello Matarazzo, 1949)].' Lovely films those were" (76/77: 11). Carmela F. (born 1917) remembers going to see *Core 'ngrato* (*The Ungrateful Heart*) (Guido Brignone, 1951) at the cinema in Spez-zano (71: 5) but apart from this she does not seem to have gone at all (72: 10–11). She and various other people interviewed in that area also remember the mobile cinema that came on the local saints' days and showed religious films (70: 15). Gustavo V., born in 1910, said these films were shown "on the festivals of San Michele or San Nicola who are the protectors of the village . . . usually they were religious films, like the *Via Crucis* [Romolo Bacchini, 1919], you know, religious stuff, very moral stuff" (75: 17). He also recalled that already in the early 1930s "Celico . . . was a holiday village, people came from Bologna, from Milan," even though it was "not comparable to what it is today" (75: 14).

Like Burcei in Sardinia (see the introduction), Celico was thus not com-pletely "cut off." It was permeated by the flows of emigration and return, by movements to other regions and back (for instance, Gustavo V. went to Rome as a student; other people were conscripted or volunteered in the wars); trips within the region (Celico-Sila, Celico-Cosenza, and so on); as well as by flows of information, sounds, and images from outside (radio, cinema). There were also excursions to the surrounding area. Gustavo V. remembers that in Celico there was "a man who hired bicycles, so we went out on a bicycle" (75: 14). As for the penetration of political events, the testimonies also register the presence of Fascist associationism (see below, chapter 8), for instance, in Casole, where Rita De L. remembers going in the late 1920s with her sister dressed in the black skirt and white shirt of the Piccole Italiane while her brothers wore the yellow and pink handkerchief of the Balilla tied round their hats (76/77: 14). On the other hand, World War II seems to have impinged only in 1943–1944 with the Allied advance northward from Sicily and the retreat of the Germans across Calabria.

Maria I., born in 1932, is a good example of someone in Celico with a "traditional" cultural repertoire who was only marginally affected by modern mass culture. Until she got married in 1955, at age twenty-three, she lived in a peasant family of four, with her parents and sister. The family worked eight months a year, from March to November, on the Sila plateau, with the father's four brothers and their wives. They kept sheep and goats there and grew potatoes. They went back and forward by oxcart; her father also sometimes went on horseback to Camigliatello, about eight kilometers from where they were in Sila. Maria made ricotta, her mother also made and sold hard cheese, and every two weeks they spent one day together baking fifty kilos of bread. During the winters they were back in Celico, where they had a house with electric lighting and running water (the latter had arrived in Celico in 1922), and an inside lavatory, whereas in Sila they used petrol lamps and Maria's father made a lavatory over a running stream. During the winters in Celico work was a little less hard. Maria did sewing and embroidery work, put out by the nuns, on trousseaux (*corredi*). After she was married she and her husband opened a veal butcher's shop in Celico (he killed the calves, she sold the meat and handled the accounts), but this closed because business was poor. The preparation of girls for marriage continued to be central at least to her planning of the family's future. Maria described how, without telling her husband, she put aside money from the shop from her own earnings to pay for her two daughters' trousseaux when they were still little, because the women who made them were getting old and she thought they might not live till the daughters reached marriageable age.

Many of the recreations Maria I. described in her life story were traditional—the *veglia* (the communal evening gathering, typical of many peasant communities), with her mother reading aloud; carnival; her own wedding feast with eighty guests (her father killed three sheep to feed them all)—but there are others that show the impact of a wider world. When she was little, in about 1942, she and her friends found an abandoned, broken-down Fiat car. They would roll down a slope in it then get a friend to hitch it to a mule and pull it up again. There was also a man in Celico who had returned from America and who had a radio set: he put it on the balcony and turned it up loud so everyone could hear the war bulletins (70: 7). She heard the news of the fall of Mussolini by oral reports of broadcasts heard by others: "We were in the Sila, but we heard rumors, rumors from people who listened to the radio, these rumours arrived: Mussolini has been brought down" (70: 7).

In the decade after the war, Calabria as a whole had one of the fastest growth rates of all the Italian regions in expenditure on cinema, sport, and radio. This rate outstripped the rates of growth in income and expenditure on necessities. This was one of the findings in a survey commissioned by the Società Italiana Autori e Editori and carried out in November 1958.[2] The growth was more rapid, the authors of the survey observed, when the source of income was temporary or short term (public works programs and special investments) and slower when the increases in income became permanent. This survey shows that the sporadic contacts with mass culture of the prewar period became more regular after the war. It also confirms the picture obtainable from other sources (for instance, the numbers of new cinemas built and private radio licenses issued) of accelerated cultural changes taking place in many rural regions in the postwar decade, particularly those areas where wage levels had been low and levels of consumption as a whole had been compressed in the Fascist period.

However, the picture of fast growth needs to be nuanced. The extent of cultural transformation in Calabria in the 1950s should not be exaggerated. In the case of cinema, although the increase in consumption in the region as a whole was certainly rapid (expenditure on cinema quadrupled between 1951 and 1958), 37 percent of *comuni* in Calabria still had no cinemas in 1958, so the growth was spatially very unbalanced. "Leisure" tended to be concentrated on Sundays, suggesting that the traditional pattern had not yet been much disturbed: 30 percent of those interviewed declared that that they had no "pastimes" on weekdays, but only 7 percent said they had no "pastimes" on Sundays.[3] The results of this survey are not entirely reliable. Like the contemporary surveys carried out by the Istituto Doxa, several of the categories used in it, notably "free time" and "pastimes," were problematic, and one wonders what some of the interviewees made of them. The authors of the report were perspicacious enough to realize that not all the people they surveyed considered the stroll (*passeggiata*) a form of entertainment or enjoyment (*diverti-*

mento). But they did not seem to follow this observation through and see that it cast doubt on the validity of the category *divertimento* itself and of their ranking of the *passeggiata* within a list of preferred *divertimenti*.

For all these limitations, several aspects of this survey are striking. For one thing, the generational differences detected are very marked, and they suggest that a significant gap had opened up between generations after the war in their patterns of cultural consumption. Conversation was more popular as a leisure activity among those over forty-five, classified as "elderly" (*anziani*) in the survey, than among the group aged sixteen through twenty-five; conversely, cinema and television were more popular with the latter than with the former. The statistical difference between generations was significant. On a Sunday, 26.4 percent of people aged sixteen through twenty-five said that they had been to the cinema and 29 percent said that they had watched television, whereas the figures for the over forty-five age group were respectively 8.6 percent and 14 percent. There are also some striking absolute figures: 55.1 percent of the total population sampled had never been to a cinema; "88.2% do not read, 72% do not read or listen to the radio, 58% do not read, listen to the radio or watch television and 57% do not read, listen to the radio, watch television or go to the cinema."[4] The resulting picture, then, is of a region where patterns of cultural consumption were already changing before the war, and where they changed more rapidly afterward, but mainly for the young generations and not uniformly across the region.

In Piedmont the penetration of mass culture was similarly limited in the poor rural areas at the beginning of our period. The life stories recorded by Nuto Revelli between 1970 and 1973 in four of these areas—the Langhe, consisting of the Langa alta (hill) and Langa bassa (plain), and three others that he designated respectively pianura (plain), collina (hill), and montagna (mountain)—are a valuable source of information about attitudes, social behavior, and consumption in these parts of rural Piedmont during a period that stretches back in the memory of most of the interviewees (the majority of whom were born between 1885 and 1920) at least to the early 1930s. The title of Revelli's collection, *Il mondo dei vinti* (*The World of the Defeated*), containing transcribed extracts of some of the 270 testimonies he taped, embodies the sense, shared by Revelli and the peasants he interviewed, of a world that was rapidly disappearing in the early 1970s due to processes that had been set in motion in the late 1950s— urbanization, new industrial plants, a labor exodus (particularly among the younger generation), and the transformation of rural Piedmont by motorways, tourism, and the new, rich, market-oriented agriculture.[5]

The deruralization process was more rapid in Piedmont in the 1950s than in most other regions. Between the two censuses of 1951 and 1961 the number of people employed in agriculture in Piedmont fell by 30 percent, and the active population in the region as a whole fell from 33 to 23 percent.[6] Yet, as the testimonies collected by Revelli suggest, up to the early 1950s in rural Piedmont, as in rural Calabria and other parts of peasant Italy, the *veglia* (evening gathering, often in a barn) remained central to the cultural life of the community: a focus of sociability and storytelling—oral, sung, or read aloud; a place for women's work, such as sewing and mending; and the usual place of courtship. One of Revelli's younger witnesses, Giuseppe Macario, born in 1929, recalled how in Robilante it was customary that, when a young man took an interest in a young woman, he would go to the *veglia*, taking two or three friends along for moral support, and then follow the girl's father as he left the stable to tell him, "If it was alright with you I should like to have a friendship with your daughter" ("Se füsi content mi l'avría l'idea 'd manteni l'amicisia cun la fia"). The father would reply that they would talk about it at home and he would let the young man know. If the courtship was not approved the father would say nothing next time and it was understood that the matter would end there.[7] Bartolomeo Spada, Revelli's oldest witness, born in 1878, remembered that boys would go in groups of eight or ten to visit a girl at a *veglia* and it was considered an honor to the girl if twenty or so boys regularly paid a visit. At carnival time those who had visited most frequently were given presents of eggs, walnuts, apples, or doughnuts. Spada saw the advent of television in the 1950s as having marked the end of the *veglia*.[8]

Frequently, in Piedmont, there circulated at the *veglie* and elsewhere stories of *masche*, women who were believed to have malign magic powers, and less commonly their male equivalents, *mascun*, to whom all misfortunes were attributed, from illness to the death of a child to a cow's failure to produce milk. Significantly, in these areas of high illiteracy (the legal obligation of school attendance was not enforced and there was mass absenteeism among the working children of peasant families), the *masche* were literate women, those who had the "power" of reading. Revelli noted that belief in the *masche* was more prevalent, indeed almost universal, among the older interviewees than the younger ones, and this suggested that the belief was tending to disappear in the newer generations. Nevertheless it was still pervasive enough in the early postwar period to be incorporated dynamically into the new realities of these areas: the legacy of the partisan struggles of 1943-1945, the implantation of the Church, the rise of the Christian Democrats, the Cold War. According to Revelli, belief in the *masche* had been exploited by the Church as part of the lucrative "exorcism industry"; it also was hitched by the Church, during the Cold War period, to the anticommunist crusade.[9] According to one of his witnesses, in the province of Cuneo in the early 1950s, the *masche* were associated by the Church with Communism because "the Communist was not seen as a political adversary but as the Antichrist, a person to fear because 'he read too many books, because he did not go to church.'"[10]

We carried out our own interviews in Piedmont in and around its capital city, Turin, not least because memory of parts of rural Piedmont had already been so well tapped in Revelli's work. The accounts we recorded vary greatly from one interviewee to another but they share certain features that mark them out collectively as different from those of the inhabitants of the rural communities interviewed by Revelli, most notably in the exposure to modern forms of cultural consumption. One of the hardest working lives recounted to us was that of Natalia, who moved with her family from the Veneto to Turin in 1927, when she was four-and-a-half years old. The family moved when her father got a job, like many others from that region, the majority of them women, in one of the Snia Viscosa plants.[11] Natalia herself started work in February 1935, when she was twelve, at the Martinin factory (later Superga) outside Turin. Her shift was eight hours a day, six days a week, with one fifteen-minute break for lunch, for 21 lire a month (the standard wage for adult women at Snia Viscosa was about ten times this amount). Her free time and consequently her cultural consumption was very limited for the first nine years of her working life. The only holidays she got were public holidays: *ferragosto* (August 15, the Assumption of the Virgin Mary), Christmas Day, New Year's Day, and Epiphany (January 6). The family lived in one of Snia's workers' villages, and her recreations at the beginning of her working life were limited to evenings and to Sundays, after mass and after helping her mother with household tasks: skipping games in the street, excursions on Sunday afternoons in the summer to the banks of the Po for swimming and sunbathing, dancing on Saturday and Sunday evenings in a hall with a pianola. The dance hall cost 1 lira, but they got free entry in exchange for cleaning the hall (4: 3–4). Gradually, as the working year was reduced (half days on Saturdays from 1944; longer paid holidays after the war) and as Natalia's pay increased her consumptions expanded: the parish cinema in Piazza Rebaudengo about once a month (entry cost 2 lire, and it was a long walk from home), and reading magazines and books, at first those bought and passed on by her brother, later those that she bought herself at the newsstand.

Sergio P., born in 1925, had a career as a draughtsman, starting as an apprentice at Fiat Aeronautica, where he remained until the end of World War II, and continuing from 1957 to 1980 at the Zerbini utensils factory. In between, however, he had another career as a professional singer with the Radio Boys quintet at RAI Torino. He earned much the same in both jobs—the Radio Boys got a lump fee of 300,000 lire that they had to split five ways, and then there were various deductions, such as company health insurance—but the lifestyles and the attractions of the two careers were very different. Sergio's story reminds us of the popularity of the new dance music in the cities in the decade after the war. The recollections of two lifelong friends, Mario C. (born 1934, also a former Fiat worker) and Roberto D. (born 1935), were full of information about this lost world of dance halls with four-piece to six-piece bands, where groups of young people of both sexes, four or five in a group, would go as many as four times each weekend (Saturday afternoon and evening, Sunday afternoon and evening), where parents were sometimes present acting as intermediaries between the sexes, where the boys thought in terms of conquests and fifteen-year-old girls would wear makeup but would not do certain dances, like "acrobatic" jiving, because they did not want to expose their thighs and pants. Roberto, with Mario present, said that the enthusiasm for dancing had sprung up in Turin immediately after the war and was connected to the new sense of freedom.

And then everybody danced.... The bombing had smashed a lot of things and there was rubble everywhere in front of us, all broken, open space. You could even see across to the opposite block, do you remember? In Via Principe Amedeo. In a number of places that had been flattened, or that they had made flat afterwards, for example in Via Po, in Via Montebello behind the RAI, they organized dancing evenings. Everyone was so happy to get back to having this that no one made a fuss, no one said: "Be home by such and such a time tonight." And from there these dancing places started to spring up. But I think that the first "working-class" dance halls, so to speak, if I remember right, started in the political party clubs, above all in Communist ones where we learned to dance. (7: 5)

Turin was also full of theaters, cafés where one could go and play music or hear music played, and the *tampe liriche,* locales hosting amateur music and singing contests. Bruno O., born in 1932, an artisan who followed his father's trade of furniture restoring, gilding, and varnishing, remembered the one in Via Sacchi:

You went there. If you knew how to play you went and played the piano. If you could sing you went with someone, with your friends, and you sang, you did a number.... You went to those cafés and performed. I knew how to play the piano. I sat there and played, someone else sang, or else they did sketches like in a variety show. None of it was professional, all amateur, amateur people having a good time. And there were lots of us, though of course most of the people there just listened, they ate and drank. They were wonderful places. (3: 4–5)

Readers

In Italy it has long been conventional to talk of a "problem" of reading. Despite a slow and continuous growth of the reading public from unification onward, it was often remarked that Italy remained a country of few readers, particularly of books and newspapers, by comparison with countries like Britain or Germany, until well into the 1960s. Five main reasons were given: comparatively high levels of illiteracy and semiliteracy until the late 1950s; low average rates and duration of school attendance by the lower classes, the peasantry in particular, until the raising of the minimum school-leaving age to 14 in 1962; limited distribution of printed paper outside towns; the relatively high cost of books (still cited as a barrier to mass book reading in the 1930s); and the insufficient number of local lending libraries. In 1927, out of 9,148 *comuni* only 1,200 (13 percent) had a public library. Survey evidence of preferred books from 1906 onward bears out what Italian publishers knew and cultural protectionists complained about, namely the predominance on the market of novels in translation over those by Italian authors. A survey of 1949 found that thirteen out of the twenty novels read most recently were translations and the most cited author was A. J. Cronin.[12] Cronin, a Scot, was known in Italy (as in many other countries, including the Soviet Union) mainly for his social novels, including two about mining communities, *The Stars Look Down* (1935) and *The Citadel* (1937). The Italian translations of these, by Carlo Coardi, were published, as were all Cronin's novels, by Bompiani (*E le stelle stanno a guardare,* 1936; *La cittadella,* 1938). They were also known through the film versions directed respectively by Carol Reed (Great Britain, 1939) and King Vidor (United States, 1938).

For three types of publication, however, a mass reading public did exist, relatively speaking, throughout our period: the sports press, illustrated magazines, and comics (*fumetti*). Antonio Gramsci had observed the popularity of the sports press during his first period of incarceration in San Vittore, Milan, where he was held for fifteen months in 1927–1928. The newspaper *Il Sole* was on sale but "the majority of the prisoners, including the politicals, read *La Gazzetta dello Sport.* Out of about 2,500 prisoners they sold, at most, 80 copies of *Il Sole;* after *La Gazzetta dello Sport* the most widely read publications were *La Domenica del Corriere* and *Il Corriere dei Piccoli*" (that is, the Sunday supplement and children's supplement of *Il Corriere della Sera*).[13] Illustrated magazines had emerged in the late nineteenth century and took on their modern appearance in the 1930s with rotogravure printing (*rotocalcografia*), which allowed high-quality, fine-mesh reproduction of photographs. Weekly magazines consolidated and enlarged particular communities of readers—for instance, young women and children—and then defined more specialized constituencies such as sports and science enthusiasts. Overall, weekly magazines had sales far larger than those of newspapers or books. In the particular case of comic magazines, already in 1938 Domenico Lombrassa estimated three million readers a week.[14] By the mid-1950s the number of copies in circulation each week was around four million, and one normally estimates three to four readers per copy.[15] By contrast, rates of book reading would not increase steeply until after the 1960s: the number of people who declared they read books doubled from twelve to twenty-four million between 1973 and 1983. The main reasons were probably that more people stayed on at school and went to university, incomes rose, and books were better distributed.

All these observations on numbers of readers can be supported by statistics, both the comparative ones produced by UNESCO from the early 1950s, which show the lower rates of newspaper sales per capita in Italy compared to the countries of northern Europe, and those produced for Italy by Istat. These figures are useful as indicators of a national average, and for broad international comparisons, and as such they are reasonably reliable. However, they are not sensitive to local variations, such as the higher average rates of newspaper reading in certain regions or cities (Genoa and Turin, for example) or among particular social groups, or to the relatively high rates of consumption of the sports press, illustrated weeklies, and comics. Additional detailed figures on the circulation of specific published materials in particular areas present a more differentiated and complex picture. And once we begin to consider the qualitative aspects of reading—that is, how people read, when and where, and what reading meant to them—the picture becomes more varied still.

Even at the quantitative level, in fact, it is harder to get a clear picture of the amount of reading taking place in Italy at any given time than it is to obtain insight into other cultural activities, for a number of reasons. First, many of the older surveys and investigations into reading were biased toward book reading, and in this they reflected the cultural prejudices of those who commissioned and carried them out. They consequently failed to pay attention to the many other kinds of reading matter in circulation and the many ways of making contact with it. Unless one wants to reproduce those same assumptions, one must not take "reading" to mean only the relatively specialized competence that is the private silent reading of a written or printed verbal text. Reading, rather, should be taken to mean the decoding of many kinds of printed artifacts, including books, illustrated magazines, comics, advertising posters, and product labels with a high ratio of image to text. For a large number of people in our period, reading meant only or mainly this: *looking at* these materials, alone or with another person, without being able to understand the written text competently. One might describe these people as "poor readers" or "weak readers," and they frequently described themselves in these terms, but readers they were, in the sense that they scanned and comprehended a good proportion of what they looked at.

Many illustrated magazines circulated, like books, from hand to hand.

Rita B. (born 1927) and Adriana A. (born 1929) recalled of the late 40s and early 50s that although they could not afford to buy magazines themselves on their wages ("if you spent your money on a magazine how were you going to eat?"), local people sometimes brought them in—*Grand Hôtel, Intimità, Tipo, Bolero Film*—and the women then passed them round (11/12: 11–12). They remember being influenced by the fashion styles in the magazines, which they would have liked to emulate:

We thought they were really wonderful. We said: "Hey, look at this, look at that, see if maybe we could . . . ." Then we said: "Alright, when we've finished work we'll go home, let's hope we have enough money for a dress like this, and then we'll make one like it." But then when we got home the money had run out and there wasn't anything left for clothes. (11/12: 12)

The same women said there was a lending library in their hometown, where on a two-week loan they could borrow novels by Liala, Carolina Invernizio, and other writers. Similarly, Clorinda said that after the war she read *Grand Hôtel* because her friends passed copies round but she would never have been able to buy it herself: "They were way beyond our means then. . . . Because it wasn't like it is now when you might spend 1,000 lire, 1,500 lire on a newspaper. Impossible! It was out of the question" (66: 8).

Since various forms of reading matter had pictures or indeed were made up mainly of pictures (illustrated weeklies, comics, photoromances), much of the reading that people describe involved looking at pictures as well as at words, or instead of words. Rosalia A. (born 1913) read *Grand Hôtel* with her daughter Lucia, who was in the second year of elementary school and who read it aloud. The magazine was "a bit cleaner than the other things let's say because I had my daughter read it too, I didn't like those more saucy ones, those kisses, things like that" (30: 10). Angela C. (born 1919), a former worker at the Ducati factory in Bologna, said, "I never read anything for a bit because I only did third grade of elementary school, it wasn't much . . . the only thing we did get were those mags like *Grand Hôtel*, things like that I got. There was *Sogno* then and *Grand Hôtel*, we passed them around at work among our women friends" (25: 6). "I was quite a comics fan but what I liked in them were the drawings as well as the stories," said Livio S., born in 1936 (17: 23), who added, "no, I've read very few books, I admit." In his case, however, the memory perhaps needs to be linked to his career, and his self-presentation, as a sculptor with a strong visual sensibility. Simonetta Piccone Stella and Annabella Rossi, in a valuable survey of reading habits in Rome published in 1964, collected testimonies of a nineteen-year-old electrician who read only comics (*Topolino, Paperino*) and a twenty-five-year-old man who said of photoromances: "I read the pictures, it's more enjoyable."[16]

Second, if we do choose to narrow the focus onto books, such quantitative data as there are on sales of popular novels (usually figures for print runs of successive impressions of a book, often referred to in Italian as *edizioni*) are of limited reliability as guides to what people actually read at any given time, still less as to how, when, or where they read. This is because book reading does not obey the same kind of predictable periodicity as the reading of newspapers and magazines. The latter are normally read soon after they are bought by one or more people and are then either disposed of or at least not read again. Books, by contrast, may be obtained from many sources other than booksellers: they may be found and read in the home or at school, lent among friends, bought secondhand on stalls, or borrowed from or read in the libraries of cultural or political associations or in local public libraries (*biblioteche comunali*). Books on average have a longer life-cycle than most other mass cultural products: a single copy of a book can last a lifetime, or even several lifetimes, passing through successive generations of the same household, or from one household to another, either directly by means of lending or indirectly through the secondhand market.

We would get to read some books by Zola, *Nana,* that sort of thing, which when we were kids was strictly forbidden. The Church always dominated, it blacked out these things and that book had got crumpled, old, it had passed among twenty or thirty kids, they had all read it, because it was strange reading things that were a bit sexual, a bit, you know what I mean? (56: 22)

For working-class people who have led politically active lives, books are often presented in memory as a means to the development of class consciousness. Fulvio M., who remembered passing this copy of Zola around as a boy, was the son of an anarchist metalworker who died in 1936, when Fulvio was nine, and there were various social novels in the house, such as those of Cronin and Jack London. Some of them were bought before the Fascists came to power, and others were found in the Fascist period on secondhand bookstalls, such as in Porta Portese, Rome's large Sunday open market, or other places outside the commercial itineraries, the "working-class shops" (*negozi popolari*) (56: 21). However, his childhood reading had consisted also of comics: *Flash Gordon, Topolino, Il Corriere dei Piccoli.*

Among the various types of popular reading matter the photoromance (*fotoromanzo*) was the one genuinely new product of the postwar years, even though it had prewar precursors in the form of sequences published in magazines of film frames or stills from popular films.[17] For the most part these publications consisted of original photographic stories but some stories were "reductions" of films released in cinemas. The original stories were made up of a series of posed stills taken either in lit studio interiors or outdoors,

1 Sul transatlantico Terry e Michel si incontrano e si amano.

2 Entrambi sono fidanzati e quindi sono attesi a New York.

3 Allo sbarco Michel incontra la ricca fidanzata americana.

4 Anche Terry deve abbracciare il suo ricchissimo fidanzato.

5 Michel rifiuta il matrimonio e raggiunge la sua libertà.

6 Egli diventa pittore e un critico incoraggia la sua fatica.

Figures 2 and 3. A prewar sequence of film stills with captions (*Tempo* 4, no. 29, December 14, 1939) and a postwar *cineromanzo* (*Bolero Film* 8, no. 293, November 21, 1954) with speech inside the panels as well as narrative captions beneath. The respective films are *Love Affair* (Leo McCarey, 1939, with Irene Dunne and Charles Boyer) and *Johnny Guitar* (Nicholas Ray, 1954, with Joan Crawford and Sterling Hayden). By permission of Arnoldo Mondadori Editore S.p.A.

as shown in Michelangelo Antonioni's ten-minute documentary *L'amorosa menzogna* (*Lies of Love*, 1948) and lampooned in Federico Fellini's feature *Lo sceicco bianco* (*The White Sheik*, 1952), whereas the reductions of actual films were made from frame enlargements or production stills. In both cases the printed photographs were laid out in panels and speech bubbles were added, exactly like a comic strip. Technically, then, as well as semiotically, the *fotoromanzo* may be considered a fusion of the comic strip (panels and speech bubbles) and the film (a sequence of shots with different distances and framings of the actors: long, medium, close-up, and so on). *Grand Hôtel,* launched in 1946, originally had drawn stories (it later switched to photographic ones), but *Bolero Film,* launched in 1947, had photographic stories from the start and, as Alberto Abruzzese put it, "derived strictly from the cinema."[18] The readers in both cases were mainly women from the middle to lower social classes.

A survey commissioned by Mondadori of the readership of eight of its magazines, conducted by the Istituto Doxa in June–July 1962, reported that 93 percent of the 868 readers of *Bolero Film* surveyed were women (49 percent were housewives) and 91 percent were from lower-middle-class or lower-class families. The age distribution of the readership was quite wide. Of the "principal readers" (those who bought the magazine and read it first in their family or peer group), a little over half (56.5 percent) were between ages sixteen and thirty-four and most the rest were between thirty-five and sixty.[19] The testimonies from our own oral history project enable us to reconstruct something of the social world of the readership of these magazines as well as the mode of reading. *Grand Hôtel* was passed round among young women (11/12: 11–12; 66: 8), and the fashions in it inspired envy and a desire for emulation (11/12: 12). Augusta R., who grew up in a strongly Catholic household, recalled that *Grand Hôtel* was forbidden in the home by her mother, along with other women's magazines like *Gioia,* although her friends read it and she sometimes looked at it (92: 12–13).

Cinemas and Audiences

The cinema was, throughout our period, as we noted in the introduction, the single most popular form of commercial mass entertainment in Italy and yet the geographical distribution of the audience remained very uneven. Many more tickets were sold in the North and Center than in the South, with the exception of Naples and a few other cities such as Bari, Catania, and Palermo. Until the late 1950s, after the end of our period, the majority of spectators in all regions were concentrated in the provincial capitals and larger towns (Tables 1.1 and 1.2). The filmgoing habits and, above all, the tastes of these audiences were also strongly internally differentiated. First, there were differences between city and country. Ennio Flaiano said that cinema in the cities was a daily event that audiences had become used to whereas in villages it was a Sunday treat, like having a cake, and remained fascinating because of its relative rarity.[20] Second, within the urban audience there were marked differences according to the type of cinema and the area in which it was located. The three-tiered distribution structure of first-, second-, and third-run cinemas corresponded in the larger cities like Milan or Rome to a concentric urban geography. New releases were shown for a limited period at high ticket

Table 1.1. Cinema tickets sold in 48 provinces during selected years from the period 1937–1951.

	1937	1942	1947	1951
Alessandria	3,799,420	7,355,750	6,120,181	6,668,860
Aosta	741,384	1,739,167	813,434	1,152,710
Bergamo	2,705,603	3,712,765	4,907,700	6,401,730
Como	1,940,537	2,821,352	4,368,829	5,697,600
Genova	12,916,596	16,755,336	19,977,632	25,816,570
Milano	33,528,867	34,672,170	38,975,530	56,089,940
Novara	2,845,172	4,354,014	4,923,821	5,670,140
Torino	18,312,114	23,187,951	22,826,230	30,517,000
Trento	1,338,985	3,581,596	2,438,373	3,939,380
Treviso	2,083,312	3,962,493	4,715,022	5,685,830
Udine	3,621,082	9,366,734	9,444,009	10,371,530
Venezia	6,971,442	9,251,333	12,363,099	14,135,640
TOTAL	**90,804,514**	**120,760,661**	**131,873,860**	**172,146,930**
Average 12 Provinces North	**7,567,043**	**10,063,338**	**10,989,488**	**14,345,578**
Ancona	2,198,473	4,593,853	5,982,427	6,164,410
Bologna	10,155,477	12,953,657	13,642,311	18,457,930
Ferrara	5,486,441	6,730,360	8,254,946	10,721,400
Firenze	12,399,488	17,263,748	20,625,916	23,466,040
Forlì	2,363,651	4,574,694	5,752,401	6,841,880
Lucca	2,787,805	3,823,331	4,721,723	6,043,860
Modena	4,250,909	5,700,345	7,678,780	10,144,750
Perugia	1,702,477	3,169,494	3,699,917	3,917,280
Pisa	2,217,476	3,801,462	4,779,704	5,366,900
Reggio Emilia	2,615,498	4,327,283	5,220,339	5,940,450
Roma	32,242,086	40,768,038	49,314,329	66,115,840
Siena	1,451,208	2,715,831	2,840,261	3,309,360
TOTAL	**79,870,989**	**110,422,096**	**132,513,054**	**166,490,100**
Average 12 Provinces Center	**6,655,916**	**9,201,841**	**11,042,755**	**13,874,175**
Avellino	654,013	1,093,051	1,426,093	2,640,630
Bari	6,393,282	13,595,262	13,950,819	20,941,240
Benevento	540,914	998,541	1,237,102	1,431,650
Cosenza	778,780	2,044,218	2,476,688	4,147,990

Continued on the next page

Table 1.1. *Continued*

	1937	1942	1947	1951
Foggia	2,481,832	4,195,726	6,350,380	8,096,290
Lecce	1,178,654	2,474,794	3,481,585	6,937,370
Matera	157,972	472,650	794,223	1,224,180
Potenza	436,985	694,443	892,925	1,709,270
Napoli	19,143,091	24,978,764	29,754,151	41,147,550
Reggio Calabria	519,087	1,194,340	1,851,843	3,339,820
Salerno	1,865,120	4,189,431	4,979,232	8,308,790
Taranto	3,010,004	4,972,049	6,226,895	8,053,650
TOTAL	**37,159,734**	**60,903,269**	**73,421,936**	**107,978,430**
Average 12 Provinces South	**3,096,644**	**5,075,272**	**6,118,494**	**8,998,203**
Agrigento	713,442	1,795,292	2,457,877	4,536,300
Cagliari	2,071,512	5,865,305	6,776,085	9,562,600
Caltanissetta	611,971	1,886,350	1,561,646	2,960,040
Catania	5,174,465	6,956,249	8,160,272	12,360,680
Enna	383,800	1,023,287	893,229	2,100,220
Messina	2,038,721	3,156,457	3,984,787	5,961,130
Nuoro	147,504	589,559	665,945	792,880
Palermo	5,357,547	6,887,035	7,040,188	12,261,980
Ragusa	531,404	1,104,444	1,844,254	2,614,810
Sassari	1,064,350	3,190,581	2,687,698	3,289,930
Siracusa	1,687,382	3,004,304	3,679,270	4,882,960
Trapani	1,237,372	2,862,669	2,734,132	5,094,890
TOTAL	**21,019,470**	**38,321,532**	**42,485,383**	**66,418,420**
Average 12 Provinces Islands	**1,751,623**	**3,193,461**	**3,540,449**	**5,534,868**

Source: Data elaborated from *Lo spettacolo in Italia* (Rome: SIAE), yearbooks for years indicated. It should be noted that the selected provinces of the region of Emilia-Romagna—Bologna, Ferrara, Forli, Modena, Reggio Emilia—appear here in the Center, whereas Istat statistics treat this as a region of the North.

prices in the city center in the *prima visione* (first-run) cinemas; the films then passed to the *seconda visione* (second-run) cinemas, and, in some cases, *terza visione* (third-run) circuits in the outer suburbs, so that the period of commercial exploitation of the same film could be up to three years, excluding reruns. Gian Franco Venè claims that there had been a class-based reshuffling of audiences from the beginning of the 1930s. Ticket prices in the first-

Table 1.2. Cinema tickets (× 1,000) sold in provincial capitals (*capoluoghi*) and rest of the provinces, 1936–1956.

	Capoluoghi	Rest of Provinces	Total	*% Capoluoghi*	*% Rest of Provinces*
1936	187,029	77,248	264,277	70.77	29.23
1937	217,312	96,663	313,975	69.21	30.79
1938	234,778	113,819	348,597	67.35	32.65
1939	241,075	118,090	359,165	67.12	32.88
1940	241,647	127,986	369,633	65.37	34.63
1941	267,057	156,921	423,978	62.99	37.01
1942	276,926	182,245	459,171	60.31	39.69
1943	275,012	184,321	459,333	59.87	40.13
1944	272,908	186,270	459,178	59.43	40.57
1945	270,917	188,295	459,212	59.00	41.00
1946	268,916	190,314	459,230	58.56	41.44
1947	305,356	220,033	525,389	58.12	41.88
1948	319,611	259,889	579,500	55.15	44.85
1949	331,015	276,548	607,563	54.48	45.52
1950	354,718	299,156	653,874	54.25	45.75
1951	373,506	323,235	696,741	53.61	46.39
1952	391,558	346,357	737,915	53.06	46.94
1953	403,736	364,487	768,223	52.56	47.44
1954	421,632	379,101	800,733	52.66	47.34
1955	427,332	392,092	819,424	52.15	47.85
1956	412,183	377,970	790,153	52.16	47.84

Source: Elaborated from *Lo spettacolo in Italia* (Rome: SIAE), yearbooks for years indicated. The figures for 1936, apart from the total, are estimates provided by SIAE, since detailed breakdown by provinces began only in 1937.

run cinemas trebled compared with 1922 from 55 cents to 1.5 lire, and this meant that the working-class audience was relegated to the suburban cinemas (*sale di periferia*).[21] The same distribution structure corresponded to an urban/rural divide as well as to that of large city/small city/small town or village. Outside cities and larger towns nearly all cinemas were second- or third-run.

Piero Santi (born 1912) gave in his book *Ombre rosse* (1954) a colorful description of the daily cycle of one second-run cinema in Florence, the Astra, from mid-afternoon to late evening in the early 1950s. It was in a building between the church of Santa Maria Novella and the Arno which in the Fascist period had housed the Party headquarters. The first to arrive are children and adolescents: "young people from the country . . . the suburbs that thickly surround the city; kids from the city . . . and often from the districts [*rioni*] across the river." If they come in groups of five or six they are noisy—"they feel that distinctly Italian need (but perhaps it's also a human need) to make their presence, their physical reality, felt to others"—but once the film begins, "the kids go quiet because they are absorbed in those adventures—maybe it is only the cinema that manages to hold their attention to that extent, giving them a reality outside themselves." When the lights go on between reels the noise starts up again. At six o'clock "the young men from the night shelter in San Frediano arrive; after having worked in the morning in the early afternoon they share the small amount of money they have earned on the cinema and some filled rolls; often they have their girlfriends." At seven the soldiers arrive: "here they are noisy, not shy like those who go to the Alhambra or the Astoria or other suburban cinemas: if they'd discovered the Astra it meant they were old lags, they almost felt like citizens of Florence."[22] Finally,

among the chatter and gestures and a few cigarettes passed around it got late, the soldiers gradually left the cinema and, at about nine or ten o'clock, the young people who worked during the day came in as if they owned the place, banging down the seats. They were in that state of excitement of someone who, having finished work, eaten, and washed, feels the whole evening and much of the night stretching out before him, open to every possible kind of adventure. The cinema was the first stage, then there would be the others, more unpredictable and thus more fascinating. The cinema was still rather standard fare, bourgeois you might say: it was the interval between work and the later evening, no more than that. Indeed these young people were those who concentrated least on the film.[23]

An oral testimony collected by Alessandro Portelli from Aurora (born circa 1915), a worker at the Alterocca printing works in the industrial town of Terni, about seventy kilometers north of Rome, represents the social scale of cinemas there in the 1930s–1950s:

The Cinema Corridoni was there, on the new street; it was a nice cinema, you paid one lira. There was also the Venezia, but you paid less because it was the fleapit [*lu pidocchitto*]; then there was the Lux and the Radium. The Moderno; and when you didn't have much money you went to the railwaymen's cinema [that is, at their *dopolavoro,* after-work club]. When they showed films, blockbusters, as they are called now, that lasted four or five hours, they showed them over two evenings, three evenings, like in installments. I saw *Purosangue,* a wonderful film. But most of all afterwards, American films. Lovely films, such lovely films. Vittorio De Sica, those lightweight films, with Amedeo Nazzari, Yvonne Sanson. But lots of American films. I saw lots of them.[24]

Third, there was a further distinction between weekday (*feriali*) films and weekend (*festivi*) films, noted by Goffredo Fofi in a 1978 essay, "Cinema 'basso' e cinema 'alto'" (" 'High' and low' cinema"), in which he recalled his own experiences of cinemagoing in the decade 1945–1955:

For me there were weekday films and weekend films. With very few exceptions, the weekday films were American and the weekend ones were Italian. The size and class composition of the audience changed and the films changed too. American genre films, including the best ones, were good for every day and for the restricted petty-bourgeois and artisan audience, while on Sundays they showed either blockbusters or Italian films. The films that made you laugh or cry or which at least stirred up strong sensations or amazement.

I am convinced that this dichotomy existed more or less for cinema audiences throughout Italy in the first ten years after the war. American films were "escapism" [*evasione*], the smoothed-over world of dreams, the exotic, and perhaps also "art." Italian films, with all their baggage of conventions, were "reality." The settings, faces and passions were recognizable and were ours. The whole schematic, reductive, repetitive fantasy of the plots had a concrete foundation in which we could take part.[25]

Fofi's point about American cinema being "escapism" and Italian cinema being "reality," and his subsequent related point about Hollywood never really colonizing Italy (demonstrated, among other things, so he claims, by the persistent strength of the left subculture), needs to be taken seriously, as does his explanation for the great popularity of Totò: "audiences loved him above all for this, for his vindictive aggression which in some way avenged their dissatisfactions and their unsatisfied hunger."[26] However, there are also some problems with this argument. In particular the polarization of "escapism" and "reality" (as Fofi's own qualifications of the terms and his placing them in quotation marks suggests) is perhaps more misleading than it is helpful. One needs to consider what the appeal of U.S. cinema might have been beyond "escapism." There is also a rather romantic notion in this article of a subproletarian interactive audience to whom Italian films (comedy, tragedy, melodrama) appealed because they spoke about material or sexual deprivation and frustration.[27]

Various other accounts have come down to us of the different perceptions of American and Italian films and actors. The actress Luisella Beghi grew up in Parma and in her early teens went nearly every day to the cinema, where she could see three films for one lira. Francesco Savio interviewed her in February 1974 and asked what she used to like:

Oh, everything. Especially American films. There were those films with Greta Garbo, and then Ronald Colman, I was crazy about Ronald Colman. There was Lilian Harvey, Clark Gable, Bette Davis, there was Katharine Hepburn, I liked her a lot and I said (you know what young girls are like?) "How I'd like to play her parts."[28]

The writer Italo Calvino, born in 1923, recalled in a text published in 1974 the sensual pleasures of his solitary adolescent filmgoing in San Remo in 1936–1942 as well as his different perception of French and American female stars:

French cinema was as heavy with smells as American cinema smelt of Palmolive, of shiny, sterile places. The women had a carnal presence that fixed them in your memory as both living women and erotic spirits (Viviane Romance is the figure who comes to mind here) whereas in the Hollywood stars the eroticism was sublimated, stylized, idealized. (Even the most carnal of the American actresses of the time, Jean Harlow, was made unreal by the dazzling whiteness of her skin.)[29]

Calvino's view was not universally shared. For example, the actor Roberto Villa, interviewed by Francesco Savio in the same period and asked about the American actors he liked in the 1930s, said, "I was particularly crazy about Barbara Stanwyck, I thought she was fabulous, she had this femininity, this unbridled sexuality, I liked her a lot."[30]

Our own witnesses provided some interesting accounts of their different memories of Italian and foreign films. Augusto C. (born 1921) recalled the 1936 Metro-Goldwyn-Mayer version of *Romeo and Juliet*, directed by George Cukor, which he saw when he was fifteen or sixteen:

we thought the Americans were brilliant at translating a story into film. I could give as an example *Romeo and Juliet* with Norma Shearer and Leslie Howard, the baronet, who acted . . . that's how I judge it now, I'd really like to see it again . . . that moment when the theater turns into cinema. I still remember those images of *Romeo and Juliet* after all these years . . . I also remember the brilliant street fight between the two clans, the way they did that clash in the square when Mercutio gets killed. I haven't read it since, I remember it like that. In our films there were these fake-looking stunts, they didn't have real stuntmen, they didn't have those advanced techniques the Americans had as soon as the talkies began. (55: 27)

Fulvio M., for many years a labor union activist, remembered his preference for adventure films over romantic films and for American actors over Italians (56: 4, 6) but he also emphasized his liking for Italian "social" films such as *Ladri di biciclette* and *Miracolo a Milano* (*Miracle in Milan*) (Vittorio De Sica, 1951), and for *Riso amaro* (*Bitter Rice*) (Giuseppe De Santis, 1949), a "social" film but also "good" (*bello*). Vita R., born in 1917, who had started working in the accounts office of the Singer sewing machine company in Trieste when she was eighteen, went frequently to the cinema from the mid-1930s with a female friend. In her recollection, she said, "For the most part the Italian films were either romantic weepies, which I didn't like, and the occasional cheerful film. I remember at the time there was the famous Sicilian, [Angelo] Musco; yes, I liked those" (65: 15). After the war she liked British comedies and the French ones with Fernandel but not the films of Totò: "they've always told me I'm an idiot because I don't like Totò, I don't like that sort of style of comedy . . . Fernandel is different, Totò is a variety act as far as I'm concerned, he's just a comic turn, not an actor" (65: 16).

Vittorio Spinazzola, in a study first published in 1974, argued that the films of the so-called *neorealismo rosa* (romantic neorealism) of the early 1950s were the first to create a "relatively homogeneous filmgoing public" in Italy in that they had good box-office returns throughout the distribution cascade from first to third run; they were "films that audiences liked both in the large city centre cinemas and in the suburbs and provinces."[31] They included *Due soldi di speranza* (*Two Pennyworth of Hope*) (Renato Castellani, 1952), *Pane, amore e fantasia* (*Bread, Love and Dreams*) and *Pane, amore e gelosia* (*Bread, Love and Jealousy*) (Luigi Comenicini, 1953, 1954), *Pane, amore e . . .* (*Bread, Love and . . .*) (Dino Risi, 1955), *Poveri ma belli* (*Poor but Good-looking*) (Dino Risi, 1955), *L'oro di Napoli* (*Gold of Naples*) (Vittorio De Sica, 1954) and *Peccato che sia una canaglia* (*Too Bad She's Bad*) (Alessandro Blasetti, 1954). These films retained the lower-class settings and speech of the films of neorealism but they had a blunter social and political edge and tended to be love stories, often comedies, focusing on the generational divide between young people and their parents. They also, importantly, featured the new female stars like Gina Lollobrigida and Sophia Loren. To demonstrate his claim Spinazzola selected three of these films released in the 1955–1956 season, *Pane, amore e . . .* , *Racconti romani* (*Roman Tales*) (Gianni Franciolini), and *La bella mugnaia* (*The Miller's Wife*) (Mario Camerini), which occupied respectively second, third, and eighth place in box-office takings on their first run, and then noted that three years later, in 1959, when they were in their third run, they were respectively in third, fifth, and seventh place. "In the move from first to last run this group of films therefore maintained almost identical positions, without the gap between first-run box-office takings and earnings in the market as a whole that normally characterizes popular films."[32]

It is perhaps inevitable that retrospective accounts of cinemagoing produced after the collapse of the second- and third-run cinema circuit in Italy in the 1970s and 1980s should be marked by nostalgia for a lost golden age. This is true of two films of the late 1980s that both present fictionalized accounts of small-town cinemas and their audiences in the postwar years and take their titles from the cinemas themselves. *Splendor* (Ettore Scola, 1988) is set in Arpino (province of Frosinone, Lazio) and *Nuovo Cinema Paradiso* (Giuseppe Tornatore, 1989) in a fictional Sicilian town, Ciancaldo. Despite the differences in generation and thus of filmgoing memories of the two writer-directors (Scola was born in Campania in 1931 in the small town of Trevico in the province of Avellino; Tornatore in Sicily in 1956 in Bagheria in the province of Palermo) and the different types of cinema (the one in Scola's film is commercial, in Tornatore's it is a parish cinema), both films, made in the period of rampant commercial television, look back wistfully at a world where the cinema was a hub of small-town life. A similar nostalgia marks Gian Franco Venè's colourful but anecdotal descriptions of the class divisions within and between cinemas in the 1930s and 1940s. The more expensive seats were separated by a stockade from the "plebs" (*popolaccio*).[33] In cinemas where the management did not want audiences to sit through more than one screening of the same film, bouncers (*buttafuori*) were employed who would go up to someone and say, "Out now you, you've been here two hours, I remember."[34] Venè claims that this shift, this embourgeoisement of the cinema audience, coincided with the advent of sound, when large cinemas were converted and new deluxe ones were built. However, it would be wrong to assume that audiences were rigidly socially segregated. Fulvio M. recalled that in the 1950s, since he then had a job with a regular income with the transport company ATAC, he preferred to go from Borgata Gordiani to the first-run cinemas in the center of Rome:

Because in the suburban cinemas when you went in there was an awful chaos, everyone whistling, every so often the film broke, the lights went on and you had to wait quarter of an hour, twenty minutes, for it to start again, so you tried, when you saw a first-run film you liked, to go a place where you could watch it in peace and enjoy it. (56: 5)

The rise of cinema coincided with the decline of variety theater. The SIAE figures on expenditure on different types of paid entertainment capture an interesting set of shifts in the regional distribution of the variety audience in our period (see Table 1.3). In 1936 54 percent of variety theater tickets sold in Italy as a whole were in the south (the mainland south plus Sicily and Sardinia), which at the time accounted for only 20.5 percent of the nation's expenditure on cinema and 14.6 percent of that on opera. Campania, the region of Naples, had by far the highest audience for variety in Italy, and both Puglia and Sicily had larger audiences than any other region apart from Lazio, the region of Rome. Lombardy had 141,000, Piedmont 107,000, and Tuscany 112,000.

Between 1936 and 1941, however, there was a large increase in audiences for the variety theater in the North and Center (with the exception of the Trentino and Umbria): an almost fivefold increase in Piedmont and Liguria, fourfold in Emilia, threefold in Lombardy, one-and-a-half times in Tuscany and the Marches, and a little less in Lazio. At the same time there was a drastic fall, probably affected by the war, in audience numbers in nearly all the regions of the south, apart from Sardinia. On average audiences fell by half, and the proportion of expenditure nationally on variety in the south fell from 54 percent to 15.3 percent. Between the war and the early 1950s the trend reversed again and the prewar geographical distribution was reestablished.

Table 1.3. Variety theater: ticket sales by region 1936, 1941, 1952.

	1936	1941	1952
Valle d'Aosta*			3,763
Piemonte	107,413	532,983	133,302
Liguria	42,466	208,101	105,337
Lombardia	140,958	471,068	333,527
Trentino	22,981	19,386	26,795
Veneto	61,517	136,256	165,746
Friuli-Venezia Giulia	16,491	143,027	59,776
Emilia	61,112	261,699	248,035
Toscana	111,581	280,643	207,434
Marche	17,218	30,066	53,453
Umbria	19,001	16,154	30,016
Lazio	184,014	240,596	232,444
Abruzzi e Molise	20,906	14,192	25,595
Campania	548,430	224,435	871,693
Puglia	154,884	58,378	110,547
Basilicata	6,556	5,945	10,787
Calabria	10,650	6,045	33,246
Sicilia	145,239	66,560	226,537
Sardegna	36,286	46,126	48,548
ITALY	1,707,703	2,761,660	2,928,533

* The Region of Valle d'Aosta was constituted in 1948.
Source: SIAE, *Lo spettacolo in Italia: 1936*, 82; *1941*, 75–77; *1952*, 36–65.

Two feature films both released in 1950 depict the swansong of the variety and *avanspettacolo* as forms of popular entertainment: Monicelli and Steno's *Vita da cani* (*A Dog's Life*) and Lattuada and Fellini's *Luci del varietà* (*Variety*

Lights). Fellini's *I Vitelloni* (*Spivs*) (1953) also deals with this subject in the story of the aspiring young playwright Leopoldo (Leopoldo Trieste). These films have an analogue in Chaplin's *Limelight* (1952), released in Italy as *Luci della ribalta* in 1953. The two Italian films show the polarization of the world of live entertainment after the war, with the more expensive live shows still doing well, and considered glamorous, and the traveling popular companies down at the bottom, their members playing to provincial audiences in smoke-filled fleapits, sleeping on trains between venues, having their takings requisitioned by people with whom they have not settled their bills, skipping out on bills from hotels and restaurants. The demonic figures in both films are the powerful impresario and the wealthy theater owner.

It is interesting to consider the problems these films pose as sources for an understanding of audiences. They show a strongly reactive audience and also what is presumably a characteristic mixture of acts—the repertoire consists on the one hand of regional and "Italian" ones, including patriotic sketches (toward the end of *Luci del varietà* Melina Amour, played by Giulietta Masina, warms the heart even of the most hostile spectator with her Garibaldi impression; there is a similar patriotic number in the theater sequence of *I Vitelloni*), and on the other hand of modern acts (the boogie-woogie and bikinis in *Luci del varietà*, the black jazz trumpeter in *Vita da cani*), and they depict a range of audience types. *Luci del varietà*, for instance, starts with a performance in front of what looks like a family audience, with children dancing in the aisles; but the next sequence of a performance, where the skirt accidentally falls off the hapless Liliana (Carla Del Poggio), is in front of a raucous and exclusively male audience. No doubt there are elements of documentary truth in these representations, and they are corroborated by other sources (memoirs of performers, oral history), but they clearly involve also a deliberate, and rather nostalgic as well as caricatural, recreation of a disappearing world. This becomes increasingly a component of Fellini's later depictions of the variety theater, for instance in *Amarcord* (1973).

The two films released in 1950 were both vehicles for established or up-and-coming cinema starlets, as *Limelight* was for Claire Bloom, whose star career was launched by her portrayal of the young dancer Terry opposite Chaplin's ageing clown Calvero. Carla Del Poggio (in *Luci del varietà*) and Gina Lollobrigida (Margherita in *Vita da cani*) play newcomers who, largely on account of their looks, rapidly break through the ceiling of the provincial *avanspettacolo* to the upper reaches of live entertainment. Like *Limelight*, too, the two Italian films contain a core relationship, made more or less explicit, and more or less erotic, between an older male comedian and a young, aspiring female performer. All three films have a seesaw plot structure in which the former declines as the latter rises, so that the displacement of the old performer by the new one, and the live stage act by the cinema, is emphasized. Both *Luci del varietà* and *Vita da cani* show a traveling company down on its heels. There is an element of self-referentiality in that the *capocomico*, the actor-manager, is played by an actor with a background in the world of live theater: Aldo Fabrizi, who plays Nino Martoni in *Vita da cani*, had been a stand-up comic and Roman variety star; Peppino De Filippo, who plays Checco Dalmonte in *Luci del varietà*, was well known from his comic performances in Naples. Thus, overall, the films' relationship to the two media, variety and cinema, is quite complex. However, we can say that they are both representations of the world of popular variety in decline in a medium, film, which had by then both partially absorbed and displaced live stage entertainment.

Radio Listening and Music

We asked many of our interviewees when they remembered first hearing a radio. If they were habitual listeners we also asked when they listened and to what. For some people who lived in villages their early radio listening fitted into preexisting social routines, such as visiting family or neighbors, so despite the novelty of the medium itself it is questionable whether it brought about any real displacement of older cultural patterns. Barbara T., who was born in 1907 in Challand Saint Anselme (Aosta) and had always lived there, remembered that before her husband bought their first radio in 1949 they used to go to the end of the village to listen at her cousins' house: "We went once a week, on Wednesday I think it was, to hear the accordion played by . . . what was his name? I think he was French, I can't think of his name now, we went to hear the accordions." Her daughter, Augusta (born 1935), described visits with her friends to listen to music on other people's sets as part of the *veglia:*

There were two or three people then who had been able to afford a radio. In the evening we went from house to house, to the *vejà*, as they were called, and it was lovely, a good reason to meet, to tell each other our stuff, our feelings, our loves, all these things in these *vejà*. (92: 10)

Barbara remembered the purchase of their first radio:

My husband wanted to buy a radio, I was sorry and I said, "It's too expensive!" Then they all got a payment from the ENEL, the SIP [electricity and telephone companies], as a bonus, and he said, "I'm going to buy a radio with that bonus." I said "What for? We won't have time to listen to it," but he bought it anyway. It was the year they elected the prince of Monaco, I remember that because I listened to the whole ceremony on the radio and I said: "Well, I'm also pleased we've got a radio!" (93: 20)

Other memories were linked to particular news events and the recollections of these were presumably affected by later knowledge. Natalia was twelve in 1935 and worked making accessories for car interiors at a branch of the Martinin factory in Via Lanzo in Turin. One day she was called outside to hear the announcement of the war against Abyssinia. As she recalled it, "They made us go outside and we went into a square and the loudspeaker announced this war and lots of people were crying. I didn't see a lot of enthusiasm for it" (4: 2). At Martinin the radios were owned by the foremen and managers.

At home, I . . . at least, there was nobody who had a radio, it was very rare, maybe the chief electrician, he had a radio. The manager of the factory who lived there, the parish priest, they had radios, and every now and then they would report the news: "I heard on the radio, this and that," but apart from that I never saw a radio. (4: 9)

Mimmo V., born in 1930, grew up in the small town of Minturno near the coast between Rome and Naples, and he remembered his father taking him in 1940 to hear Mussolini's speeches announcing Italy's entry into the war: "In that area there was only one person who had a radio and we all went to listen to it, he turned it up to full volume so everyone could hear" (58/59: 13). His father bought their first radio, a Magnadyne, in 1951, by which time they were living in the Tor Pignattara district of Rome. Since his father was very keen on Neapolitan songs and his sister Mena (born 1935) had a good memory for tunes on the radio, she would buy *Il Canzoniere della radio,* in which song lyrics were published, and she and her father would sit together in the evening learning the songs (58/59: 31–2). It was also in 1951 that, in Burcei, Mariarita P.'s uncle was given a radio as a wedding present, a few months before electricity came to the village. She remembers neighbors coming to listen and friends asking, "And today what did they say?" (41: 11–12). She too remembers the songs she heard on the radio in that period, such as "Rosamunda"; hearing it then triggered her memory of having first heard it during the war sung by an evacuee in Burcei whose home in Cagliari had been destroyed by an air raid.[35]

Others had a radio in the home already before the war and they commented on the purchase of a radio as a significant life event. In Turin, Sergio P.'s family bought a Superla, a set manufactured in Bologna, around 1939, when he was fourteen and had already started working as an apprentice at Fiat. It was through this radio that he discovered the world of popular song that he was later to join as a professional singer for twelve years of his working life:

I began listening to songs. There were already the bands, Angelini, Barzizza, I'm talking about 1939–1940. For two years running they had singing contests and the first year the winners were Otello Boccaccini, Gilberto Mazzi, and Dea Gar-baccio. The next year it was Oscar Carboni, Alfredo Clerici, and many others who later went on singing with both Angelini and Barzizza. I was crazy about those songs and sometimes I stood there and learned them, I learned them very easily and I let myself go by singing them in the bathroom. (1: 1)

Radio listening was distinct from other forms of cultural consumption at this time in that people habitually did it while carrying out another activity such as eating, drinking, or working. Adriana A. worked from the late 1940s as a domestic servant for a professional couple (the husband was an engineer who had an office at home, the wife was an elementary schoolteacher), and she listened to the radio during the daytime while washing, cleaning, and looking after their children. "At that time there was a lot of music, really a lot, it's not like now when you get for example fifteen minutes of drama; no, there was a lot of music then and I liked it" (11/12: 30). When she heard the husband come in she would turn it off but he would say, "Adriana, instead of turning it off why don't you leave it on? If you really like it leave it on. Keep it quiet, though, otherwise I can hear it in the office" (11/12: 31). Adriana bought her own first radio, a secondhand set, in 1952 when she was twenty-three and had been married for two years (11/12: 22). Giuseppe M. was a hairdresser in Aosta and after the war he had a radio in his salon: "I played music, news, information, the bulletins. I liked the news, the bulletins, because I read it in the papers, then I heard the comments. And I always tried to keep up to date from that point of view" (53: 13). In Burcei, Mariarita P. helped her aunt with sewing in the early 1950s and they listened to the radio together. She remembers she particularly liked the midafternoon broadcasts of readings from the *Divine Comedy*, as well as songs by Giorgio Consolini and others (41: 12–13).

The radio audience, like the cinema audience, can be approximately quantified for our period, because the monopoly broadcaster EIAR (Ente Italiano Audizioni Radiofoniche) and its successor RAI (Radio Audizioni Italia—the name was changed in 1944 to mark the refounding and reorganization of the company after the fall of Fascism) collected regular statistics, province by province, of numbers of paying subscribers (see the tables in chapter 6) and they also conducted, periodically, their own surveys of radio listening. In addition, RAI commissioned the Istituto Doxa to carry out surveys of radio listening in 1952 and 1955. The official company statistics are approximate because there were always many more listeners than there were subscribers. This was both because an unquantifiable number of people evaded payment of the license fee (*abbonamento*) and because most sets had more than one listener: either the other members of a family in the case of a private subscription or members of the public in the case of a special or institutional subscription

Figure 4. A house in Canolo, Sunday afternoon, early 1950s. The radio occupies a place of honor in the salotto (sitting room). Note also the covered-up fireplace, later replaced by stove heating. Photo by permission of Egeo Ferretti.

(the ones taken out by schools, *dopolavoro* clubs, bars, and so on). For private subscriptions there is no agreed coefficient for working out the ratio of subscribers to listeners, since the EIAR/RAI did not collect information on the average family size of subscribers. The EIAR reckoned six listeners per private subscription in 1940, but Alberto Monticone considers this an overestimate and assumes four people per household.[36]

The various surveys conducted since the early years of the medium give us a partial picture of audience tastes and opinions but they are also like distorting mirrors. Those before 1939 were based on very small samples; they were commissioned by *Radiorario* (later renamed *Radiocorriere*) and tended to reflect the opinions of the limited universe of readers of this program listings magazine rather than the wider radio audience of private subscribers as a whole, let alone that of collective listeners in public places.[37] They also gave no demographic information about audiences. It is clear, nevertheless, that the audience whose tastes were sampled consisted of the small, solid, middle-class public who formed the backbone of the private subscribers. The majority of respondents to the 1927 "Radioreferendum" said they wanted more classical music and cultural talk programs and less jazz, light music, and advertising.[38]

The referendum of 1939–1940 was significantly different from the earlier ones, primarily because of the large size of the sample. It was given a massive promotional push, with a special documentary made by the Istituto Luce (the state-funded nonfiction film production company) about the referendum screened in cinemas and with billboard and newspaper advertisements, songs distributed on vinyl records, over three million leaflets, and incentives to return the questionnaires in the form of cash prizes for the first replies extracted: a first prize of 100,000 lire, ten prizes of 10,000 lire, and hundreds of smaller prizes. Around 900,000 replies were received, representing over 75 percent of the total 1.2 million private radio subscribers at the time. It was, as Antonio Papa noted, the largest public opinion survey conducted in Italy in the first half of the twentieth century.[39] It was also the first survey of the radio audience to require detailed demographic information. As well as being invited to indicate, as in the earlier questionnaires, their favorite programs (a list of twenty-eight program genres was supplied, including news, sports reports, school programs, light music, opera, and religious music; preferences were to be marked "yes" or "no" and expressed on a numerical scale), respondents were now also required to fill in the number of members in the household, their ages, and the occupation of the subscriber, normally the main breadwinner. The referendum also asked how many hours one listened each day and which stations one listened to.

The 1939–1940 referendum had some serious limitations, however, most of which have already been remarked upon in earlier studies. In confining its universe to private subscribers and their families in the home, the poll once more left out the large number of collective listeners in public places who constituted the bulk of the radio audience at the time. Papa drew attention to the "fragmentation and ambiguity" of the social categories used, which made it difficult to correlate them with social classes.[40] These categories included state employees (*impiegati dello Stato*), two types of accountant (*commercialisti e ragionieri*), "farm-owners" (*proprietari di aziende agricole*, but that term could cover a wide variety of economic activities in 1939–1940), "well-off people" (*benestanti*, presumably those living off private inherited incomes), pensioners (*pensionati*), and housewives (*casalinghe*). The last of these categories, which accounted for just under 10 percent of the audience polled, flattened out a complex array of social realities, from wives of professional men with domestic servants to working-class women in the home. Papa also noted that although the results gave numbers of listeners in each category and their relative proportions as percentages of total listeners, they did not indicate the total numbers of these categories in the population as a whole and thus one could not see clearly which categories were overrepresented and underrepresented.[41] Anna Lucia Natale attempted to rectify this by grouping the forty-two occupational categories used in the referendum into a small number of larger sets (upper, middle and lower class, students, housewives), based loosely on the model of social stratification proposed by Paolo Sylos Labini, and then correlating these with numbers in each grouping in the active population according to census data for 1936.[42]

Whatever the shortcomings of Natale's method, which are partly those of Sylos Labini's work itself (one may question both his allocation of certain occupational categories to class groupings and the groupings themselves), her elaboration nevertheless shows very clearly that the "upper classes" (including, among others, company directors, the higher professions, and *benestanti*) were still in 1939–1940 overrepresented in the total audience of private subscribers while the "lower classes" (peasants, agricultural laborers, artisans, factory workers, transport workers, and so on) were greatly underrepresented. The "upper classes" and "lower classes" as a whole each accounted for around 28 percent of replies in the referendum but the former were just 2.5 percent of the active population and the latter 84.5 percent. The referendum also confirmed the uneven regional distribution of the private radio audience, with 73 percent of replies coming from the North and Center and only 27 percent from the South and Islands. The two northern regions of Piedmont and Lombardy alone accounted for 35 percent of the total returns.[43] Finally it confirmed, as earlier surveys had, and as was common to most countries in the pre-transistor era of the fixed domestic radio set, usually located in middle-class homes in the living room or dining room, that the peak listening times in the home were around family mealtimes, in the middle of the day (12:30 to 2 P.M.) and the mid- to late evening (8–11 P.M.), with low listening figures in the early morning and midafternoon.

In explaining the aims of the referendum, the EIAR said it wanted to collect detailed information on audience demographics and program preferences: "Each category, for various reasons that can easily be set out, has a particular mentality and specific habits, and the EIAR needs to understand this if it wants to give everyone, as far as it can, what they want."[44] The fact remains that this was not an independent survey but an in-house poll designed, conducted, and processed by the radio company itself, and significantly, despite the huge promotion, the detailed findings were not made widely available but were published in a deluxe, leather-bound volume of only 300 copies. For this reason, recent studies have described it as an EIAR "plebiscite" rather than a proper opinion poll or market analysis.[45]

The promoters were interested not in creating a new schedule of programmes but in showing how good the existing one was. They were not looking for suggestions but for confirmations. They were not concerned to make the audience active in relation to the radio but simply to get their approval and understand their habits.[46]

Gianni Isola was right to see this as a reflection of the paternalism of the EIAR in this period and as such of the close ties it had formed by 1939 with the Fascist regime. Yet for this very reason it is interesting that this large-scale referendum still registered a significant degree of dissatisfaction among the audience, just as the earlier surveys had done, with some of the EIAR's more political and pedagogical program content. It is true that some factual programs, such as news (*giornale radio*) and the overtly propagandistic *Commento ai fatti del giorno,* registered very high approval votes (97 percent and 85 percent, respectively). Others, however, had a significant number of "no" votes. These included the programs for the armed forces, sports broadcasts, and school programs (24 percent, 33 percent, and 44 percent of "no" votes, respectively) and the program for farmers, the *Ora dell'agricoltore* (27 percent of "no" votes).[47]

One needs to take care in interpreting the disparity between these two sets of results: the high "yes" votes for news bulletins and news commentary, the high "no" votes for other kinds of factual programs. Natale uses the terms "consent" and "dissent" in discussing these results and, even if with some qualifications, tends to identify the "yes" and "no" votes respectively with acceptance and nonacceptance of "fascist values."[48] Yet, while it is true that the yes/no form of the question, designed to elicit responses on a scale of approval, and the high percentages of declared approval for news and news commentary both reveal, as Isola suggested, the plebiscitary character of the referendum and the close formal ties between the radio company and the regime, it seems harder to explain what was actually being expressed in the "no" votes for other program types. It is unlikely that it was "dissent" from the regime or its values as such or even strong disapproval. What is more likely is that it was lack of interest by middle-class adults in talk programs targeted at social or occupational groups (peasant farmers, soldiers, schoolchildren) with whom they felt they had little or nothing in common. The farming programs, for instance, had a fairly large following in the form of collective listening through the Ente Radio Rurale, but this audience's views were not solicited or reflected in the referendum. At the other end of the spectrum, the referendum showed that private radio subscribers by and large rejected one of the EIAR's "prestige" genres, namely poetry readings, which scored 60 percent of "no" votes. The results thus appear to confirm that the sector of the radio audience dominated by middle-class adults with a fair degree of education wanted the radio for information (news was a popular genre) and entertainment, in particular good-quality music, but they also wanted their high culture in small doses.

An altogether different type of "dissent" in the radio audience, one which can be unequivocally interpreted as political, was that expressed by "clandestine listening" to antifascist broadcasts from outside Italy, both from foreign-language stations and by the Italian antifascist parties. There had been repression of clandestine listening by the Fascist authorities as early as 1930. Isola mentions the first victim, an anarchist from L'Aquila, Francesco De Rubeis, who was sentenced to five years of *confino* (internal exile).[49] The Spanish Civil War, in which the Fascist government intervened from the autumn of 1936 on the side of Franco's nationalist Falange and in which Italian antifascist volunteers fought with the Republicans, marked a turning point, with a significant take-up of clandestine listening to the antifascist broadcasts in Italian of Radio Barcellona (Giustizia e Libertà) and Radio Mosca (Italian Communist Party). This was also the time when hammer-and-sickle and "viva Stalin" graffiti appeared in industrial cities. A police report from Turin dated September 4, 1936 mentions the latter appearing in public urinals.[50] Later, during World War II, Radio Londra (the Italian language service of the BBC) would have a significant clandestine audience.

Radio did much to spread a taste for light music, as we shall discuss in chapter 6, but it was not until after the war that this became visibly linked to other forms of social behavior. The years immediately after the war saw a mushrooming of dance halls (*sale da ballo, balere*) in the cities, while dancing to records in the home continued as a parallel form of recreation with different meanings. In Rome Fulvio M. remembered going from Borgata Gordiani to dance halls in Porta Pia and Via XXI Aprile, but he said that in the suburbs too there were open-air dance floors in the summer where they did both ballroom-style dancing (*ballo liscio*) and the newer, more energetic boogie-woogie. The young women who went to the dance halls, however, were the "more emancipated girls" and he would not take his own girlfriend there:

We danced with our girlfriends in our apartments, we organized dances at home and you danced with your girlfriend or the girls from the neighboring apartments . . . with a record player. But when you went to the dance halls you always went with a sense of adventure because you found all sorts of things. . . . Also you'd come home late so you couldn't take your girlfriend, your girlfriend was someone who was attached to the family and if you got back late there would be trouble, so these girls had to be home by seven or eight, whereas we would get home in the small hours, because you had adventures there, maybe you'd meet a servant girl who had some time off, that kind of thing. (56: 9–10)

Mena V. (born 1935) met her future husband in 1956 after inviting him to join a dance party at her home in Rome. He had a girlfriend at the time but left her for Mena. She hastened to point out that she was not a flirt and that in her home she was under the surveillance of her mother and brothers:

When I was twenty-one it was as if I was thirteen, I didn't understand anything, anything. There was this guy's sister, the usual thing, you know, and she said, "Why don't you invite my brother over to dance?" [She said,] "If you invite him I can come too," you know these things girls arrange between them. The great thing about my husband, I must say, because I remember, he lived in this alley where we lived here in Tor Pignattara, and I saw him looking all sharp and I had to do this embarrassing thing of going up and asking if he would come to dance at our place. I said, "Excuse me, my brother told me that . . ." But I knew he had a steady girlfriend, I only went up to him because they'd said, "Ask him if he'll come and dance too, he's my brother so we can be together, I'll come and dance with your brothers," the usual things you do. "Excuse me, would you like to come and dance at our place, my brother said if you come too we'll have fun, Liliana is coming too you know," and of course he couldn't say no. He said: "Yes, yes." This was the first time I met my husband, and afterwards he left that other girlfriend, and that was fate, that's how it had to be, it wasn't because I was a flirt, God forbid. . . . So that's how it was, a few dances at home, because when we were invited to dance at someone else's place it was not allowed, because at our place there was my mother who could keep her eye on us, there were my brothers who also took this protective role despite everything, because it could have been a scandal for the family, a girl who allows herself to do something . . . . (58/59: 29–30)

Roberto R., who recalled the dance-hall phenomenon in postwar Turin, also remembered that around 1950, when he was fourteen or fifteen, they had parties in his parents' apartment, which was larger than those of his friends, and they danced to records. His parents were sometimes present, though not always, and these were occasions for the first courtships among this group: "Someone would bring along a few records . . . there were a few cakes, soft drinks, a few nervous words exchanged with a girl, in other words one thing led to another" (7: 25).

Some recollections of dancing to records were of earlier childhood and did not carry the same connotations. Luisanna D., born 1928, daughter of the local doctor in the village of Sardara in the province of Cagliari, used to go to the house of her father's cousins with the other children and they would dance the waltz, tango, and Charleston to a gramophone with a trumpet loudspeaker.

It was a good time, a great time, because . . . my aunts and also my parents really enjoyed watching us dance and teaching us to dance, probably because they could relive their own dancing days. . . . For them Friday was the day [they looked forward to], there was a lot of excitement in anticipating it, as there was for us too. (52: 17)

It was in such ways that the consumption of mass culture became a part of everyday life for many people, even before the arrival of mass consumption toward the end of the 1950s. It provided rhythms and occasions, opportunities and information. But it acquired meaning only when it was absorbed into patterns of behavior that were sometimes generational, at other times familial, regional, class-based, or gender-specific. In the next chapter we shall examine in more detail how this absorption worked in relation to various forms of cultural consumption centered on the body and on the communication of new forms of appearance or behavior to others.

2 Practices of the Self

In a pioneering work on material culture and consumption, Mary Douglas reminded her readers: "It is standard ethnographic practice to assume that all material possessions carry social meanings and to concentrate a main part of cultural analysis on their use as communicators."[1] The consumption of various mass cultural products—films, recorded music, advertising images, clothes, cosmetics, branded foods and drinks—is closely related to changing social uses of the body and involves the communication of these changes to others. In the act of consuming cultural products, people assimilate their socially shared meanings by literally incorporating them, that is, by taking them into or onto their bodies: eating, drinking, listening, reading, watching, dancing, dressing, doing their hair, putting on makeup. In many cases they then

also communicate these meanings to other people in the form of a modified physical appearance (clothes, hair, makeup), new gestures and movements
(dancing, walking, sports), or new attitudes and ways of speaking. This chapter is about how the processes of incorporation and communication of meanings worked in mass cultural consumption in Italy during our period and how
they contributed both to new "practices of the self," to use Michel Foucault's
expression, and to changes in collective cultural behavior.[2]

One illustration of these processes at work is to be found in Fulvio M.'s
description of the effect of the new American dance music on his male peer
group in Borgata Gordiani after the war: "We really liked it because the boogie-
woogie in particular as a dance shook up all the old customs here in Italy and
all the young people danced, as well as dances in pairs, but the boogie-woogie
was more fashionable." His married friend came home from the dance hall
with a vest dripping with sweat, which his wife took off and wrung out (56:
17). For girls, a typical form of incorporation was the first use of makeup,
marking the passage into adolescence and often linked to staying out later in
the evening. Maria Occhipinti was thirteen in 1937–1938 when her friends in
Ragusa "stole some money from their mothers to buy perfume and lipstick
and they put them on secretly when they went out. At home my mother didn't
use any make-up apart from a tiny bit of powder."[3] E. P., born in 1930, daughter of middle-class parents in Cagliari, was fourteen in 1944 when she put on
an improvised lipstick—an iridescent lip salve made of pink cocoa butter. She
was discovered by her mother, who gave her "a big slap because at fourteen
you weren't allowed to wear cocoa butter, it wasn't a real lipstick" (50/51: 11).
Agnese S., born in 1920, grew up in Rome under the vigilance of her father:
"He was very frightened of me so he kept me locked up at home, I couldn't go
out and enjoy myself outside, but I went out sometimes with school friends,
even boys sometimes, we'd go to a bar and buy an ice cream or to a cinema"
(67: 2). When she was eighteen she put on lipstick, encouraged by friends. Her
father found it and threw it out of the window (67: 9). Elsa, born in 1937, the
daughter of an army officer, recalled the "parties at home . . . under my parents' eagle eyes" (13: 7–8). In 1954, when she was seventeen, she still had to be
home by 8 P.M. (13: 31). However, dancing to records in her home or in friends'
homes was one of the ways in which she could experience physical contact
with boys: "I liked dancing, because I liked this first contact with boys when
you could get close up and that's really why we liked dancing, the kinds of
dances that you did in those days" (13: 11).

It was in ways like this that the spread of mass culture, including mass leisure and sport, challenged and changed existing norms of acceptable bodily
display, sexual behavior, intimacy, and dress. It also modified earlier notions
of what constituted a clean, healthy, and attractive body. Over time, mass cul-

ture helped break down the barriers that had prevented young people from adopting certain "adult" forms of consumption and behavior before a certain age. However, the timescale of the changes by which the barriers were eroded could be quite protracted, and it is important to recognize that in certain areas they were still largely in place at the end of our period, 1954. Our interviewee E. P. said that she and her younger sister, F. P., born in 1935, remained "children until we were thirteen or fifteen." According to F. P. there was no real dialogue with their parents or with their mothers' friends: "It wasn't even allowed to interrupt when they talked . . . if the women were speaking to each other you simply didn't interrupt or ask something" (50/51: 11). Magda Baiesi, who was a teenager in Bologna in the 1960s, still had to wait for her father's permission to wear makeup. She recalled that "this happened fairly late," though as soon as permission was granted her makeup was "extremely violent" with dark eye shadow and heavy mascara.[4] These changes as a whole also presupposed some fundamental shifts in basic levels of consumption that took several decades to reach the majority of the population but which, once they had done so, could alter people's cultural thresholds and mentalities very rapidly. For example, in the late 1960s the introduction on a mass scale of running water and lavatories in working-class homes moved thresholds of hygiene so fast that by the end of the 1980s, as Chiara Saraceno observed, "as soon as people can afford it they want two bathrooms."[5] These changes, as this example suggests, had other sources and channels apart from mass culture: rising incomes; public interventions in education, hygiene, and recreation; scientific and medical writings on health and fitness; books on conduct; the associationist activities of the political subcultures; and the thick web of horizontal oral communications within families, neighborhoods, and local communities. However, the mass media and advertising nearly always interacted with these other channels; they served to publicize and promote cultural change, and they were often decisive in shaping its form.

The picture that emerges between the 1930s and the 1950s, given the still limited impact of consumer culture and the persistent strength of the traditional social forces, is one of tension between "liberalization" and "repression." This tension frequently took the form of a conflict over boundaries: in this case over such measurable entities as length of skirt, time of evening when a son or daughter was expected home, demarcations between what was considered appropriate feminine and masculine behavior, and places where it was permissible to go out on one's own or with friends. Cecilia Dau Novelli, in her study of the Italian family between the wars, sees the underlying conflict as being between, on the one hand, "an ideology founded principally on the conservation of the traditional family," fostered both by Fascists and by Catholics, and on the other a modernization process that the Fascist regime partly furthered and partly opposed but which ultimately ran beyond its control.[6] Victoria de Grazia, in her chapters on "Growing Up" and "Going Out" in *How Fascism Ruled Women,* uses a variety of expressions to describe these respective attitudes and tendencies: "conservative," "conventional," "official culture" on the one hand; "modern," "secular," "commercial culture" on the other.[7] The subtitle of her later essay, "Nationalizing Women," represents the relationship even more starkly: "The Competition between Fascist and Commercial Cultural Models in Mussolini's Italy."[8] In other words, de Grazia links liberalization explicitly to commercial culture, which she sees as working to deflect or undermine the more conservative and containing tendencies of the Fascist and Catholic elites. She focuses in particular on women because, she argues, their leisure was more bound up with the home, the family, and consumption than men's leisure activities, whose forms of sociability remained largely within public spaces: the bar (*osteria*), after-work club (*dopolavoro*), and stroll (*passeggiata*).

As evidence that new attitudes toward traditional gender roles were pervading parts of Italian society under the Fascist regime, both de Grazia and Bruno Wanrooij cite a 1937 survey of a thousand female school students aged fourteen through eighteen in *scuole professionali* and *istituti magistrali* in Rome. The survey appears to suggest that the Fascist and Catholic promulgation of an ethos of subservient feminine roles and large families had largely failed among this social group (young, urban middle-class women) and that self-determination, or an aspiration toward self-determination, was the norm. Only 10 percent expressed an interest in housework and 27 percent were negative about it; the majority were uninterested in knitting and sewing. More of them preferred "to command rather than to obey," valued self-confidence over tractability, and said they were studying in order to get a job and did not expect their husbands to support them. Very few said they liked looking after children and only a few aspired to become mothers of large families. Their favorite pastime was going to the cinema.[9]

It would be rash to conclude from findings like these that mass culture and the attractions of modernity worked simply to undermine the disciplinary projects of Fascism and Catholic culture. In the first place, the sample may not have been representative of the age group as a whole and the replies might have been partly ironic or provocative. For instance, it seems on the face of it odd that these young women, many of whom were training to be schoolteachers, would have had so little interest in looking after children. Secondly, sport and gymnastics, which the same girls mentioned as their next favorite pastime after cinema, were actively promoted by the regime and the promotion of these activities, along with mass tourism, seems to have been one of the regime's areas of relative ideological success (see chapter 8). Nevertheless the survey does seem to bear out the view that the cinema, which was only partly controlled and channeled by the state (see chapters 5 and 7), played an important role in the emotional and sexual development of adolescents, exposing them to adult behaviors and modern attitudes.

Informality and Intimacy

Between the 1930s and the 1950s a gradual extension of informality can be observed in relations within and outside families. This was a complex and by no means unilinear process but it is one that can be related to other forms of interpersonal relations involving intimacy as well as to geographical mobility and increasing exposure to the mass media. "Intimacy" covers here relations such as modes of mutual address, forms of physical contact, and other displays of affection both between family members and among members of couples. One measure of the change in both types of relation is the use of pronouns of address, about which Marzio Barbagli published valuable findings in his history of the Italian family since the fifteenth century, *Sotto lo stesso tetto* (*Under One Roof*).[10] In 1974 he coordinated a team of research assistants, all of them young women, to carry out surveys in eight regions of the North and Center.[11] The researchers interviewed a total of 801 older women, born between 1890 and 1910, from various social classes. They found that approximately two-thirds of the interviewees born into peasant families had addressed each of their parents with the more formal pronoun for "you," *voi*, or its dialect equivalent, while their parents had always addressed them with the more intimate form *tu* or its equivalent. It was, Barbagli comments, "also through the use of these linguistic forms that parents maintained the social distance between themselves and their children."[12] In the next generation of peasants, those born between 1920 and 1940, the proportion of those who addressed their mother or father as *voi* had fallen to less than a third.

Such an asymmetrical system of address had been typical until the beginning of the nineteenth century, Barbagli noted, in aristocratic families (where parents were addressed with the polite forms *lei* or *vostra signoria* [your lordship] rather than *voi*), and also in the upper bourgeoisie (where they were addressed as *lei*), but it had then begun to be replaced in both classes by a mutual use of *tu*. By the end of the nineteenth century the asymmetrical system had also started to be displaced in urban working-class families: in about two-thirds of the latter *tu* was being used reciprocally between parents and children born between 1890 and 1910. Barbagli concluded that the new codes of intimacy traveled from higher to lower social classes and from city to country, and that consequently they arrived last among those social groups most insulated from exchange with others. Thus, within the different categories of agricultural workers, it was the sharecroppers (*mezzadri*), whose family structure was more hierarchical and who typically lived in large peasant houses, known as *case coloniche,* which were physically distant from one another, who were the last to adopt *tu* as an acceptable way for children to address parents. Smallholders, tenant farmers, and day laborers (*braccianti*) had begun to switch over a little earlier. Whereas in the generation born between 1890 and 1910, 82 percent of children of *mezzadri* addressed their father as *voi,* compared to 64 percent of *braccianti* and 57 percent of smallholders and tenants, in the generation born 1920–1940 these percentages had dropped respectively to 33, 21, and 13 percent.[13] Looked at another way, however, these figures show that at the beginning of our period roughly a third of children of *mezzadri* and a fifth of children of *braccianti* still used a deferential form of address toward their parents. In other words, the shift toward greater intimacy was very much still in process in rural Italy between the wars, and there was still a notable gap between the respective usages of the lower and higher social classes. This gap remained for several years after World War II. Chiara Saraceno has recalled of her own adolescence in a middle-class household in Milan in the 1950s that she used to write letters home for the family's maids, who lacked the requisite literacy skills. The letters

had to follow a very rigid code of expression so that the senders, as well as the recipients, would recognize them as expressing due respect: "With this letter I tell you [*voi*] that I am well and so I hope are you. . . . Your most devoted daughter." From me they accepted superiority in grammar, but not the ability to judge how one ought to behave. I found this hard to understand, just as I did not understand why they addressed their parents as *voi*.[14]

It is worth observing of Barbagli's findings that the spread of *tu* followed the same pattern as many other linguistic innovations—higher to lower class, city to country, plain to hill or mountain—and, although he does not make this point himself, it can, like these other innovations, be correlated in part with the diffusion of means of communication and the spread of mass culture, that is, with the enhanced mobility and the opening up of windows onto the practices of other classes and cultures that we discussed in the introduction.

This leads us to the difficulties for young people of finding opportunities for intimacy when most of them had no private space of their own either within the home or outside it and when so much of their life was carried on under the gaze or surveillance of parents, kin, companions, or neighbors. Recollections of control and surveillance by parents recur frequently in our testimonies. For young women in particular most social life took place within the family home or in spaces that were accessible to parental regulation. Several female witnesses, like Lina C., born in 1919 in Cagliari, recalled that they were never left alone (46: 10). Also in Cagliari, F. P. and her sister F. P. were even forbidden to receive friends of the same sex in their rooms ("what secrets have you got to tell?" was the justification offered by their mother) (50/51: 13). Women and men both recalled that it was very difficult to meet members of the other sex. Even at the Catholic *oratorio*, girls and boys were divided for Mass, day trips, and all recreational activities. Anyone who, like Roberto R. (born Turin 1935), "messed around with girls at thirteen or fourteen," found himself banned (7: 20–21). In consequence some boys resorted to stopping girls in the street, a desperate tactic that did not always receive the desired response: "You stopped them in the street, you waited there, did that, and sometimes you had to give up because some of them reacted badly, there was that way of thinking," recalled Augusto M. from Rome (62: 20). Even if a young man did manage to engage a young woman in conversation, there was always the possibility of parental intervention. As Agnese S., born in 1920, reminisced bitterly: "Once my father found me near our home talking to a boy and he came up and said to me, 'You go home right now.' I might have been eighteen—yes, I was eighteen. And he said, 'And try not to see that boy again'" (67: 9). Consequently, exchanges often occurred furtively at Mass or, at a distance, between boys in the street and girls who would stand at the window (73: 14–15). Girls would sometimes receive declarations of love by letter from boys they did not even know and, since letters were not regarded as private, the whole family would immediately know they had an admirer (46: 9; 41: 7).

Despite the persistence of some patterns of control during World War II, conscription, evacuation, foreign occupation, and economic crisis brought about a major disruption of family-based customs, especially in the larger cities. The absence of men during the war was followed by a dramatic collapse of conventional sexual mores in Rome and Naples as poverty and hunger forced many thousands of women into prostitution. The example of the wives of Catania who, according to Adelia Q. (born in 1924), went into convents to avoid any suspicion that they had cuckolded their husbands, does not appear to have occurred elsewhere—not even in Calabria, where she lived with her parents (57: 16). During and after the war, there was also a change in patterns of representation as more sexually explicit images and subjects also appeared in the mass media. Two trends in particular marked the liberation period, both of which would leave traces on the customs and practices of the population. The first was a huge increase in commercial and voluntarily organized leisure activities, particularly dancing and cinema. The second, short-lived but significant, was a more widespread display of young bodies as entertainment and as a result of financial inducement. These heralded the beginning of a different social articulation of the body in which family, religious authorities, and the state were obliged to negotiate and respond to a range of novelties that marked a gap between the experiences of the generations.

Sex and the Cinema

In a context in which social control was tight, the movie theater was one of the very few places where young people went as groups of friends and where courting couples could experiment sexually away from the gaze of their parents. Gino G., born in Rome in 1920, was living in the late 1930s with his antifascist parents in an apartment on the side of the Cinema Palazzo in San Lorenzo:

When I went to the cinema with a girl, to be honest I didn't watch the film. I'm not a hypocrite like so many other people . . . . It was dark, a good place because I couldn't go to a hotel, they would have arrested me because I was an antifascist and I didn't have any money, so we sometimes went to the cinema. It was in the dark; we did something a bit more . . . (16: 17–18)

These practices persisted at least into the 1960s. A notable fictional account of a working-class cinema courtship is that of the young Tommaso, in Pier Paolo Pasolini's 1959 novel *Una vita violenta,* who goes with his date Irene to see *Quo Vadis* in a cinema near her home in the Garbatella district of Rome. She is frightened as they watch the scene of the Christians walking out to the arena to face the lions, and Tommaso takes advantage of her absorption to make a sexual advance. When she pushes him away he becomes aggressive, since he feels he has earned the right to touch her after paying for her seat and buying pumpkin seeds (*bruscolini*). She gives in, tears filling her eyes.[15]

These stories illustrate what Chiara Saraceno has called the "paradoxes of privacy" in the history of the family: in a period when low-income families typically lived in overcrowded dwellings, privacy could exist only in "public" places,

in the spaces and relationships of external society: the *osteria* for the men, the game of bowls, the dance floor, the Sunday stroll for young people, or in Church, at pilgrimages or at the washing places for the women—in public places, to be sure, but ones that were outside the control or just the excessively close presence of family and neighbours (so that one can suspect that for both men and women, adults and young people, their chance of having a private life was inversely proportional to the amount of time they spent in the domestic space).[16]

The increased visibility of intimacy in cinemas and other public places was noted with alarm by Catholic writers and moralists from the 1920s.

Giovanni Agnese, in 1929, deplored the behavior of couples "who make a spectacle of their amorous intimacy in every public place, sit indecently close together in cafés and embrace in theatres and public parks."[17] He proposed that screen kisses be prohibited, public meeting places closed at midnight, no girls under nineteen allowed to dance in public, short dresses banned, overcrowding on trams prevented "so that indecent contact, voluntary or otherwise, may be avoided and the sensitivity of the flesh may not be pointlessly exercised," beauty contests stopped, and woods patroled by *carabinieri* and *guardie forestali* (forest rangers) to root out lovers.[18] These prescriptions may have been extreme, but they show the anxiety among traditionalists about the changes in sexual behavior, the lowering of the age at which people were exposed to sexual display and contact, and the public places where transgressions were taking place: beaches, woods, parks, public transport, cafés, dance halls, theaters, and cinemas. In a pastoral letter of 1934 the Archbishop of Cremona, Giovanni Cazzani, criticized the current dance craze (*danzomania*) and the new women's fashions: "This habitual immodest display of the female figure increasingly stimulates and goads in men, particularly young men, the base instinct of sexuality, and causes them to lose the idea of the woman's dignity, respect for her virtue and the chaste cult of her beauty."[19] The risk of the cinema was, for moralists, that it tantalized young spectators with fantasy images before they were ready for mature sexual relations. As Mario Bernabei put it in his *Educazione del sesso,* published in 1933: "The adolescent does not yet know in reality the joy of the female kiss and embrace; the cinema offers him a musical vision of them which is therefore all the sweeter."[20] The notion that the cinema was a place of danger for susceptible young audiences was most influentially expressed in Pope Pius XI's encyclical to the American bishops, the *Vigilanti cura* of 1936:

The motion picture is viewed by people who are seated in a dark theatre and whose faculties, mental, physical and often spiritual, are relaxed. One does not need to go far in search of these theatres: they are close to the home, to the church, and to the school and they thus bring the cinema into the very centre of popular life.

Moreover, stories and actions are presented, through the cinema, by men and women whose natural gifts are increased by training and embellished by every known art, in a manner which may possibly become an additional source of corruption, especially to the young. Further, the motion picture has enlisted in its service luxurious appointments, pleasing music, the vigour of realism, every form of whim and fancy. For this very reason, it attracts and fascinates particularly the young, the adolescent, and even the child. Thus at the very age

when the notions and sentiments of justice and rectitude, of duty and obligation and of ideals and life are being developed, the motion picture with its direct
propaganda assumes a position of commanding influence.[21]

Few individual films of this period were recalled in detail in the testimonies of our witnesses, but it is reasonable to suppose that the cumulative effect of the erotic suggestions and situations that cinema communicated, in
combination with magazines and other media products, provided a widening
of their horizons beyond what they had immediately experienced. Rosalia A.
(born Bisceglie, province of Bari, 1913) told us that the cinema taught her that
it was possible for a young woman to exercise choice in personal relations and
that this led her to reject an "arranged marriage" (30: 20). At a time when parents intervened as a matter of course in a girl's choice of fiancé, with betroth-
als occurring formally at home in the presence of relatives with exchanges of
gifts (46: 9), this was a bold act. The cinema in this way seems to have helped
give expression to forms of longing and individuality that otherwise might
have remained dormant, and in this case to have helped nurture an idea of romantic love and personal choice that allowed the young woman some leverage
in relation to custom. The cinema also communicated ideas about fashion and
behavior that were close in some respects to the reality experienced by its audiences. This proximity in fact served to highlight the plausibility of the novel
situations it sometimes proposed.

Our testimonies show that cinema was less subject to parental bans than
dancing or other unsupervised pursuits outside the home. Although boys
were more frequent spectators than girls, the latter were often able to go to
the cinema with friends in the afternoon, or in the evening with their family-
approved fiancé provided they were back home by 8.30 P.M., so young people
could enjoy relative privacy there for a few hours. Gian Piero Brunetta quotes
the account in Ermanno Olmi's *Il ragazzo della Bovisa* (1986) of the narrator's
first experience, as an adolescent, in 1945, of seeing an adult film after a friend,
Pedrini, lets him in through the safety exit. The two are more interested in
what is happening in the auditorium than what is on the screen.

"Can you see those two kissing?"—and he pointed out several couples separated
from the others along the sides of the auditorium—"they go in the corners so
they won't be seen."

The flickering from the screen lit up their outlines and you could work
out their positions and movements. He showed me some others: "Look at them!
What are they up to, do you think?" I could make out some heads, I realized
they were holding each other, but I could only guess what they were doing from
Pedrini's suggestions.[22]

It would be unwise to generalize too freely, but we might suggest that such be-havior was an effect of three distinct processes: first, the liberalization of het-erosexual mores; second, the weakening of repressive practices and institu-tions; and third, the arrival after 1945 of more explicitly sexualized films from the United States. In particular *Gilda* (Charles Vidor, 1946), starring Rita Hay-worth, and *The Outlaw* (1943), Howard Hughes's Hays Code–busting picture featuring Jane Russell, signaled a new departure in the representation of the heroine as a physically alluring woman. Pasolini wrote a fictionalized account of the reaction of a working-class audience in Caorle, on the coast between Venice and Trieste, to *Gilda,* in which the young men shout obscene remarks: "Attento che ti si spaccano i bottoni!" ("Watch out, your fly buttons are going to burst!") and "Quante te ne fai stasera?" ("How many [wanks] are you go-ing to have tonight?").[23] Italian cinema broke with the past too, although its depictions of prostitution, situations involving extramarital sex, and sexual temptation and manipulation were cruder and more realistic than the dis-tilled sex appeal of American cinema.

American movies were part of a variety of experiences that included new sounds and also new dances, notably the boogie-woogie. The latter became a symbol of the liberation, not only in Italy, but its fast pace, physical nature, and general acrobatics limited its broader acceptance. Within a short period it disappeared and more traditional dances once more reigned unchallenged until the vogue for Latin American dances arrived in the mid-1950s. For E. P. the boogie-woogie was "a dance for Americans and loose girls [*ragazze poco serie*]; none of us ever danced it" (50/51: 18). According to Fulvio M. "it could catch on more in the *borgata* . . . because it was a livelier dance, livelier because you could do things that you shouldn't to get a girl, even treat her a bit rough, sling her around here and there; these things were fun" (56: 17–18).

Star Cults and Care of the Body

At a time when Fascists and Catholics were united in promoting conven-tional roles for women, cinema offered an alternative. The many young women who worked in cities as typists, shopgirls, secretaries, seamstresses, and fac-tory workers found in film stars an attractive modern example of fashion, style, and consumption. Indeed, the only modern models supplied to women in fields such as beauty, courtship, behavior, and dress were to be found in magazines, cinema, and advertising. Consequently, for some Italian women, Hollywood exercised a strong fascination. Greta Garbo, Jean Harlow, and Joan Crawford were the great models. The ideal consumer of the Hollywood ro-mance, the sort of person producers had in mind, was a young, single female secretary or shop assistant. In Italy as elsewhere such people responded to the movies with enthusiasm. Referring to the 1932 film *Grand Hotel*, in which Crawford played the part of a socially aspiring typist courted by wealthy visitors at the hotel where she worked, Irene Brin wrote:

There was a Crawford style, a Crawford Club, millions of Crawford fans; above all there was a Crawford mouth, with the upper lip in the form of a liver sausage and the lower one like a slice of watermelon. This was deplored at first but then much imitated. . . . Secretaries left their offices in the evening certain that they resembled her and that, like her, they deserved a villa in California with a swimming pool.[24]

Magazines featured photographs of current starlets to give people an idea of the sort of look that was desirable and in fashion. *Cinema Illustrazione* in October 1930, for example, featured the long-forgotten names of Leila Hyams, Mary Philbin, and Alice White. Alongside their pictures were photographs sent in by readers who claimed a resemblance to the stars. The pictures are a remarkable testimony to the penetration of the star culture into everyday life in this period. There was great attention to hair, pose, and expression. Permed hair (sometimes bleached), plucked eyebrows, makeup, and careful dress were common among women, although there were also photographs of simple girls who used little or no artifice to improve on their natural appearance. Young men often appear with their hair brushed straight back and brilliantined. They often have cigarettes dangling from their mouths, pencil moustaches, and the look of a dark, handsome stranger. Hollywood-style toothy smiles, halfway between a laugh and a smile, are common. Most of the photographs are of face only or of head and shoulders, but there were also a few full-length portraits of young men and women wearing swimming costumes. This was a reflection of the image of the Hollywood life conveyed by the magazines as being one of leisure, sport, healthy outdoor pursuits, and the cult of the body and physical beauty.

Evidence such as this shows that the whole idea of beauty and of attractiveness was being redefined in a way that tended to displace traditional evaluations. A new emphasis was being placed on exterior appearance, on the physical, and on the whole body. Moreover, new international standards of beauty were being introduced. In this process, people were subtly encouraged to alter and shape their appearance to some degree, to choose an image and to make the best of themselves. As Jackie Stacey observed in her study of women and stars in Britain, people did not just copy stars to try and be thought of *as* them; they also took stars and star looks as a starting point to redefine their own appearance and hence also sometimes their identity.[25]

Several of our witnesses, mostly those of middle-class or north Italian origin, recalled the special qualities of American film stars. Gualtiero (born in Turin in 1927), who used to work as an actor and then as a theater director and manager, said: "Regardless of whether the film was good or not, you saw performances by extraordinary actors. Bearing in mind that they were edited they probably were not quite at that level, but they really knew how to hold their place as stars" (5: 19). "The American actor was more spontaneous," said Sergio M., "you could see that he fitted the part, he really seemed to have lived it" (107: 32). Giuseppe M., born in 1914, who worked as a barber in Aosta, remembered how the standard hairstyle changed following Valentino: "We used lots of brilliantine to keep hair straight, Valentino-style; they used to make a three-quarter parting and then pomade it, with all the hair pulled tight. The service basically consisted of that" (53: 4). Screen actors also influenced moustache and sideburn styles. Those who found that they bore some resemblance to an American actor felt they had been touched by fortune. Ottavio F., born in Spresiano (Treviso) in 1909, recalled, "They said I had the features of Ramon Novarro, that I really looked like him here and there, and that I could exploit it as a career" (69: 21).

Even though the typical American movie stars in the 1930s were dream figures, who had little in common physically with most Italians, there were many attempts to imitate their hairstyles, makeup, attitude, and dress, especially but by no means only among the lower middle classes. Jean Harlow, the platinum blonde whose star career took off in 1930 and who was dubbed "the most beautiful woman in Hollywood" by the women's magazine *Eva* in 1935, inspired many Italian girls to bleach their hair. As an adolescent in Benevento in the 1930s, Rosalia A. used a homemade concoction of hydrogen peroxide and drops of ammonia to lighten her hair so that she would seem "more elegant, more sexy than the others. I saw myself with my friends with this hair, even just a small plait, and I liked to be a girl who was a bit special" (30: 13). However, her father reacted to her decision with intense wrath:

He wanted to kill me. I had to run away and stay with my aunt for a week. "I'll cut it all off," he said. "As soon as you come back I'll cut it off with the hair clippers." I said, "Dad, I swear that when my hair grows back I won't do it again, I'm sorry, I didn't know," and I started crying. But he meant it. If he had collared me he would have cut it all off. (30: 14)

Italian cinema had less impact on appearance in the interwar years. It was not unknown in the 1930s for well-to-do audiences to whistle and laugh at fashions that were either out of date by the time they made it on to the screen or looked plain. Although this problem was the subject of continuous debate and it was widely agreed that what was needed was a systematic link-up between the film industry and the fashion world, this never came about, because of the desire of the former to economize on costumes and the unwillingness of the latter to accept that it would benefit if it donated time, skills, and costumes that would then be promoted onscreen. Thus, with the partial exception of Clara Calamai (who was known for her glamorous *toilettes*) and Vivi Gioi (an actress known for her elegance, who was dressed by the Milanese designer Biki), film star glamour was largely absent. One of the few Italian stars who attracted the sort of imitative dynamic that was routine with the Americans was Alida Valli. A former student of the Centro Sperimentale di Cinematografia (see chapter 5) from Pola (Istria), whose real name was Alida von Altenburger, Valli won her preeminent position as a result of her performances in light comedies such as *Mille lire al mese* (*A Thousand Lire a Month*) (Max Neufeld, 1939) and *Ore 9, lezione di chimica* (*9 A.M. Chemistry Lesson*) (Mario Mattòli, 1941), costume films like *Piccolo mondo antico* (*Little Old World*) (Mario Soldati, 1941), and dramatic films such as *Noi vivi-Addio Kira* (*We the Living*) (Goffredo Alessandrini, 1942). Valli's appearance can be located within the broad frame of beauty as defined by the cinema of the period. She was young and fresh-faced, with long, medium-brown hair. Her high cheekbones and slightly slanted eyes gave her an air of mystery that betrayed her middle-European origins. Valli evoked special memories from our interviewees, particularly from women who had been adolescents in the early 1940s. "People were really keen on her, she was very good," said Germinia Z. in Rovereto (104: 21). Natalia in Turin said of *Noi vivi-Addio Kira:* "That film launched a hairstyle, I remember, because she [Valli] had shoulder-length straight hair, completely straight with a parting on one side and quite full; everyone tried to copy it" (4: 71).

Innovations tended to follow the rapid diffusion of new inventions like the permanent wave or brilliantine for men, both of which owed their popularity to cinema. Loris C. (born near Bologna in 1925) used brilliantine and a hairnet to keep his hair straight and in place: "That brilliantine gave you that nice slick hairstyle, you comb it in place and it just stays put" (26: 15). However, while the resulting look might have been appreciated, there were drawbacks such as oily collars and cuffs. The "perm" arrived first due to a French invention of heated irons called "the Marcel wave." According to Giuseppe M., "at first you heated them on a petrol flame, then there were electric irons and you did waves, wavy hair all over. . . . But these didn't last long, then we got the permanent wave, the steam perm." The process was not without risks:

Sometimes when a rubber hairband broke you had to stop straight away because it could easily burn; the pressure in the dryer was four atmospheres [about sixty pounds per square inch], it went all round the head. . . . It went from . . . a roller with a hole in it and the hairbands linked together from one roller to the next. There was a chain that went in and out, in and out, and every now and then a

Figure 5. Alida Valli in a photograph from circa 1942.
Stephen Gundle collection.

band broke and you had to protect the customer's face because it would burn: terrible it was. (53: 5)

Avelina G. (born near Bologna in 1919) had her first perm at the age of twenty in 1939:

When you had a perm then, those were the first ones, you had it all curly and for a month you couldn't comb it because your hair was so curly and then afterwards you washed it all the time because when you washed it it came down a bit. So you had it for a year, a year and a half, because you had it short and then your hair came right down to here [the shoulders]. (24: 1)

As regards the cultural consumption of adolescents, one of the most significant differences between the cohort born in the 1920s and the one born before World War I is that the later cohort embraced distinctive appearances in a way the earlier one had not. The first cohort had grown up largely emulating the consumptions of their parents whereas the next began for the first time to differentiate themselves from their parents, to adopt distinctive consumption patterns designed to mark them off both from children and elders. Again, Vasco Pratolini provides valuable examples from working-class families in Florence. The group of young people in *Il Quartiere* were mostly "war babies," conceived when their fathers had come back briefly from the trenches in World War I. When the narrator Valerio turns sixteen his father allows him to wear long trousers for the first time; he also puts brilliantine on his hair. The girls make a similar rite of passage to adulthood by wearing high heels, using scent, tying up their hair, and wearing pink pendant earrings. Their cultural routines become similar to those of their parents: an espresso coffee in the Bar San Pietro, card games, smoking Xantia or Serraglio cigarettes.

The expansion of cinema as a leisure experience brought with it new aspirations and parallel rituals. Beauty contests had been held in Italy since the early years of the century (the first was in 1911), and they were also held in the 1930s until the Fascists banned them. After 1945, however, they took a different form. The American troops were the first to organize improvised beauty contests, importing the custom of the bathing costume parade. In contrast to the photogenic competitions of the prewar period, where the emphasis was always on the face, the postwar focus shifted to the body. Those who took part almost uniformly desired a film career, viewing it as an easy route to fame and riches. Photographic evidence shows that, among the contestants, star poses and personal grooming were common, though by no means universal. In a climate of poverty, the prizes, even if modest, were a huge attraction. Such competitions were widely imitated by Italian commercial organizations, which ensured a high level of participation by promising goods or money as prizes. Evidence suggests that often it was not ambitious girls who put themselves forward but family members including mothers who saw that the beauty of a sister or daughter might help resolve a situation of penury. More conservative sections of the press and public opinion were critical of these practices, which were seen as undermining traditional ideals of modesty and beauty. In place of more gentle and individual notions, a standardized American-influenced ideology of commercial beauty was seen to be making headway. The Sunday supplement of *Il Corriere della Sera, La Domenica del Corriere,* put itself at the head of a campaign to resist such trends and restate conventional ideals. It denounced the fact that Italy's news kiosks and theaters were "full of legs" and deplored the spread of "make-up, swimsuits . . . and ambiguous and studied little smiles accompanied by jazz."[26]

The shift from face to body in the representation of women did not occur simply or without specific Italian factors. In *Roma città aperta* (*Rome Open City*) (Roberto Rossellini, 1945), the Roman actress Anna Magnani created a type, the woman of the people, which she then recreated in a series of films, including *Abbasso la ricchezza!* (*Down with Riches!*) (Gennaro Righelli, 1946) and *L'onorevole Angelina* (*Angelina*) (Luigi Zampa, 1947). She was the exact opposite of the Hollywood star, a real woman, in her late thirties at the end of the war, not in any way typically beautiful, with an indifferent figure and scruffy hair. Yet she was authentic, passionate, instinctive, and strong. She had a vital energy and human warmth that was without parallel. Tito A. in Bologna said, "I think Anna Magnani was a great actress, she got into your bloodstream when she made a film, in the way she made them" (28: 15). While Magnani is remembered as the most original face of postwar Italian cinema, other actresses who were popular at the time have been forgotten. One of these was Elli Parvo, a half-German, though decidedly Mediterranean-looking, actress who appeared in a series of films between 1942 and 1947, usually taking on the part of the vamp. She was seen as the number-one starlet at the end of the war, a sensual, full-bodied presence who featured prominently in the press. Another, similar actress was Franca Marzi. Like Paola Barbara, Marisa Vernati, and Greta Gonda before 1943, these full-figured women attracted significant male interest. Their first successor was Silvana Pampanini, runner-up in the first Miss Italia pageant in 1946 and a regular presence in low-budget films from 1947.

The emphasis on the body and the image of eroticism that Pampanini projected owed a great deal to America, but the lesson of Anna Magnani and of neorealism was also forcefully present in postwar cinema's pursuit of a natural, earthy, deglamorized look. Indeed the focus both on the female body and on landscape constituted a distinctive trait that signified a new starting point for Italian cinema.[27] In *Riso amaro* the barefoot Silvana Mangano, her feet firmly rooted to a specific geographical place, the rice plains near Vercelli, set the pattern for a whole series of female actors chosen by male directors and producers. Gina Lollobrigida and then Sophia Loren would become the best known of several women who would associate Italy with a new idea of sex appeal and beauty. These performers embodied the erotic fantasies of the men of the time and their images were shaped by producers such as Carlo Ponti (who would later marry Loren) and Dino De Laurentiis (who married the nineteen-year-old Mangano in July 1949, two months before the release of *Riso amaro*), directors like De Sica, and screenwriters like Cesare Zavattini. Because of the aura of sexuality that was overtly associated with these actors, the Catholics disliked them intensely and they were largely ignored in the Catholic press.

By no means all the women who appeared on screen were *maggiorate fisiche* ("physically advantaged"), to employ the term widely adopted in the media to refer to female stars whose main distinguishing characteristics were ample breasts and curves.[28] There were many delicate, modest, childlike young women too who on screen represented tranquility, love, and the aspiration for marriage and a family. These women, whom Stefano Masi labels *fidanzatine* ("girls-next-door"), had much in common with the quiet, respectable girls of Fascist cinema. However, they were wholly overshadowed by the more assertive, physically striking *maggiorate*. The latter, almost all of whom were of working-class or lower-middle-class origin, were very popular with the public. Their looks were at once traditionally Italian (especially their uniformly dark hair) and American. They offered a contrast to Fascism's masculine emphasis and a vitality that went beyond the privations of the present to hold out the prospect of an Italian recovery.

Sport and the Seaside

The emphasis on the display of the female body in the postwar years was not the result only of commercial influences and the impact of American mass culture at a time of social and political flux. It was also shaped by the earlier development in Italy of sport and bathing. The Fascists believed in fitness as a means of promoting readiness for war and of organizing and disciplining the young generations. Their many initiatives in this area need to be seen in relation to other measures adopted to promote health and hygiene, eliminate longstanding health problems such as tuberculosis and malaria, and tackle infant mortality. Women, as well as men, were drawn into sporting activities. The Catholic Church was unequivocally hostile to this. *L'Osservatore Romano* argued that sport for women involved immodest sexual display and was both unsuitable and dangerous for those whose primary function was to become wives and mothers. After the Concordat of 1929 these conflicts came to a head. A meeting of the Grand Council of Fascism was convened in October 1930 to look into the question of women's sport. It concluded by distinguishing between "women's physical education," of which it remained firmly in favor, and "women's sport" (*atletismo femminile*), into which it agreed to set up an official enquiry to be conducted by the Federazione dei Medici Sportivi (Federation of Sports Doctors). Rosella Isidori Frasca has reconstructed in detail the results of the ensuing discussions within the medical profession, and among the Fascist elites, over women's physical exertion, and has found divisions that parallel almost exactly those described above over the sexual question between "repression" and "liberalization."[29] Everyone involved in the debate (which remained unresolved during the lifetime of the regime) concurred, at least in their public pronouncements, that women's reproductive role was paramount, but whereas some Fascists and medical experts warned that prolonged strenuous exercise could jeopardize this role by causing amenorrhea and possible permanent damage to women's reproductive organs, others argued that, provided certain safe limits were observed, such exercise could make women more fertile by improving their general health. There was also a division of opinion over the propriety of women displaying their "naked" bodies in public. On the one side were the arguments of the arch-ideologue of Fascist anti-feminism, Ferdinando Loffredo, in his *Politica della famiglia* (1936):

In all countries women's sports have proved to be one of the most decisive factors in drawing women away from the family, and thus causing a decline in the population and a loss of modesty. . . . Women's sport is a potent factor in what is now called the ideal of nudity, whose general effects on morality in family life and on the demographic trend nobody denies.[30]

On the other side were ranged the equally staunch (and again usually male) advocates of women's sport, like Poggi Longostrevi, a doctor and member of the International Women's Sporting Federation, who argued in 1933 that sport could have for women the same virtuous effect it was widely claimed to have for men, namely to be "excellent as a corrective against the excess of stimuli that modern city life offers to a precocious and excessive sexual activity," or like Sisto Fevre, who wrote in the periodical *Lo Sport Fascista* in 1942 that women's health and fertility could only benefit from fresh air, sun, and exercise: "Let nobody be shocked by agile naked limbs thrashing about under the lash of the sun or wind."[31]

Sport and work could provide legitimate excuses for women to wear clothes that in any other context were considered improper. Various prefectural ordinances in 1941 stated:

To prevent attitudes that are incompatible with correct clothing women are forbidden to go out in public or travel wearing long or short trousers. This ban does not apply to sporting activities requiring the use of particular clothing (horse-riding, tennis, skiing). Culottes are permitted for cycling and female overalls with trousers for accepted work requirements.[32]

Transgressors could be fined. In Novi Ligure in November 1941 a young woman was fined 350 lire for wearing "men's-style short trousers" (*calzoni corti da uomo*) and a fifty-year-old woman 200 lire for wearing a pair of men's trousers in the courtyard where she lived. As a fashion item, trousers for women were seen as an "Anglo-Saxon" import to be resisted. An article in *Tempo* in July 1939, illustrated with fashion pictures of models wearing trousers, commented:

This wearing of trousers by women is one of the saddest and most laughable chapters in the democratic doctrine.

We do not wish in this article to state a politics of the wardrobe, but the fact is that women's trousers emerged on the gluttonous and blasphemous terrain of equality and liberty and, remarkable though it may seem, came into the world in the very country, England, where the Puritans came from, the country where the Suffragettes thought they could claim equal social rights by wearing men's clothes.[33]

The anti-feminist and anti-democracy points here are partly being made seriously but the style is supposed to be witty. The Mediterranean peoples, the article claims, have an "innate aversion" to trousers. The Romans and Greeks, both sexes, covered themselves with loose tunics and togas and men practiced sport naked. The anonymous (but evidently male) journalist ends with a consistently hot-blooded defense of skirts: "The ancient pleasing and fair skirt seems to be quicker: it can be undone in one go, it slips to the ground in one go."[34]

For the Catholics, there was a dangerous slide between sport, nudity, and sexual license. In May 1941 Pius XII received 4,000 members of the women's youth movement of Catholic Action and invited them to launch a "purity crusade." He complained of the rise of

a fashion for being daring that is immodest in a young woman raised in a Christian way; clothing that is skimpy or seems designed to show off what it should keep hidden; sport, dance, shows, music in which the obsession with enjoyment and pleasure stores up the gravest dangers. So long as provocative clothes are the sorry prerogative of women of dubious repute and almost their identifying mark no one will dare wear them, but the day they start to be worn by people above suspicion one will not hesitate to follow the trend, a trend that will perhaps drag women to their greatest downfall.[35]

The term "nudity" was used in Catholic publications up to the 1950s to designate the exposure of men's bare chests and women's shoulders and legs. As well as prescriptions on men's bathing costumes, one may cite as examples some of the classifications of the Centro Cattolico Cinematografico, the Catholic censorship body founded in 1934 (see chapter 7), from its condemnations of the "nudity" of Tarzan films to its ruling over Carlo Campogalliani's sport film *Stadio* (1935) that "the excessive nudity of the athletes makes it not to be recommended to young people."[36] In the summer of 1941 *Il Messaggero* reported that young women were increasingly seen traveling scantily dressed on buses and trains back to Rome from the Lido di Ostia (this had developed in the 1930s into a popular weekend destination for working-class and lower-middle-class Romans, in contrast to the more upmarket Fregene, still only accessible by road) and approved the measures taken by the Ministry of the Interior to clamp down on these "displays of itinerant nudism" (the state in fact adopted a similar broad definition of nudity, at any rate on paper: Article 794 of the 1942 Penal Code, the Codice Rocco, prohibited the exposure of "shameful nudity in public places"). In the summer of 1941 the Catholic newspaper *L'Italia* reported:

On Sundays for the last few weeks a group of loafers of both sexes have chosen the locality of Canonica Lambro as a place to sunbathe without caring much about the morality of their clothing. To put a stop to this not very edifying celebration of nudity (of varying degrees of attractiveness) a group of local residents challenged the unwelcome guests with bunches of stinging nettles. The remedy has had a positive effect: since then, nobody has taken such liberties again on a Sunday.[37]

The testimonies of women collected by Miriam Mafai in 1987 suggest that there was a growing freedom at the seaside for those who were fortunate enough to go away on holiday.

My mother seemed distracted, far away. Every afternoon we nibbled a bit more freedom, we went back home a little later in the evening. Let's be clear about it, by suppertime we had to be back home, there was no flexibility over this. But my mother was certainly more indulgent than my father, particularly when we were on holiday.[38]

According to another:

At Forte dei Marmi we had a lot of friends. My mother let me go alone to the house of people we knew. They were friends from Milan and they were rich. They had a gramophone and sometimes we danced. My mother's friend wore these very smart white silk pyjamas. She looked like Marlene Dietrich and she was pleased when we told her so.[39]

In the 1930s the opening of the seaside to mass excursions, encouraged from 1931 by the *treni popolari*—cheap train journeys subsidized by the Fascist government—and from 1935 by the non-working Saturday afternoon (the so-called *sabato fascista*) and by the building of new *colonie marittime*, holiday camps for the children of manual and white-collar workers, was accompanied by a pushing back of boundaries of propriety also for the middle and lower classes. On beaches, women's bathing costumes, which in the early 1920s still typically had a sewn-in skirt and separate knickers covering the tops of the thighs, now left the arms and legs fully exposed and were either one-piece with a low-cut back (worn in Italy from the late 1920s) or two-piece (introduced in the early 1930s). The latter, featured in *Vogue* in 1935 and shown in newsreels and feature films, such as the sequence on the beach at Alassio in

De Sica's 1942 film *I bambini ci guardano* (*The Children Are Watching Us*), were the precursors of the skimpier bikini, designed by Jules Renard and launched in Paris in July 1946.[40] However, the mass adoption of these costumes was a slow process. The sisters E. P. and F. P. recalled that at Poetto, the public beach of Cagliari, in the early 1950s there was just one woman who wore a two-piece costume, "a middle-aged woman who was considered beautiful, with a nice body but a very ugly face, a mature woman who was considered good to look at, but we wore these very modest one-piece costumes." Their own mother always remained fully dressed at the beach, in sleeves (50/51: 52, 53).

There was resistance to the changes in bathing costumes, in particular by Catholic moralists. Giovanni Agnese had recommended in 1929 that at seaside resorts women and men should be separated by "a thick and impenetrable palisade going down from the beach where the sand begins and continuing into the sea to where the water is at least two metres deep at low tide"; women's bathing costumes should include a knee-length skirt and men's costumes should cover the chest and back.[41] But such recommendations were far too extreme to be generally acceptable and the trend toward greater exposure of the flesh proved inexorable, assisted as it was not just by the international movement in this direction and by the glamour attached to beachwear and tanned skins in fashion magazines but also by the widely held belief in the tonic properties of prolonged exposure to the sun: in this period heliotherapy was being extensively used in sanatoria for the treatment of tuberculosis, a disease associated with dark, damp urban dwellings.

Catholic definitions of "nudity" or "nakedness" were affected to some extent by changing secular norms of costume and propriety, but otherwise they remained remarkably stable over time. In the seventeenth century the neck, shoulders, and upper breasts were thought of as constituting a single area (in French termed *la gorge*), the public exposure of any part of which was considered indecent. If what was scanty but permissible costume on the beach became unacceptable "nudity" anywhere else, the beach came easily to signify a lowered sexual threshold. We find an example of this as early as 1933 in Raffaello Matarazzo's film *Treno popolare*, where Carlo (Carlo Petrangeli) and Lina (Lina Gennari), who have first met only that day on a Sunday outing from Rome to Orvieto, capsize in a rowing boat in the country and come ashore soaked. He tells her she must take off her clothes and dry them in the sun. "Take them off?" she protests. "You must be joking." "Pretend we're by the sea," he replies. "It's easy." The resulting sequence when they undress behind separate trees must have produced a sexual *frisson* for the contemporary spectator. It cements the couple's intimacy: after it Carlo switches from "lei" to "tu" in addressing Lina.

Anxieties among Catholics persisted in the postwar years and indeed were fueled by the collapse in some areas of social controls and the rise of the swimsuit beauty contest. Even more than before, an issue that was the object of particular attention on their part was wider display of the body in holiday resorts. In August 1954, fourteen women on holiday in Miramare di Rimini signed a letter of protest to the Interior Minister against "the degeneracy of the bathers who don't hesitate to display shameful nudism on the beaches, on trams and trolleybuses and in the public streets, nudism which has now reached the highest degree."[42] The prefect of Forlì, asked by the minister to give an explanation, replied that transgressions of the existing by-laws on dress codes were indeed taking place: the offending swimmers were nearly always foreign tourists; as well as being scantily clad on the beach or in the sea, "even in the vicinity of the beach they insist on wearing clothes which are often excessively skimpy." In other words it was this crossing of the threshold between beach and town that made their "nudism" (which meant in this case naked shoulders, backs, waists, and legs) both more visible and particularly offensive to the sensibilities of the complainants. He added that attempts to clamp down on the offenders had met with resistance on the part of the local authorities and tourist boards, who were concerned that it would damage the tourist trade, and that in any case the police were not always able to intervene decisively, "both because of the difficulty of being able to determine the point at which a swimming costume or item of clothing becomes licentious and because of the extreme delicacy of the interventions." In the past, he noted, these interventions had given rise to "fierce protests, deplorable publicity . . . ironic and generally unfavourable remarks about the police who are accused of being heavy-handed." In 1954 Emilio Cassone of Turin complained to the prefect about the statuettes of naked or seminaked women displayed in artisans' workshops and shop windows. The prefect sent police officers to photograph the statuettes, provoking a complaint by the local artisans' union of unwarranted intrusion. In the same year, a group of Christian Democrat members of parliament called for the abolition of beauty contests.

Dancing and Fashion

We have already mentioned dancing with reference to the specific disruptive impact of the boogie-woogie. This was a field in which the tension between repression and liberalization was marked, especially among members of the middle class. Some parents seem to have banned dances altogether, although enterprising daughters nevertheless sometimes found a way to take part (92: 4; 102: 11). Avelina G. recalled, "I always went dancing on the sly. In the afternoon when I had to go I told my parents I was going to a blessing in church and we went off in a group. We had two or three men's bicycles. We got on them and went to another village to dance" (24: 2). Public dances were often declared off-limits by parents who could no longer exercise appropriate control. Given these restrictions, parties and private dances were precious occasions that afforded rare opportunities for interaction between the sexes. Suspicion of strangers prevailed, however, and most dances occurred within the family or the close neighborhood. As Leandro N. of Cosenza confirmed: "The girls from your extended family came, and those from the neighborhood, but they had to trust the boys, otherwise they wouldn't send them, it was all a particular ritual" (73: 15). At dances, strict rules prevailed. In Cagliari, as elsewhere, it was the boys who invited girls to dance (52: 18), the only exceptions occurring during carnival (50/51: 20–21):

There were also fixed rules. What were these rules? That we couldn't dance with boys we didn't know, so we had to say no, because this was strongly instilled in us. And we couldn't dance twice with the same boy. (52: 18–19)

To have danced with the same boy would have given rise to gossip or to damaging accusations of being "loose" (*poco seria*). In Rome, Mimmo V. recalled that the rarity of these moments was such that you had to move quickly to extract the promise of a further meeting from a girl you liked (59: 34–35). Surveillance was pronounced because parents were aware that there was, beyond the limits of acceptable prescribed behavior for girls and young women, an area that went from having a bad reputation to prostitution. Even a small step into this area was perceived as fatally damaging to a girl's marriage prospects. Maria P., born in 1935 in the village of Rogliano in the province of Cosenza, said: "Here if you were engaged to a young man and the relationship ended you would never get married. The fiancé would say, 'She went with that guy and I don't want her any more.' Parents were afraid: 'Be careful because you won't be able to get married; careful what you do'" (81: 10). Mothers sometimes began collecting and making items for a girl's trousseau very early, from the age of five or six, and this investment required protection. Fears over transgressions were plentiful. Wanrooij comments on anxieties about the "flirt," a phenomenon initially perceived in the higher social classes; the moral anxiety was not just about the greater visibility of flirtatious behavior but about its spread downward to the lower classes.[43]

Our testimonies suggest that established patterns of parental control persisted over the first postwar decade, with young people effectively being chaperoned whenever they encountered members of the opposite sex. Some parents continued to ban their daughters from attending dances, especially where these were open to all. In any case girls in particular did not always find the latter appealing. In Rome after the war Laura S., born in 1930, whose middle-class Jewish family had survived the German occupation and who loved jazz and swing, avoided outdoor dancing places because "they were really at a very low level, I don't mean this in a negative sense, of course, but you couldn't go there, there was real rabble there." Instead she and her friends danced to records in their homes (101: 25). Enzo P., who lived in Rovereto with his family above a bank, the Cassa di Risparmio, where his father was the custodian, had a large room in which he was able to organize regular dances. However, these took place in the afternoon and under the "assiduous control of my mother," who, unlike her freethinking husband, was "more tied . . . to religious dogma, rules of behavior more in tune with the Catholic religion. So when we had parties she kept an eye on us, and every so often we tried to turn off a few lights to dance closer together but she noticed and came out" (110: 6). Nevertheless the greater frequency of parties, facilitated by the wider availability of the gramophone, can be said to have rendered them a normal rather than an exceptional aspect of the experience of young people. Most of these spontaneous afternoon dances, moreover, were specifically held by and for the young, not for intergenerational groups.

The use of cosmetics was a relative novelty that gave rise, as we have seen, to hostile reactions from some parents. For many girls makeup consisted of a little face powder and nothing else. Rita B. (born 1927) found that any use of makeup led to difficulties: "If my mother or even my aunt saw us wearing makeup there would be big trouble. They didn't want us to" (11/12: 57). An area where there was more room for maneuver was hairstyles. *Famiglia Cristiana* and other Catholic periodicals regularly denounced not only beauty contests but also cosmetics, fashion, and dancing. The frequency with which such issues were raised suggests that these things were becoming more widely practiced. A conception of the body as a part of the self that could be adorned, fashioned, and displayed according to an individual's will was taking shape. Long a feature of upper-class femininity, after 1945 it gained a wider hold among the lower classes.

Before that, things were different. Although even poorer people were aware of fashion, attractive or even new clothes were usually out of reach. Lisa G. (born in Turin in 1921) remarked that if you were lucky enough to have good clothes, you only wore them outside the house and removed them as soon as you got home (32: 16). Before the mass consumption of fashion, clothes, and cosmetics, there was a period when working-class and some peasant women sought to emulate the appearance of women with higher incomes but could do so only in a rough and ready way. It was easier for city dwellers to approximate fashionableness. For example, Avelina G. observed that "if a woman came from the town you could tell, because she came wearing a hat even if she was a maid, she came with a hat on her head and gloves on her hands" (24: 11). Clothes were often poor and usually homemade. Only middle- and upper-class women enjoyed more varied wardrobes (8: 12–14; 13: 16–18; 14: 29). Victoria de Grazia quotes a report of 1931 on the families of sharecroppers in the Chianti valley, which noted that the girls would go to the market on Saturdays to sell their crochet work in exchange for "gewgaws—wool and ny- lon stockings, ribbons, hairpins, combs and such, the likes of which they had never before even dreamed of."[44] Loredana Donini Negrini, who worked in the 1930s as a hairdresser in Bologna, said in an interview in 1989:

I wanted clothes, because you saw these people who were better off, they were well off, they dressed differently from us who worked in factories or as dress- makers or in fashion shops or who did the ironing or worked as hairdressers. I never had a dress, we were dressed in clothes people gave away to my mother where I worked: "Excuse me, madam, would you like this dress for your daugh- ter?" "Yes, please give it to me." We didn't buy clothes, hardly any. But we did put on makeup. I . . . was a hairdresser [and] made myself blonde . . . so I went and got all the lotions, the dyes, from this so-called hairdresser who sold soap and perfume in Via Marsala, Manzolini, everyone in Bologna knew him, so I made do with him. He gave me samples of this perfume called Revedor. I always got by with creams, a few samples, because I was a hairdresser, but my friends never used them, we sometimes gave each other creams but mostly people put olive oil or seed oil on their faces.[45]

The young people of the years after World War II marked out some of their own practices with the aid of the mass media and greater access to some consumer goods. Young working-class men regarded Saturdays and Sundays as a temporal territory that was their own. According to Fulvio M., "When Sunday came round you tried to do something different, you might have had only one suit but it was a good suit, you dressed well, you put on some scent, you smoked a more sophisticated cigarette because we came from poverty so that day was a day when you wanted to have fun, so it was different from all the other days" (56: 12). For Roberto R. in Turin:

Your weekday clothes, whether you went to school or out to work, were modest, super-modest. But on Saturday, or on Thursday night when you went dancing, you put on a dark blue double-breasted suit, white shirt, and dark blue tie. For a time . . . when you went to dance halls it seemed almost everyone was in uni- form. Everyone had dark blue double-breasted jackets, but everyone. . . . There was a time when, out of a hundred boys, seventy to seventy-five dressed in dark blue. Those few boys who weren't in blue almost clashed. Then that time ended, but you still dressed smartly. But perhaps then there was the fact you had to go, because they made you go with a tie so you made a point of turning up well dressed, because maybe you'd be going out with a girl and you wanted to go for a walk down Via Roma, so when you were well dressed you could walk down Via Roma and show that even you, poor sod that you were, had a smart enough suit to walk down Via Roma, this was how it was then. (7: 36–37)

As for girls, although it remained true for many that, in the words of Angela C. (born in Sasso Marconi, province of Bologna, in 1919), "You put on a smart dress not to go dancing [but] to go to mass" (25: 12), there was an engagement with the wider world that was new. Fashion and appearance took on a greater importance as a result. The photoromance magazine *Grand Hôtel* was influential as were sightings of desirable items in shop windows or other magazines. Natalia, whose mother was a dressmaker, would often ask her to reproduce a skirt or blouse she had seen in a shop window or a magazine.

I remember . . . in the first issue [of *Grand Hôtel*] there was a smock on the cover in red and white gingham, I still have a piece of it, because I made a shirt for Beppe [her son] when he was little. I bought the same material, I found it, it was easy to find this gingham, and I went home and said: "My mother has to make me this smock." It was all buttoned in front, a smock dress, it was lovely. Wow! And she made buttonholes and the buttons just the same, she made it exactly like that. Just like in *Grand Hôtel*. (4: 25–26)

For poorer girls like Rita B. and Adriana A. the magazine was purely aspirational: "We would say: 'Look at her, look at that one, look whether we could have this too'" (11/12: 12). At first *Grand Hôtel* used drawings for its stories, then it switched to photographs in 1947. Angela C. said, "The photos were better because we could see the clothes; those drawings seemed artificial" (25: 6). Although this publication was aimed at the lower classes, its appeal extended more widely. Thanks to its seductive covers, accessible fashion, and romantic stories, even middle-class girls like Elsa (born in Turin in 1937) read it, borrowing copies from servant girls (13: 25). Young women of all classes were well aware of the advantages of being well turned out and in tune with fashion. It would seem that this greater familiarity with goods and their uses was accompanied by a certain increase in privatization. For example, Maria I. (born in Celico in 1932, married in 1955) broke with the custom of inviting all the neighbors to view items from her trousseau laid out on a bed in the days before her wedding: "On Thursday you would make the bed tidy and put out all the bridal stuff, sheets, blankets, underwear, and everything, and people would come and look. But they didn't come to me, I wasn't interested. . . . The neighbors wanted to come and see the stuff I had but I didn't show it to any one. Only to the people closest to me" (70: 9).

In terms of fashion and beauty, both Sophia Loren and Gina Lollobrigida were role models for girls, especially those of provincial or working-class origin. Lollobrigida was more popular with women on account of her relatively modest off-screen demeanor. Both initially had found work in the photoromances that were read by many women who rarely went to the cinema. Their hairstyles were copied and so were their looks, such as the high belt pulled in tight to emphasize the feminine shape. One Roman witness, a former hairdresser, said that the short, curled, and permed style that Lollobrigida adopted in 1954 became very popular with young women: "all permed they were, Lollobrigida-style" (20: 25). Girls ceased to bleach their hair too as dark hair became more fashionable. However, middle-class women, like E. P. and F. P., the two sisters interviewed in Cagliari, always preferred elegant American stars. F. P. said, "I hardly ever went to see Italian films, the neorealist films, with the Italian man in his vest and the woman in an underskirt" (50/51: 37). The full-figured *maggiorate* were also considered to be "excessive" and vulgar. Silvana Pampanini, E. P. noted, was "all bosom and bottom" (50/51: 51). For inspiration for an evening gown, she looked instead to Grace Kelly. This shows that the Hollywood model of beauty was not eclipsed as far as the middle classes were concerned. The magazine *Estetica,* a trade paper for hairdressers and sellers of beauty products, never mentioned the new Italian cinema stars. The beauty ideal was very much the glamorous, polished, Hollywood one and reference was only made to performers like Deborah Kerr, Audrey Hepburn, and Elizabeth Taylor. The new styles continued to emanate from Hollywood—including, for example, that of short hair for women stars from 1949, which both Lollobrigida and later Loren would adopt. But for some fans, the Americans still seemed far away. Bruno O. remembered writing in 1950–1952, when he was about twenty, to various actresses, including Abbe Lane and Doris Day, to ask for an autographed photograph: "nothing ever arrived of course" (3: 42).

For Italian audiences, Lollobrigida and Loren were appealing because they represented an Italian adaptation of the commercial star type. They followed the Americans in publicizing a range of products like Lux soap and Chlorodont toothpaste (a rare practice in the 1930s). They were groomed and dressed by a top-ranking couturier, the "Italian Christian Dior," Emilio Schuberth, who specialized in elegant gowns that emphasized the bust. The magazines pictured them at numerous receptions and other social events. Their highly publicized participation in American productions and sojourns in Hollywood were taken as a symbol of Italy's economic recovery and reemergence on the international plane. With their taste for ostentatious jewelry and Beverly Hills–style homes, they mirrored a significant change in material aspirations that was taking place in Italy by the early 1950s.[46]

Mass Culture and the Self

In this chapter we have tried to reconstruct a picture, drawing on our own oral history research and other sources, of the diverse ways in which mass culture interacted in our period with practices of the self and forms of bodily display. What has emerged is a mosaic with pieces missing, fragments of a more complex whole, but with sufficient information, we hope, to capture a sense of that whole in all its dynamism. This was a period riven by tensions and contradictions between old and new practices, challenges to some established beliefs and behaviors, acceptance of others. What is striking about many of the testimonies is the relationship between mass cultural consumption and other changes taking place in Italian society: challenges to "traditional" norms of Church and family, changes in relations between men and women and in rituals of courtship, and increased freedom and autonomy for young people in relation to their parents' generation. In all these ways, films, magazines, fashion, radio, recorded music, advertising, and sport were important in driving a wedge between generations and between old and new practices of the self. In the next part of the book, we turn from the consumption and demand for these products to their supply and the industries that produced them. Our aim is to see what presence these cultural industries established, to examine their approach to markets and audiences, on the one hand, and to consider their relationship with political forces on the other.

Part 2.

Cultural Industries and Markets

3 Publishing

BOOKS, MAGAZINES, AND COMICS

One of the most characteristic features of cultural modernization is the increasing presence in society of mass-reproduced leisure goods such as films, paperbacks, glossy magazines, radio programs, and records, offered to consumers through the market. The industries that produce and distribute these goods come increasingly to mediate and shape people's cultural repertoires, determine which products are available, and stimulate demand through promotion and advertising. At the same time these industries need to respond to various forms of regulation and intervention by public bodies. This chapter and the three that follow it in this part of the book deal with different industries and aspects of this process in Italy between the mid-1930s and mid-1950s.

In all the major Italian cultural industries, despite the upheaval of the war years 1940–1945, with occupation, resistance, and the change in regime and form of the state, many of the commercial strategies established in or before the 1930s persisted into the 1950s. We suggest two main explanations for this. The first is that cultural firms, like other kinds of firms, tend to develop a continuity in their way of operating, a "house style" that is strongly shaped by their key players, that is, their directors or management boards. The second is that, as we shall show in more detail in chapter 7, the Italian state was fragmented in its operations, and political influence and decision-making in the cultural sphere were devolved to different ministries and agencies that rarely acted together in a coordinated way. This fragmentation generally worked to the advantage of the cultural industries, enabling them to pursue their strategies relatively unhindered, whereas the ruling elites tended, with a few exceptions, to have weak, inconsistent, or internally contradictory cultural policies. The international context in which the cultural industries operated was also of major importance. There was a constant tension in Italy between, on the one hand, openness to flows of information from outside, an openness that the cultural industries either permitted as a technical possibility (as in the case of radio receivers) or pursued as a conscious policy (in film distribution and exhibition and in many areas of publishing) and, on the other hand, closure within the nation's borders, which was sought either by political forces or by protectionist elements within the cultural industries themselves. One finds this tension again and again, from industry to industry, in the 1950s as in the 1930s, despite the different political and ideological frameworks.

In neither the Fascist nor the postwar period did the Italian political elites act as a coherent bloc in their responses to modern commercial culture and to the "Americanization" with which it was often associated.[1] Fascist traditionalists, the advocates of cultural autarky and of a specifically Italian cultural identity, Church leaders, and, after the war, the leading cadres and intellectuals of the Socialist and Communist parties were all, for the most part, hostile to the new forms of commercial mass culture (see chapter 8), whereas those who advocated free trade, economic modernization, and renewal, both in Fascism and among the postwar elites, were generally sympathetic to the new forms. Italian cultural firms that sought to modernize could attempt to use these differences in outlook, sometimes successfully, sometimes not, as a lever in their dealings with the state. Their importation or mediation (for instance, by translations or emulations) of foreign products or styles involved cultural firms repeatedly in conflict with protectionist or xenophobic elements both in the state and in other, more traditionalist, firms. Ultimately, the attempts to contain cultural development within national boundaries failed and the pattern that prevailed throughout the period was one of openness. All this has important implications for the assessment one makes of the degree of popular "consent" to Fascism and the ideological success or otherwise of the Fascist political project, that of the Center-right coalitions of the Cold War and those of other political forces operating in civil society. We shall examine these in the last part of the book.

In this chapter we focus on publishing. We start with an overview of the industry and its modernization from the 1930s to early 1950s. We then examine a case study of the presence of a foreign cultural industry in the Italian publishing market—Disney comic strips published by Mondadori—and end, in a brief coda, with a glimpse of the Italian fortunes of *Reader's Digest* during the Cold War years.

The Modernization of Publishing

Publishing was the oldest of the major cultural industries operating in twentieth-century Italy. In the 1930s it underwent an important process of technological modernization and growth, particularly in the glossy magazine sector, under a regime that often did not officially favor or support what it produced. After the war there was a huge expansion of weekly magazines (*settimanali*), which put Italy, traditionally a country of few readers (see chapter 1), in the lead in Europe for magazine circulation figures.[2] There was also a significant development, with the return to democracy and pluralism after 1945, of publishing houses linked to the parties of the left. Overall, the geography of Italian publishing changed between the mid-1930s and mid-1950s. Milan's position as leading city for both books and magazines was consolidated; that of Turin was strengthened, while that of Florence, which had been a strong publishing city until the 1940s, declined, along with its status as a literary and artistic capital.

The transformations of the 1930s and 40s are best understood if placed in a longer historical perspective. Italy had lost its early dominant position in the European book trade during the eighteenth century. It fell behind Germany, France, and Britain in the transformation of its production processes and had a much smaller mass reading public. There was a partial modernization in the nineteenth century, including the purchase in Turin in 1830 of the first fully mechanical press by Giuseppe Pomba and the development in Milan of the first popular Italian publishers, Sonzogno (founded 1818) and Treves (1861). But in spite of these developments, by the early twentieth century there were still many small family firms using artisanal methods of production, including hand presses. By 1915, when Italy entered World War I, several new firms had emerged that would become market leaders, including Laterza, Vallecchi, Mondadori, and Rizzoli. Yet even these had started as printers, and in the early twentieth century a clear separation in the book trade between publishing and printing, characteristic of an advanced publishing industry, still did not exist. The Laterza family had set up a printing firm in Bari in 1896 (they had initially been paper sellers in Putignano from 1885). Attilio Vallecchi had started out as a printer in Florence around 1900. Arnoldo Mondadori had founded his first printing works in Ostiglia in the province of Mantua in 1907; he became a publisher from 1911, and transferred his offices to Verona in 1917 and to Milan in 1921, but he retained printing (at Verona) as a parallel and important part of his overall commercial operations. Angelo Rizzoli became an apprentice in the printing trade while living in the Martinitt orphanage in Milan and set up his own firm in 1909.

At the end of the 1920s, Franco Ciarlantini noted, there were still a number of "mixed" enterprises alongside the fully fledged publishers: "bookshop-publishers, printer-publishers, even paperseller-publishers."[3] As president from 1927 to 1940 of the Federazione Nazionale Fascista dell'Industria Editoriale (National Fascist Federation of Publishers, FNFIE), Ciarlantini debarred these "hybrid" firms from membership and sought to develop publishing, to put it on a par with other Italian industries. In his articles and speeches of this period he outlined what he saw as the main factors that would allow the emergence of a modern publishing industry in Italy: reduction or elimination of the widespread and unprofitable practice of giving away large numbers of free or cut-price copies (*omaggi* and *sconti*), reduction of postal tariffs to make distribution cheaper, promotion of book fairs and festivals, and development of advertising. Overall, Ciarlantini's desire was to create a new attitude to publishing and bookselling:

The book should be treated the same as any other commodity. It must be supplied, in other words, with the same means used to supply any other product. The publisher cannot stand outside the iron laws of commerce. The reader needs to be grabbed by the collar no less than the hypochondriac who makes the quack's fortune. In Italy we are particularly badly organized in this field.[4]

It was Mondadori and Rizzoli who spearheaded the modernization of publishing during the 1930s. Mondadori concentrated primarily on books, with magazines as a secondary division, whereas Rizzoli at first concentrated on magazines. Although Rizzoli had published a few bestselling books in the late 1920s, he only moved decisively into books in 1949 with the creation of the cheap classics series Biblioteca Universale Rizzoli (BUR).[5] Credit for inventing the BUR, modeled on the Reclam paperbacks in Germany, was claimed by

Luigi Rusca, who had left Mondadori for Rizzoli after the war, although this claim has been challenged.[6] The books, printed with cheap, grey paper covers, cost 50 lire for a volume under 100 pages and 100 lire for one up to 180 pages. The innovation consisted not just in this "modular" pricing structure but also in the commissioning of prefaces by established scholars and the addition of critical bibliographies. However, it has been pointed out that in other respects the BUR followed a traditional concept of popularized literary culture and excluded, for example, science, philosophy, and politics.[7] Mondadori's first equivalent series of low-priced quality texts was the more expensive (250 lire per title) Biblioteca Moderna Mondadori (BMM), launched a year before the BUR in 1948, with which the firm pioneered the practice of selling books in news kiosks (*edicole*) that was later to be extended in the 1960s with the hugely successful Oscar series.[8]

Both publishers diversified in the 1930s to create large, integrated firms. Rizzoli expanded into cinema, founding the production company Novella Film, whose first film, *La signora di tutti* (*Everybody's Lady*), directed by Max Ophuls and released in 1934, was also a vehicle for launching Isa Miranda as a star (see chapter 5), as well as the distribution arm Cineriz. Rizzoli later moved into newspapers. Mondadori expanded into paper production and both Mondadori and Rizzoli subsequently diversified into bookselling. They were both quick to recognize the changing nature of the publishing market. Arnoldo Mondadori and Angelo Rizzoli also happened to be exactly the same age (born in 1889) and, despite their intense rivalry, their early fortunes were intertwined and some key individuals, including Indro Montanelli, Luigi Rusca, and Cesare Zavattini, worked for both at different times during the period we are examining (Rusca also played a central role in the reconstruction of EIAR at the time of its transition to the RAI in 1944 and in its first phase of wartime exceptional management (*gestione straordinaria*), until he was forced to resign by the unions on April 20, 1945). The career biographies of these and other individuals, in publishing as in the other cultural industries, are illuminating for an understanding of the continuities of cultural strategy across the political watershed of the war years. Although some of them changed their political allegiances, or became politicized for the first time, as a result of their wartime experiences (Zavattini is a case in point), there was often a continuity in their professional self-image and their "technical" outlook, for instance in their conception of the design, format, and marketing of a publication.

Rizzoli had first become successful as a publisher after acquiring in 1927 four magazine titles—*Il Secolo Illustrato, Novella, Donna,* and *Comoedia*—jettisoned by Mondadori when his firm was losing money after having taken

Figures 6 and 7. The makeover of *Novella:* the cover of an early "note-book-sized" issue (vol. 1, no. 10, December 10, 1919, 17.5 x 24.5 cm), published by Casa Editrice Italia, and the later broadsheet magazine (vol. 23, no. 26, July 1, 1942, 28 x 37 cm), published by Rizzoli. The latter shows film star Vivi Gioi alongside the beginning of a short story by Luciana Peverelli. By permission of RCS MediaGroup S.p.A.

over the ailing Milanese newspaper *Il Secolo*. Rizzoli modernized the appearance of these magazines and targeted them toward a mass public. The Mondadori version of *Novella*, for instance, had more or less followed the model of the earliest issues (it was originally launched in 1919 by the publisher Italia): a small-format (*formato quaderno*) monthly, called *Novella, Rivista letteraria* (*Novella, Literary Review*) containing short stories, mainly

by Italian writers, plus a small section called "Gli altarini del Parnaso" (Dealings on Parnassus) consisting of captioned photographs of writers. There
were advertisements of a traditional type, aimed mostly at women: depila-
tory cream, breast-developing pills, and so forth. When Rizzoli took over the
title he turned it into a weekly *rotocalco* (that is, printed with a rotogravure
press, called in Italian *stampa a rotocalcografia*) with a broadsheet format,
and changed the subtitle to *Settimanale di novelle e varietà* (*Weekly magazine of short stories and variety*), and subsequently to *Antologia di novelle* (*Anthology of short stories*).[9] The magazine's editors inserted photographs of film
stars in the text of the short stories and added a two-page center spread, consisting in most weeks of production shots or publicity shots from Hollywood films. Overall the number of photographs and advertisements (still directed at women: beauty treatments, eau de cologne, and so on) was greatly
increased. A new column called "Hollywood" was also introduced, as well as
an advice column, "Botta e risposta" (Back-chat), signed by "Dottor minimo"
(Doctor Minimus). The style of the Rizzoli *Novella* thus anticipated the later
formula of the photo-weekly and the *fotoromanzo* (see chapter 1). It had cover
photographs on the front and back, usually of beautiful women, couples, or
film stars, and its stories mainly had a romantic content. The Hollywood material often focused on the everyday life of female stars. The issue of July 7–
14, 1929, for instance, carried on the cover a picture of Norma Shearer and
her puppies and inside (in the "Hollywood" column on page 7) a story of
how she had been issued with a court summons after her neighbor, a retired
general, had complained that the puppies were ruining his flowerbeds. Rizzoli understood the size and structure of the female reading public and he
later sought to transform *Il Secolo Illustrato* along similar lines. Zavattini, who
had started working as a proofreader on the latter magazine before being appointed editor, wrote in 1935 to Valentino Bompiani: "My boss delivered quite
a blow this morning: he says he wants it to be for women, that they are our
target readers, and that it has to be popular ... he tells me in no uncertain
terms that he wants nice legs on the cover."[10] All this stoked opposition from
moralizers. In March 1934, for instance, the intransigent Fascist organ *Ottobre*,
edited by Asvero Gravelli, denounced the Rizzoli firm as a "thriving and well-
fed publishing system ... an ominous game of immorality, banality and bad
faith."[11]

On April 3, 1937 Rizzoli launched Italy's first modern-looking illustrated
weekly, *Omnibus*, edited by Leo Longanesi. Although it was more literary and
elitist in content than the better-known weeklies that followed it, its innovative design (a broadsheet with photographs and drawings and a modern type-
face) had antecedents in the photo-weeklies published in Germany by Ull-
stein (*Berliner Illustrirte Zeitung* and *Die Dame*), France (*Vu*), and the United

States (notably *Life* magazine, an established title that had folded and been relaunched in 1936 as a photo-weekly by Henry R. Luce, publisher of *Time* and *Fortune*). Although *Omnibus* ran for less than two years before being suppressed in January 1939, it reached a weekly circulation of 70,000 and gave rise to two other prewar *rotocalchi*, both launched in June 1939: Rizzoli's *Oggi*, edited by two journalists from *Omnibus*, Arrigo Benedetti and Mario Pannunzio; and Mondadori's *Tempo*, edited by Arnoldo's son Alberto.[12] Mondadori had reentered the adult periodicals market in November 1938 with the women's magazine *Grazia*, after having branched into children's comics in 1935 with two Walt Disney titles (discussed in more detail below). The photojournalistic format of *Tempo* was fiercely attacked by the cultural autarky lobby as being a more or less transparent copy of *Life*.[13] By 1940 Mondadori was publishing nine periodical titles: for adults *Tempo*, *Grazia*, and *Ecco*; and for children the weeklies *Topolino* and *Paperino* (*Mickey Mouse* and *Donald Duck*), the fortnightly *Nel regno di Topolino* (*In Mickey's Kingdom*), and three non-Disney titles: *Albi d'Oro* (*Golden Albums*), *Albi di Salgari* (*Salgari Albums*), and *Albi di Avventure* (*Adventure Albums*). According to Enrico Piceni, who began working for Mondadori in 1924, the latter had entered the children's weeklies sector on little more than an inspired business hunch.[14] The comics too would come under attack from cultural protectionists as examples of deleterious foreign influence, in this case on the grounds that they were diseducative (see chapter 7).

One could cite many more examples from other parts of the publishing industry of these cosmopolitan tendencies in the 1930s and the conflicts they engendered in parts of the Fascist political and cultural apparatus. Valentino Bompiani, who had left Mondadori in May 1928 to set up his own firm, was one of the publishers with a high proportion of translations in his book lists. He engaged in a celebrated piece of haggling in 1940–1942 with Alessandro Pavolini, Minister of Popular Culture from October 1939 to February 1943, over the proposed publication of *Americana*, the anthology of American literature from its origins to the present edited by Elio Vittorini.[15] Pavolini at first refused permission to publish the book, then acceded to Bompiani's suggestion that it appear with a preface by Emilio Cecchi, a literary scholar more acceptable to the regime than Vittorini. Cecchi was the author of, among other works, *America amara* (*Bitter America*), published in 1939, which had contained many criticisms of American society. However, Pavolini only agreed to publication on condition that Vittorini's own introductions to each section of the anthology were removed and replaced by an anthology of critical writings by others. After the end of the war Bompiani would describe his firm in a letter to Erskine Caldwell as "perhaps the greatest publishing concern in Italy for Anglo-American Literature, ancient and modern."[16] Like Mondadori, he had been criticized since the late 1930s not only by the Ministry of Popular Culture but also by more autarkic publishers such as Attilio Vallecchi, who was proud of his record of publishing Italian authors, many of them profascist, like Ardengo Soffici, Giovanni Papini, and Giuseppe Prezzolini. The argument that Italy imported and translated too many books had been voiced for many years by cultural protectionists under Fascism but it acquired a new urgency after 1937 when pressures toward cultural autarky started to come directly from the Fascist government (see chapter 7). It is interesting to note, nevertheless, that there was initial resistance to autarky even among authors aligned with the regime. In July 1937, for instance, Papini sent Vallecchi the following memo, headed "Autarky," for the latter's forthcoming audience with Mussolini:

The principle of autarky in the field of ideas [*nel campo spirituale*] is dangerous. The only concrete form it can take is a ban on translations. We would be seen as barbarians. There are already too many economic barriers; to set obstacles to the circulation of ideas would be madness. And to prevent intellectual relations between countries is an impossible task, beyond the powers of any man, even a very powerful one. I don't think that M. [Mussolini] would be in favour of this kind of autarky.[17]

The pressure against excessive translations continued to mount nonetheless and publishers had to find ways of dealing with it. Mondadori, whose firm published the most translations of all, argued in his own defense that the importation of foreign titles was part of a successful system of exchange that he had painstakingly set up with partner publishers abroad, by which they took and translated some of his Italian titles. He thus argued that any move to restrict imports would damage exports. In an article published in May 1938 he proudly reported an increase in the number of Italian books exported—bought mainly by Italians residents abroad, particularly in North and South America, but with a secondary market among foreigners able to read Italian (according to Giuseppe Prezzolini, who had become director of the Casa Italiana at Columbia University, there were around 30,000 students of Italian in North America). The number of exported books had gone up by 40 percent from 5,727 in 1934 to 7,957 in 1937, with a corresponding 50 percent increase in the value of exports from 7.7 to 11.5 million lire.[18] Mondadori suggested four main reasons for the increase: interest in Fascist Italy ("They can love us or hate us, but today there is no civilised country in the world where they are not interested in what is happening here"); improved design (Italian books at this time stood up well in their graphic appearance against foreign books); quality of content ("in every field Italian publishing has produced works worthy of the interest of those who live abroad"); and better organization of book export.[19] Mondadori also argued that the publication of translations provided work for Italian translators, typesetters, and printers so that to cut them would jeopardize Italian jobs.

The clampdown, however, finally started to take effect in 1940. In February of that year Attilio Vallecchi became president of the FNFIE and called on publishers to restrict translations. This call was put into practice after Italy entered the war in June and then, with even more force, after the United States joined in December 1941. Table 3.1 shows the proportion of translated books out of the total published in Italy from the mid-1930s to the mid-1950s and Table 3.2 shows the proportion of translations in Mondadori's lists. Comparison between the two sets of figures shows the high percentage of translations published overall by Mondadori. Table 3.2 registers the sharp drop in that percentage during the war years (from around half the titles to less than a quarter between 1942 and 1945, when there was also an overall reduction in titles published) but it also indicates that, apart from these aberrant years, there was substantial continuity in the proportion of translations in Mondadori's lists for the rest of the period.

The period immediately after liberation in 1945 saw a mushrooming of small publishing houses, some of which survived for only a few months, and an increase in book production, despite residual paper shortages. At the same time some existing publishers sought to take advantage both of the market opportunities and of the chance for cultural renewal opened up by the liberation. Einaudi, founded in 1934, was the rising star of so-called *editoria di cultura* (cultural publishing) and had strong antifascist credentials. Like various other cultural firms, Einaudi had decentered its operations during the war into three different cities: Turin (its original home), Milan, and Rome. Giulio Einaudi was determined after the end of hostilities to expand the Milan office and thereby mount a direct challenge to Mondadori, Rizzoli, and Bompiani. On May 16, 1945 he wrote to two of his editors, Cesare Pavese and Felice Balbo, who were skeptical about his strategy: "The most important thing is to organize the struggle against the Milan publishers. If we win this battle we will be at the head of the progressive cultural front. Don't be hesitant about financing Milan. If necessary slow down the production of other books."[20] Einaudi envisaged as part of this cultural front a political-cultural weekly published in Milan, and he decided to transfer the firm's administrative and commercial offices there.[21]

Vittorini, a consultant at the time for both Einaudi and Bompiani, was the lynchpin of Einaudi's Milan operation. It was he who would edit the periodical that Einaudi launched on September 29, 1945, *Il Politecnico*. Despite his efforts to get his contributors to write accessibly about demanding subjects—current affairs, history, Marxism, literary criticism—and despite his use of

Table 3.1. Book production in Italy, 1936–1954.*

	Istat figures	BNCF figures	Number of translations (BNCF)	% Translations (BNCF)
1936	10,238	10,015	n/a	n/a
1937	10,745	9,938	1,172	11.8
1938	10,838	9,736	919	9.4
1939	10,160	9,683	705	7.3
1940	10,489	9,330	659	7.1
1941	10,762	9,427	544	5.8
1942	9,062	8,414	402	4.8
1943	8,162	6,832	228	3.3
1944	2,248	1,895	124	6.5
1945	4,307	4,068	439	10.8
1946	5,614	5,466	731	13.4
1947	5,230	5,477	882	16.1
1948	7,430	7,592	772	10.2
1949	9,985	10,054	1,170	11.6
1950	8,853	8,539	896	10.5
1951	7,101	9,613	1,220	12.7
1952	8,949	9,047	1,150	12.7
1953	6,642	8,599	1,258	14.6
1954	8,234	8,514	1,172	13.8

Source: *Statistica delle pubblicazioni italiane ricevute per diritto di stampa* (Florence: Biblioteca Nazionale Centrale, appendix to *Bollettino delle pubblicazioni italiane ricevute per diritto di stampa* for years indicated); "Opere pubblicate per materia trattata," in *Sommario di statistiche storiche 1926–1985* (Rome: Istat 1986), 97. All figures are for numbers of titles, not numbers of volumes.

* Statistics for book production in Italy are not entirely reliable for this period, for reasons that have been well explained by Elisabetta Carfagna and Pierfrancesco Attanasio, "Fonti statistiche per la storia dell'editoria libraria in Italia," in Gianfranco Tortorelli, ed., *Fonti e studi di storia dell'editoria* (Edizioni Baiesi, s.l., s.d.), 137–62. The BNCF figures are for the year in which publications are received by the library, which is not always the same as the year when they are published. There was also a widespread evasion, particularly by smaller publishers, of the legal requirement to deposit a copy of each work at the BNCF, so the figures are always underestimates, and the BNCF did not report or include all publications it received. From 1951 Istat began to collect and publish statistics of book production using a different method from the BNCF, namely collecting data from the *Ufficio stampa* of each prefecture, where a copy of each work also had to be lodged (from 1967 Istat's method changed again and it started to collect data directly from publishers).

Table 3.2. Total books published annually by Mondadori 1936–1954, with number and percentage of translations.

	All Titles	Italian Works	Number of Translations	% Translations
1936	159	73	86	54
1937	189	105	84	44
1938	193	94	99	51
1939	182	86	96	53
1940	177	93	84	47
1941	153	86	67	44
1942	109	80	29	27
1943	66	52	14	21
1944	61	45	16	26
1945	59	46	13	22
1946	141	63	78	55
1947	125	49	76	61
1948	155	56	99	64
1949	195	95	100	51
1950	210	103	107	51
1951	161	75	86	53
1952	141	68	73	52
1953	159	66	93	58
1954	166	68	98	59

Source: Elaborated from Patrizia Moggi Rebulla and Mauro Zerbini, *Catalogo storico Arnoldo Mondadori Editore, 1912–1983*, vol. 5, *La Cronologia* (Milan: Fondazione Arnoldo e Alberto Mondadori, 1985). "Italian works" include, in addition to works written by Italian authors, art books edited by Italians. "Translations" include, as well as translated books, anthologies consisting mainly of translations (e.g., the "Super-gialli" albums of detective stories), biblical translations, and a very small number of translations of Latin and Greek texts with or without the originals on facing pages.

various formats from the popular press, such as a serialized novel (Hemingway's *For Whom the Bell Tolls*), Vittorini knew that *Il Politecnico*'s sales were never going to compete with the high-circulation magazines. It had particular difficulty picking up readers in the Center and South. 12,000 copies of the first issue were dispatched to Rome, half of which were to be sent on to Naples, but 50 percent of these were returned unsold.[22] The decision to switch to monthly publication (from May 1, 1946) and increase the number of pages was partly a response to this failure—even with the price raised from 12 to 15 lire the weekly was not covering its costs—but it did not suffice to salvage *Il Politec-nico*. A further nail in the coffin were attacks on the magazine by leading members of the PCI, including party leader Togliatti, over its alleged hetero-doxy and lack of a clear political direction. These criticisms had a direct im-pact on sales, not least because the PCI federations stopped putting copies on sale at party festivals and meetings. But although it was never a mass circula-tion magazine, *Il Politecnico* was unique for its time in attempting to combine a pedagogic mission with formats borrowed from popular photo-journalism, such as Luigi Crocenzi's "photostories" (*racconti fotografici*), and in the mod-ernist graphics and page layouts created by Albe Steiner for the weekly.[23]

The leading personnel and consultants at Einaudi included Partito d'Azi-one members as well as Communists, so, although friendly toward the PCI, it was not a party publisher but independent. Despite the conflict over *Il Politecnico* the relationship between Einaudi and the PCI generally proved beneficial to both sides. In particular the decision by Togliatti to entrust the publication of the works of Gramsci to Einaudi rather than to one of the two publishing houses directly controlled by the party, Edizioni Rinascita and Edizioni di Cultura Sociale (these merged in 1953 into Editori Riuniti, di-rected by Roberto Bonchio), showed that the PCI wanted Gramsci to have an ecumenical status as a national cultural figure beyond the immediate cultural orbit of the party. This decision was almost certainly a factor in gaining such a status for Gramsci.[24] Indeed, it was partly by means of the PCI's links with publishers, as well as its galaxy of directly produced or affiliated newspapers and magazines—*L'Unità, Paese Sera, Vie Nuove, Noi Donne, Il Calendario del Popolo*—that the PCI became a major subcultural force in postwar Italy (see chapter 8), despite being excluded from government after 1947. The PCI was involved in various publishing innovations. One of these was the production and distribution of the cheap paperback series of classics of philosophy and political ideas Universale del Canguro, produced by the Cooperativa del Li-bro Popolare (Colip) in Milan and launched in June 1949, a month after Riz-zoli's BUR, with a program that stated: "Every week a book. A library in every home" and "A book a week against obscurantism."[25] The series and its kan-garoo symbol would subsequently be taken over by one of Colip's founders, Giangiacomo Feltrinelli, at that time a PCI member. Feltrinelli used his con-siderable inherited fortune to fund a research center for the labor movement in 1951 and to set up one of the most successful new publishing firms of the postwar era in 1955 along with a major bookstore chain.[26]

Publishing is the only one of the major cultural industries in our period to have been dominated by family firms and dynasties. In the film industry, for instance, the only comparable case was that of the Lombardo family, founder of the Titanus studio, where control passed from father Gustavo to son Goffredo. This dominance of particular families in publishing firms is important in explaining their longevity, their internal dynamics, and their attitude to markets and to political forces outside them. Arnoldo Mondadori and Angelo Rizzoli were parallel figures as well as rivals. They were dissimilar in temperament, appearance, and public self-presentation but similar in their approach to publishing as a commercial venture, in the control and influence they exercised within their own firms, and in their ability to keep in touch with each of their various divisions. Both also founded dynasties. Angelo Rizzoli brought his son Andrea into the firm at quite an early age but subsequently infantilized him and would not delegate any real power to him (after Angelo's death at the age of eighty-one in September 1970 Andrea took over but soon afterward the Rizzoli firm encountered serious financial and management problems). Mondadori gave his two younger brothers, Remo and Bruno, important positions early on, and although Remo died in 1937 at age forty-six, his son Andrea remained involved in the printing division and Bruno became the firm's commercial director. The four children Arnoldo Mondadori had with his wife Andreina Monicelli also became involved in different ways. The eldest son, Alberto, took charge of the firm's magazine division, API (Anonima Periodici Italiani), at the age of twenty-five, replacing Zavattini. Arnoldo had imagined that Alberto would succeed him after his death as head of the firm, but a bitter conflict sprang up between them, exacerbated by Alberto's wartime espousal of antifascist politics and rejection of Arnoldo's conception of the firm's ethos and style of management.[27] Alberto subsequently split off and founded his own publishing house, Il Saggiatore, in 1958. The second son, Giorgio, became Mondadori's technical director. Of the two daughters, Laura (called "Mimma" in the family) became a co-director and Cristina ("Pucci") married Mario Formenton, who became a vice-president. Mimma's memoir, written in the 1980s, sums up Arnoldo's outlook:

My father was the publisher for Italy as it was; he did not claim to invent a different Italy. This was the job of the cultural publishers, the intellectual publishers driven by strong political or ideological beliefs. . . . Dad was a "pure" publisher, in the terms of a definition that is often used to distinguish those publishers, above all of newspapers, who publish in search of profit from those who publish for example with political aims. For him publishing books and magazines was not a cover for other aspirations or aims; it was an industrial activity in its own right, which customers would reward or punish according to what they were offered. . . . My father was a much-loved publisher because the Italian people felt he trod the same path as most of them, with the ups and downs of history, the changing seasons, Christmas coming round, free time to be filled with simple things to read, children to be educated, and with high culture and good literature reserved for the privileged few who could understand it or those who studied it professionally.[28]

After the war Alberto Mondadori played a key role in opening out the firm to American writers, including Ernest Hemingway, with whom he maintained a personal correspondence. In 1948 he succeeded in persuading Hemingway to sign an exclusive contract with Mondadori after having shared him with Einaudi, who had acquired before the war the rights to two of Hemingway's novels, *To Have and Have Not* and *The Sun also Rises*. He was also instrumental in developing the new magazine, *Epoca,* launched in 1950, which built on the prewar innovations of *Tempo*. The dimensions, graphic design, and layout were again explicitly indebted to *Life* magazine (Bruno Munari as graphic director was responsible both for *Tempo* and for the first issues of *Epoca*) but there was a more extensive use of photographs, including color ones, and the quality of both paper and printing was higher. Here the magazine benefited from two Marshall Plan loans in 1948–1949 to Mondadori's printing division for new machinery: a Cottrell offset press able to print in five colors and a Champlain. The ratio of pictures to text varied according to the feature but in the special reports it was particularly high and in some cases the pictures were by internationally renowned photographers such as Robert Capa and Henri Cartier-Bresson who, since founding the Magnum photographic agency in 1947, held the copyright of their own negatives and could sell them to more than one magazine. In the tenth issue of *Epoca,* for example (December 16, 1950), there was a nine-page report on Israel by Irwin Shaw with photographs by Capa. On seven of these pages the photographs occupy 50 percent or more of the page and on three of them the photographs are in color. Overall, as is generally the case with this kind of feature, the images with their captions may be "read" independently of the continuous written text. As for the content of the magazine, the most innovative aspect of the early issues was their declared emphasis on representing and reflecting the lives of ordinary Italians. The policy with the early covers was to show faces of working people rather than famous personalities. On the cover of the first issue (October 14, 1950), over the caption "Liliana, ragazza italiana," was nineteen-year-old Liliana De Mario, a shop assistant who served ice cream in the Motta shop in Milan's Piazza Duomo. The unsigned article inside, a photo-story about her Sunday outing with her boyfriend on a boat on Lake Como, said:

Why have we put the gentle face of this girl on the cover? She is just an ordinary girl, one of the many who work in Milan and earn between 25,000 and 30,000 lire a month. She belongs to the common people, in whose lives nothing exceptional happens, only the little events of everyday life. We chose Liliana and a Sunday afternoon on the lake because the ice-cream girl and her day off are part of daily life, and this is the magazine that tells your story, that comes looking for you in a crowd, picks out your face and brings it to the surface, in other words makes you a protagonist of the time.[29]

This ideology of ordinary life was also present in the "Italia domanda" (Italy Asks) column, conceived and initially edited by Zavattini. Readers were invited to write in on any topic and address their questions to experts in the relevant fields. The concept reflected Zavattini's postwar commitment to showing and giving voice to the "many Italies" and the ordinary people who had been barely visible under Fascism as well as the new interest in public surveys and polls. The opinion poll, which had been developed in the United States between the wars by George Gallup and Elmo Roper, was first used in Italy in 1946, when the statistician Pierpaolo Luzzatto Fegiz and others founded the Istituto Doxa.[30] Zavattini had originally conceived of a whole magazine called *Italia domanda* but this project was whittled down to the feature in *Epoca*. As with the cover stories about ordinary lives, there was also a degree of populism and paternalism in this column, particularly in the use of "experts" to provide the answers to the people who wrote to the magazine. Nonetheless it was an innovative idea, anticipating the later idea of radio phone-in programs, and it left as a permanent legacy an invaluable set of records of popular attitudes and beliefs of the early 1950s. The "Italia domanda" column, according to an Istituto Doxa survey, accounted for 80 percent of sales of *Epoca*. However, Zavattini left the magazine after the first four weeks of "Italian domanda" as a result of differences with Arnoldo Mondadori: he disagreed with a strongly pro-American column signed by the latter.[31]

Epoca was an instant success in a rapidly expanding market for weekly magazines, most of them published in Milan, which had reemerged after the war as the uncontested "capital of the weekly magazine."[32] Between 1950 and 1955 its circulation rose from 200,000 to 500,000. In the same period that of *Tempo* (relaunched in January 1946 under the editorship of Arturo Tofanelli and now published by Palazzi) increased from 150,000 to 420,000, while that of *Oggi* (relaunched in July 1945 by Rizzoli and edited by Edilio Rusconi, who was to leave in 1957 to set up his own magazine publishing firm) rose from 500,000 to 760,000.[33] According to the figures produced by the Biblioteca Nazionale in Florence, a total of 9,244 separate periodical titles were registered as having been published in 1955, of which 650 were published for the first time in that year.[34]

The publishing market that developed after the war was diversified enough to have room for established niche publishers, such as De Agostini in Novara (founded in 1901) for maps and atlases and Zanichelli in Bologna (founded in 1859) for reference works and school texts, as well as for the large generic houses like Rizzoli and Mondadori and for others that acquired "industrial" dimensions by the end of the 1950s in terms of employees, internal organization, and size of market, like Garzanti and Bompiani in Milan, Sansoni and Marzocco (later Giunti) in Florence, UTET and Einaudi in Turin.[35] It was, nevertheless, a changing market, and a number of more traditionally minded firms found it difficult to adapt. A case in point was Vallecchi, which began to fail after the war when it was taken over by Enrico Vallecchi (1902–1990). His father had been tried by partisans, accused of having taken subsidies from the Fascists; he had been exonerated but died soon after, in 1946.[36] The firm's failure had various causes, including Florence's loss of its strategic position to Milan and Turin, the decline of its café-based literary culture, and the migration to other cities of writers formerly based there, such as Montale and Gadda. However, as Geno Pampaloni, who was brought into Vallecchi by its parent company Montecatini in 1962 to help pull it out of financial crisis, recalled in 1991, the decline was attributable at least in part to the attitudes of the firm's founder.

Attilio Vallecchi, who was a man of great culture and energy, was not however a great businessman, and he was content to balance the books by printing rail tickets. Naturally this got him into difficulty and allowed his two great rivals—Rizzoli and Mondadori—to get on the winning horses. He never understood the role of weekly magazines, or of the mass media; he remained entrenched, faithful to literature in a world that was changing profoundly. There was an exodus of his writers, who one by one left for other publishers: Palazzeschi, Pratolini, then Papini died, but Papini's complete works were published by Mondadori, not Vallecchi. He lost practically all of them.[37]

Italy and Foreign Publishers: The Case of *Topolino*

Foreign publishers and publications had a more significant role in Italy in the period we are examining, including the autarkic late years of the Fascist regime, than is often realized. They indirectly influenced graphic design and layout (*Life* magazine influenced the *rotocalchi* of the 1930s and *Paris-Match*, launched in 1949, those of the 1950s) but they also played a more direct role through the syndication of American comic strip material, handled worldwide by King Features Syndicate, through deals to publish material under license, and through direct control of Italian subsidiaries. A notable case was the marketing of Walt Disney comics. It is also an instructive illustration of continuity in an Italian cultural industry from the 1930s to the 1950s.

Disney-related publications and merchandise had begun to appear in Europe at the end of the 1920s with the debut of Mickey Mouse (1928) and the Silly Symphony sound cartoons. Distribution of Disney's films (all of which were short cartoons until 1937) was handled initially by other American film companies and their overseas agents, first Columbia (1928–1932), then United Artists (1932–1937), then RKO (1937–1953), until in 1953 the Walt Disney Studio took control of its own distribution, setting up for this purpose a subsidiary called Buena Vista, named for a street in Burbank where the studio had relocated before the war. By contrast, foreign distribution of Disney materials in print was delegated to local firms abroad. Whereas in the United States and Canada, as well as in Britain, the Disney characters were known mainly through the animated films screened in cinemas, and the Disney comic strips were very much a secondary means of diffusion, in Italy, as in many other countries and regions (such as Latin America), the comics came to have a very substantial market. Hence, when Disney more or less wound up production of the short films in the early 1950s the comic strips remained an important source of foreign earnings for the company.

From the early 1930s to the end of World War II Disney's practice for periodicals was to sign a deal, through its agents, with publishers abroad to whom it granted an exclusive license. In other words, the rights to publish material featuring Disney characters were given to a single company in each country, and in turn that company agreed to pay Disney either a fixed sum or a percentage of revenue from sales or both. The granting of exclusive rights was part of a wider move by Disney to clamp down on a growing piracy of its characters abroad from the late 1920s. Vigilance over piracy and copyright would remain thereafter a constant feature of the company's international operations.

The Disney-Mondadori connection began in 1935 when the two parties signed a contract giving the Milanese firm exclusive Italian rights to publish periodicals containing Disney material. The first Disney comic in Italy, *Topolino,* had in fact been launched by the Florentine publisher Nerbini in December 1932, with a masthead and front-page strip featuring Disney's mouse. The stories and illustrations were by Italian artists and were done without authorization either from Disney or from King Features Syndicate. Nerbini, who claimed not to know that Disney's characters were protected by copyright, got out of the ensuing legal tangle by signing a three-year contract in which he agreed to be supplied with authentic Disney material through King Features Syndicate. On the expiry of this contract, and for reasons that are not entirely clear, Nerbini was prepared to relinquish *Topolino.* Mondadori, on the other hand, was just then diversifying into children's comics and beginning to take an interest in Disney. In 1935 the firm launched its first Disney title, *I tre por-*

cellini (*The Three Little Pigs*), which included a Mickey Mouse strip. Later the same year it took over the *Topolino* title from Nerbini.[38]

The terms of the 1935 contract with Disney, dated June 25, gave Mondadori an exclusive license for an unlimited period for the use of the name and the character Mickey Mouse/Topolino in children's comics. Mondadori undertook to give Disney a first payment of 250,000 lire plus an annual lump sum of 40,000. A further agreement, of July 31, between Mondadori and the Rome office of King Features Syndicate gave the publisher exclusive Italian rights for Disney comic strips.[39] These early agreements also regulated Disney stories created by Italian writers and artists. The 1939 contract for *Paperino* gave Mondadori the right to publish, subject to Walt Disney's written approval, material based on Disney characters created under license by its own artists.[40] These and subsequent transactions between Disney and Mondadori were conducted through Disney's European agents rather than directly with the parent company in Burbank. The role of these agents (Creazioni Walt Disney was founded in 1938; Disney had offices also in London, Paris, and Brussels) was to represent the company's interests in Europe, handling local licensing and merchandising deals and generally exercising vigilance over its affairs. In the 1930s, the policy on publishing was to grant exclusive licenses to reliable European companies. Just as Mondadori got the Italian rights, so another established publisher, Hachette, got the French rights, and began to publish *Le Journal de Mickey* and other Disney titles.

The Mondadori *Topolino* in the 1930s was a newspaper-format weekly of eight (subsequently sixteen) pages consisting of a mixture of Disney-originated material, other material imported from the United States, and material created by Italian artists. The majority of strips were American, even if only a minority were based on Disney characters, In 1938, when the Fascist government moved to curb what it claimed were diseducative popular cultural products imported from the United States, and the first general circulars against American comics went out, the editors of *Topolino* sought to protect themselves by increasing the proportion of Italian material. By January 1941, apart from the Mickey Mouse strip on the cover page and one inside page and Popeye (Braccio di Ferro) on page 11 (Popeye had started life in 1929 as a comic strip character and in 1933 became a star of short films, produced by Disney's rivals the Fleischer brothers and distributed by Paramount), the remainder consisted of original material by Italian artists and writers: Pedrocchi, Albertarelli, Martini, Merlini, Caprioli, and Leporini. Consequently, by the time the Ministry of Popular Culture, then under Pavolini, came to order Mondadori directly to suppress its Disney strips, the publisher was able to cite in his defense this preponderance of homemade materials. He wrote to the Ministry on March 18, 1941:

With reference to the instructions we have received from the Italian Press Division to suppress the Walt Disney stories in our weekly magazine *Topolino*, we should like to point out the following:

1) We do not feel that Walt Disney can be considered in the same light as those run-of-the-mill American artists who in the last few years have invaded the pages of Italian publications dedicated to young people.... He is an authentic creator of fables, a most delicate poet, a painter of great taste.... Walt Disney, like Aesop, Phaedrus, La Fontaine, Gozzi, Collodi, De Amicis, has been translated into every language: he is not an "American" but an artist worthy of being known and admired everywhere.

2) Each issue of *Topolino* contains only three pages of Disney-created material: this is very little, considering that the periodical as a whole is 16 pages long.

3) The three Disney-created stories justify the title *Topolino*; if we removed them we would risk bankrupting the periodical and losing a good proportion of its 140,000 readers. This cannot but be a grave cause of concern for us, given that *Topolino* has cost us around half a million lire. In other words, the suspension of Disney would lead to an enormous loss for us.

4) Some of the panels in *Topolino* containing Disney stories are not created by Walt Disney but are drawn, with the latter's permission, by our own artists, namely the Fascists Enrico Pinochi and Federico Pedrocchi. In other words these panels are not even imported.

5) Other panels created in America are published by other children's comics, for example The Katzenjammer Kids, Felix the Cat and Jiggs and Maggie appear regularly in the *Corriere dei Piccoli*.[41]

Mondadori won the argument. On December 11, 1941, four days after Pearl Harbor, he wrote to thank Pavolini for having allowed him to continue to publish Disney strips in *Topolino*. However, he added in a show of patriotic spirit that since Italy was now at war with the United States he was going to remove the signature of Walt Disney from future issues and, once the supply of material already imported from America had been used up, he would publish in *Topolino* only stories written and drawn by Italian artists.[42]

In fact, imported Mickey Mouse strips continued to appear in *Topolino* until February 1942, and even when they disappeared (the strip was replaced by the adventures of a boy called "Tuffolino") the masthead, with the name "Topolino" and the head of Disney's mouse, remained.[43] It was not until the end of 1943 that the wartime economic crisis and the German occupation of the north of the country forced Mondadori to shut down a good part of its operations, including *Topolino*. All the same, *Topolino* appears to have survived Fascist censorship better than any other American-originated comic in Italy, and this survival gave it a presence in the Italian comics market that would be greatly to its advantage when the time came to relaunch it after the war.

On September 9, 1943, the day after Italy's separate armistice with the Allies was announced and as German troops swept over the north of the country, Arnoldo Mondadori and his sons Alberto and Giorgio fled to Switzerland, taking with them 85 percent of the firm's shares, worth 17 million lire. Arnoldo's personal holding was 45 percent of the total. Only 12 percent stayed in Italy, in the hands of Arnoldo's brother Bruno and other relatives.[44] Arnoldo would later cite his self-imposed exile as evidence of his refusal to collaborate with the Nazis and the Repubblica Sociale Italiana (RSI), the reconstituted Fascist regime set up on September 23, following Mussolini's rescue from arrest by the Germans, which claimed jurisdiction over north and central Italy. The Mondadori offices in Milan and the firm's printing division in Verona, the Officine Grafiche Arnoldo Mondadori (OGAM), fell into the hands of an Extraordinary Commission of the RSI, which introduced a new management based on corporatist principles: the share capital was to be distributed among the employees, who would also receive a proportion of the firm's profits. In fact, these proposals could not be put into practice with the flight abroad of so much of the share capital and with the firm's activities severely curtailed by the war. Yet the fact remains that for the employees this period was experienced as one not just of Nazi and Fascist occupation but also of socialized management. This experience contributed to the radical demands they made when the country was liberated.

Meanwhile, Arnoldo Mondadori took up residence in a hotel in Lugano. "I didn't waste time in Switzerland," he later recalled. "I kept in close touch with foreign authors, planned series, took notes and thought about the future."[45] He used part of his share capital to gain control of a Swiss firm, Helicon, with which he had had dealings for several years, and he set up an office at the back of a bookshop at number 4, Via Vegezzi, Lugano. From this base of operations Arnoldo and Alberto began to make their plans for peacetime. Alberto, as we have noted, corresponded with Ernest Hemingway, among others, offering him the Italian rights for his unpublished and forthcoming work. On February 22, 1945 Arnoldo wrote to Walt Disney and the following day to Disney's European headquarters in London, proposing, as Helicon, to handle Disney merchandising and to publish Disney books and periodicals in German for distribution in Switzerland and, when the war was over, in Germany and Austria.[46] In other words, even before the war ended Mondadori was hatching plans to expand his operations outside Italy and was trying to use Disney as a way into this expansion.

When the north of Italy was liberated in April 1945 the workers at the Mondadori offices in Milan and the OGAM works in Verona set up firm-based branches of the Comitato di Liberazione Nazionale (CLN), the official coalition government of the Resistance. After the formation at the end of 1944 of the free labor union confederation CGIL, the firm's employees in Milan established a self-management council (*consiglio di gestione*) onto which they invited Bruno Mondadori as a "representative of capital." Arnoldo was accused, in his absence, of collaboration with the Fascist regime and was prevented from reentering the firm. In May 1945, the firm-based CLN received a letter in favor of letting him back in, signed by the writers Dino Buzzati, Arnaldo Fraccaroli, Elio Vittorini, and others, but the employees were not persuaded and Arnoldo, who by now had returned from Switzerland, had to sit out the end of the war in Italy in his villa by Lago Maggiore.[47]

For several months after the end of the war in Italy the Mondadori firm was severely hampered by being divided administratively into two halves (a part of the management had been moved to Rome when the country was divided in two) and by the difficulty of getting sufficient supplies of paper. On June 20, 1945 the *consiglio di gestione* met to discuss the situation. It decided to take "emergency measures . . . to give the maximum impulse to publishing, in order to ensure the necessary rhythm of sales and guarantee sufficient work for the Verona print shop." To achieve this, one of the council members recommended the resumption of relations with Disney. Bruno Mondadori argued that, given the shortage of paper and the high costs of reconstructing the various parts of the firm's operations, periodical publication should in the first instance be limited to the weekly *Topolino*, of which the firm had "various materials ready consisting of stories and illustrations."[48]

So it was that on December 15, 1945 *Topolino* reappeared on the newsstands after an absence of two years. A few months earlier, on July 25, Arnoldo Mondadori had been let back into the firm after agreeing to recognize certain fundamental principles of corporatist management, including a 50 percent profit share among workers and the participation of equal numbers of workers and managers on the board. In fact, as the reconstruction and the postwar social and political settlement took shape these principles progressively became a dead letter. The ban on sackings was rescinded, the *consigli di gestione* were depoliticized and reduced to mere "technical" advisory bodies, and labor unions were expelled from the firm.

From his Swiss exile, Arnoldo Mondadori had already nosed out postwar business prospects based on the Disney connection. He now moved rapidly to seize the new market opportunities that were opening up with the cessation of hostilities, not only in Italy but elsewhere in Europe, seeking to make himself a Europe-wide publisher and printer of Disney books and periodicals. Noting that Disney lacked its own subsidiary in the German-speaking countries he offered, under the Helicon label, to become that subsidiary himself.

He tried to obtain for Helicon an exclusive license, similar to that he already had for Italy, to publish German-language Disney books in Switzerland for distribution not only there but also in Germany and Austria.[49] He also wanted to function (and in this there was a difference from his Italian operations) as a merchandising agent, that is, he wanted Helicon to have the same role in the German-speaking countries as Creazioni Walt Disney had in Italy.[50]

Disney's response to these proposals was cool. At the end of the war its European operations had changed tack. Its policy was now no longer to grant unlimited or exclusive licenses to a single firm in each European country, such as it had granted to Mondadori in 1935. Instead it reserved the right periodically to review all contracts and to cancel them if the licensee failed to satisfy its conditions.

Mondadori was one of the first victims of this new policy. In 1946, under pressure from Disney, the Italian firm was forced to dissolve the old *Topolino* contract and replace it with a much less favorable one, which, although it still gave Mondadori an exclusive license for Italy, took away the unlimited time clause and restricted the license to eight years, reserving to the American firm the option of subsequent renewal. Under the terms of the new contract Mondadori had to undertake to keep sales above a minimum of 100,000 copies a week, to pay Disney a 2 percent royalty on each copy, and to advance against this a fixed sum of 400,000 lire a year, making over to Disney each month any difference between the 2 percent and this amount.[51] An appendix to the new contract, added in 1949 at the moment when *Topolino* changed from a fortnightly to a monthly with a smaller format (it would later change back to a weekly), insisted on a minimum of 80 percent Disney material. At the same time the license was renewed for a further five years.[52]

In this way, Disney imposed its own identity far more markedly on the postwar *Topolino* than it had on the prewar version, and this was part of the firm's new course in the sphere of promotion, marketing, and merchandising. The new type of relationship with its licensees can be seen from an agreement dated November 6, 1947 between Kay Kamen International—Disney's New York licensing agent—and Mondadori's Helicon. The latter is granted a non-exclusive license for just three-and-a-half years, until June 30, 1951,

to translate into German, print and sell in Switzerland, Germany, Austria and any other German speaking country, the publications published abroad in the form of juveniles (namely non-periodical publications, with pictures in black and in colours) derived from the artistic characters of Walt Disney.[53]

Arnoldo Mondadori, however, was not to be outdone. He tried to turn Disney's new rules to his advantage. In 1946 he told Disney's Paris representative, Walter Feignoux, that he was considering entry into the French market:

he wanted to publish Disney books and albums in competition with Hachette. The proposal did not succeed, partly because it was resisted by Meunier, the president of Hachette, and partly because Feignoux himself blocked it. Yet Mondadori kept up the pressure on the proposal and eventually struck a more limited deal with Meunier by which he would print deluxe French-language Disney editions at Verona on the latter's behalf.[54] Mondadori's other proposals to publish Disney material outside Italy had a similar outcome. For example, despite getting the contract for Helicon to market German-language publications, Mondadori had great difficulty making inroads into the German market and in 1949 he was forced to explain to Disney's European agents that progress on this front had been much slower than he had anticipated.[55] One reason for this was precisely Disney's new European policy, which worked in practice both to arouse and to frustrate Mondadori's German ambitions by first declaring the market open to all bids, including those of established German and Swiss publishers (Bertelsmann, Delphin of Zurich, and others), and then giving preferential treatment to just one publisher.[56] For example, in 1950 the publisher Bluchert paid Disney a $10,000 advance for the rights to the book version of *Snow White and the Seven Dwarfs;* Disney then put pressure on Mondadori to withdraw his own edition of *Snow White* from the German market.[57]

Mondadori's tenacious courtship of Disney may be explicable on economic grounds alone but it seems likely that the ideological affinity between the two also played a part. There are various pieces of evidence, beyond the letter of 1941 quoted above, that Mondadori was strongly attracted to the Disney ethos and saw it as a highly congenial brand with which to expand the popular end of his operations after the war. Disney was a conservative whose values were stamped onto his films and television shows and onto the two pet projects of his later years: Disneyland, which opened in Anaheim, Los Angeles, in 1955, and the futuristic EPCOT (Experimental Prototype Community Of Tomorrow) that he planned for the new Disneyworld near Orlando, Florida, constructed after his death in 1966. He was nostalgic for days gone by, for the ethos of the frontiersman, for lost childhood innocence, and for nature unspoiled by human intervention. At the same time, he was besotted with the "magic" of scientific exploration and technological gadgetry, particularly such technologies as "audio-animatronics," which allowed a "perfect" technical replication of human beings. His films and theme parks invited adults to share these sentiments, to enjoy healthy adventure, the call of the wild, and a protective nurturing feeling toward children and animals, to marvel at the "wonders" both of the natural world and a technologized future and to eschew sentiments that were pessimistic, misanthropic, antifamily, dirty, or otherwise deviant according to this code. Disney thus incarnated the middle-American, middle-class values of Church, family, and patriotism and he was always suspicious of intellectuals, socialists, and communists. In 1941 his employees went on strike after he tried to introduce a "yellow union" and fired Art Babbitt, the representative in the studio of the free labor union, the Screen Cartoonists' Guild. During the strike Disney took photographs of the pickets that he later showed to the FBI and the investigators of the California Un-American Activities Committee to help them identify Communist activists. In 1964 he supported Barry Goldwater and contributed to the campaign funds of two other right-wing Republicans, Ronald Reagan and George Murphy.[58]

On the face of it, Mondadori was a different kind of character. Whereas Disney distrusted intellectuals, Mondadori cultivated them; he had a profound and enduring admiration for the world of high culture. And yet his courtship of intellectuals seems to have been less a matter of his personal taste as a reader (which ran as much, if not more, to the popular fiction and nonfiction authors he published from the 1930s onward) than of the kind of publisher he wanted to be. What was distinctive about Mondadori in this respect is that he sought to be both a commercial and a cultural publisher, on the one hand opening up new markets with popular fiction and magazines and on the other having his prestige list of modern authors and producing deluxe leather-bound editions of literary classics. Beneath his high-cultural appearances Mondadori was primarily an entrepreneur who was nostalgic for tradition but also eager to be a media innovator, a believer in the ethos of the family-firm but at the same time the builder of a diversified mass cultural enterprise. In all these respects he was similar to Disney.

In addition, he too was politically conservative. He did not hesitate to support Fascism, not only because he and Mussolini shared common socialist origins but because he realized that, once it came to power, the Fascist government could be useful to him: it could help him get into foreign markets by reducing export tariffs, assist him with tax concessions, and reduce the price of paper. After 1945, when Mondadori, like so many others, threw a democratic cloak over his shoulders and fell silent in public about his profascist past, there was a deep continuity in this attitude, which now came to embrace the economic liberalism of Luigi Einaudi, the architect of reconstruction economic policy, and the political centrism of Alcide De Gasperi.

In 1955 Henry R. Luce (whose wife, Clare Boothe Luce, was then the U.S. ambassador to Italy) asked Arnoldo Mondadori to contribute to his *Fortune* magazine a survey of opinions on America's future prospects in the world. Mondadori's reply is one of the few records we have of his political outlook as the Cold War began to recede:

You know that Italy is in a key position for the defence of the frontiers of the free world. And yet I believe it is essential for all of us to recognize that this position can only be held by reinforcing the home front within Italy. This depends closely in turn on our allied peoples' recognizing the vital necessities of our own people. . . .

The experience of the last few years has shown that the free circulation of goods within the frontiers of the free world, within a framework of rational economic organization and opportune financial cooperation, is an ideal we must pursue if we wish to increase our level of collective well-being and take our stand against the systems in force in the other half of the world.[59]

In the end, Mondadori gave up the attempt to penetrate European markets outside Italy as a publisher of Disney. Instead he offered himself to other European publishers as a printer of their Disney editions, with competitive labor rates at OGAM and an unrivaled store of high-quality color negatives. In the 1950s a first important agreement was reached for the book series *The Living World,* a spinoff from Disney's new diversification into nature films, in which Disney supplied Mondadori with color photographs that had remained unused from the films and Mondadori then used these to create dozens of volumes, printed at Verona, both for its own firm and in other languages for foreign firms. These operations were not limited to Disney materials. A similar deal was struck in 1960 with Time-Life Books on the one hand and a number of European publishers on the other, including Thames and Hudson, Editions du Seuil, and Rowolt, as a result of which OGAM printed Time-Life editions for European distribution by these publishers. By the end of the 1960s, 50 percent of the printing work undertaken at Verona was for other publishers.

The postwar success of OGAM was due in no small measure to the aid it received under the European Recovery Program (ERP) or Marshall Plan, which we mentioned above in relation to *Epoca.* In 1948 the firm was guaranteed a loan of $9 million and in 1949 a further sum of $940,000 was agreed for the purchase of machinery following a visit to the United States by Giorgio Mondadori in November 1948.[60] Since most of the machinery damaged or removed from the Verona plant by the Germans during the occupation had been in the periodicals division, the ERP aid was aimed primarily at relaunching this sector. The loan enabled OGAM to acquire the most up-to-date American machinery, including the Cottrell that would be used to print *Epoca.* Giorgio Mondadori wrote of the Cottrell: "with a machine as powerful as this we will crush them [our competitors] on prices."[61] The Cottrell also enabled the Mondadori firm to undertake major contract work for third parties, including the Italian edition of *Reader's Digest,* which first appeared in October

1948 and on which we will conclude this discussion of foreign publications in Italy.

Selezione in the Cold War

The full Italian title, *Selezione dal Reader's Digest* (*Selection from Reader's Digest*), was quirky, given that a "digest" already means a selection or précis (as in one of the magazine's main innovations, the "condensed book"). However the magazine became generally known in Italy simply as *Selezione,* just as the French version (founded in 1946) was known as *Sélection.* These national editions were among several launched in Western Europe after the war; others were published in West Germany, Austria, Belgium, and Switzerland. In exchange for using Mondadori's presses, *Selezione* carried advertisements for its magazines and book series. During the Cold War the magazine, whose parent edition had been founded in 1922 by the American Presbyterian DeWitt Wallace and his wife Lila Bell Acheson, became an important international organ of pro-Americanism and anticommunism. In June 1953 the *Reader's Digest International Editions Newsletter* reported that the French Communists had daubed the front door of the magazine's Paris office with the slogans "*Sélection* go home" and "Propagande de Guerre."[62]

The *Reader's Digest* art of persuasion was generally of the "soft" type, inherent in the appearance and values of the magazine itself: the pocket format; the sobriety of the use of drawings rather than photographs; and the emphasis on the family hearth, self-help, and intellectual betterment, as exemplified in its long-running feature, "It Pays to Increase Your Word Power." However there was also propaganda of a more overt kind. Cesare Pavese drew out the various ideological strands in an acerbic article published in the PCI's monthly *Rinascita* in February 1950:

We are all agreed that the magazine *Selezione* is a good example of how culture should *not* be popularized. The pretentious booklet, coloured and shiny like a packet of cigarettes or stockings, gives off a clear odour of a bathroom made of plastic, neon and chrome, and this gives it away for what it really is: a mirror of "Americanist" propaganda. Its contents alternate between exhaustive paeans to ever new facets of the "American dream" and denunciations of ever new iniquities in the socialist world.[63]

Among the condensed books, which readers' polls regularly put on top of their lists of favorite features in the magazine, were "Eleven Years as a Prisoner in Russia" (September 1951) and "I Was a Slave in the Russian Mines" (April 1956).[64]

The success of *Selezione* was a measure of the modernization of the periodicals sector in Italy by the end of World War II as well as the implantation of "American values" in the reconstruction and Cold War years and the rise of a mass middle-class reading public. It was the first successful example of a magazine sold largely through direct marketing (most copies were mailed to subscribers) on the basis of market research, rather than through news agents or news kiosks. A readership survey conducted in 1962 established that subscribers were fairly well educated (nearly 40 percent had a high school diploma and 11 percent a degree), largely middle class (40 percent were white-collar employees and only 10 percent were workers), and aspirational (over 60 percent already owned a television and 43 percent a car, and a further 17 to 18 percent intended to buy one of each in the future).[65] The partnership with Mondadori, which printed the magazine until 1967 and supplied its first Italian editor (Mario Ghisalberti had been director of Mondadori periodicals from 1946 to 1948), was fundamental to its success and beneficial to both parties. *Selezione* was printed by OGAM, it carried advertisements for Mondadori's book series and magazines, and it funded the purchase of additional machinery at OGAM.[66] Arnoldo Mondadori's sympathy with conservative American values thus provided the ideological conduit for what would become the highest-selling monthly magazine in postwar Italy.

4 Film Production

The film industry, more than any of the other cultural industries, with the possible exception of recorded music (see chapter 6), has always been international. Its history has been one of internationalized consumption and movements and exchanges between countries—trade in films, but also in technologies, actors, directors, technicians, stories, and styles. Film audiences, except in cases where protective restrictions have been put in place or where there is a very strong domestic production sector (like in the United States or India), have always been consumers of films from more than one country. In Italy, the arguments during the Fascist period and after the war in favor of protection for the domestic film industry, the efforts in the 1940s of neorealist filmmakers to create national alternatives to Hollywood, and the Catholic complaints throughout our period about the negative influences of certain American films all presupposed a situation in which non-Italian films dominated the

Table 4.1. Number of films passed for public projection in Italy, 1936–1954.

	Italian		Foreign		Total	
	Number	%	Number	%	Number	%
1936	43	18.7	187	81.3	230	100.0
1937	33	10.2	290	89.8	323	100.0
1938	45	16.4	230	83.6	275	100.0
1939	77	31.4	168	68.6	245	100.0
1940	86	32.0	183	68.0	269	100.0
1941	71	31.7	153	68.3	224	100.0
1942	96	43.0	127	57.0	223	100.0
1943	66	39.1	103	60.9	169	100.0
1944	37	41.1	53	58.9	90	100.0
1945	48	28.7	119	71.3	167	100.0
1946	62	21.0	233	79.0	295	100.0
1947	60	11.4	467	88.6	527	100.0
1948	54	11.6	410	88.4	464	100.0
1949	76	13.0	509	87.0	585	100.0
1950	104	21.2	387	78.8	491	100.0
1951	107	21.6	389	78.4	496	100.0
1952	148	26.9	403	73.1	551	100.0
1953	163	32.6	337	67.4	500	100.0
1954	201	40.3	298	59.7	499	100.0

Source: *Lo spettacolo in Italia nel 1952* (Rome: SIAE, 1953), 148; and *Lo spettacolo in Italia. Statistiche 1994* (Rome: SIAE, 1995), 163. Figures are for films over 1,000 meters (approximately 3,330 feet or 37 minutes running time). The discrepancies between these figures and those collected from other sources are mainly because films were sometimes released in the year following that in which they were passed. For 1946 there is a significant discrepancy largely because the PWB (see chapter 7) released films not approved by the Italian authorities.

Italian market (see Tables 4.1 and 4.2). The only time in the history of Italian cinema when this was not so, and when the dominance was temporarily reversed, was outside our period, in the 1960s, when a surge in Italian film production was accompanied by a sharp decline in U.S. film production and export. To be sure, the period (1939 to 1945) in which the Monopoly Law (see chapters 5 and 7) was in force also saw a big drop in the number of American films imported and an increase in the production of Italian films, but there was also a partial substitution of those absent American films with films from

Table 4.2. Percentage of cinema receipts in Italy by nationality of film, 1937–1954.

	Italy	United States	France	Britain	Other or Not Specified	Total
1937	15.9	65.6	5.9	1.4	11.2	100.0
1938	13.7	73.6	5.0	2.8	4.9	100.0
1939	35.1	29.2	18.6	9.1	8.0	100.0
1940	45.0	22.9	17.6	4.0	10.5	100.0
1941	45.8	n/a	n/a	n/a	54.2	100.0
1942	56.5	n/a	n/a	n/a	43.5	100.0
1947	10.7	n/a	n/a	n/a	89.3	100.0
1949	17.3	73.3	0.7	4.8	3.9	100.0
1950	29.2	63.7	3.1	2.7	1.3	100.0
1951	30.1	63.0	2.3	2.4	2.2	100.0
1952	36.8	56.7	2.7	2.7	1.1	100.0
1953	38.2	54.1	3.0	3.0	1.7	100.0
1954	39.0	53.3	1.6	3.4	2.7	100.0

Source: Lorenzo Quaglietti, *Storia economico-politica del cinema italiano 1945–1980* (Rome: Editori Riuniti, 1980), 289. Quaglietti's figures are based on SIAE data for new films passed for exhibition in the years indicated, not all films in circulation (i.e., they exclude second and subsequent runs). For 1943–1946 and 1948 there are no reliable data. For 1941, 1942, and 1947 there is no available breakdown by country of the non-Italian percentages and the latter therefore appear aggregated in the last column. It is known, however, that the number of films imported from the United States, and thus the percentage of receipts earned by American films, remained low for the duration of the Monopoly Law and the war and that it rose again rapidly after the law was rescinded and U.S. films reentered the market in 1945.

France, Germany, and elsewhere. A new form of cinematic cosmopolitanism temporarily took over during our period.

Studies of the film industry in Italy generally stress the deficiencies of the businesses operative in the sector. These deficiencies, along with inadequate protection, are blamed for the subordination to the American film industry that marked the whole period following the end of World War I. Studies have drawn attention to the way much of Italian film production was narrowly profit-oriented and many companies were extraordinarily flimsy and short-lived. There was, it is noted, a lack of serious capital inputs, a reliance on state aid and assistance, and a lack of strategy. The producers themselves are seen to have been responsible for this situation. It is often claimed that Stefano Pittaluga might have saved the Italian industry through his Cines company (established in 1927) if he had not died in 1931. But apart from Pittaluga, most producers have been damned as ignoramuses, comical eccentrics, or megalomaniacs.[1] Only two elder statesmen, Riccardo Gualino of Lux Film and Gustavo Lombardo of Titanus, who both cautiously developed businesses of different styles in the interwar years, are seen as having played a positive role over a long period.[2] But even here it has been questioned whether their role was properly industrial. For example, Lux in the 1940s has been described as "a bit of a family and a drawing room and not much of a factory or office."[3] The gap between this style of operation and the Hollywood studio system or even the German UFA company could scarcely have been wider.

The reasons for this negative view of film production in Italy are fairly evident. On the one hand, almost all those who have written about the film industry have done so from the left or from a left-liberal standpoint.[4] The explicit aim of these critics was not only to document or analyze, but to denounce a series of specific failings including the entanglement of the film industry with the political sphere, the suffocation of neorealism by the political elite, the subservience after 1945 to the Americans, and the poor quality of many of the films produced. Insofar as the presence of an industrial role was acknowledged, this was seen as having been inimical to the creativity of the director, who was viewed as an intellectual with a quasi-Gramscian duty to guide and educate audiences.

In her economic history of Italian cinema, Barbara Corsi criticizes this approach and argues that the Italian film industry was not so different from that of many other European countries. By any standard, its achievements were remarkable. However you define it, she argues, whether "artisan's workshop, assisted industry, mix of capitalism and marginality," it produced people and practices that proved remarkably able at creating an "artistic miracle with little money" by "finding a golden point of equilibrium between political pressures, artistic impulses, market requirements and expressive innovation."[5] Italian cinema included a great array of creative talents, not just directors but actors, writers, directors of photography, editors, set and costume designers, and others, yet the activities of these people were financed from different sources and harnessed in a variety of ways. When the Americans started to make films in Italy—sometimes using Italian producers as a front—and various European co-production agreements broadened the nature of domestic filmmaking, it became clear that in Italy the industry depended on the interaction of a series of domestic and foreign, as well as public and private, factors.

This sort of interrelationship, which was an unavoidable fact of life for the economy of film production and distribution throughout most of the period under examination, conditioned the development of the sector. The Americans provided the Italians with benchmarks and some technical know-how, as well as an organizational model in some spheres, but they also proved a limiting factor, since the American industry's outreach into the Italian industry made it a vampire-like presence in the Italian market, which in some respects confined the Italian industry to a provincial level. In considering the general character of the industry, two other factors need to be borne in mind: first, that it was not isolated from the rest of the economy and that in some respects its circumstances were dependent on other sectors including the press, the music industry, and the retail trade; second, that the consistency and stability of the film industry were always related to the size of the market for films, and in Italy this market, although it was large relative to markets for other forms of mass culture, was still quite restricted before the rapid growth of the exhibition sector in the postwar years.

Structure and Organization

Several continuities can be traced in the workings of the film industry between the 1930s and the 1950s. Over the whole period, the interests of producers were most visible and were often taken as synonymous with those of the industry as a whole. Matters of distribution and exhibition, which will be considered in the next chapter, were seen as secondary. This was because film production became a matter of national prestige as governments everywhere realized the internal and external propaganda potential of film. Thus producers were able to win the ear of government and often secure the adoption of measures (such as obligatory programming of Italian films) that went against the pure interests of many exhibitors who were simply concerned with attracting customers. Corsi has highlighted the organizational effectiveness of the producers' lobby and the skill and persistence with which it secured favorable treatment. She has also underlined the way in which the post-1945 industry organization ANICA (Associazione Nazionale Industrie Cinematografiche e Affini) acted to extend the market for Italian films by means of agreements with the Americans and alliances with their opposite numbers in other European countries.[6] Yet such successes were not without costs. Throughout the period the rewards that these approaches secured led to compromises over the content and quality of films.

Italian film production was not concentrated in the hands of a small number of large enterprises but was spread among a vast number of mainly small companies, many of which made only one film, and sometimes not even that. This proliferation of tiny, short-lived companies was an endemic feature of film production that was attenuated in the late 1930s but was soon resumed in the postwar years. Between 1945 and 1957 no fewer than 287 production companies started up and went bust.[7] Nevertheless there were a small number of enterprises that had something approaching a continuous life and acquired a certain importance. In the early 1930s, Pittaluga's Cines company, whose modern, sound-equipped studios had been opened with much fanfare in 1930, was the only enterprise of any note. In 1930 ten of the total of just twelve Italian films produced that year were made by the company while the following year twelve out of thirteen were.[8] Among the companies that emerged to challenge the Cines monopoly were the Tirrenia studios, established in Tuscany by a close artistic ally of Mussolini's, Giovacchino Forzano; Titanus, which moved from Naples to Rome; Lux film, founded in 1934; the Rizzoli publishing company's film arm, Novella Film; the Scalera studios; and other companies established by Carlo Roncoroni, Peppino Amato, and Giulio Manenti.

Gian Piero Brunetta suggests that Cines was the only one of these companies to have had a clear production strategy, formulated by the critic Emilio Cecchi during his brief period as artistic director. Various writers and directors collaborated with the company and enjoyed a relative freedom of expression.[9] Other companies operated very much in relation to the encouragements and financial incentives made available by the Fascist regime as it started to take a systematic interest in film production. Political clientelism and financial speculation were the two factors that together led most people to enter the otherwise risky realm of film production.

Pittaluga led the way in establishing the practice whereby film business representatives engaged in dialogue directly with representatives of the state and sought to win support for their commercial activities in the name of the national interest. Although the initial responses were cold, his efforts alerted the Fascist government to the importance of film and led the state to develop through the 1930s a series of laws and institutions designed to protect, coordinate, and promote national film production (see chapter 7). But while the regime encouraged stability among commercial companies it did not favor concentration or lay the conditions for industrial development. By privileging medium-sized enterprises, offering generous subsidies, rewards for profit, and compensation for losses, it removed the need for strategic business development.[10] For example, despite a decision in 1941 to limit the number of production companies to twenty-five, ninety-one films were released by fifty-four different companies.[11] Nonetheless, the volume of production did increase markedly, especially from 1937, and producers learned to make films in series and according to a system of genres that reflected something of an industrial mentality. Production ceased to be entirely sporadic even if it never truly became systematic. The absence of heavy-handed totalitarian directives concerning the content of films meant that commercial considerations broadly had pride of place. The opening of the state-dominated Cinecittà studios in 1937 took political involvement to a new level but it also heralded a qualitative leap in terms of the technical possibilities of filmmaking.

The Fascist regime institutionalized the production branch of the film industry by turning its representative association into an official corporation, the Federazione Nazionale Fascista degli Industriali dello Spettacolo (FNFIS). This gave the producers a legitimacy that they used to press their case ever more forcefully with the authorities. The most striking example of the power that the producers acquired in the later 1930s was the isolation and removal in 1939 of Luigi Freddi (who, as head of the Direzione Nazionale per la Cinematografia, set up in 1934, had made clear his preference for dignified and inspiring quality films) and the subsequent appointment as director general of the head of the FNFIS, Eitel Monaco. Business leaders never liked the powers of discretion in the distribution of funds to underwrite film production that Freddi had sought to reserve to the state. These gave him significant control over the content of films and legitimated the favoritism he practiced. When it became clear that his draft of what would become the "Alfieri law" of 1938 (by which each Italian feature film would receive from the state a sum linked to its gross box-office earnings) amounted to little short of the nationalization of cinema, the producers objected. Freddi was overruled by Dino Alfieri, the Minister of Popular Culture, and Mussolini himself, who both accepted the need for strictly economic criteria to prevail in the distribution of funds.[12]

During the war filmgoing increased in Italy, as it did in the other belligerent countries. Film production also expanded very significantly (see Table 4.1). In the three years between 1936 and 1938, 121 Italian films were released; in the three years between 1939 and 1941, when the Hollywood majors' withdrawal from the Italian market reduced American films to a trickle, 234 were. After reaching a peak of 96 in 1942, however, the war and political events dramatically impinged on production. With the downfall of Mussolini in July 1943 and the flight from Rome of the king and prime minister Badoglio in September, film production in Rome came to a virtual halt. The whole network of state institutions ceased to function, and above all the financial support for cinema ceased to apply. Freddi made attempts to persuade producers, actors, and other personnel to join him in Venice to reconstitute the film industry under the RSI regime based at Salò, but with very limited success. Despite the relocation of equipment rescued from the Germans and the keen support of the Salò authorities, just thirty films were made and several of those did not find a release before the war ended. In the German-occupied North of Italy, audiences were mostly fed a diet of German and Hungarian films.

The amount of disruption to filmmaking during the transitional period of 1943 to 1946 was extensive but Italian films continued to be released: 66 in

1943, 37 in 1944, 48 in 1945, and 62 in 1946. What was very different were the conditions in which the business operated: no Cinecittà (used during the war first as a munitions store then as a refugee camp and back in production only in late 1947); no subsidies or privileges, except under the RSI in the North; few producers willing to invest in film; some cinemas destroyed or damaged; the massive return of American competition after 1945; and the increasing difficulty of making films. The striking originality of some of the films made in Rome after the fall of Fascism should not obscure the fact that in important respects the film industry emerged little altered from the conflict. Virtually all those who had gone to Venice were quickly pardoned and were allowed to resume their previous activities "without [anyone] demanding from them any gesture of condemnation concerning the past or attributing any guilt."[13] Even more than in some other areas of public life, a purge was avoided and people turned to the future.

The opportunities of the immediate postwar period were considerable. With the popular appetite for film developing as never before, in theory Italian cinema should have been looking forward to a significant period of industrial development. In fact the political situation was not propitious and businesses were left exposed to unfettered competition. Nevertheless, there were a number of figures who, while far from being movie moguls along Hollywood lines, were able to give shape to a sustained program of film production. Of these, the most prominent were Lombardo at Titanus and Gualino at Lux, the production company that led the way in reviving Italian cinema and that spawned two of the most active new producers of the postwar years: Dino De Laurentiis and Carlo Ponti.

Although the pioneer neorealist Roberto Rossellini often acted as his own producer, most cinema continued to require conventional financing and facilities. Alberto Farassino has demonstrated that in most cases the costs of neorealist films were higher than those of other films due mainly to location shoots, the consequent transport of personnel and equipment, and the payment of daily allowances to the crew.[14] Despite the general rejection of the idea of a film "industry" among socially committed filmmakers and critics, the experience of neorealism did not give rise to any stable new system of making and distributing films. Lux produced several of the more popular neorealist films including *L'onorevole Angelina* (Luigi Zampa, 1947), *Molti sogni per la strada* (*Woman Trouble*) (Mario Camerini, 1948), *Riso amaro*, and *Non c'è pace tra gli ulivi* (*No Peace among the Olive Trees*) (Giuseppe De Santis, 1950). Farassino has shown that the mode of filmmaking was scarcely industrial in the sense that Gualino preferred gentlemen's agreements to detailed contracts and much was left to improvisation, but at the same time criteria such as casting and budgets were considered seriously in relation to the perceived market for a film. There was undoubtedly also something of a star system of directors, which included not just the new figures whose films were winning worldwide recognition but old masters such as Mario Camerini and Alessandro Blasetti.

Lux made five films in 1945, each costing under ten million lire—and produced for seventeen million lire in 1946 one of the first postwar star vehicles, *Il bandito* (*The Bandit*), directed by Alberto Lattuada and starring Amedeo Nazzari and Anna Magnani.[15] Films like this gave Lux a recognizable brand name that signified popular, quality films. Titanus was a more cautious company, embarking on a program of production only from 1950. In contrast to Lux, it pursued a two-pronged strategy, making popular films, such as Raffaello Matarazzo's; semirealist melodrama *Catene,* which appealed especially to provincial and southern audiences, and prestige films by art directors that aimed at more sophisticated audiences. Other companies included Rizzoli, which made the Don Camillo series, based on the stories of Giovanni Guareschi, before embarking on larger-scale productions, and Excelsa-Minerva.

The Americans and the Italian Film Industry

The conditions of film production changed considerably from 1949–1950 as the political, legislative, and economic situation altered. Squeezed by the American presence and suffering from the absence of the aid and privileges that had been available under Fascism, all sectors of the film industry united to pressurize the government to intervene. The result was Law 958 of December 29, 1949, "Disposizioni per la cinematografia," popularly known as the "Andreotti law" (Giulio Andreotti, the Undersecretary of State responsible for cinema, was largely responsible for framing it). Corsi has suggested that the law was "a daring synthesis of the ideas of Freddi and Alfieri."[16] Within the broad principles insisted on by the Americans after the war, it gave rise to the partial rebirth of the state controls over the cinema and the state-regulated cinema market that had prevailed under Fascism. The DC evidently realized, as is quite apparent from its move to occupy the state in other spheres, that, as it was firmly in power, it did not have to embrace a pure free-market line to undermine the left in the state and para-state agencies; it could simply purge these of leftists and reshape them as tools of its own hegemony. Sometimes this facilitated the return of officials who had occupied positions of responsibility under the regime, including Vincenzo Calvino and Nicola De Pirro (dubbed "the anti-fascist fascist, the partisan fascist party official").[17] Eitel Monaco, Director General for Cinema at the Ministry of Popular Culture before 1943, became president of ANICA, in effect the successor of FNFIS, over which he had presided in the 1930s.

The law guaranteed producers protection and subsidies while centralizing all power of decision on cinema matters in the Central Office, a close relation of the Fascist Direzione Generale per la Cinematografia. Prior to granting subsidies and confirming the nationality of a film, the government demanded approval of scripts. This marked the return of key aspects of the Fascist system of control over cinema with two differences that worsened the situation. First, no measures were adopted to limit the proliferation of unstable, speculative enterprises.[18] Thus, Italian producers were obliged to operate in a legislative context that exacerbated the defects of the film business.[19] Second, in contrast to the prewar regime, postwar governments demonstrated a low level of commitment to the state institutions operative in the cinema sector with the result that these were left to decline or were forced to seek foreign funding.

The Andreotti law, which remained in force until 1954, favored three developments: industrial expansion, depoliticization, and Americanization. It has been widely remarked that from 1950 Italian cinema finally underwent a transition from an "artisanal" stage of development to a properly "industrial" one,[20] although the effects of this are not universally seen as positive. The lack of a coherent commercially driven practice of film production meant that, according to Mino Argentieri, "The practice of subsidies, from which Italian cinema would never again free itself, became routine with the result that entrepreneurs were continually subject to blackmail (a simple gap between legislatures was enough to unleash panic and reduce production) and Italian cinema was forced in the domestic market to wrestle with American competition rather than engage with it in a constructive way."[21] Such a system also had an effect on the type of cinema that flourished. A market that was heavily conditioned by imports demanded certain types of film and insisted that these were provided. "The result," Otello Angeli has argued, "was a progressive decline of quality production in favour of middle-brow production marked by little artistic and cultural commitment, the vigorous revival of 'genre' cinema and the birth of a cinema of imitative costume spectaculars."[22] In fact, quality cinema remained something that the larger companies valued for reasons of prestige and because of the access it gave them to foreign markets. But there can be no doubt that the market was indeed dominated by "middle-brow" entertainment films.

One of the most striking by-products of the law was the development of American location or "runaway" productions in Italy. One of the great aims of the Italian authorities in the 1930s had been to persuade foreigners to come and produce in Italy. On grounds of equity, it was argued that those who profited from the Italian market should also invest in it. Initially the Americans were reluctant. Metro-Goldwyn-Mayer's filming of the 1926 version of *Ben-Hur* in Rome had gone way over budget and the company had run into difficulties with the authorities, suppliers, and labor organizations. It had been resolved not to let a film be produced again at such a distance from studio control.[23] The feelings resulting from all this are captured in a 1929 note in which a State Department officer replied to a suggestion from the Rome embassy that Fox, Paramount, MGM, and UA "might do well to try a little production here." The officer wrote that "all indicated that they would sooner withdraw from the market entirely than do any such thing as this."[24]

The extreme reluctance persisted throughout the 1930s, although various efforts were made to lure leading film people to visit the new Cinecittà studios after they opened in 1937. Several prominent Americans expressed interest in working in Italy. The most sustained and well-documented negotiations concern the projects of the United Artists producer Walter Wanger, and the Hal Roach–Vittorio Mussolini tie-up, RAM (Roach and Mussolini).[25] Neither of these came to fruition but they illustrate well the way politics could interfere with business interests in relations between Italy and the U.S. film industry.

The first attempt to get Americans involved in Italian productions began when Mario Luporini, one of the leading representatives of the American film industry in Italy, suggested that United Artists become involved in Italian production. In a letter dated June 25, 1936 to A. H. Giannini of the Bank of America, he said that "in order to protect American pictures here it is essential that foreign companies show some spirit of cooperation otherwise it is only a matter of time before life will be made more miserable for us."[26] He reported that Wanger had been over to visit, had inspected the plans for Cinecittà, and had taken stock of the exhibition situation. He also had an audience with Mussolini. However, Wanger never proceeded with a deal, leaving Luporini fearing that he would be "looked upon as a bag of wind" as he had talked up prospects to Mussolini, Freddi, the Bank of Italy, and Cinecittà boss Roncoroni.[27] The failure was due to political reasons. Wanger, who was Jewish, admired Mussolini for his apparent lack of racism and his interest derived in part from the hope that he would act as a counterbalance to Hitler. He rapidly disengaged when racial policies started to find support in Italy.[28]

The Hal Roach episode was less disappointing for the regime, which was not involved with it officially—indeed, some leading figures strongly opposed it. But it was more embarrassing on account of the involvement of Mussolini's twenty-one-year-old son Vittorio. Roach and Vittorio Mussolini formed RAM with the intention of producing in Italy five opera films for release through MGM. Freddi was ferocious in his criticism of the initiative. He felt that Vittorio risked causing considerable damage, coming as he did, after having fought in Ethiopia, to the complex question of cinema "without preparation and with the expertise of a habitué of first-run cinemas."[29] Freddi (not least, it must be said, because he feared that Vittorio aimed to take his place) warned the Duce against his son's trip. He also prepared a long memorandum in which he set out a stern critique of the whole RAM enterprise.[30] He was particularly annoyed that the proper state organs had not been consulted or involved. He took the view that the whole operation was disadvantageous and would lead to the "destruction of the reborn Italian cinema."[31] An agreement with the American film industry was necessary, "but not in conditions of slavery."[32] In the end this initiative also came to nothing. When Vittorio visited Hollywood in October 1937 as Roach's guest, a few days before taking tea with President Roosevelt at the White House, he encountered a hostile reception from antifascists in the film community.[33] In the wake of this, and the threat of a boycott of RAM and possibly of his other activities, Roach dropped the idea of the joint project.

As a consequence of the war and their role in the liberation of Italy, the Americans became directly involved with the Italian film industry. When the Allies entered Rome in June 1944 all the public organs of cinema were still under state control. The Allied command moved with great speed and determination to strike down the protective barriers, purge all Fascists, and overturn the pattern of state control, actions they did not believe could safely be left to the Italians. A Film Board was set up in March 1945 with two representatives each from the Allied Control Commission, the Psychological Warfare Branch (PWB), and the Italian government (on the PWB's activities in this and other sectors, see chapter 7). Admiral Stone's opening remarks on March 21, as reported by Lorenzo Quaglietti, have frequently been taken to represent the true intentions of the Allied authorities on film questions.[34] According to Quaglietti, Stone declared that Italian cinema was a Fascist invention and should be suppressed; Italy was an agricultural country that had no need of a film industry (this line of interpretation was subsequently taken over by Brunetta).[35] Quaglietti cites no source for these comments, which find no correspondence in the American archives, and he gives the impression that Stone spoke extemporaneously. In fact a statement had been prepared before the meeting for Stone to read and this formed the centerpiece of a press release which said something quite different:

The task before you gentlemen is not an easy one. The problems to be considered are complex. The former Italian Fascist regime created a state-financed motion picture industry which by a series of unfair and discriminatory measures soon made competition impossible for foreign companies. Taking advantage of its monopolistic position the industry became riddled with corruption and graft at the expense of the Italian tax payer. Through its films it preached hatred and war in an effort to overthrow and conquer Democratic and peace-loving countries of the world.

We trust the new Italian government will not tolerate such a condition to occur again and will see to it that these unfair Fascist measures are immediately revoked and free competition is again restored. It will be one of the duties of this Board to transfer the film industry back into Italian hands in such a way that we will be assured this will not happen again.

I hope the Board can be really TEMPORARY. Its main task should be to lay down, in agreement with the Italian government, the principal conditions under which the production, review and distribution of films, Italian and foreign, shall be transferred from the control of the PWB to the Italian Government. In my opinion the Italian Government should form a Film Commission composed of non-Fascist members representing the Government, the various elements of the industry and the public, to carry out the recommendations of the Temporary Film Board.[36]

The Board formed three subcommittees to deal, respectively, with the revision of legislation, the derequisitioning of property, and the fate of Italian films that had been banned by the PWB. The line quickly prevailed that all existing Fascist laws regulating and supporting cinema should be abrogated. The Italian government accepted abrogation, but no sooner had this occurred than its representative, the Liberal politician Francesco Libonati, began to press the case to allow financial support for the industry to help it on its feet again.[37]

The legislative vacuum that followed the abolition of Fascist laws created serious difficulties that worked to the advantage of the Americans. With subsidies abolished and Cinecittà occupied by refugees, the level of production in Italy was limited. As a result, film workers of every category experienced unemployment and hardship and began to engage in agitation. The first few months of 1949 were perhaps the most tense since 1945 in this area. They saw the first systematic involvement of the left parties and the labor unions in the campaign to defend the Italian cinema. Cinema workers appealed publicly to the government to do something to save Italian cinema from annihilation, most memorably in a rally held in Rome's Piazza del Popolo on February 20, 1949 at which Anna Magnani, Vittorio De Sica, and Gino Cervi, among others, forcefully stated their case. The trigger for the demonstration was the announcement by Andreotti that the government would shortly legislate to defend national cinema. This period was also marked by intense American lobbying and negotiation.

In contrast to the extreme reluctance to engage in any form of production in Italy in the 1930s, the postwar years saw a blossoming of American filmmaking in Rome. There were several reasons for this: low costs, blocked funds, the encouragement of the U.S. government, and the increasing importance of European markets to Hollywood. Although Hollywood had become enough of a part of the American establishment during the war for it to be intimately involved in the general effort to win over Italians and propagate a positive image of the United States, it would not be correct to imagine that the Allies, the U.S. government, and the film industry had identical aims and interests. The mere fact that there were several elements involved, not necessarily in direct and immediate contact, created the potential for differences. More particularly, there was a strategic difference between the aim of the U.S. government to create stability and economic recovery in Western Europe and the desire of Hollywood to maximize profits. As Ennio Di Nolfo has shown, in 1946, when money was lacking in Italy for more immediate necessities, Washington came to accept, against Hollywood, the Italians' view that they did not have sufficient foreign exchange to allow dollars to be exported for films.[38]

With the American government taking this view, the film companies had no choice but to adopt a more conciliatory approach. At the same time, they realized that in such circumstances they needed more than ever before to maintain a united front to extract concessions. It was just the sort of difference of interest that occurred over Italy that contributed to the creation by the Motion Picture Producers and Distributors of America (MPPDA) of the Motion Picture Export Association (MPEA), an organization that functioned as a legitimate cartel and represented the movie industry in negotiations with foreign governments, earning itself the unofficial title of "the little State Department."[39]

Twenty-five years after the débâcle of Ben Hur, MGM returned to Rome to make a blockbuster epic of the ancient world, Quo Vadis. Following numerous doubts about personnel, the film was directed by Mervyn LeRoy and starred Robert Taylor and Deborah Kerr. Although Twentieth Century Fox had been the first U.S. company to use the Cinecittà studios (for Prince of Foxes), MGM took over "virtually all the Cinecittà facilities."[40] Even though it was the largest production ever made in Rome, and a rare blockbuster even for MGM, "not a dollar of American money needed to be spent; the equivalent of $6 million in frozen lire from 1941 was being used for the production."[41] In effect, it was a way of converting blocked lire into cash, because the film could be exported and used to gain profits for MGM around the world. Quite exceptionally, the right was granted to use blocked lire that were greater than the amount of MGM's current balance, by drawing on future receipts. A variety of other concessions were granted, including waiving the screening quota provision for 15 to 20 first-run cinemas in order to allow Quo Vadis to be screened for more than three months continuously, and the speedy release of equipment from customs.

The occupation of most of Cinecittà was widely seen as a flagrant ex-

Figure 8. Photograph of set of *Quo Vadis* (Mervyn LeRoy, United States, 1951) showing Peter Ustinov as Nero. The film was the first major U.S. "runaway" production in postwar Italy and it tied up Cinecittà for eighteen months. By permission of Fototeca-Manifestoteca, Centro Sperimentale di Cinematografia, Rome.

ample of cinematic imperialism, since it meant that for around eighteen months Italian film production was virtually shut out. An additional source of anger was the fact that MGM made use only of very low-level Italian technical staff; the only Italian actor to have a speaking part in the film was Marina Berti, who played the slave girl Eunice. Nevertheless, the Americans took the view that, by making a top-level color film in Italy, they were helping the Italians to raise the quality of their own productions. Embassy staff reported that "as a result of financial support made available through these productions . . . the studios have been refurbished, and now have a modern well-equipped plant. In addition the technical staff have had an opportunity to observe and learn about American techniques in the production of a major Technicolor film."[42]

Quo Vadis was a blockbuster intended to raise the profile of Italy as a world center of filmmaking and say something about the country's perception of its place in the world. At its core was a message not of grandeur and conquest, like the 1937 Fascist spectacular *Scipione l'africano* (*The Defeat of*

Hannibal) directed by Carmine Gallone, but of Christian piety. It was appropriate that, whereas the Fascists had boasted of the autarkic production of Gallone's films, the Christian Democrats were happy to allow the Americans to supply their message by proxy. This was in keeping with the way in which the DC delegated certain cultural functions to America and accepted U.S. world leadership.

Quo Vadis had nothing in common with the new realistic style of filmmaking that flourished in Italy in the immediate postwar years. Yet the Americans were anything but insensitive to the revolution in filmmaking that films like *Roma città aperta* and *Paisà* (*Paisan*) (Roberto Rossellini, 1946) represented. The very antithesis of Hollywood studio productions, these offered an alternative that was appealing not only to radicals but also to some big-league producers who saw them as offering a new avenue to be explored. One of the first to see the potential was David O. Selznick, who set his sights on bringing Vittorio De Sica to Hollywood. This was negotiated and discussed for much of 1947, with De Sica learning English and making considerable progress, despite what, in October, was referred to by Selznick's representative as "an atrocious accent."[43] However, De Sica went cool on the idea of going to America and instead negotiations focused on the possibility of an English-language version of the film he was preparing to shoot, *Ladri di biciclette*. Selznick liked the script, which he saw as "very charming and very touching . . . another demonstration of De Sica's extraordinary humanity."[44] But the gulf between De Sica's vision and Selznick's was apparent in the telegram discussion of possible stars for the principal role. As a Hollywood producer Selznick could not conceive of a film that was not made according to commercial criteria with the best stars available. After proposing Cary Grant, and encountering De Sica's polite suggestion that Henry Fonda might be more appropriate (turned down because Fonda was "not big enough" and because of fears that his performance would "incline to dullness and heaviness"),[45] Selznick went through a bizarre string of possible alternatives that included Danny Kaye, Bing Crosby, and William Powell (deemed "absolutely perfect for the role" by Selznick, in spite of the reputation for suave, debonair roles he had acquired thanks to the *Thin Man* series with Myrna Loy).[46]

This project folded but collaboration did occur in 1952 on *Stazione Termini*, a film scripted (originally) by Zavattini, the principal screenwriter of *Ladri di biciclette*, and directed by De Sica, with two American stars, Jennifer Jones and Montgomery Clift. The aim was for "a neorealist type film crossed with American appeal and stars."[47] The very impossibility of such a thing was manifest in Selznick's contradictory memos, which on the one hand said that "so much of the quality of the picture depends upon getting the type of atmosphere that has contributed so much to the quality of films like *The Bi-*

cycle Thief, Shoeshine, The Open City etc." and on the other demanded that
the film be made "in the American spirit."[48] A particular problem was posed
by the American insistence that, for censorship reasons, the love between the
protagonists be of a purely platonic nature. In the end the film was something
of a hodge-podge and it came out in the United States, completely reedited by
Selznick and with the addition of theme songs, under the title *Indiscretion of
an American Wife.*[49]

Soon a more routine formula was found for the many location films that
were shot in Italy in the 1950s. American companies not only used Italian studios but also shot in picturesque places, with the blessing and encouragement
of the Italian government, which saw movies as a useful promotion for tourism. What this meant was that Italy was turned into a movie set for Americans
as the techniques of U.S. filmmaking were imported into the country. *Roman
Holiday* (William Wyler, 1953), *Beat the Devil* (John Huston, 1953), *Three Coins
in the Fountain* (Jean Negulesco, 1954), *Summer Madness* (David Lean, 1955), *It
Started in Naples* (Melville Shavelson, 1960), and many others were all breezy
romantic comedies that set a mature male Hollywood star (such as Gregory
Peck, Humphrey Bogart, and Clark Gable) against a young and usually Italian female star (with the variation of Rossano Brazzi and American women
in *Summer Madness*). The films were shot largely outdoors and made full use
of the Italian countryside, monuments, and the appealing ways of Italian life.
They all showed the Italy Americans wanted to see and which, in increasing
numbers, they experienced as they came to the country as tourists.

The presence of American majors in Italy pushed up considerably the
costs of production. *Helen of Troy* (Robert Wise, 1956), *War and Peace* (King
Vidor, 1956), and other blockbusters were so expensive that they created difficulties for a cinema accustomed to low costs. However there were some benefits from the direct contact with American runaway productions. Many Italian
technical and production personnel learned, through their work on American
films, how filmmaking could be organized more efficiently. Once filming had
never begun before midday in Italy. Now an eight-hour working day was fully
exploited. By the same token, people were employed on the basis of their skills
rather than who they were related to or how little money they would accept.[50]
Later some film workers acknowledged that working with the Americans had
given them new skills that were then transferred to Italian films.

Italian Film and International Markets

As the Italian film industry recovered after the war, producers regained con-
fidence and negotiated directly with the American MPEA through the Italian trade organization ANICA. Led by the evergreen Eitel Monaco, this asso-

ciation included some 180 companies (among which, perhaps paradoxically, were the distribution affiliates of the U.S. majors). It acted strategically to secure alliances and collaboration and exploit opportunities to promote Italian film abroad. Producers and others did not object to the complex network of legislation governing cinema—after all, they had been the first to seek guarantees—but instead sought to draw maximum advantage from the situation that resulted. In 1958 Libero Bizzarri and Libero Solaroli published supposedly secret accords between ANICA and MPEA that enshrined a series of mutual favors. In essence these involved ANICA approving the export of 50 percent of earnings on American films while the Americans agreed to invest 40 percent of their blocked funds in the production and distribution of Italian films.[51] The relationship with the Americans was not, of course, one between equals. Indeed, in some respects the American companies were more powerful in the Italian market than they were in the United States after the American law of 1940 that ended the monopolistic domination of production, distribution, and exhibition by requiring "divorcement," that is, the same company could not operate simultaneously in all three sectors of the industry. No such divorce was required in Italy. Thus not only did the Americans gain a strong influence in distribution and exhibition but also part of Italian film production was financed by them. By this means they could pass films off for Italian and receive the economic benefits that Italian nationality afforded.[52]

The careers of Ponti and De Laurentiis need to be seen in part in relation to these circumstances. Both men began their production careers with Lux before setting up on their own. Of the two, De Laurentiis was the more ambitious, but both indulged in a flamboyance (fast cars, splendid villas) that was closer to American practice than Italian customs. They produced films, often on a grand scale, such as *Ulysses* (1955), directed by Mario Camerini and starring Kirk Douglas alongside Silvana Mangano, De Laurentiis's wife, and also King Vidor's *War and Peace*.[53] In some cases they acted on behalf of Paramount.[54] These were never co-productions in a formal sense but rather American productions or "co-participations," that is, collaborations in which the exact nature of the artistic or financial exchange was determined on a case-by-case basis. Although both men would eventually move abroad (Ponti to France, De Laurentiis to the United States), their joint company produced many interesting and popular films in the early 1950s. They gave opportunities to new directors and cultivated stars, notably Silvana Mangano. They even produced films featuring the Neapolitan comic actor Totò whose fans were largely confined in this period to the poor population of the South.

In some respects the Italian market, as we shall discuss in the next chapter, was a provincial one that absorbed many low-budget films with a strong local flavor. Titanus, a company so cautious that it did not make more than eight to nine films per year (many of them co-produced with other companies so as to share costs) specialized in these. But the influx of foreign capital provided opportunities for development. According to his biographers, De Laurentiis was the most ambitious of Italian producers, the first to aim directly at the U.S. market, to think in terms of big budgets and international casts, and to shoot in English.[55] Italian cinema in the 1950s possessed many of the characteristics of an industrial cinema. There might have been serious weaknesses and distortions that in later years would lead to profound problems, but these were at least temporarily covered by the fever of activity in all spheres that accompanied the expansion of the domestic market for film. Producers copied the American formula and made costly spectacular films aimed at export markets. Foreign stars, color, lavish settings, and costumes were all key elements of the recipe. Two such films were *Fabìola,* the 1949 biblical epic directed by Alessandro Blasetti starring Michèle Morgan, and the already mentioned *Ulysses.* The use of foreign stars, especially American ones, became routine practice in Italian art films, although the sheer quantity of actors, including has-beens and young hopefuls, who arrived in Italy meant that some appeared even in low-budget films for the home market.

The international dimension of Italian filmmaking was further reflected in the very large number of European co-productions made in these years. From 1946 sectors of the film business were busy cultivating links in Europe that would lead to a long series of co-productions, most notably with France, with which accords were signed in 1949 and renewed in 1954. After the early foreign successes of the first neorealist films, Italian producers sought to build on the prestige they had acquired. The European initiative was a concerted one to share costs and multiply the nationality of a film to derive maximum advantage from the legal privileges available in different countries. Its products were less eye-catching than some of the American-style costume spectaculars but it was more a collaboration of equals that also offered the prospect of diminishing the specific reliance on Italian state finance and therefore interference. By 1954 a quarter of all Italian films were co-productions.[56] Thomas Guback has noted that between 1950 and 1965, Italy co-produced 1,149 films: 764 with France, 190 with Spain, 46 with Germany, 141 tripartite, and 8 with others.[57] The purpose of co-productions, other than to gain guaranteed access to a second market, was to raise budgets and share costs.[58] It would not be entirely true to say that the national qualities of films produced in this way were obscured or eliminated, because there was usually a major (normally 70 percent) and a minor share in a co-production and very often the best aspects of national cinema were maintained. But the definition of what was and what was not a national film became highly indeterminate at this time.

The American market, as Christopher Wagstaff has noted, was the most profitable and therefore most desirable.[59] With few exceptions, in the early postwar years Italian films in the United States were limited to art cinemas, which showed subtitled films, and circuits for immigrants, which showed original versions. Together this constituted a small market, equivalent to Argentina or Brazil. It later became a more important market, with the establishment of Italian Film Export (IFE), an association formed with the express purpose of assisting the entry of Italian films into mainstream circuits abroad. One of the clauses of the 1951 ANICA-MPEA accord provided for the use of 12.5 percent of the earnings of U.S. films in Italy to promote Italian films in the United States. Italian Film Export, with offices in both Rome and New York, had the role of advising producers, facilitating dubbing, promoting Italian films in America, and subsidizing subtitled showings for Italian-Americans. However, its history was brief (it was dissolved in 1957) and complicated. One major problem was the hostility it encountered from independent American distributors who regarded its subsidized status as a threat to free competition. To get round this its activities were limited to providing for dubbing and promotion; no direct distribution was engaged in.

In order to get into major circuits in the United States, Italian films had to meet the standards of the Production Code Administration. This was not easy given the different attitudes to sex, morality, and the body. The rejection of the neorealist masterpiece *Ladri di biciclette* caused outrage in Italy and was seen as deliberate discrimination.[60] What caused offense were two scenes, of the boy Bruno urinating against a wall and his father's pursuit of a suspect into "what appears to be a bordello."[61] Without the PCA's approval, the film could only be shown with local approval. However, many other films were censored on grounds of taste and morality. The alleged vulgarity and emphasis on poverty in Italian films could not be justified by reference to their realism. The reaction to Giuseppe De Santis's left-wing melodrama *Riso amaro* was unilateral. The PCA's secretary, Joseph Breen, wrote that he was horrified that a leading official of the MPAA had agreed to help promote the film in the United States.

It is utterly inconceivable to us that anyone connected with this Association would undertake, even in the slightest manner, to appear to support a picture of this type. This Association, in the first instance, was started with the purpose—among other things—to put an end to the exhibition in this country of pictures of this type.[62]

The film was on the Legion of Decency's condemned list, and, in his office report, Gordon White wrote, "I have seldom, if ever, seen a more morbid and depressing moving picture." Confirming this, a further in-office report stated "about every important tenet of the Code is broken. Girls are living with men without the benefit of clergy or apology. The relationship between them and the continuous and flagrant—purposeful—exposures of thighs and breasts flaunts [*sic*] decency."[63] An amended version was submitted but was still denied approval. However, the film was released in the United States despite the direct challenge to the authority of the PCA. This and other cases contributed to the latter's eventual demise.

It was precisely the sexually daring and explicit qualities that horrified the official guardians of American morality and ensured the success of Italian films in the United States. "Silvana Mangano is nothing short of a sensation on the international film scene," Bosley Crowther wrote in the *New York Times* on September 19, 1950.

Full-bodied and gracefully muscular, with a rich voice and a handsome, pliant face, she handles with vigor and authority the characterization of a tortured libertine. It is not too excessive to describe her as Anna Magnani minus fifteen years, Ingrid Bergman with a latin disposition and Rita Hayworth plus twenty-five pounds.[64]

The IFE file held at the American Academy of Motion Picture Arts and Sciences suggests that, in seeking to promote Italian films, the company laid heavy emphasis on sex appeal. The first issue of *I.F.E.*, a special publication for exhibitors, featured Sophia Loren on the cover and promised "sex, spectacle and showmanship." Italian films, it said, "thrilled by provocative picture layouts revealing the off-beat allure of Italian beauties." The back cover feature proclaimed "Italy's Secret Weapon—Fresh New Faces and Box-Office Figures."

Since Silvana Mangano first electrified the screen with her sensational debut in *Bitter Rice,* the delectable Roman lovelies—presented in all sizes and a variety of sensuous shapes—have opened the doors of US theatres and the eyes of American fans to the very special delights of Italian-produced films. This new and apparently inexhaustible source of pulchritudinous pin-ups has given new lustre to theatre marquees and accelerated the tempo of box-office cash registers. With some of these Latin beauties coming over to make pictures here, Italy has emerged as the testing ground for modern star beauties with half a dozen answers to Marilyn Monroe in each new crop of signorinas.

The appeal of Italy's new female stars was considerable, but the Italian films in which they appeared rarely broke out of the art-house and immigrant circuits (*Riso amaro* was an exception). Their biggest successes in America came in Hollywood films with an Italian or European setting. Two examples were the Ponti-Columbia collaboration *Woman of the River* (*La donna del fiume*) (Mario Soldati, 1955) and the Fox film *Boy on a Dolphin* (Jean Negulesco, 1957), both of which starred Sophia Loren. James Powers wrote in the *Hollywood Reporter* of April 11, 1957 that

Sophia Loren ... may not bring any new dimension to sex appeal but certainly expands those already existing. There are many underwater and diving sequences ... and the sight of Miss Loren dripping wet in a water-soaked dress—a frequent sight, happily—will be a powerful attraction to the picture for those who might otherwise class it as a semi-art production.[65]

"Miss Loren, particularly, with that now well-identified and highly merchandisable Italo-style 'build', will be something for the boys (and girls) at the wickets," drooled *Variety* of April 11, 1957.

In the years that followed World War II, the production sector remained fragmented, as it was before 1939. Its development was no less shaped by the influential presence of the Americans and the example they provided. Indeed, the absence of a government that was explicitly nationalistic in its policies meant that the American presence in the Italian industry expanded considerably. Further aspects of this will be explored in chapter 5. Nevertheless, the balance was beginning to change. Italy's early postwar penetration of the American market, and other foreign markets, was a clear indication both of the international critical prestige and commercial success earned by a number of Italian films in the late 1940s and of the strengthening of at least some sectors of Italian film production in industrial terms. Foreigners, and especially the Americans, were better disposed toward the Italians, but stronger producers with a more professional and aggressive approach to markets and foreign distribution were a vital factor in this development. Italian films became, for a short period, a regular part of the programming of mainstream cinemas in the English-speaking world and a more stable part of the film diet of audiences in Western Europe and other countries.

5 The Film Market

The film exhibition sector experienced controlled growth through the 1930s as cinema became the leading commercial entertainment in the country. Because the granting of licenses for new movie theaters was resisted by existing exhibitors and, from 1936, required approval from a commission of the Ministry of Press and Propaganda, the expansion was significant but not massive. From 2,450 cinemas in 1930, the figure rose to 2,700 in 1938 and 2,876 in 1942.[1] Only after the war did the market increase substantially as new cinemas were built in the South and in rural areas. By 1955 Italy had 10,570 screens, approximately double the total in France (5,688) and Britain (4,483) and over half the total in the United States (18,700).[2] The vast majority of films exhibited in Italy in the period between the 1920s and the 1950s were American, with the exception of the period between 1939 and 1945. This dominant position was established after World War I and was stubbornly defended by the American companies in the decades that followed. By 1925 American films took up 70 percent of exhibition time in Italy. By 1928 the figure had risen to over 80 percent. Germany accounted for 9.6 percent, Britain and France for less than 4 percent each, and Italian films for just 2.6 percent. American films were often marketed by companies that bore the names of major studios and were entirely dependent on them. In fact six of the twelve leading distribution companies in Italy were American.[3]

This does not mean that cinema was tied into networks of consumption in the same way that it was in the United States. In the United States, the histories of cinema and consumerism were intertwined; the development of the exhibition sector was part of the chain store revolution. In Italy, movie houses were not generally modeled on department stores, as was the case in the United States, nor were films seen as having consequences for the retail industry, even though the cream of the exhibition sector was concentrated in the centers of the large cities of the North and Center. Here several first-run movie theaters were typically located in close proximity to one another and the clientele was a modern urban one with certain expectations of quality and comfort. Admission prices were also highest and profits greatest. Yet, the limited development of consumerism meant that cinemas were modeled on theaters designed for live performances—indeed, they were often converted theaters—and the only product on sale was the film itself. For this reason, American attempts to introduce into Italy promotional techniques tried and tested in the United States encountered little success. Commercial tie-ins were rare. In order to promote their films successfully, American companies were obliged to rely heavily on the press and on posters created by Italian illustrators who developed ways of connecting films with the cultural codes of the audience. Pasted on billboards and cinema fronts, posters played a vital role in communicating the themes and attractions of a film to its potential spectators. They indicated the genre of a given film and typically placed special emphasis on the stars who were featured in it.

Although Italian films were relatively weak in the market, they were not without advantages. There was some resistance to them among sophisticated audiences who deemed them second-rate, but large sectors of the public found Italian films more familiar in cultural terms and enjoyed them for that reason. For example, Italian film stars were often able to connect more fully with audiences because they possessed specific physical and behavioral traits. While the idea of the film star was shaped largely by Hollywood (see chapter 2), the Italian adaptation of the phenomenon was less manufactured and commercial. Moreover, the state-owned distribution company Ente Nazionale Industrie Cinematografiche (ENIC) was a significant force that prioritized Italian films. Through its ownership of the Cines film company, the state also acquired a network of cinemas in large cities. The simultaneous presence of the state and of foreign companies meant that distribution and exhibition, both of which usually receive far less attention than production, were no less political than the former and were no less subject to negotiation and conflict.

American Companies and the Italian Market

In Italy, as elsewhere, it was common for companies involved in production also to engage in distribution and sometimes, as in the case of Cines, in exhibition. In other cases, such as that of Titanus, distribution was the core of a company's activities and was the sector that it developed most consistently. For American film companies, distribution was crucial and abroad it was the area in which they asserted their influence most strongly. By the end of the 1920s, four major Hollywood companies—Metro-Goldwyn-Mayer, Paramount, Twentieth Century Fox, and United Artists—had established their own distribution companies, or strong links to companies with exclusive rights to sell their product in Italy, and each maintained offices in the fourteen leading cities. This network was vital in developing and promoting the market for American films. United States companies typically sold packages of films in which eye-catching titles were matched with less appealing product. Italian distributors were constrained to bid against each other to secure the films audiences wanted to see, thus raising costs sometimes unrealistically. As a result, the whole terrain of distribution became one on which competition was skewed to the advantage of the Americans. Their domination of the country's screens meant that Italian films were exceptions that had to struggle for screen time.

Italians, and other foreigners, often had the impression not only that the American film industry was one big conglomerate but also that Hollywood and the U.S. government effectively functioned as one as well. There were good reasons for thinking this, for the degree of coordination within the industry and between industry and government was, at some moments in particular, remarkable.[4] This was especially so abroad when American interests were threatened. The industry organization, the Motion Picture Association of America (MPAA, also known as the "Hays Office" after its first head, William Hays), negotiated directly with governments when such situations arose. Yet, in fact, U.S. companies not only competed with other countries' film industries; they also competed among themselves. They were effective abroad to different degrees, they operated and marketed their films in different ways, and they sometimes took different attitudes toward restrictions.

This meant that the conglomerate sometimes failed to function and that domestic forces could exploit this to divide and rule.

What distinguished American companies overall was the strategic view they took. They saw themselves as trading overseas year after year. In consequence they aimed to accumulate as much information as possible about foreign markets and, as far as possible, to control those markets. They went about this by taking as big a share as possible of the distribution sector, operating through foreign subsidiaries, not through local agents. The distributors occupied a powerful position in relation to exhibitors as American product was so desirable and lucrative. Control of this sector meant that profits could be maximized with minimum bother.[5]

Stars were one of the key levers by which audiences were attracted to American films. Whereas the Italian stars of the silent era had been remote, fantastic creatures, exotic and extreme, the American stars of the 1930s were more down-to-earth. Even the most famous (Gary Cooper, Errol Flynn, Clark Gable, Ronald Colman of the men; Jean Harlow, Greta Garbo, Joan Crawford, Carole Lombard, Myrna Loy of the women) conformed to types and were manufactured by a remarkable, industrially organized studio system in which every aspect of the process of star recruitment, grooming, launch, response, and utilization was meticulous and "scientific." Studios like Metro-Goldwyn-Mayer and Paramount invested huge resources in the creation and promotion of stars and were well aware of the extraordinary imaginative appeal they exercised. Audiences in Italy as elsewhere loved and admired them, even if there were difficulties in pronouncing their names and the process of dubbing leveled out some of their individuality.

Information about how the American film industry viewed the market in Italy and about its operations there is quite rich from the mid-1930s due to the documentation contained in American government archives. It is less revealing concerning the on-the-ground activities of the various companies. Even publicity material for the prewar period is exceptionally difficult to come by, and only occasional issues of the various bulletins that were published by the Italian subsidiaries of the majors, such as MGM's *Il ruggito del leone* (*The Lion's Roar*), are available for consultation. The most detailed records available are those for United Artists (UA); consequently much of the material presented here is drawn from them.[6] United Artists was different from the other companies in that it never produced films. It was founded in 1919 as a distribution company for independents, that is, for those actors, directors, and producers who were opposed to the studio system and who made at their own risk pictures that reflected their individual talents. It was not intended as a profit-making company but rather as a service organization, primarily for the work of the four "famous names" who founded it: Charlie Chaplin, Douglas Fairbanks Sr., Mary Pickford, and D. W. Griffith. In consequence it was never a major player in a strict sense—UA was considered one of the "little three" along with Universal and Columbia. Nevertheless it carried great prestige on account of the names whose films it distributed, which included (apart from those of the founders) the Marx Brothers, Walt Disney (from 1932 to 1937), David O. Selznick, Howard Hughes, and Hal Roach.[7] Abroad, the differences between UA and the majors were less pronounced as they were all simply distributors. United Artists set up its first foreign subsidiary in 1920 and by the mid-1920s it had subsidiaries in all the important countries.

In Italy UA did not operate a company of its own. Instead, after a satisfactory trial with two pictures in 1922, it used a local company to distribute its films on a salary and commission basis. Mario Luporini formed Artisti Associati (AA) for this explicit purpose and it distributed UA's films in Italy throughout the period up to America's entry into the war in December 1941.[8] There were various difficulties and changes in the structure and ownership of the company in the 1930s, as a result both of UA pressures and changing conditions under the Fascist regime, but these did not stop the creation and functioning of a highly effective distribution network that in general terms was deemed to be very satisfactory by the head office. Artisti Associati had eleven direct distribution outlets in Italy, as well as various agencies. From 1944 to 1946 the company used the services of a Swiss national, Fred Mueller, to protect its interests. After the war, it concluded a distribution deal with an industrialist, Ferruccio Caramelli, who in the meantime had become the owner of AA. This deal occurred only after various other possibilities had been considered. A crucial factor in the decision was that Caramelli owned a dubbing plant in Rome and a printing and developing plant in Turin. Meanwhile, Luporini found employment with Twentieth Century Fox.

Although the Italian distributor was a separate, autonomous company (apart from a 2 percent UA stake in it from 1929), the parent company kept a close check on its operations, both from New York and Paris. There were constantly matters to discuss, negotiate, or resolve. The mentality and business practices of the Italians and the Americans were so different that frequently there were clashes and misunderstandings. The Americans often distrusted their Italian collaborators and they also had difficulty in adapting to some Italian business practices. In particular, they disliked the practice whereby negotiations were never concluded once and for all; any matter could always be reopened for discussion even after an agreement had apparently been reached. The UA files contain various allusions to theft and blackmail and also to late payments and to Caramelli's annoying habit of going into hiding periodically and rendering himself untraceable (usually when monies were due). United Artists kept a close watch, like all the film companies, on the political and market situation of the foreign territories in which it did business. It kept data on the cultural patterns, business practices, and laws that affected the foreign subsidiaries and licensed agents of the corporation. For example, in 1934 it was recorded in the Italy file that the most popular types of pictures were dramas, action films, and costume films. The biggest Hollywood stars were Greta Garbo, Joan Crawford, Eddie Cantor, Leslie Howard, and Laurel and Hardy.[9] Most contracts for pictures in the 1930s were handled through United Artists (Export) Limited, based in London. This corporation acted for the UA Corporation of Delaware, which supervised overseas operations through a foreign department. In the postwar period, the UA Corporation also maintained an office in Rome, of which Mueller was manager. He was accountable to a representative of the New York home office. Mueller worked with AA to assess the market and ensure that appropriate films were chosen for release at appropriate times. He also sought to coordinate publicity and advise on strategy, although AA had to put up the cost of materials.

From Monopoly to Free Trade

Because of the dominant position they occupied in the market, American companies often acted as though they had every right to dictate conditions of trade to foreign governments. They were happy to negotiate over the terms under which films should be imported, and they even discussed the number of American films that should be distributed annually, but all the while the assumption was that, as a norm, they should be able to carry out their business with as few impediments as possible. In the case of Italy, however, cordial relations broke down over the introduction of the Monopoly Law of 1938, which granted a monopoly on the distribution of foreign films in Italy to the state-owned ENIC. The deliberations surrounding this law are considered from the Italian side in chapter 7 in the context of the state's role in relation to mass culture. Here we shall concentrate on the American responses to it.

The major studios reacted to the Monopoly Law by simultaneously closing their Italian distribution subsidiaries on January 1, 1939 and boycotting the Italian market. Their expectation was that this would send the Italian exhibition sector into crisis. In fact this did not happen, for three main reasons. First, Italian production increased and the films were of sufficient quality to satisfy most audiences. Second, imports from other countries, notably Germany and Hungary, also increased. Third, the Americans were not fully united. While the majors were firmly behind the boycott, minor American companies were more flexible. The Italian authorities perceived this and attempted to break the unity of the U.S. producers, work around the boycott, and fill the gap that arose in the short term in the domestic market. For example, it was expressly decided not to undertake reprisals against the studios or distributors linked to them. By fostering a conciliatory atmosphere, the authorities encouraged minor companies to trade with Italy. United Artists is an interesting case here. An internal communication of November 9, 1938 reported that there was unanimous support among producers for maintaining a solid front with all other Hays Office members and refusing to deal with the Monopoly Law. However, the rider was added that if any other company were to make a deal with the Italian monopoly distributor ENIC then the London-based head of UA Export would be authorized to negotiate all of UA product on the best basis possible.[10]

The united front was in fact short-lived. Negotiations were started on behalf of ENIC to buy films from Monogram and Republic, two small companies that were not under the regulation of the Hays Office. Their output was low, but this breach was a blow to the majors. It meant that other minors came in and that the boycott did not provoke the desired desperation and recantation in Italy that the majors had hoped for. The circulation and exhibition of American films were finally banned by Italian government decree only in February 1943. However even after this some continued to be shown. A file entitled "American films—infractions" held at the Archivio Centrale dello Stato contains cuttings from newspapers in the Veneto region advertising films such as *Frankenstein* (James Whale, 1931) at the Marconi cinema in Padua and *Streets of New York* (*Gli eroi della strada*) (William Nigh, 1939) at the Patronato cinema in Vicenza, both in July 1943.[11]

The withdrawal of the major American studios did not lead to the complete eradication of the cult of American stars. This had first developed among young middle-class people in the 1920s and had been sustained through the 1930s by a specialist press. The illustrated weekly *Cinema Illustrazione* still featured American actors on the cover in 1939 and in *Film* as late as August 1940 there were pictures of Joan Crawford, Maureen O'Hara, and others. The quantity steadily declined, however, as the agencies were no longer supplying new material, and derogatory captions were often placed beneath the images. *Cinema Illustrazione* of March 1, 1939 reported, for example, that Joan Bennett "is considered the most elegant of the Hollywood actresses, but this elegance is often artificial, 'sophisticated'; it is very different from the spontaneous elegance of our actresses." Without regular new material, the film magazines grew poorer, printed fewer photos, lost color print, and were reduced in pages (after 1940 this was also a result of the wartime paper shortage). Yet, for real fans, the American cult went on; fans continued to adore their idols in secret, Viniccio Marinucci confessed in August 1944. They whispered items of news to each other and passed photos around. They also lovingly leafed through their collections of past issues of film magazines.[12]

The initial public reaction to the American films that hit Italian screens after World War II has generally been depicted as positive. According to Gian Piero Brunetta the return of Hollywood movies was greeted, at first at least, like the first drops of rain following a drought.[13] Large curious crowds flocked in Naples and Florence to see *The Great Dictator* (Charles Chaplin, 1940) and *In Which We Serve* (Noël Coward, 1942), as well as war documentaries and news. The major features that followed also did well. Lorenzo Quaglietti, however, who was old enough to remember the reception of these and other films, strongly challenged the view that Italians were enthusiastic.[14] Indeed, he claimed that this whole perception derived from an article that one critic, Libero Solaroli, had written. Audiences, Quaglietti said, did not favor American films; if anything they preferred Italian films. If they actually saw more American movies, it was because in many instances they were forced to see them for lack of alternatives. Quaglietti was probably right up to a point. Although Hollywood films did certainly have a wide and general appeal, their reception was not entirely unproblematic. An Allied Propaganda Report dated March 3, 1945 revealed that some films were found boring, too war-oriented, unsuited to Italian tastes, or simply second-rate. Problems also emerged with the subtitles, which were not popular, and with dubbed films: with Italian postproduction houses not yet back in action, the Americans had resorted to the earlier practice of dubbing films in the United States before marketing them in Italy. The Italian-American accents and pronunciations were not well received by educated Italians.

While Brunetta stresses the enthusiasm of the initial response, he has described the enormous influx of American films that followed the relief of the drought as a flood that was detrimental to Italian cinema. It was "a veritable continuation of the state of war for the Italian film industry [that] prevented it from re-establishing regular contacts with its own audience."[15] He also refers to the close surveillance of Italy (and other countries) by the Hollywood production companies and American government departments as "an aggressive policy, aimed at total destruction of the adversary [which has] no precedents in the history of cinema politics and economics." These judgments require some qualification. It is true that the American film industry was immensely powerful after 1945, not just because of its economic strength and the unique fascination exerted by its products, but because it became part of the U.S. government's campaign to convert Europe and the world to Americanism.[16] It also found itself faced with a situation in which many of the protective barriers of the 1920s and 1930s were removed and national film industries had been disrupted or destroyed by the war. Hollywood had no concern whatever for national needs and set about occupying as much space as possible in foreign markets. However the extent to which this was achieved and to which the Italian industry was stifled and denied contact with audiences needs reassessment.

Neorealism, for example, was quite well received in Italy at the outset; indeed *Roma città aperta* was the biggest grossing film of the 1945–1946 season.[17] Box-office returns also revealed a persisting taste for Italian costume films and comedies. Perhaps surprisingly, there is some evidence that audiences missed the Italian stars they had grown to love during the war years. Up to 1948 and after, film magazines like *Star* and *Hollywood* often published letters asking for news of favorites who had slipped out of view. The names of stars like girl-next-door Maria Denis and the dependably heroic Fosco Giachetti, who had appeared in many successful costume dramas, war films, and comedies since 1936, still had a certain attraction for them. These actors continued to appear in popularity polls and they also constituted a reference point for those fans who sent in photographs to the look-alike competitions, run by various magazines, which were so popular in the postwar period. It is striking to find pictures side by side of young women who modeled themselves both on the sultry actress Luisa Ferida (who was executed for collaboration by partisans together with her lover, the actor Osvaldo Valenti, in 1945) and on the face most identified with neorealism, Anna Magnani.[18] There were always crowds present whenever famous film actors appeared in the live theater or at the publicity football matches, featuring teams of actors and actresses, which also took place from time to time in 1945–1946. There were also many requests in the press for the autographs of actors who continued to enjoy a following.

Despite all this, Brunetta is right to stress the resolve with which the United States employed global and local pressures to create the trading conditions it wanted. The Hays Office was extremely alert to any reappearance of protectionism and negotiated hard to avoid any obstacles to the studios' activities. In Italy, it strongly objected on principle to the government's proposal in 1945 that cinemas should reserve time for the showing of Italian films. The Italians secured the backing of the British on this issue, but the Americans continued to object to what they saw as an illegitimate attempt to give an artificial prop to an industry that they felt should stand on its own feet. The seesaw continued over the question of a sixty-day quota (the proposal to require exhibitors to screen Italian films for a minimum of sixty days a year), with the measure reappearing in the new legislation that was approved by the Council of Ministers in September 1945 before being struck out again, along with the producers' subsidy, when legislation was definitively approved on November 3. The Americans could take comfort, for the time being, that their concept of free enterprise appeared to have been accepted. The only legitimate restrictions in their view were voluntary ones.

The American industry's concern to shape events did not manifest itself only on the commercial plane. Despite the difficulties it had experienced, it set about finding political allies and, in keeping with the U.S. government's position, it took an anticommunist, pro-DC line. Relatively little is known about the contribution of the film companies to the highly divisive 1948 Italian general election campaign, except that the anti-Russian comedy *Ninotchka* (Ernst Lubitsch, 1939) was strategically released in the weeks prior to the vote. There was also a poster, "The Stars of Hollywood are Against Communism Too," featuring pictures of John Wayne, Tyrone Power, and Gary Cooper among others (an embassy report of December 3, 1948 refers to the U.S. companies' "aid [in the] pre-election period and overall US aid to Italy").[19] The American companies certainly had a sense of the potential and actual political impact of cinema. From 1949 there is evidence in the archives of films deliberately being withheld or, more rarely, promoted respectively because of their liberal or anticommunist content. To give just a few examples: in February 1949 the spy thriller *The Iron Curtain* (William A. Wellman, 1948) was released to vociferous Communist protest; in August John Ford's 1941 Depression-era drama of poor southern farmers, *Tobacco Road,* was withheld on the grounds that it lent support to Communist propaganda; in 1950 UA withheld *Home of the Brave* (Mark Robson, 1949), which raised the issue of racism during the war; there was concern about a positive review in the PCI newspaper *L'Unità* of *Pinky* (Elia Kazan, 1949), another film that treated the question of racial discrimination; and a story of the corruption of a rural politician, *All the King's Men* (Robert Rossen, 1949), was held back because it showed the U.S. political system in a bad light. All of this shows the desire of the film companies to contribute to U.S. foreign policy.

In the wake of the victory of the Christian Democrats in the election of April 18, 1948, the companies probably felt that they could exact some concessions. They hoped for the removal of the few barriers that obstructed their market domination. They resented the privileges accorded to Italian producers and continued to treat the market as a potential fiefdom. Also, they hoped that some of the administrative methods that had been employed to delay film releases or limit the number of American films on exhibition at any given time would be set aside. Repeated delays had occurred in the normal application of censorship procedures to imported films, causing much American anger.[20] In the absence of any formal restrictions, such delays were a way of allowing some Italian films to get onto the country's screens.[21]

In contrast to Britain, France, Spain, and Germany, Italy remained an open market throughout this period. However, the continued flooding led to further cries from the Italian film industry that the United States was deliberately seeking to saturate the market as a policy of pressure. For example, in 1949 the U.S. companies distributed 400 films under the system of block booking. In the same year there were also 100 Italian and 80 other foreign films in distribution, whereas the market capacity was reckoned to be between 300 and 400. So many American films from the war and prewar backlog were being sold below cost that the leading trade periodical, the *Araldo dello spettacolo*, attacked the practice as an example of dumping.[22]

Although the Hays Office gave undertakings that imports would be contained voluntarily, in fact they were allowed to expand without limit. The exponential increase in U.S. films in the market between 1946 and 1949 (from 188 to 369) suggests one or more of the following: that the undertakings were given in bad faith; that the trade association could not guarantee the behavior of its members; that extra numbers were made up by direct sales which were considered not to count in the United States, but which inevitably did in Italy; that the difference was partially accounted for by smaller U.S. companies that were not part of the Motion Picture Export Association (MPEA). In fact all of these explanations were probably true.

To this extent the Americans themselves brought about the situation that made the Andreotti law necessary (see p. 132). Yet, the law was not formally protectionist since, while it provided indirect support to Italian producers, it introduced no limitations or restrictions on the import of American films. The free trade doctrine that the Americans regarded as a sine qua non was not disputed since no one advocated a return to autarky. However, Libero Bizzarri has argued that, even within this framework, Italy could have adopted a measure like that promulgated in France in 1953, under which foreign films were granted visas that restricted the period of their circulation.[23] Instead the only limitations imposed by the law concerned the export of capital, with the consequence that the money earned on American films rapidly infiltrated nearly all aspects of the Italian film industry leading to qualitative developments in some areas and distortions, subservience, and dependency in others. It is possible to interpret this soft official response to flooding as an effect of the relationship of complicity between the Christian Democrats and the Americans.

In March 1950 the Italian government formed a Motion Picture Consultative Committee representing all the voices and interests concerned. The government wanted to keep the film trade free, but was embarrassed by the continuing high volume of U.S. imports. After talks, an agreement was finally reached in June 1951 on three main points. First, it was formally stated that there would be no restrictions on imports or distribution of U.S. films in Italy. In return the U.S. industry agreed to refrain from "flooding the market" (the definition of this was agreed upon as not going above a ceiling of 225 films per year for MPEA companies and 50 for independents). Second, provision was made for an agreed percentage of the lira earnings in Italy of the U.S.

film industry (subsequently fixed at 37.5 percent) to be exported in dollars. Third, a further proportion of lira earnings (12.5 percent) was to be used to give financial assistance to the Italian film industry in promoting its product in the United States, as we saw in chapter 4. The remainder of the U.S. film industry's Italian earnings (50 percent) was to remain in blocked accounts for approved, mostly film-related, uses. It is indicative of the way in which the United States, as the world's leading economic power, was able to impose its own conception of free trade in international agreements, such as the IMF and GATT, that the U.S. Federal Trade Commission subsequently insisted on the reference to market flooding being struck out of the accord. The reason given was that it was restrictive of free trade purely for protectionist reasons and not because of balance of payments issues (a point the United States had accepted in 1946). Thus the limitation of imports into Italy remained purely voluntary and was to be determined by agreement between the Italian trade association ANICA and the MPEA.

Paolo Bafile has argued that this "self-limitation" provided proof of the "wisdom, far-sightedness and clear vision" that the American majors had of their own interests. This was because to export too many films would have been counterproductive, resulting in American films competing with each other and earning less. It is quite wrong therefore, he argues, to see the companies' acceptance of limitation as "a sort of victory of the power of persuasion and of the negotiating ability of Italian industrial delegations."[24] This view may be questioned because the objections raised by Italian interests to continued flooding, and the threats of reprisals that were made if action was not taken, were decisive in forcing the U.S. companies to accept a limitation. Although the MPEA could think strategically, the single companies that comprised it were much more geared to short-term selfish gain. The high-profile new releases of large companies were not damaged by the presence in the market of a large number of older or low-budget films, but Italian films were affected, since it meant that they either struggled to get on the screen or were not fully exploited. Therefore the agreement to limit imports to Italy was good for the U.S. majors because, without damaging mainstream U.S. interests, it brought a halt to the threat of other sanctions and to the use of strategies of delay.

Despite their protests, it is clear that some U.S. companies repeatedly engaged in irregular exchange practices to remit blocked funds to the United States both before and after the accord of 1951. Eitel Monaco raised this with a Rome embassy officer in November 1950,[25] referring to lira advances made by U.S. companies to religious institutions in Italy and to the companies' policy at the time of accepting payment in dollars at a black market rate in the United States. He also referred to permits to remit dollars being obtained fraudulently from the Ministry for Foreign Trade (established in 1945). Evidence on such a topic is obviously not easy to come by, but the archives do provide some backup. Minutes of a special meeting of the MPEA board of directors held in New York on December 9, 1948 mention a deal with a Catholic educational institution that was keen to buy lire at a more favorable rate than the official one, and to the dioceses of New York and Chicago that were also happy to negotiate on this matter.[26] On March 9, 1949, the *Hollywood Reporter* headlined with a story about blocked lire being used to build a seminary in Rome, in return for the release of three million dollars by the Catholic Church in New York.[27] In September 1956 negotiations were entered into with Finmeccanica and Piaggio for the laundering of blocked lire.[28] Apparently, in the past, the MPAA had agreed to purchase dollars held by Finmeccanica as a way of transferring from the blocked accounts more than the amount that was officially allowed. The American ambassador at the time regarded this as irregular. Further irregularities occurred when the MPAA's representative, a man named Van Dee, who was seeking to get a better deal from the company, demanded a rake-off. Although he had received such payments on previous occasions, this time he was fired.

Stars and Audiences

We have already mentioned the importance of stars in creating a bond between audiences and films (see chapter 2). The Italian case shows that stars were found highly attractive even in contexts where the full apparatus of consumerism was absent. American films offered high-quality comic and dramatic productions, skilful cinematography, and lavish sets and settings that had a unique capacity to capture the attention of filmgoers. However, their greatest selling point was the alluring personalities that filmgoers admired and followed. The American star system was promoted in Italy by local agencies of the U.S. majors; by the film press, which they supplied with photographs and material; by posters; and by related minor parallel media, such as signed photographs for fans and collectable cards (*figurine*).[29] Metro-Goldwyn-Mayer, Paramount, and, to a slightly lesser extent, Twentieth Century Fox, which invested heavily in the star appeal of their movies, also employed a range of techniques to enhance the identification of young people with the stars. Competitions of one sort or another linked to particular films were commonplace, as were recruitment and look-alike contests. These began after the death of Rudolph Valentino in 1926. Convinced that Italy was the breeding ground of beauty and talent, the major studios indulged in periodic searches. Twentieth Century Fox launched a hunt for "the new Valentino" and held a competition for this purpose. Over 300,000 young people took part and 500 were selected for a screen test in Rome. The winner, Alberto Rabagliati, went to Hollywood and made one silent film, but his career there, like that of many foreign actors, ended with the arrival of the talkies at the end of the 1920s. In 1932 Metro-Goldwyn-Mayer held a Greta Garbo look-alike competition for promotional purposes that was won by Sophia Loren's future mother, Romilda Villani, who did indeed bear a striking resemblance to the Swedish actress.

Because American stars were the dominant examples of the type, Italian actors were often considered as substitutes for, or equivalents of, the more attractive and powerfully projected but faraway Americans. They were regarded as second-rate above all by the audiences of first-run cinemas, who generally viewed Italian films in the same way. Magazines reinforced this by habitually matching up Italian actors to their supposed American equivalents. For example, Maria Denis was dubbed the Italian Janet Gaynor and Gemma Bolognesi the Italian Mae West. Assia Noris was matched with Claudette Colbert, Mino Doro with Clark Gable, Erminio Macario with Eddie Cantor, and so on. Italian actors were viewed in terms of a lexicon of stardom that was of unequivocally American origin.

In the press, Italian screen actors and actresses occupied at best a marginal position. A popular publication like *Cinema Illustrazione* offered occasional pictures of the actress Dria Paola, who took the lead role in the first Italian sound film, *La canzone dell'amore* (*The Love Song,* Gennaro Righelli, 1930), or of Rabagliati, who cultivated the look and dress of a film star even after his return from America. Despite his physical ordinariness, Vittorio De Sica became a focus of attention with the release of the 1932 film *Gli uomini, che mascalzoni!* (*Men, What Rascals!*), directed by Mario Camerini.[30] He played average, lower-middle-class or working-class guys although he soon acquired the veneer of charm that would mark his screen persona in his postwar career. Elsa Merlini, the star of Goffredo Alessandrini's 1932 success *La segretaria privata* (*The Personal Secretary*), a remake of a popular German film, was also featured. She became an idol for young working women and for those who aspired to be such. Chirpy and spirited, her bouncy step, extroverted manner, and fringed hairstyle were much imitated.[31] For the most part, though, Italian actors were given marginal treatment in the 1930s.

Italian stars were recruited in various ways. Many actors and actresses had a background in stage plays. Others, particularly some of the young women who embarked on film careers, won competitions organized by commercial companies to find protagonists for given films. For example, Isa Miranda was selected to star in Max Ophuls's *La signora di tutti* (*Everybody's Lady*) in 1934 after winning a magazine competition, and Dina Sassoli won the competition launched by Lux Film in 1940 to find a Lucia Mondella for the film version of Manzoni's novel *I promessi sposi* (*The Betrothed*) directed by Mario Camerini (released in 1941), a search that was billed as the Italian equivalent of Selznick's much-publicized hunt for Scarlett O'Hara. In the early 1940s it was the structures established by the state that undertook the tasks of selection and grooming. The film school of the Centro Sperimentale di Cinematografia (CSC), founded in 1935, became the forging house for new talent until the war, after which it lost this role. It provided a stream of young actors to Cinecittà, which functioned as the equivalent of a big film studio, like UFA in Germany or the Hollywood majors. Luisa Ferida, Alida Valli, Carla Del Poggio, Luisella Beghi, Elli Parvo, and many others took courses at the CSC on generous grants and in some cases began their film careers before ending their studies. Articles on the CSC regularly appeared in the press and it acquired a mythical aura. However, star careers were still not planned or constructed in the way they were elsewhere.

Considerable success was achieved in molding actors and actresses who could prosper in the absence of the Americans. People grew to like Italian stars, who were unstandardized, sometimes plain-looking, human, and endearing. There was a whole category of actors whose pictures appeared frequently in the film press and who became familiar. In order to arouse interest, the press office of Cinecittà distributed thousands of photos. There were also features on the actors in women's and general-interest magazines, including leisure shots and behind-the-scenes articles reporting from the sets of films.

The journalist G. V. Sampieri was one of those who maintained that stars had been the key to the success of American films; indeed the Americans had transplanted their own stars into Italy, leaving little or no space for homegrown products. While some took the view that Italian cinema could—or should—do without the corrupting influence of stars, he argued that a "genuine Italian *divismo*" needed to be created.[32] He called for a halt to the circulation of news and photographs of American stars after the withdrawal of the American majors because it was unpatriotic and cultivated nostalgia for the absent stars. For their part, Italian actors needed to be persuaded that publicity relied on a dose of fantasy. They should not respond angrily if they were approached to pose for bathing-costume shots, or if there were news and gossip about imaginary love affairs, as these were a necessary ingredient if curiosity and interest were to be aroused.

The old film actors Francesco Savio interviewed in the 1970s were reluctant to admit that there had been any star culture in the interwar years.[33] Many said that they had been able to lead normal lives without having to worry about personal gossip in the press or other forms of intrusiveness. Such retrospective statements, which inevitably included comparisons with the postwar years, cannot be accepted at face value. But what is certain is that stars in Italy did not deliberately court controversy in the way the Americans did. They did not function in any perceived way as a "transgression elite," by offering irregular or opulent lifestyles.[34] "I think we expressed the Italians of that time," Maria Denis told Savio, "and in those days the consciousness of the individual was a bit dormant. We did nothing to try and say anything new; we were not encouraged to say new things."[35] The pictures of stars in their homes, which appeared with some regularity in Italian magazines in the 1940s, revealed that their standard of living was modest. Their well-furnished apartments and cozy living rooms may have represented an aspiration for lower-middle-class and working-class cinema audiences but they were really quite banal and ordinary. The stars were internal to a framework of norms that was deemed acceptable under the regime and that, for the most part, they endorsed. There was a preference for modesty and down-to-earth traits in stars, qualities that were taken as signs of Italianness.

Yet, viewed from another perspective, the relationship between the stars and their audiences was quite intense and took various forms. Stars received avalanches of letters, requests for autographs, and even marriage proposals. The blonde comedienne Assia Noris claimed that she received 400 to 500 letters per day at the height of her popularity and employed three secretaries to deal with them. Episodes of what might be called "movie star mania" were on the whole rare but by no means unknown. Autograph hunters descended on Venice in large numbers at the time of the film festival and laid siege to stars' hotels. When the premiere of *Piccolo mondo antico* (*Little Old World*) was held in Vicenza in April 1941, the magazine *Film* reported that a mass of students tried to force their way into Alida Valli's hotel, not realizing that the actress was not there.[36] In August 1940 the same magazine published on its back cover a map of Rome with the faces and addresses of the stars, indicating where they lived (as *Novella 2000* would do from time to time several decades later). Among our witnesses, women evoked memories of Noris and Valentina Cortese, while the ill-fated Luisa Ferida had more impact on men. For Sergio M., "she had a strong way of acting, of performing her role in a film, she had a certain personality" (107: 33). Both Fascists and Catholics were concerned about the growth of the phenomenon of star veneration. In the 1940s, restrictions were placed on the earnings of stars and on the quantity of information about them in the press. Efforts were made to Italianize the names of actresses and, without success, to recruit leading actors to the Fascist Party.

The nature of the connection between stars and their admirers was explored in two articles published by *Film* in 1941 under the title "Lettere d'amore," in which the journalist Alessandro Ferraù read and analyzed fan mail. He deduced that the authors were largely drawn from the audiences of first-run cinemas as the quantity of letters received went up when the recipient was appearing in a film on its first release and declined after it had finished.

Authors also seemed to be young and educated to some degree, suggesting a middle-class background. The actor Roberto Villa, a Leslie Howard/milord type, who appeared in *Luciano Serra pilota* (*Luciano Serra, Pilot*) (Goffredo Alessandrini, 1938) and in *Il fornaretto di Venezia* (*The Fornaretto of Venice*) (Duilio Coletti, 1939), received letters mainly from schoolgirls who tended to write in groups of two or three after having been to the cinema together several times to see one of his films. If a girl was especially timid an older person would write on her behalf. Letters were addressed "to the nicest actor in the world," "my beloved actor," "illustrious actor," "to Roberto," suggesting different levels of presumption of intimacy. They asked what shoe size the actor wore or what brand of toothpaste he used. A few of the letters were obviously written during school lessons; one, for instance, informed Villa that "your photograph did the rounds of the class between the pages of a Latin text book."[37] Carla Candiani received letters from students and soldiers who wrote to her from the front confessing their love, asking for signed photographs, or offering advice. Some confessed to having been tempted to steal posters of her, Ferraù wrote, while "others declare that they do not want actresses who are blonde 'like your American colleagues' on the screen and they sing the praises of brunettes. 'Now we want stars that belong to us, to our country: beautiful brunettes like you who are endowed with the charm of our peninsula.'"[38]

Although several personalities remained popular, any chance of perpetuating the Italian star system was undermined by the interruption of production and the massive invasion of American cinema that accompanied the Liberation. There was no sharp break in the star system between Fascism and the postwar years, but there was a progressive unraveling of an established hierarchy that affected those involved in various ways. Some stars simply disappeared, either because there was no space for them in a cinema that was rapidly changing its sense of purpose or because their natural cycle of popularity had come to an end. Others decided to take advantage of offers that came from abroad, from Hollywood in the best of cases, from Spain and Argentina in a few others. Still more were able to find a role in the postwar cinema, although only a few actually found that their popularity increased. Most had to adapt to a somewhat reduced role.

None of these changes arose from competition on the part of new Italian stars since few emerged in the immediate postwar years. One very significant exception was Anna Magnani, whose distinctive look we briefly discussed in chapter 2. She had been Luchino Visconti's original choice for the role of Giovanna in *Ossessione* (filmed 1942, released 1943), but was unable to take it on because she was pregnant at the time (the role passed to Clara Calamai, whom Visconti at first did not want, but who managed to act against her usual glamorous type). Magnani became a national symbol, the symbol of the Italy that emerged from the war and looked with faith to the reconstruction. She conveyed an idea of femininity that was new to cinema—earthy, maternal, distinctively Mediterranean—and extremely influential. The ethereal, bourgeois, restrained appearance and mannerisms of the "white telephone" films—as the romantic comedies and melodramas of the early 1940s had come to be known, on account of the luxurious environments and objects featured in them—were canceled almost overnight. A new reference point was laid down for the rebirth of Italian cinema. This image was not at all undermined by Magnani's luxurious off-screen wardrobe and extravagant lifestyle, which were always tempered by her untidy hair and explosive, authentic character. Her emergence was proof that, even in difficult circumstances, Italian cinema could connect with its audience.

With Italian integration into the Western bloc, sanctioned by the outcome of the dramatic election campaign of 1948, a series of codes and practices were implanted that changed the nature of stardom. The idea of the American star and the star lifestyle had been strongly present in Italy in the 1930s, but as an external and rather distant influence that people experienced through the cinema and film and fashion magazines. In the postwar climate of economic recovery and growing personal and familial aspiration, the relationship became more dynamic. American elegance, grace, wealth, prosperity, and health were regarded with deferential admiration as the product of a superior, more developed society.

The influence of Hollywood was widespread. No one was exempt from its charm and appeal, even though magazine articles started to appear expressing disappointment with the large number of low-quality films that arrived and bemoaning their detachment from the Italian situation. The two biggest star cults in Italy of the postwar years were those of Rita Hayworth and of Tyrone Power. Hayworth, a product of the glamour alchemy of Harry Cohn's Columbia Pictures,[39] introduced something that had been absolutely unknown in Italy and was sensationally new, namely a mixture of two previously separate qualities—innocence and sex appeal. She was not a vamp, yet neither was she a girl-next-door.[40] In *Blood and Sand* (Rouben Mamoulian, 1941), *Cover Girl* (Charles Vidor, 1944), and *Gilda* (Charles Vidor, 1946; see also chapter 2), she had a tremendous impact. It is notable that in *Ladri di biciclette* the protagonist Antonio Ricci is briefly employed putting up posters for *Gilda* in Rome until his bicycle is stolen.

Tyrone Power, the Latinate hero of *Blood and Sand*, was the number-one male star of the postwar years, an idol especially with adolescent girls. Pier Giorgio Amerio noted in *Hollywood* that, when "Ty" visited Turin in November 1947, his hotel was besieged by schoolgirls aged between twelve and eighteen (Italian "bobby-soxers," as he described them): "The girls shouted his name (they did not chant Tee-ro-nay, but Ty-rone: the high school element made its superiority felt)."[41] His wavy hair was imitated by boys. But, as so often occurred, the physical arrival on Italian soil of the star did not compound the cult but rather diminished it. When the crowds saw the personalities they had dreamed of, they were often surprised to find that they were smaller in stature and older than they had imagined. The same occurred with Hedy Lamarr, Rita Hayworth, and others who came to Italy later: their mystery was suddenly reduced. Power's popularity came to an end finally with his marriage in 1949 in Rome to Linda Christian. Although the event aroused enormous interest, it was more a wake than a new beginning.[42]

While the popularity of individual American stars was often brief, the phenomenon heralded a new idea of stardom: a more complete and commercialized version that was accompanied by new rituals and new identifications. The dominant American presence was thoroughly evident in cinema's parallel media: posters, fan press, and comics. It was extremely rare to see an Italian face on the front or back cover of *Star, Hollywood,* or any of the other magazines that flourished at this time. News of Veronica Lake, Rita Hayworth, Dorothy Lamour, Humphrey Bogart, Robert Taylor, and other American stars dominated, even though numerous articles dealt with Italian cinema and demonstrated a passionate commitment to its rebirth. Yet the workings of an industrial star system were not fully apparent since the film press of the period reveals imperfect attempts to adapt to the American model. Whereas, in America, only aspirant models and starlets did cheesecake shots, in Italy several of the young stars of the 1940s—Maria Denis, Elli Parvo, Elsa De Giorgi, Clara Calamai—posed after the war in bathing suits. Their pictures appeared here and there amid the mass of anonymous American flesh, depriving them of all distinctiveness and situating them in the eye of the reader on a level several degrees below that of a star. The distance with respect to the American stars was also reinforced by the magazines' habit of asking Italian actresses to write "Letters to" columns. For example, in *Star* of March 24, 1945, Mariella Lotti "wrote" to Veronica Lake, almost apologizing for having succeeded while the Americans were absent by force.

In particular, the experience of "Hollywood on the Tiber," which saw hundreds of American movie personnel arrive in Rome to shoot on location, witnessed the emergence of new links among film, fashion, publicity, advertising, and stardom. The phenomenon of stardom was extended in the Italian context along Hollywood lines as a result of this unprecedented American presence. Although not immediately, earlier difficulties in systematically creating strong and distinctive film personalities were resolved.

In the 1950s, Hollywood presented a series of new male stars like

Figure 9. Amedeo Nazzari in a photograph from circa 1950. Stephen Gundle collection.

Montgomery Clift and Marlon Brando who were often troubled and intro-spective.[43] In Italy too, there were some changes in the representation of mas-culinity, although the innovations were less marked. The most interesting case was that of Amedeo Nazzari. Before the war, he had been the leading male star. A tall Sardinian of rugged appearance, he forged a heroic persona in cos-tume dramas and war films that appealed widely. The film *Apparizione* (*Ap-parition*) (Jean de Limur, 1943) was striking for the fact that the actor played himself, Amedeo Nazzari the movie star, and even corrected a common mis-pronunciation of his name (it was in fact Nazzàri, not Nàzzari). He was fre-quently mentioned by our oral witnesses, especially in the South and Sardinia. Several remembered school screenings of his best-known film, *Luciano Serra pilota* (*Luciano Serra, Pilot*). Sometimes the memory was linked with that of a loved one: "My husband looked like Amedeo Nazzari . . . handsome he was, handsome and tall," said Lina C. from Cagliari (46: 21). Nazzari was the one great star whose popularity continued undiminished into the second half of the 1950s. Between 1949 and 1954 he made no fewer than twenty-eight films. However, his postwar career was rather different in tone from his prewar one. He appeared immediately after the war in two second-rank neorealist films— Alessandro Blasetti's *Un giorno nella vita* (*A Day in the Life*, 1946) and Alberto Lattuada's *Il bandito*—playing a partisan leader in the first and a soldier returning from a prison camp in the second, and then in a series of historical costume dramas mostly shot in Spain. Critics deplored these films but they were liked by working-class audiences. Nazzari then reached great heights of popularity in the early 1950s in a trilogy of low-budget melodramas directed by Raffaello Matarazzo—*Catene, Tormento* (*Torment*, 1950), *I figli di nessuno*—set in realistic southern milieus. Nazzari was partnered in these films by Yvonne Sanson, an actress of Greek origin who stood as a sensuous, maternal counterpart to his highly traditional masculinity. These films turned Nazzari into "a sort of Clark Gable of the backward areas."[44] So popular were they that Nazzari became the special idol of the rural and provincial audiences that were encountering cinema for the first time. One of our interviewees, Teta, in Rome, told us: "Yes, I cried a lot, I went to see all the tearjerkers. When Amedeo Nazzari was on, when there was Yvonne Sanson, *Catene, Tormento*, all those films, we went out with our eyes like this [filled with tears], but we were all happy" (20: 14). Three male interviewees (85, 86, 88) in San Giovanni in Fiore (Cosenza) remembered seeing Nazzari and Silvana Mangano in person, when they were in the area for the shooting of *Il lupo della Sila* (*The Wolf of the Sila*) (Duilio Coletti, 1949). "I was a small boy, of course. I saw him as a great man," said one of them, Antonio C. (88: 5).

Did the policy of star creation actually generate a star-led pattern of consumption of Italian cinema? To answer this question, it is necessary to refer to the analyses published in *Cinespettacolo*, a trade journal edited and largely written by Alessandro Ferraù. The journal argued that there was no active unified phenomenon of star veneration across Italy's four major film-going cities (Rome, Milan, Turin, Genoa). Most stars enjoyed a predominantly local appeal; the Neapolitan comic actor Totò and the rising Roman actor Alberto Sordi, for example, were capable of raising takings in Rome but not in the other three cities. Comics of all types, who mostly came from the South and Center, performed badly in Milan. In 1953 Ferraù argued that few names had sufficient drawing power to affect the success of a film. These were Nazzari, Silvana Mangano, and Totò.[45] By 1956 Gina Lollobrigida and, to a lesser extent, Sophia Loren had joined this list.[46] The women stars were the only ones whose draw was evident in several cities and therefore was tendentially national. In general there were many names that received a high degree of press attention that was not matched or merited by box office performance.

What this reveals is that, by the end of our period, the Italian film market was organized along industrial lines that were distinctive and reflected the differentiated levels of development in the economy and the existence of different intensities of media consumption. Italian cinema was advanced enough to generate and sustain personalities, who in certain instances functioned as full-fledged stars. But in other respects people who looked and behaved like stars relied solely on the print media for their prominence. This was one effect of a situation in which American companies had played a dominant role for the best part of thirty years and in which the media themselves were more developed than the general economy. This situation was not restricted to cinema but was also manifested in the way popular music became a commercial product and a media phenomenon through radio, as we discuss in the next chapter.

6 Radio and Recorded Music

Radio had various cultural uses and meanings in the period we are examining. We saw in chapter 1 how some of our interviewees spoke about their first contact with a radio set and what it had meant to them. As radio gained a mass audience, it became one of the most important channels for unifying diverse local and regional publics and creating a sense of national belonging, through regular appointments such as news bulletins and the coverage of popular sports events like the Giro d'Italia, discussed in the introduction, and international football matches. As the number of listeners expanded, radio also became, increasingly, a means of disseminating news and other kinds of information quickly to large numbers of people, first in the closely controlled political environment of Fascism, then under the political tutelage of the Christian Democrats. We shall examine these political uses and controls of radio in the wider context of state intervention in chapter 7. Here we concentrate on how radio functioned as a cultural industry with various branches: the production of programs and the employment both of permanent staff and contracted performers, the manufacture and sale of receivers or sets, and the delivery of audiences to advertising clients. Radio had a potentially very large market both as an information medium and as a medium for entertainment and became, by 1940, the main source for the circulation of popular music. It is on these entertainment functions, and in particular the role of music distribution, which has been relatively neglected in the academic literature on Italian radio, that this chapter concentrates. We shall examine here the close interrelationship of radio with the recorded music industry as well as the role of musical performers and their audiences.

The Broadcasting Industry

Radio broadcasting had started to develop in Italy in the same period as in Britain and Germany—the early 1920s—but its initial growth was slow and geographically uneven. By 1934, after ten years of regular transmissions, there were still only 440,000 licensed subscribers, just over one percent of the population, compared with five million at the same time in Germany and nearly six million in Britain,[1] and the majority of these were in the North and in cities and towns. Commentators in Italy were attentive to these international comparisons. In December 1934, "Radio-critica," the weekly page devoted to radio in *La Stampa* (the articles were unsigned but were attributed by Gianni Isola in 1990 to Santi Savarino), noted that with only ten subscribers per thousand people Italy was in thirty-first place in a list of fifty-eight countries. In December 1937, when the number of domestic subscribers had risen to just under 800,000, "Radio-critica" observed not only that Germany still had over six times more but also that even "small countries" like Belgium and Czechoslovakia already had a million subscribers.[2] In considering these figures it is important to bear in mind, as we noted in chapter 1, that there were always more actual listeners in Italy, as there were in these other countries, than there were licensed subscribers. Each private set normally had several listeners (there were between four and six family members in the average middle-class household), and there were also forms of public or semipublic group listening (in Italy in *osterie* [drinking places], dopolavoro clubs, and so on) as well as license-fee evaders and "radio hams" (*radioamatori*) who built their own crystal sets (*radio a galena*). Nevertheless, these international comparisons certainly have some validity, and they are striking as an indication of the relatively restricted radio market in interwar Italy.

The slow and unbalanced growth in the take-up of radio licenses may be partly explained by the spatial unevenness of the market for all cultural goods

Table 6.1. Radio license subscriptions in Italy, 1936–1954.

	Private	Special	Total All Subscriptions	Per 100 Inhabitants	Per 100 Families
1936	654,522	28,134	682,656	1.62	7.13
1937	782,418	40,453	822,871	1.94	8.48
1938	946,248	51,047	997,295	2.33	10.14
1939	1,106,982	62,957	1,169,939	2.70	11.75
1940	1,301,814	73,391	1,375,205	3.14	13.63
1941	1,556,300	82,017	1,638,317	3.71	16.02
1942	1,740,435	87,515	1,827,950	4.10	17.65
1943	1,697,759	86,487	1,784,246	3.97	17.00
1944	1,546,348	61,899	1,608,247	3.56	15.12
1945	1,596,431	50,035	1,646,466	3.62	15.28
1946	1,801,752	48,727	1,850,479	4.04	16.95
1947	1,961,153	50,301	2,011,454	4.37	18.19
1948	2,186,554	55,953	2,242,507	4.76	20.01
1949	2,544,721	66,609	2,611,330	5.53	23.00
1950	3,092,316	75,382	3,167,698	6.70	27.53
1951	3,617,056	86,085	3,703,141	7.82	31.76
1952	4,129,498	93,034	4,222,532	8.89	35.74
1953	4,661,832	99,200	4,761,032	9.98	39.72
1954	5,073,026	88,572	5,161,598	10.88	42.44

Source: *Gli abbonamenti alle radiodiffusioni nel 1981* (Rome: Rai Radiotelevisione italiana, 1982), Serie annuali, 217–18. "Special" subscriptions are those at institutional rates for public places: schools, *dopolavoro*, *osterie*, and so on.

in Italy, the result of wide variations in income and patchy distribution, but there were three further reasons peculiar to the radio market. The first was the determination of the manufacturers of radio sets, which persisted well into the 1930s, to keep the price high and sell to a high-spending, geographically restricted audience.[3] In January 1934 the "Radio-critica" column in *La Stampa* complained that the campaign by EIAR to win new subscribers, in which the prizes for persuading one's friends to buy a radio included a Fiat 514 and a prefabricated villa, was evidently designed to enlarge the existing middle-class audience rather than to create a mass one. "Italian industry still thinks of radio as a luxury toy. This is an unforgiveable mistake: to put it as straightforwardly as possible we need radio sets that cost no more than 400 lire, including the licence, payable in ten instalments."[4] The second reason was

Table 6.2. Regional distribution of radio license subscriptions, 1936–1954.

	1936	1938	1940	1942	1944	1946	1948	1950	1952	1954
Piemonte	93,376	128,817	172,707	227,351	219,124	246,979	289,217	395,638	504,062	584,618
Valle d'Aosta	3,046	4,508	6,354	9,669	9,631	3,386	5,038	7,361	9,903	12,185
Lombardia	149,904	211,127	284,819	366,505	364,330	406,143	505,809	702,426	906,154	1,043,875
Trentino Alto-Adige	12,218	18,612	24,516	33,205	33,854	40,215	43,532	58,723	77,552	93,793
Veneto	44,373	63,149	87,818	121,174	117,383	132,707	149,277	219,830	296,788	370,671
Friuli-Venezia Giulia	25,214	35,873	45,337	57,621	55,215	63,318	78,805	106,919	138,647	164,909
Liguria	51,226	67,732	88,572	108,859	88,275	96,696	116,626	164,936	212,255	252,238
Emilia-Romagna	48,029	75,037	104,437	150,774	123,553	150,066	187,946	268,853	356,208	443,309
NORTH	**427,386**	**604,855**	**814,560**	**1,075,158**	**1,011,365**	**1,139,510**	**1,376,250**	**1,924,686**	**2,501,569**	**2,965,598**
% North	**62.60**	**60.65**	**59.23**	**58.82**	**62.88**	**61.58**	**61.37**	**60.76**	**59.24**	**57.45**
Toscana	51,533	73,279	100,564	136,205	95,710	122,188	155,957	233,965	319,455	385,654
Umbria	6,725	10,766	16,927	23,277	17,560	21,487	26,450	40,258	55,987	69,792
Marche	10,408	16,357	24,863	35,354	28,476	33,711	43,239	68,981	97,116	121,643
Lazio	66,145	97,265	140,961	183,711	142,062	166,061	200,667	267,870	354,342	414,153
CENTER	**134,811**	**197,667**	**283,315**	**378,547**	**283,808**	**343,447**	**426,313**	**611,074**	**826,900**	**991,242**
% Center	**19.75**	**19.82**	**20.60**	**20.71**	**17.65**	**18.56**	**19.01**	**19.29**	**19.59**	**19.20**
Abruzzi	6,611	10,841	15,477	21,130	13,331	17,189	24,473	37,850	58,853	82,895
Molise	2,204	3,170	4,373	5,618	5,020	5,198	6,954	10,582	15,010	20,771
Campania	43,074	67,789	92,653	122,894	102,829	123,061	140,375	197,219	268,090	355,926

Continued on the next page

Table 6.2. Continued

Puglia	23,072	35,253	49,958	68,799	64,545	76,894	95,450	124,363	171,210	234,002
Basilicata	2,883	4,227	5,379	6,538	6,961	6,523	8,662	12,818	18,987	27,058
Calabria	8,158	14,383	20,195	26,711	21,831	24,380	27,733	41,527	63,715	88,008
SOUTH	**86,002**	**135,663**	**188,035**	**251,690**	**214,517**	**253,245**	**303,647**	**424,359**	**595,865**	**808,660**
% South	**12.60**	**13.60**	**13.67**	**13.77**	**13.34**	**13.69**	**13.54**	**13.40**	**14.11**	**15.68**
Sicilia	27,335	47,251	71,231	97,181	78,308	91,564	109,532	164,750	237,980	317,135
Sardegna	7,122	11,859	18,064	25,374	20,249	22,713	26,765	42,829	60,218	78,963
ISLANDS	**34,457**	**59,110**	**89,295**	**122,555**	**98,557**	**114,277**	**136,297**	**207,579**	**298,198**	**396,098**
% Islands	**5.05**	**5.93**	**6.50**	**6.70**	**6.13**	**6.17**	**6.08**	**6.55**	**7.06**	**7.67**
TOTAL ITALY	**682,656**	**997,295**	**1,375,205**	**1,827,950**	**1,608,247**	**1,850,479**	**2,242,507**	**3,167,698**	**4,222,532**	**5,161,598**

Source: *Gli abbonamenti alle radiodiffusioni nel 1981* (Rome: Rai Radiotelevisione italiana, 1982), Serie annuali, 226–227, 230–231. These figures may be compared with the distribution of the population as a whole. In the 1951 census this was: North 44.5%, Center 18.2%, South 25.1%, Islands 12.1% (Antonio Golini, *Distribuzione della popolazione, migrazioni interne e urbanizzazione in Italia* (Rome: Università di Roma, Istituto di Demografia, 1974).

that high taxes were imposed initially, and not reduced until 1934, on anyone who installed a radio for use in a public place such as a bar or restaurant. The third was lack of impetus from the state, whose relationship with the new medium until the early 1930s has been aptly described as one of "benevolent neglect."[5] The beginnings of a concerted attempt by the state to expand radio listening came only with the launch in 1931 of the Ente Radio Rurale (ERR), an organization that aimed to take the medium beyond its overwhelmingly urban, northern, middle-class audience and to create a new, nationwide mass audience, particularly among schoolchildren and small farmers.

Like the British government and the BBC, which started as a private company in 1922 (as the British Broadcasting Company) and became a public corporation in 1927, the government in Italy had given an "exclusive concession" (in other words, a monopoly) to one private broadcasting company, called URI (Unione Radiofonica Italiana) from 1924 to 1927, EIAR from 1928 to 1944, and RAI (Radio Audizioni Italia) thereafter. Unlike the BBC, however, this company was, from 1926, dual-funded, that is to say its activities were paid for out of commercial advertising revenue (like the two main American networks NBC and CBS, launched respectively in 1926 and 1927) as well as from the license fee paid (in theory) by subscribers (*abbonati*) to the Ministry of Posts. Both in its legal status and in its mode of funding, broadcasting in Italy was therefore a mixture of public and private, with a tension between political and commercial interests built into its very structure.

While various sectors of Italian industry had strong commercial interests in radio for the manufacture of equipment for transmission and reception—electricity, electronics, glass (vacuum tube valves), chemicals (plastics), steel (antennae and cables), rubber (cable sheaths), and telephones (landlines)—the "radio industry" as such consisted of two main branches: one that produced and distributed programs (EIAR/RAI) and another that manufactured radio sets. The Società Idroelettrica Piemontese (SIP), a Turin-based company involved in electricity and telephony, had in the early 1930s extended its control over the radio sector. It became the major shareholder in EIAR, acquired the shares of the radio advertising concessionary SIPRA (Società Italiana Pubblicità Radiofonica e Affini), and launched the record company Cetra. At the time of the takeover of SIP by the state holding company IRI (Istituto per la Ricostruzione Industriale) a decree law, dated July 29, 1933, allowed representatives of the electrical and other industries to sit on the EIAR's board but expressly prevented the EIAR from manufacturing or selling sets.[6] As in some of the other cultural industries, a conflict of interests consequently arose among the different branches of the radio industry. From the late 1920s the program makers aimed at a mass broadcasting market and wanted to help create this by putting a cheap set out for sale, but the manufacturers at first resisted, fearing that the market take-up of cheap sets would not be sufficient to offset the increased total production costs and the reduction in revenue per item. It was only when the state began to be directly involved in radio that a real impetus was given to the sale of cheap sets and the manufacturers' fears started to be assuaged. In July 1934, shortly before his death, Enrico Marchesi, president of the EIAR and ERR, exhorted the society of radio constructors to market a cheap set, and they came up with a design for one costing 350 lire. However, it was not until May 1937 that the first "popular" radio set, costing 430 lire and bearing the distinctly Fascist name of Radiobalilla ("Balilla" was the name of the Fascist boys' organization), was actually put on sale. The EIAR's weekly magazine *Radiorario* welcomed the new set in pedagogical rather than political terms. The Radioballila would open the door to "culture" for the masses:

This attractive coinage should be understood in the sense that it is a set for the people, sold at a very reasonable price, constructed essentially with the aim of allowing all the working classes of the city and the country to buy a radio ... made by an Italian company using Italian materials and for the Italian people. Although it serves a specifically national purpose it does not exclude the universality of culture because through the programmes it receives all of human knowledge is put at the disposal of the masses, like a spoken word encyclopedia, a universe for the people.[7]

The relative lack of state involvement in the early years has been widely attributed to a delay on the part of the Fascist government in recognizing the political potential of the medium, despite the fact that an Italian engineer, Guglielmo Marconi, had played a leading role in its development and in the international marketing of the technology. While it is true that the Fascist government did not really capitalize politically on radio before the 1930s, it is not really correct to speak of a "delay," since no other government before the 1930s recognized the political potential of radio. Radio technology had initially been used (until around 1920) for point-to-point communications, first as "wireless telegraphy" and then with voice transmission. The first clients for radio equipment were merchant shipping firms and the armed forces, which used the medium to exchange messages at sea, in the air, or on the battlefield. When the technology was adapted to broadcasting in the early 1920s it was almost universally conceived of as a medium for entertainment or "culture" and the large majority of broadcasts consisted of music. Moreover, before an effective use could be made of the medium for political broadcasts a potential mass audience already had to be in place. The development of broadcasting predominantly as a medium for music, the type of music that was broadcast, and the high cost of sets meant that in Italy radio became locked initially into a pattern of middle-class cultural consumption, which, not surprisingly, in turn affected the government's perceptions of the nature and potential of the medium itself.

When the Fascist government did become more involved with radio it did not control it directly or totally, but rather appropriated it for certain uses. It still had to negotiate against the commercial interests of the broadcasters and radio manufacturers, who were interested in transmitting programs that would encourage people to buy sets and take out subscriptions. The key personnel in the EIAR were representatives of the industry rather than party nominees and Fascist personnel were outnumbered by Catholics. Gianni Isola has spoken of the "massive presence of Catholics among the personnel and external collaborators of the EIAR at every level and rank."[8] It is true, nevertheless, that the Fascist state's involvement in radio increased during the 1930s and that a model of direct governmental control of informational broadcasting was established then that would be resumed after 1945. The postwar RAI retained from the prewar EIAR an articulated structure in its personnel, which consisted of three main categories: *tecnici* or representatives of the industry, journalists (of whom political journalists were a discrete and important subcategory), and musicians, including the various radio orchestras and bands.

Another important continuity was in patterns of radio listening, which we looked at in chapter 1. Radio had been, from the beginnings of broadcasting, an international medium both in that its flows of signals did not respect national borders and in that its listeners often picked up foreign stations, which were sometimes marked on the tuning dials. For listeners with homemade crystal sets it was a point of pride to find and identify distant stations, and many of these were listened to, mainly for their music programs. When the antifascist broadcasts from outside Italy began during the Spanish Civil War they therefore grafted themselves onto an existing pattern of "exotic" listening from the consumer's point of view.

Radio contributed greatly to the growing popularity of sport. Cycling, which had been promoted in the 1930s, was especially popular. As we noted in the introduction, it was the sport of a rural society that admired the strength and determination of cyclists who were often men from poor backgrounds reflecting the hopes and desires of ordinary people. Radio added a dimension to the celebrity of sports champions, who were described and praised as well as being interviewed. The commentator Niccolò Carosio became himself a personality thanks to his competence and enthusiasm; letters to the *Radiocorriere* asked for his photograph to be published.[9] The cyclists Fausto Coppi and Gino Bartali, the two great champions and rivals of the period, had been well known before the war but it was only from 1946 that they became

Figure 10. Cover by Gino Boccasile for *Il Canzoniere della radio,* 1941. By permission of Messaggerie Musicali, Milan.

a focus of passion and the country divided into two in support of one or the other. They were symbols of hope and rebirth, strong, "real men" who won through sacrifice and willpower.

Both figured prominently in the memories of our male interviewees, whereas the great rivals of the early 1930s, Learco Guerra and Alfredo Binda, evoked few specific observations even among older men. Aldo B., born in 1912, said, "I was a fan of Binda but I had no preference between Coppi and Bartali" (9: 11). Augusto A. in Rome, born in 1922, recalled "there were rumors that Binda was antifascist, whereas Guerra [was not]. . . . It was said that Coppi was a socialist and that Bartali was a Christian Democrat, so I was for Coppi, that one was a socialist. . . . He was closer to my ideas; Guerra no, I didn't like him" (62: 23). However, allegiances were not always related to politics. Although he was a Catholic, Livio S. preferred Coppi because he considered him to be the better athlete:

I think that even by today's standards he was a complete man athletically, because he was strong going uphill and an excellent track performer, whereas Bartali was extremely strong going uphill but on the straight, whether because of his build or for some other reason I'm not aware of, I thought Coppi was stronger than Bartali. (17: 27–28)

Bartali's particular strength in ascents, however, led others to regard him as the better of the two (18: 18). Aside from political and strictly sporting considerations, Coppi attracted identification because "he used his brain" (85/86: 17–18) and because he was the perennial underdog.

There was a transitional situation in Italian radio during the war, when broadcasting reproduced the divisions of the country into two (the EIAR and some of its personnel were absorbed by the Republic of Salò; antifascist stations transmitted under the supervision of the Psychological Warfare Branch of the Allied Military Government in the liberated cities: Palermo, Bari, Naples in 1943; Rome in 1944, and so forth). Broadcasting was briefly decentralized at the time of liberation, and then was soon "normalized" with a resumption of the old centralized system and a return of many of the old personnel (see chapter 7). It is true that the so-called wind from the north, that is, the influence of antifascist ideologies, the partial turnover of personnel in the radio, and the now officially permitted openness to foreign influences, all meant that there were some noticeable changes to program formats and contents. One example were the experiments with a "people's theater" in the late 1940s, which fitted with contemporary experiments on the stage. Nevertheless, the dominant pattern from a managerial and organizational point of view was that of continuity.

Recorded Music

In their international history of the recording industry, Pekka Gronow and
Ilpo Saunio noted that up to the 1930s "the Italian record industry had been
almost entirely in foreign hands."[10] The foundation in 1933 of the EIAR's
Cetra record division—effectively a form of state intervention, given the absorption of EIAR by the state holding company IRI in the same year—was
designed as a partial corrective to this. Nevertheless, the record industry remained dominated by a combination of non-Italian companies and companies with Italian names that were owned or controlled by foreign ones.

The evolution of the market in Italy for both record players and discs
followed a similar pattern to that of radio receivers. In the 1930s ownership
of gramophones and records (78 rpm discs) began to expand, as had that of
commercially manufactured radio sets, beyond the elite market to which they
had been largely restricted since the early years of the century, when the cost
of record players had been high and they had been designed as luxury pieces
of furniture for the middle-class living room (*salotto*). The expansion continued into the 1940s, with a notable rise after World War II. In 1924, only
1,314 gramophones and 10,458 records were sold in Italy.[11] In the United States,
by contrast, about 150 million records were sold in 1929 and about 30 million
each in the same year in Britain and Germany, the two largest European markets.[12] By 1948 the number of records sold in Italy had risen to about three
million. It expanded further through the rest of the decade and very considerably in the 1950s.

The prehistory of the record industry up to the 1930s may be rapidly
summarized. Internationally, after a first phase (1870s–1890s) of technological
startup, patenting, and refinement of the techniques for recording and re-
producing sounds with a needle on either a rotating cylinder (Thomas Alva
Edison's phonograph) or a flat disc (Emile Berliner's gramophone), a second
phase had followed, from the 1890s to the early 1920s, of the first mass marketing of records worldwide. In the United States, where both the phonograph
and the gramophone had been patented, this was the period when records became the main source of technically reproduced music in the home. As in the
film industry, though from an even earlier stage, U.S. companies, and notably
the two largest firms Victor and Columbia, dominated the international market, directly or through their subsidiaries. In Europe the main record producing and distributing countries were Britain and Germany, where Emile Berliner (who had grown up in Germany before emigrating to the United States at
nineteen) was instrumental in founding, respectively, the Gramophone Company (in London, but with its presses in Hanover) and Deutsche Grammo-

phon. There were, however, also autonomous local record companies. In Germany in the 1910s the Carl Lindström conglomerate, consisting of various record labels managed by Max Strauss, became a strong international force, capable of competing in certain markets (such as South America) against Victor and Gramophone. The leading French company was Pathé, which had diversified from cinema into recorded music, initially with its own patented "vertical cut" records that could be played only on its own machines since they were incompatible with both the Edison and the Berliner players.

In Italy, the first companies to be established, in the first years of the century, were Fonodisco Italiano Trevisan (renamed Fonit in 1926), Fonotecnica, and the Neapolitan firm Fonotipia. The last of these, founded in 1904, was subsequently taken over by the Lindström group and in fact the history of the Italian record industry from a very early stage was one of fusions with or takeovers by foreign companies, who were keen both to exploit the Italian market for their own records and to record Italian singers, both operatic and popular. Neapolitan song was very successful, particularly among the Italian-American communities in North America, but also with a wider non-Italian public. Italian-Americans were among the early audiences for recordings of opera arias (early records lasted no more than two to three minutes, so the distribution on disc of longer highlights, let alone complete operas, was unthinkable).

The domestic market leader in the 1930s and 40s was La Voce del Padrone-Columbia-Marconiphone (VCM), the result of a merger in the late 1920s of the Società Nazionale del Grammofono (founded in Milan in 1912) with two British companies that were themselves linked to American companies. Columbia in Britain had been set up originally as a subsidiary of the Columbia Graphophone Company, founded in the United States in 1894, but when the latter's fortunes fell badly in the early 1920s against those of its market rival, Victor (The Victor Talking Machine Company), it was bought out (1924) by its former British subsidiary, which thus became the parent company. His Master's Voice was the trademark name (from the painting by Francis Barraud of his brother's dog, Nipper, listening to a gramophone, used extensively in the company's publicity) of Victor in the United Kingdom and its British affiliate, the Gramophone Company. The creation of VCM in Italy was part of a wider international pattern of mergers and takeovers between record companies and between these and broadcasting companies in the first decade of broadcast radio and microphone recordings (as opposed to direct recordings onto wax). In the United States, Victor itself was bought by the Radio Corporation of America in 1929 to form RCA Victor; in Britain, the Gramophone Company and Columbia merged in 1931 to become Electric and Musical Industries (EMI).

Other companies operating in Italy were Durium, founded in the 1940s, and Odeon-Parlophon and Eterofon, both subsidiaries of German companies. In 1943–1945, VCM fell into the hands of the Salò regime and underwent a period of interim wartime administration (*gestione straordinaria*), after which, with the Liberation, it came under the more or less direct control of the British parent company in Hayes, southeast of London. Franco Crepax, who worked for VCM for one year in 1952–1953 before moving to Ricordi, recalled in an interview with Marcella Filippa that after the war VCM

reopened with British personnel or personnel directly dependent on the parent firm. I remember that the managing director when I arrived was Roger Degois, who had been the manager of Columbia in Beijing for twenty-five years.... The other top directors were British, but the lower levels of management were all Italian. This was the first firm to produce long-playing records and I was particularly lucky to have been with them at the time. The long-playing record emerged during the war. The first LPs that arrived in Italy came with the Allied troops. They did not last very long, but the technique was that of the microgroove, and above all they were unbreakable.[13]

The period after 1945 marked a decisive change in the recorded music market, with the reentry of American jazz and dance music, now newly popularized by the Allied occupation, and the important technological advances of the early 1950s: the rise of the microgroove disc and of variable-speed gramophones, 33 and 45 rpm. Mario De Luigi, in what remains the only history published to date of the postwar Italian record industry (his main source was the trade journal *Musica e Dischi*), suggested that the late 1940s were also watershed years between two systems in the light music sector. The earlier system centered on the figure of the music publisher, who would launch a song or dance tune on the radio and, if it was successful, would have it cut on disc and distributed, parceling work up among the different record companies, each of which had its own artists under contract.[14] The later system came to be driven more by the record companies themselves, which began after the war to develop more distinctive house styles and to compete to get major domestic and foreign artists into their catalogues. In 1948 two new companies were founded, Compagnia Generale del Disco, the first to be run by a light musician, Teddy Reno, and Celson, founded by the Swiss brothers Walter and Ernesto Guertler, which specialized in jazz. At the same time the existing companies started to buy and launch foreign catalogues and this laid the basis for the "catalogue war" of the late 1950s.[15] Microgroove records took off after 1954. According to Giulia Baldi, by 1957 45 rpm records accounted for 55 percent of RCA Italiana's sales in 1957 and 33 rpm for 16 percent.[16] After 1950 others emerged: Angelicum and Italmusica (both in 1950) and Music (in 1951). In 1951 two other European companies also set up subsidiaries in Italy: Pathé and DGG (both distributed by VCM).

In 1953, RCA Italiana was founded (originally with the name Radio e Televisione Italiana) as an Italian subsidiary of RCA Victor. The factory was built twelve kilometers out on the Via Tiburtina on the eastern outskirts of Rome and, like the American parent company, it manufactured hardware—record players, radio sets, television sets—as well as records. The founding of RCA Italiana, according to Mario De Luigi, "marks the end of the first phase—the pioneer phase—of the history of recorded music in Italy and the beginning of a new phase where marketing acquires unprecedented importance and the American philosophy of music as business develops alongside the search for artistic production."[17] For the first three years of its activity it made a loss. Its fortunes were turned round in 1956 when P. J. Casella, president of the Canadian RCA, came in as chief executive officer and reorganized the firm, cutting staff by 35 percent (eighty-five employees went) and appointing new managers to the firm's creative and commercial divisions. In 1956, 74 percent of its turnover of 529 million lire came from records and the remainder from hardware. Italy was also geographically placed to target export markets for RCA Victor records elsewhere in Europe as well as in Africa and Asia. In 1957, 7.3 percent of its turnover came from exports.[18] In that year total turnover had risen to 953 million lire (760 million from records, 193 million from hardware); by 1958 it was 1,379 million, with a net profit of 55 million. By 1958 the company was producing over 20 percent of the national total of records.[19] Fundamental to RCA Italiana's success in the popular Italian song market was its recording of singers from the Festival della Canzone Italiana in San Remo, launched in 1951. Radio remained fundamental for the diffusion of music and thus for enhancing record sales, but the record industry now also developed synergies with sport and cinema. The first magazine devoted to singing stars, *Sorrisi e canzoni,* started publication a few months after the first San Remo festival.

Franco Crepax recalled an interesting case in 1953 of VCM marketing its own recording of a piece of music that had already become a hit in the United States:

It so happened that the year I was at La Voce del Padrone . . . a Charlie Chaplin film called *Luci della ribalta* [*Limelight*] arrived in Italy. In this film there was a famous dancer, I don't remember her name, and Chaplin had written the music for the film, he was an amateur composer and he wrote a piece which in Italian was called "Arlecchinata," I don't know what it was in the original. The Voce del Padrone was the licencee of this recording through American contracts and there was a lot of commotion because we had heard that in America the record was a big hit, for the first time a record had a mass success, so to speed things up our artistic director, who was called Dino Olivieri, went to the cinema to see the film, since they hadn't sent us the recording yet, and with a flashlight he wrote down the music in the cinema and we cut this tune very quickly and it sold 45,000 copies, which was a huge number at the time because normally a record would sell two or three thousand copies.[20]

Popular Music and Society

Radio made popular personalities of several of its announcers, commentators, and singers. In most cases their fame derived simply from familiarity and was circumscribed to their professional role. Nevertheless, it is important to relate the phenomenon to the broader context of radio. The medium covered sports events and musical and theatrical performances and it also invented quizzes, competitions, and entertainment shows. Anna Lucia Natale suggests that the paternalism of the Fascist regime and the censorship it practiced were such that the purely entertainment broadcasts had no significance other than distraction or escapism. They were not, she argues, part of the development of mass culture as it manifested itself in the United States and France at this time.[21] Yet it is misleading to imply that these programs were devoid of implications other than indirect subservience to the regime. The creation of patterns of interest and identification that were tendentially national and had nothing to do with political imperatives signaled the emergence of a commercial culture that bore some of the characteristics of mass culture. Gianni Isola argued that "more than an instrument of propaganda" radio was "a great machine for dreams, enjoyment and entertainment for a society in profound transformation."[22] The linkages and mutual reinforcements among radio, the recorded music industry, manufacturers, film production, and publishing were part of a trend that would develop further in the postwar years.

Nevertheless, there were some peculiarities in the Italian experience of radio. Isola recalled that a Franciscan monk, Vittorino Facchinetti, reached such popularity in the interwar years that "he was in fact the first real popular star of Italian radio."[23] His wide appeal was demonstrated when, after receiving an insulting letter from a listener who declared himself ready to set about the monk "with kicks up the backside," he invited his listeners to express their support. The avalanche of over four thousand letters he received began a dialogue with the audience that was aided by Facchinetti's radiophonic eloquence.[24]

Despite this example, it was mostly quizzes and entertainment that aroused keen interest. Many of the shows were sponsored by companies, which also used the medium for advertising. The most famous series in this regard was *Quattro moschettieri* (*Four Musketeers*), a parody of the Dumas novel mixed with Italian elements drawn from the *commedia dell'arte* that was aimed at a youth audience. Broadcast on Thursday lunchtimes in 1934 (with a second series in 1936), it was jointly sponsored by two foodstuff manufacturers, Buitoni and Perugina (a collaboration that by itself showed the limited nature of Italian consumption). The show was a complete entertainment: it was a radio play, it contained humor and music, and it was accompanied by a book and by discs. It also gave rise to a film. The second season was linked by the sponsors to a collection of illustrated cards (*figurine*), one of which could be found in the packaging of each of their products. With prizes including books, sports equipment, record players, and even a Fiat Topolino for multiple completed albums (200 in the case of the Topolino), the cards, drawn by Angelo Bioletto, became much sought-after and the hunt for the rarest of all, depicting the characters of Ferocious Saladin and Beautiful Sulamita, drove fans to desperate measures.[25]

Film and theater actors acquired an additional platform with radio series like *Le attrici e la moda* (*Actresses and Fashion*), broadcast in 1935, and programs of entertainment news. The expansion of radio ensured that film was not the only medium in which the state took a hand in the construction of stardom. The competitions launched by EIAR in 1938 and 1939 to find new singers to front in-house light music orchestras attracted vast numbers of entries: 2,500 entered the 1938 competition from whom 14 were chosen, while 3,000 took part in the second competition. Some of the new names, such as Oscar Carboni and Ernesto Bonino, were popularized through mechanisms such as vocal "duels" on the radio. The Barzizza and Angelini orchestras released many discs in addition to being radio regulars and they toured Italy promoting the 1939 film *Viva la radio!,* which featured and made visible the singers who otherwise were known to many only by their voices. The two orchestra leaders were distinguished by a difference of style and repertoire. Barzizza was "the more daring," recalled former EIAR and RAI employee Cesare G. (89: 21). For accordion player Aldo G. (115: 17) he "had another culture musically, he played . . . more challenging and jazzy pieces, whereas Angelini found this way of pleasing the simple folk more."

Despite the case of Facchinetti, the general climate was not favorable to an excessive emphasis on personality. Praise was reserved for actors and singers who lacked star quality and who exhibited frugality and ordinariness. "Bonino is surely no Adonis but he is certainly a dear, good boy," wrote one observer. "He does not adopt the attitude of star and when he is not behind a microphone he is among friends . . . in the barracks or keeping company with the oarsmen and swimmers of his native Turin, on the River Po."[26] But this comment appeared in the weekly, *Il canzoniere della radio,* published from

1939, which catered to music fans and brought them news of their favorites. Some of the most popular singers of the period were men like the Florentine Carlo Buti who popularized the operatic *bel canto* style. His warm tones and falsetto capabilities were demonstrated in a series of songs that contrasted city and country life (the most celebrated was "Reginella campagnola" [Country Queen]). He made several musical films as well as being a radio favorite and a top record seller. According to Gianni Borgna, "He became the hero of the working-class suburbs of the cities and of small villages which, starved of operatic music, satisfied their taste for opera with a repertoire that swung between modest rustic trysts and violent urban passions."[27]

While some singers drew inspiration from Italian musical traditions, such as opera, Neapolitan popular song, and local repertoires, others looked to France or to the United States for sounds, attitudes, and rhythms that possessed a modern edge and more easily inspired listeners to dance. After his return from Hollywood, Alberto Rabagliati (mentioned in chapter 5) built a career as a crooner of the American type and became a radio favorite (he had his own show every Monday evening in 1941) with songs that included the self-referential "Quando canta Rabagliati" (When Rabagliati Sings), which named many of his colleagues, similar to Bonino's "La famiglia cantarina" (The Singing Family), which contained references to all the famous singers and orchestras of the day. Natalino Otto traveled regularly between New York and Genoa and developed a modern, jazz-inspired repertoire that caused controversy because it seemed directly based on black music. These singers were sustained by the fashion for swing that began in 1934 and that saw some American artists, including Louis Armstrong, perform in Italy. However, Italian versions generally took their inspiration more from white swing orchestras like that of Paul Whiteman.[28] The Trio Lescano, three sisters of Dutch origin, were EIAR favorites, whose American-style vocal harmonies and witty lyrics showed the limits of innovation. Mostly their songs had an artificial, infantile feel. Only "Maramao, perché sei morto?" (Maramao, Why Did You Die?) was controversial on account of a possible, but in fact inadvertent, allusion to the recent demise of the senior Fascist Costanzo Ciano. Quite unlike the American Andrews Sisters, the Trio Lescano never tackled sleazy themes; even the upbeat "Ma le gambe" (But The Legs), in Gianfranco Baldazzi's view, "turned into the kind of homespun and cheeky eroticism palatable to the Fascist petty bourgeoisie."[29]

The Trio Lescano were one of the few acts to suffer as a result of the Nazi occupation. Banned from the radio on account of their mother's Jewish background, they continued to perform live until they were arrested in Milan in late 1943 and imprisoned. At the end of the conflict they emigrated to Argentina. During the liberation there was no purge or internal review of the music business. Only the opera star Beniamino Gigli found himself accused of collaboration after the arrival of the Allies.[30] Many singers had performed and recorded propaganda songs such as "Faccetta nera" (Little Blackface Girl) about the colonial seizure of Abyssinia, which was made into a hit by Buti, and war songs, including "Vincere" (Victory), among others. Gigli, however, had worked in Germany and had sung for Goebbels, Goering, and Hitler on their visits to Italy. The tenor claimed in his memoirs that, concerning Hitler, "I knew nothing about his political activities and I never had occasion to exchange more than a few words of circumstance with him."[31] He claimed to have sung indiscriminately for everyone but nevertheless he was placed under investigation and only resumed performing in late 1945.

The liberation, as we noted in chapter 1, heralded an explosion of American music and of dancing, both of which had been banned since 1940. Jazz and swing, which were most associated with the big band swing of Glenn Miller and Benny Goodman, set the tone while modern crooners like Tommy Dorsey, Bing Crosby, and Frank Sinatra enjoyed enormous popularity for several years. Since Italian adaptations of swing had been popular in the war years, domestic orchestras, like those headed by Angelini and Barzizza, were able to adapt. The period also saw the arrival of novel Latin American rhythms and sensual dances including the rumba and the raspa, which were joined in 1954 by the mambo and soon after that by the cha-cha. The demand for entertainment and distraction produced numerous opportunities for musical performers. Dance halls, radio stations, and Allied entertainment organizers all needed talent. While this provided opportunities for emerging performers, some established singers interrupted their careers or fell out of fashion. Natalino Otto remained popular and so, with a little less fortune, did Rabagliati.

Italian melodies were never entirely displaced during the postwar years, even in a climate that American music seemed to capture best. Gradually, Italian passions and interests won out and reasserted themselves. Radio won a wider popularity than ever before at this time because it matched this trend and positioned itself as a desirable object and status symbol. Competitions were held to relaunch radio as a national medium and increase subscriptions. An ever greater share of programming was given over to light shows, while the popularity of the Giro d'Italia and its undisputed aces, Coppi and Bartali, owed much to the fact that the race was covered on radio nine times every day and that the broadcasts incorporated songs, music, and quizzes.[32] Cinema too received ample coverage. After the war the RAI's two networks, the Rete rossa and Rete azzurra (Red and Blue networks), featured a variety of film programs introduced by critics while the program *Polvere di stelle* (Stardust) had interviews with foreign and national stars.[33] The medium acted as an entertainment training ground and created a number of personalities who would later achieve wider success in cinema. The Roman actor Alberto Sordi first came to public attention by performing sketches during the interval of the Barzizza orchestra's Friday evening show on the Rete rossa. He developed a series of comic characters that he would further elaborate in his early cinema work with Fellini (*Lo sceicco bianco* and *I vitelloni*) and Steno (*Un americano a Roma*).

Radio was responsible for the initial success of a song contest that would rapidly become an annual event and an institution: the San Remo song festival. Like many radio phenomena of the period, this contest had a precursor in the prewar years. But only the democratic climate, the growth of the market for records, and the recruitment of singers from the social groups that were coming to the center of national life for the first time sealed the success of an event that was in fact highly defensive. The competition was the invention of a RAI musical director, Giulio Razzi, who brought together song publishers to defend Italian song against the tide of foreign music and the rhythmic contaminations of jazz and South American dance music. A commission selected twenty songs from 250 submitted that would be performed by the Angelini orchestra and singers associated with it. The audience itself was called to vote to choose the winning three songs. From the beginning the festival was broadcast live over three evenings from the ballroom of the San Remo casino, starting in January 1951. It attracted only minor interest in the coastal resort itself, but the audiences and public involvement in the radio broadcasts were very substantial and they grew by leaps and bounds in the years that followed. The festival relaunched Italian song, creating tunes and lyrics that were repeatedly played on the radio and that sold huge numbers of records.

Various observers have questioned the value of the bland and disengaged songs that the festival blessed and that became synonymous with mainstream light music. For Borgna, the absence in Italian music of a current of renewal like that which ran through postwar cinema led to a situation in which nostalgia, patriotism, and conventional amorous and familial sentiments provided the main source material for songs.[34] Baldazzi argues that when it came to song, republican Italy "does not seem all that different from the Italy that preceded it." The return of melodic escapism was wholly retrograde, a "triumph of mediocrity, framed by violins and showers of rose petals."[35] The conservatism of the content of the festival, especially in the first few years, was striking but it was vital as a promotional mechanism for Italian music and for a new generation of singers. The audience in the postwar years was no longer mainly middle-class but far broader. The specialist weekly, *Sorrisi e canzoni,* catered to public curiosity about singers, the most popular of whom became lower-class idols who would remain successful for decades.

The first winner of the festival, Nilla Pizzi, had taken part during the war in the EIAR's search for new voices and had debuted on the radio in 1942. In 1946 she won a two-year recording contract from the Voce del Padrone and scored several successes singing for the Angelini orchestra. Her winning song in the first San Remo festival was "Grazie dei fiori" (Thank You For The Flowers), in which she competed with the Duo Fasano and Achille Togliani. The following year her songs "Vola colomba" (Fly, Dove), "Papaveri e papere" (Poppies and Ducks), and "Una donna prega" (A Woman Entreats) won respectively first, second, and third place, a phenomenon that led to her being dubbed "the queen of song" (*la regina della canzone*). In the years that followed she won the festival several more times and consolidated her position as one of the most popular singers in the country. A solidly built young woman from the province of Bologna with a warm manner and spontaneous personality, Pizzi possessed a voice that Borgna describes as "modern, exotic and sensual."[36] Married and separated in the space of two years at the start of the war, she became Angelini's lover before beginning a tumultuous liaison with fellow singer Gino Latilla.

Thanks to *Sorrisi e canzoni*, which regularly published photographs of her and other singers, Nilla Pizzi became an all-around personality. To the initial consternation of the singers, the magazine gossiped frequently about their private lives, with articles on Pizzi and Latilla and on Togliani and his then girlfriend Sophia Loren (their engagement was announced in the issue of September 20, 1953 but then denied the following week). In 1954 two regular features were entitled "La loro vita privata" (Their private lives), which pictured performers in their homes, and "Microfono pettegolo" (Gossip microphone), which contained a mix of fact and rumor. The professional lives of the singers were of great interest; for example, when Pizzi declared in December 1953 that she was leaving the Angelini Orchestra and RAI, the magazine received thousands of letters.[37] When she reappeared shortly afterward, with a new slim physique, blond hair, and a contract with the new company RCA Italiana, her fans breathed a sigh of relief and were undisturbed by the brusque change of image.

The film industry, which at this time of expansion was ever ready to capitalize on popularity, was not slow to see potential in Pizzi. Ever since the 1930s, musical films had contributed to the celebrity of a select group of singers including the heir of Caruso, Gigli, who appeared in his first film, the Italo-German production *Non ti scordar di me* (*Forget Me Not*), directed by Augusto Genina, in 1935. The success of this led the tenor to make over fifteen more films, most of which, including the 1940 film *Mamma,* launched songs that became famous. He also starred in several American movies. Gigli acknowledged in his memoirs that the films were of poor quality, yet they brought him "sizeable fees."[38] In addition:

They guaranteed me a huge audience, which I could not have reached otherwise. In every part of the world the films were shown in towns and villages that were too small or too remote to be included on a concert tour. Even in large cities they got my songs heard by people who for one reason or another—lack of money or culture or interest in music—had never seen the inside of a concert hall or opera house. This was brought home to me by the thousands of letters I received, so wildly enthusiastic that after a certain point they stopped being flattering and became worrying, like when a lady wrote from Berlin to say that *in one month* she had seen *Non ti scordar di me* no fewer than *seventy-seven* times![39]

Such a testimony shows above all the power of cinema, but through cinema a new audience was attracted to music and to musical personalities. Numerous films of the period featured signature songs and often these were sung not by recognized singers but by well-known actors who, in this way, added a dimension to their personalities and helped, through radio plays, to plug their latest films. An example is Alida Valli, who never possessed a good voice, but she sang the melancholic "Ma l'amore no" (Anything But Love) in *Stasera niente di nuovo* (*Nothing New Tonight*) (Mario Mattòli, 1942), while De Sica broke into song in many of his films of the period, starting with "Parlami d'amore, Mariù" (Speak To Me Of Love, Mariù) in the first film in which he had a starring role, *Gli uomini, che mascalzoni!* (see chapter 5).

In the 1953 film, *Ci troviamo in galleria* (*Let's Meet in the Arcade*), directed by Mauro Bolognini, Pizzi was cast, alongside variety star Carlo Dapporto and Alberto Sordi, as Caterina Lari, a cashier in a village pharmacy who is endowed with a beautiful voice. By recruiting her, Dapporto's failing troupe suddenly returns to its former glories. Pizzi made several similar films, in which she played singers closely modeled on herself, before deciding to concentrate on building an international career and taking on engagements in the United States and the Soviet Union. Her enterprises were followed with great participation by her fans, who wanted to know everything about her. Like other female singers, she was regarded as a fashion leader and her theater costumes were eagerly studied by ordinary girls. *Sorrisi e canzoni* always featured detailed interviews with singers, and in the column called "La posta dei divi" (Postbag of the stars) a different singer was invited to respond each week to the questions of readers. The questions included many requests for advice on matters of the heart.[40]

The singer who attracted the most devoted fans was Claudio Villa, a cobbler's son from Trastevere in Rome who emerged from the vibrant entertainment world of the immediate postwar years to establish himself as the leading exponent of the suboperatic variant of Italian melody. He did shows for Allied troops, radio broadcasts, and night club and concert engagements; he performed in theaters, revues, and outdoor and beach festivals. He also took part in the many song competitions that burgeoned at this time, including the San Remo festival. As with other singers, it was radio that was crucial to his success rather than the recordings he made for Parlaphon. People flocked to live performances because it gave them a chance to see their favorites in the flesh. Villa's repertoire was eclectic: he sang Roman *stornelli,* Neapolitan songs, emigrants' laments, and nostalgic and melancholic love songs such as "Buongiorno tristezza" (Good Morning Sadness), the song that won San Remo in 1955. For Borgna, his voice, "rich in slight, agile nuances, all modulated in his throat, with open vowels . . . was magical."[41]

One of the most striking features of all accounts of commercially organized musical activities was the presence of massive crowds. When Villa went on a tour of Sicily in 1951, after receiving the Microfono d'argento (Silver Microphone) prize, he was mobbed everywhere, as he later recalled: "In every location a huge festive crowd turned out to cheer me enthusiastically. Road blocks, police cordons, fireworks in my honour, endless bunches of flowers and baskets of oranges and prickly pears."[42] The first Giro d'Italia della canzone, in 1953, a precursor of the more famous Cantagiro of the 1960s, which saw a variety of second-rank singers and an orchestra perform a show of twenty-four songs in seventy locations, was a similar success. The public, which was invited to vote for its favorite songs at the end of every evening, was enthusiastic and drawn "from every social class."[43] According to a press account, Tino Vailati was "literally assaulted, every evening he performed, by female fans hunting autographs" while another singer, Almarelli, "gets at least fifty marriage proposals a day."[44]

Villa took part in song competitions; went on domestic and international tours; made musical films including *Serenata amara* (*Bitter Serenade*) (Pino Mercanti, 1952), *Canzone d'amore* (*Love Song*) (Giorgio Simonelli, 1954), *Serenata per sedici bionde* (*Serenade for Sixteen Blondes*) (Marino Girolami, 1956), *Ore dieci lezione di canto* (*Ten o'clock Singing Lesson*) (Marino Girolami, 1956), and *Primo applauso* (*First Applause*) (Pino Mercanti, 1957); released numerous records; endorsed household products; and appeared in photoromances. Although he was a supporter of the Italian Communist Party, he sang for Catholics as well as Communists at their respective festivals and for anyone else who paid. If Pizzi was the queen of Italian song, Villa became, following a "coronation" staged by some fans, "the little king of song" (*il reuccio della canzone*). A controversial figure owing to his assertive and boastful manner, he both courted and despised the press. In 1953, he acquired an enormous American

car that ensured that his movements in the peninsula never escaped attention ("Just imagine what it meant in 1953 to travel around Italy in a powerful
American car," he later boasted).[45] This was not the only concession to Americanism on the part of a musical traditionalist. The singer's most audacious
move was to establish American-style fan clubs that flourished especially in
the South following his San Remo victory in 1955. Although their organization was sponsored by a brand of shampoo, clubs had some of the characteristics of "party branches" and "organized Sunday outings and other leisure
activities."[46] Although the fans of other singers followed the example, none
were able to rival the ingenuity and industry of Villa's mainly female followers, who in one province even organized a "Miss Claudio Villa" beauty contest.
Not everyone liked him, however. "I didn't think much of Claudio Villa," said
Lina A. in Rome: "Perhaps it was his personality I didn't like. Listening to him
sing without seeing him was one thing, but to see him . . ." (68: 13).

Observers in the 1950s believed that the enthusiasm and dedication
aroused by musical performers was far more intense than that aroused by film
or theater stars. This probably reflected the fact that songs were widely sung in
everyday life and that there were many local competitions for keen amateurs.
The greater reach of the medium of radio was also a factor since many fans
hailed from the lower rungs of the social ladder (the organizer of the fan club
called "Roman's Girls di Claudio Villa" [sic] was Irene Di Nardo, a fruit seller),
from the outskirts of cities, and from small towns and villages. It was also
significant that popular music after the war was depoliticized. In the view of
Piero Palumbo, who conducted an inquiry into musical fandom for the illustrated weekly Lo Specchio in 1958, the associations

seek to dispel the boredom of the interminable evenings that hang over provincial Italy by feeling they are active members of society, using a membership
card to legitimate enthusiasms and ideas that otherwise would remain boxed up
inside the walls of their home. To do this Villa's fans and the female members of
the supporters' "circles" organize fund-raisings, excursions, dance parties and
demonstrations that are eloquent signs of the birth of a rhetoric that is destined
to bury the memory both of the Roman eagles [Fascism] and the workers' protest movement.

Palumbo also highlighted the economic aspirations of fans:

Our homespun fans reject the expressions of collective delirium that are aroused,
for example, in America by the stage performances of Elvis Presley. They are the
humble footsoldiers of an army full of problems and rich only in hopes: they are
the representatives of a suffering humanity that has consigned its destiny into
the hands of the kings and princes of song.

Figure 11. Claudio Villa with female fans in the Pasticcieria Ruschena, Rome, July 12, 1956. Photo Giuseppe Palmas, by permission of Roberto Palmas.

In their ranks there are no teddy boys, but only honest tomato-sellers and telephonists. There are deeply unhappy small farmers and lonely radio-listeners. For all of them the singing star is their only comfort and one of their few hopes. They turn to him for handouts, radio sets, wheelchairs, artificial limbs and wedding dresses. They ask him for autographs, photographs, records, letters, visits, or just some material sign of his presence on earth.[47]

Through popular song a form of national unity was established that crossed class, political, and regional barriers. Few singers succeeded in winning recognition outside the realm of the San Remo festival, which "transformed popular song into a national sport and a business."[48] Although Neapolitan songs continued to enjoy popularity, the hegemony of northern business in the music industry meant that not even the annual Festival of

Neapolitan Song, which was founded after San Remo with a specific promotional mission of its own, could act as a distinct platform. It was a subsidiary event that never acquired the same prominence, and which singers used merely to consolidate the success they had won elsewhere.[49]

The only forum that constituted an alternative were night clubs. This was the realm of irony and invention that witnessed the triumph of offbeat character singers including the Neapolitan Renato Carosone, whose celebrated "Tu vuo' fa' l'americano" (You Want To Play The American) mixed a Neapolitan rhythm with lyrics poking fun at Italians who mimicked the fashions arriving from the other side of the Atlantic. The Turinese Fred Buscaglione, whose adult songs of whisky, smoke, guns, tough guys, and molls were diametrically opposed to the flowers and church bells of San Remo, was another who took American elements, in his case mostly from cinema, only to rework them and combine them with a series of stylistic innovations (notably his rapid-fire delivery of lyrical stories) and various musical genres.[50] Buscaglione owed his success to the clubs, radio, and subsequently to television and jukeboxes. He also made a number of films, including *Noi duri* (*Tough Guys*) (Camillo Mastrocinque, 1960), in which he played an American FBI agent who poses as a singer to infiltrate the world of Paris night clubs. According to Aldo B., Fred Buscaglione appealed because he was unconventional. He "had this sense of independence and 'fuck you!' [*sfottitura*] attitude towards the world." He especially appreciated the singer's "hoarse voice, the whisky...." He added, "I have always liked whisky a lot" (9: 24).

Cultural Industries and the Italian Market

Let us now review the picture that has emerged from this section of the book on cultural industries. In the second half of the 1930s the Italian cultural industries presented a contradictory picture. They were, at least in part, technologically modernized but they operated in a smaller and poorer national market for cultural goods than their counterparts in other European countries with similar population sizes, such as Germany, France, and Britain. There were various reasons for the relative underdevelopment of the Italian market. First, average per capita income was low. Levels of individual consumption were nearly stagnant during the Fascist period as a whole and they were approximately halved during World War II.[51] Although the regime did attempt to maintain purchasing power by offering "political" (that is, subsidized) prices and defending the value of the lira up to 1936, most people had little or no disposable income to spend on commercial cultural goods. Before the 1950s, significant levels of expenditure on recreational activities and cultural goods were concentrated in urban populations, and within these largely among the middle and upper classes. We therefore believe it is incorrect, despite the growing contact that most people had in this period with some of the products of commercial culture, to speak of a "mass" consumer culture in a quantitative sense in Italy at this stage. One index of this is the very circumscribed extent of the modern retail sector. The department store chain UPIM (founded in 1928) had fifty-five branches by 1943 and Standa (founded, as Standard, in 1930) thirty-nine, but in 1938 these chain stores as a whole still accounted for a mere 1 percent of retail sales nationwide.[52] Second, the communications infrastructure—roads, railways, electricity, telephones—on which all the cultural industries depended to varying degrees for distribution was underdeveloped. The market for commercial culture therefore remained mainly limited to the larger cities until the 1950s, when a more significant penetration of small towns and rural areas began. Third, the educational level and the level of literacy outside main towns were low, and this reduced the potential market for print media. Fourth, geographical mobility was also relatively low, despite labor migrations, which meant that many people's cultural repertoires remained partly or wholly unaffected by the products of the modern cultural industries. In short, mass culture, together with the technologies that mediated it, was being produced but it was not yet being distributed or consumed on a mass scale. By the mid-1930s the EIAR's signals covered most parts of the country, but there were still many areas lacking electricity to run radio sets, a problem that only started to be overcome in 1938 when the first battery-powered models came onto the market. Distribution of printed paper was also uneven, with few retail points outside urban centers. In all provinces, the majority of cinemas were concentrated in the provincial capitals; in many rural provinces films were seen only occasionally, if at all, by means of a traveling film truck (carro-cinema), which carried portable projection equipment. One reason why there was no development of a national television service before the war was the high cost of the early sets, which would have limited the market to such a small group of consumers that the costs of launching a daily service would have far exceeded the returns.

In the ten years after the end of the war this situation changed. There was a very rapid growth in the domestic radio audience (licenses more than trebled, from 1.6 million in 1945 to 5.6 million in 1955) and in the number of cinemas and cinema tickets sold (the peak year was 1954 with 801 million tickets, putting Italy ahead of Germany, with 736 million, and well ahead of France, with 383 million, though still far behind Britain, with 1,276 million), with the largest percentage increases in rural areas of the Center and South. Total sales of weekly magazines in 1952 (including glossy magazines, children's comics, and the new fotoromanzi) were 12.6 million, over three times the amount of daily newspaper sales: this proportion would remain constant and, as we have seen, it was a distinctive characteristic of the structure of the postwar reading public in Italy. Largely as a consequence of this expansion of the market, the RAI decided in the summer of 1949 to introduce a television service with nationwide coverage. A regular service officially started on January 1, 1954 (on April 10 that year the company, although it continued to be known by the abbreviation RAI, changed its name officially from Radio Audizioni Italia to Radiotelevisione Italiana) and, although at first it only covered the North and part of the Center, a service area inhabited by less than half the total population, by 1956 nationwide coverage was complete.[53]

Despite the relatively limited size of the domestic market and low average purchasing power of consumers, the changes that took place in the cultural industries in Italy from the 1930s onward were to a considerable extent synchronized with what was happening in other industrialized countries. This was in part because of the growing internationalization of cultural markets in mass entertainment after World War I, in particular U.S. domination of the global film market. Related to this was the development of faster forms of transnational mass communications, notably radio, and the development of advertising and the international marketing of a number of brand-name goods. But it was also because governments were anxious to modernize communications and overcome what political élites perceived as inherited cultural backwardness. The period around 1930 saw the beginning of a long wave of transformation in the industrialized world, both of cultural industries and of popular cultural repertoires and tastes, which would last to the 1970s. It was a turning point both because of a cluster of technological innovations that were internationally commercialized during the mid- to late 1920s—sound films, rotogravure printing, and audio broadcasting—and because of a more concerted intervention by governments into the economy, including the cultural industries, during the interwar years. In the next section of the book we examine these political interventions in Italy as they affected mass culture, looking first at the state and then at the activities of political parties and social movements in civil society.

Part 3.

Politics and Mass Culture

7 State Intervention in Cultural Activity

Despite the emphasis we give overall in this book to the cultural industries and consumers, we do not underestimate the role of the state in shaping the way mass culture was received by the public. However, we argue that this shaping took many forms. Our intention here is to move discussion of the subject beyond the reductive accounts of state–culture relations that have dominated the historical literature until now. As we shall show, in both the Fascist regime and the postwar Republic parts of the Italian state, as well as some of the legitimated political forces in society—the Fascist Party and pro-Fascist intellectuals in the former case, different parties and interest groups in the latter—sought to carry through a transformative agenda, while other parts sought to conserve stable relations with nonstate bodies and élites, and others pragmatically defended their own niches of power. There were also many different types of interaction and interdependency, as well as conflict, between state institutions and the cultural industries.

In order to provide a sense of the overall "shape" of the state, this chapter begins with an examination of its structure and evolution in Italy from Fascism to the Republic. Our discussion considers what is meant in this context by the expression "continuity of the state" and reflects on approaches to culture under Fascism that presuppose a strongly interventionist state and a "manufacture of consent." In the rest of the chapter we put forward an alternative view by examining and illustrating in turn the five main forms of state intervention in the activities of the cultural industries in our period as a whole: subventions and premiums; protectionism; promotion of exports; propaganda; and censorship.

Questions of Continuity

It is now generally accepted that there was a degree of "continuity of the state" from Fascism to the Republic, to use the phrase introduced by Claudio Pavone in the early 1970s and widely adopted since by other historians.[1] The historical controversy on this subject has centered not so much on the idea itself but on how much continuity there was, what parts of the state it affected, and how much significance to give it—in particular, whether it effectively outweighed the discontinuities. It is agreed that if some parts of the state were able to continue unchanged from Fascism to the Republic, this was because the state was not wholly colonized or transformed by Fascism. Despite its self-advertisement as a "totalitarian state," Fascism is probably more accurately described as a "limited totalitarianism" or a form of authoritarian state in which the party's occupation of the state, although extensive, was never total.[2] When the Fascists came to power in 1922 they acquired a preexisting state bureaucracy. They did not so much transform it as maintain it—for instance, retaining the system, which dated from 1865, of prefects in each province appointed from Rome and accountable to the Interior Ministry—and renew its personnel: from the late 1920s the old functionaries of the Liberal era, recruited mainly from the South, were replaced with a new generation largely from the North and Center, where the Fascist movement had a stronger implantation.[3] At the same time, the Partito Nazionale Fascista (PNF) duplicated the state with its own parallel party structures, for instance the *federazioni,* the party associations at provincial level, with their bosses (*federali*) operating alongside the prefects.

There were limits also to the Fascist state's colonization of society. In his classic work on the Fascist state, Alberto Aquarone listed five groups, areas of social "residue," which it did not fully integrate: the Church and the Catholic movement; leading Fascist activists themselves (because of their ideological heterogeneity); the industrial, financial, and agrarian élites; the working classes; and the intellectuals. Writing of the last of these groups, Aquarone said that Fascism "was not even able to prevent Italian culture, in its most significant expressions and the majority of its best exponents, from gradually acquiring increasingly antifascist features."[4] Aquarone's argument about Fascism's non-total presence in civil society has stood up well over time, although his last assertion is both rather dated and questionable, restricting "Italian culture" as it does to the intellectual subcultures and defining, in a circular way, the "most significant expressions" of culture as those that were or became antifascist. If we widen the meaning of "culture" to include the mass media and the cultural industries then we may say that they were never fully integrated into the state either (see chapters 3 through 6), but neither did they have, as a whole, an antifascist character.

Despite the weight of historical argument against the view of Fascism as a wholly exceptional phase in the history of the Italian state, a number of studies of mass communications and mass culture under Fascism have suggested that they were harnessed more or less efficiently to a totalizing political project that used them as instruments to organize "mass consent." Philip V. Cannistraro's book *La fabbrica del consenso* (*The Factory of Consent*), published in 1975, was, as its title suggests, an example of this "instrumentalist" approach.[5] As the first well-documented account of the controls exerted over the press, radio, and cinema by the Ministero della Cultura Popolare (MCP) and its antecedent organizations, it remains an important work and its appendices of documents are of considerable interest. Yet its overall heuristic value is compromised by the author's founding assumption that "each sector of cultural life was overshadowed and intimately influenced by the politico-moral imperatives of the totalitarian state and the single party."[6] Cannistraro sought to prove this by looking in the archives for political directives operating propagandistically or censorially in the cultural sphere. He found many such directives in the files of the MCP (held in the Archivio Centrale dello Stato, Rome) and he also found that their number increased in the late 1930s and early 1940s. These documents are certainly accurate records of some of the state's activities. However, by focusing exclusively on them, Cannistraro's book exaggerated their overall significance and deflected attention from the other forces influencing cultural products and consumption.[7] These other forces included, first (as we discuss below), other parts of the state than the Ministry of Popular Culture and, second, non-state forces, forces in the cultural economy. In the case of cinema, for instance, as we have seen (see chapters 4 and 5), the efforts of directors to make a certain kind of film, the market calculations of producers and distributors, and the demand from exhibitors for Italian films that could stand up against American imports all played a part in determining the kinds of film that were actually made, alongside the sometimes conflicting directives of different parts of the state and the PNF and the structures of censorship. The point is that *all* these constraints need to be looked at. They are like so many vectors pushing the cultural product in different directions. In order to reconstruct a more complete picture of how they interacted one has to use a variety of sources, including information about the role of different ministries and the operations of cultural firms, evidence about audiences and their tastes, and the kinds of pressure exerted by all these factors on production.

Although the idea of Fascism as a successful totalitarianism went through a period of disfavor among historians in the late 1970s and early 1980s, it has since returned, notably in a body of work on the Fascist regime as a form of "political theater" involving the public in a "collective performance," as creating a form of "society of the spectacle," being a "lay religion" or carrying out a "secularization of politics."[8] This line of interpretation has had an influential exponent in the historian Emilio Gentile, who seems to have taken more or less at face value the regime's own claims to have been an effective totalitarian system, integrating society into its political project by means of mass rituals and other forms of collective belonging generated from above.[9] Jeffrey Schnapp's well-documented work on the Mostra della Rivoluzione Fascista adopts a similar interpretive stance.[10] Simonetta Falasca-Zamponi, in her book *Fascist Spectacle* (1997), develops into a full-scale analysis Walter Benjamin's often-quoted statements of 1936 about Fascism aestheticizing politics, examining in detail the emphasis on beauty and form in the regime's self-representations.[11] Although she weighs some of the evidence offered by Luisa Passerini and Gianpasquale Santomassimo for popular dissent and non-acquiescence to Fascism, she concludes: "Through festivals and images, rituals and speeches, Mussolini narrated fascism's story and naturalized the regime's history. These symbolic practices then reflected back and affected the reality Mussolini had articulated in the first place."[12]

Against these and similar approaches we would invoke the work of scholars such as Steven Lukes, James C. Scott, and Michel de Certeau, all of whom pay attention, on the contrary, to the limitations of political rituals and to ruses of popular non-acquiescence. Lukes, in a classic essay of 1975, exposed the weakness of neo-Durkheimian accounts of political rituals (marches, demonstrations, state funerals, and the like) as producing "value consensus" or "value integration" on the grounds that they work with too simple a model of how societies hold together, they attribute to political rituals an implausible plurality of functions, and they pay attention only to the public or official account of the ritual and do not consider that it may have different meanings for each of the various groups who take part in it.[13] Scott, a historical anthropologist, deals with "the most severe conditions of powerlessness and dependency," namely societies in Southeast Asia based on slavery, serfdom, or colonization, but his methodological premise is very similar to Lukes's, namely that one must be extremely wary of taking the official accounts of rituals in these societies at face value.[14] Scott uses the same kinds of theatrical metaphors as those who argue for the integrative effects of public rituals—he talks of them as "spectacles," "performances," "displays," "staged events"—but unlike the others he devotes most of his attention to what happens "behind the scenes," "backstage," "offstage," "in the wings where the mask can be lifted," and he sees a disparity between the two sets of actions. "Every subordinate group creates, out of its ordeal, a 'hidden transcript' that represents a critique of power spoken behind the back of the dominant."[15] As for Certeau, among his most important propositions is that even the weakest and most subjugated of peoples have networks of "microrésistances" and "microlibertés," in his colleague Luce Giard's terms, a number of "ruses" (the conception here is similar to Scott's) by which they may resist or evade surveillance and domination from above.[16] Certeau called for an analysis of the everyday practices that swarm in the interstices of a surveillance society.[17]

All these approaches seem to us to account in a more sensitive way for how people actually behave under situations of political coercion like that of Fascism. They allow us to get beyond the "consent" model and to begin to enquire into the complexity, the "thickness," of social attitudes, beliefs, and behaviors, of which cultural activities and consumption are a part. One of the implications of an approach such as ours, which seeks to reconstruct on the one hand the complexity of the state's role in relation to mass culture and on the other the degree of agency possessed by audiences, is that it obliges one to address the question of just how "exceptional" the state's role was in Italy, that is, how far it did or did not conform to a pattern shared by other European countries at the same time. Between the early 1920s and the neoliberal turn against Keynesianism in the late 1970s and early 1980s, most states in Europe increased their involvement in cultural activities. Most of them exercised control over flows of information through monopolistic or restrictive licensing arrangements in the case of broadcasting, through press offices and press commissions in the case of print media, and through censorship and obscenity laws for all media. Most of them used the public purse to provide recreational and leisure facilities and to subsidize arts and cultural industries. They used import controls to protect the home markets of these industries, such as the quota systems used in many European countries to ensure that a minimum number of domestic films got screened alongside U.S. films, and in some cases they passed antitrust laws to foster internal competition and protect plurality of opinion. In all these respects, state intervention in culture in Italy was part of a wider European pattern.

This is not to say that the particular coercive context of the Fascist dictatorship did not have specific consequences. There was a significant tightening of control over all areas of mass culture in successive waves: in the late 1930s; after entry into the war in June 1940; from September 1943 to April 1945 in those parts of Italy that were under the Repubblica Sociale Italiana and German occupation. As for the postwar years, despite important institutional and operative continuities in the state, the changes brought about by the work of the Constituent Assembly (June 1946–December 1947) that were embodied in the 1948 Constitution of the Italian Republic were also very significant. The presence of a legal opposition meant, for instance, that government policies toward the cinema, or the way the state monopoly over radio was managed, could now be challenged legally both in parliament and outside, in publications or in mass demonstrations. In other words antigovernmental public opinion could be openly articulated after 1945, unlike under Fascism, even though there was no real alternation of parties in power from the end of the war until the mid 1990s, given the proportional electoral system, the dominance of all government coalitions by the Democrazia Cristiana (DC), and the permanent exclusion of the Communists from these coalitions from 1947.

Types of State Intervention

Modern nation-states interact with cultural activity in different ways, some of them enabling, others repressive. The enabling role may take the form of direct subsidy or subvention to cultural firms, promotional campaigns, assistance with distribution and export, tax and tariff concessions, or protectionist measures such as import quotas or restrictions on translations. Repression can operate at different stages in the life of a cultural product: the forced revision of theatrical plays or screenplays before a production gets underway; the refusal to let a play be performed or a completed film be screened; the seizure of publications.

These different modes of intervention involve different parts of the state, that is, separate ministries or agencies. In Italy, the successive incarnations of the body responsible for overseeing the activities of the press, and subsequently also of publishing, theater, and cinema—Sottosegretariato di Stato (later Ministero) per la Stampa e Propaganda, Ministero della Cultura Popolare, Sottosegretariato di Stato per la Stampa, lo Spettacolo e il Turismo— were of central importance, but there were limits to its sphere of influence, and other state bodies were influential too. The Foreign Ministry (Ministero degli Affari Esteri) handled matters relating to exports of cultural goods and, through the embassies, could attempt to apply diplomatic pressure abroad. The Interior Ministry (Ministero dell'Interno) dealt with questions of policing and public order, such as the sequestration of censored materials and the banning of certain performances. Since 1861, responsibility for public order had been devolved to prefects at provincial level, and the power to license or ban the publication or public performance of a work lay in their hands. In principle, a prefect in one province could prevent the publication or performance of a work that had been permitted in another. In practice, the arbitrariness was contained by central government guidelines on what were permissible grounds for censorship. In this respect, as in others, the prefecture was an ambiguous institution in which bureaucratic decentralization was coupled with political centralization: the prefects were direct emanations at provincial level of the executive power and were accountable to the Interior Ministry, but they had a certain de facto autonomy in the powers devolved to them.[18] Other ministries had specific responsibilities, such as Communications (Ministero delle Comunicazioni), which was responsible for radio licensing; Finance (Ministero delle Finanze), which included the Treasury; and Exchange and Currency (Ministero per gli Scambi e le Valute) for matters concerning currency export. These different ministries and agencies did not necessarily express coherent or preformed policies; they sometimes acted in ad hoc fashion, or were driven by personal ambitions or rivalries among the officials who worked for them, and their respective interests sometimes conflicted with one another. In the following five subsections of this chapter we shall look at different modes of state intervention. In each case we shall give specific examples to illustrate how the interventions worked, drawing mainly from two cultural industries, cinema and publishing.

SUBVENTIONS AND PREMIUMS

The main form of direct economic support to the film industry was the payment of a premium or bonus to Italian films. The premium was linked to box office receipts and it thus rewarded commercially more successful pictures. The first legislation introducing premiums was introduced in 1927. The timing was determined partly by the wider state intervention in the Italian economy during the world recession but also in this particular case by the coming transition to sound. Synchronized sound, using the sound-on-film system developed in the United States and launched commercially there in 1927, was to push up the costs of domestic film production. Studios would need sound stages equipped with microphones, cables, "blimps" to isolate the noise of the camera motor, and so forth. These changes led Italian film producers to seek increased financial support from the state; in turn, the production abroad of films spoken in other languages forced the question of cultural protectionism and control onto the Italian state's agenda.

A law of 1931 set up a fund of 2.5 million lire to be distributed among producers of Italian films as a percentage of their earnings. In 1934 Luigi Freddi was appointed to the newly created post of Director General for the Cinema in the Sottosegretariato di Stato per la Stampa e la Propaganda, on the strength of a long report he had written for Mussolini setting out a strategy for renewal of the Italian film industry. He held this post until 1939. In his self-justificatory memoirs, *Il cinema,* published in 1949, he proudly recalled that his first measure had been not to set up a state production company but to create competitive conditions that would force the small, commercially nonviable production companies out of business and thus rationalize and strengthen the private production sector. He had also stressed that the state's role vis-à-vis the film industry should be to encourage and persuade producers to create certain kinds of film, those that were ideologically aligned, artistically worthy, and commercially robust, not to impose its own pet projects on them.[19] The state's relation with the cinema under Freddi was thus one of relatively indirect control of a cultural industry that still remained largely in private hands. It was nonetheless resented by many film producers, who disliked what they saw as the ideological molding that Freddi was imposing on Italian production and who felt that his directorate was not doing enough to support their interests in the face of foreign competition. In March 1939 he criticized the introduction of the Monopoly Law (see chapter 5 and below) and was removed from his post.

In book publishing the background to the state's interventions in the 1930s was on the one hand the so-called crisis of the book (*crisi del libro*) of the previous decade, caused by rising costs of paper and labor after World War I, which had led publishers to turn to the state for support,[20] and on the other the drive by publishers and political elites to promote the book as a cultural good or an educational resource for which state support was considered appropriate. Publishers were economically hampered at home by the relatively small market for books, which they attributed not only to persistent illiteracy and semiliteracy but also to the lack of a book-reading habit outside the relatively small number of regular readers and to inefficient distribution and retail networks. They were also frustrated in their efforts to export books by high postal tariffs. The main forms of economic support sought by publishers and given by the state were consequently subsidies, control of paper prices, and various initiatives to help book distribution such as tariff and postal concessions, promotion of local and traveling libraries (*biblioteche comunali e ambulanti*), and an annual book fair, the Fiera del libro.

With the creation of the state holding company IRI in 1933, direct financial aid was given to publishing firms in the form of loans, with IRI paying out to seven publishers, including Mondadori, Treves, Vallecchi, and Bemporad, a total of 17.1 million lire.[21] In June 1937, at a national conference of publishers and booksellers held in Florence, the delegates concurred that the "crisis of the book," at least with regards to the quantity of books produced, was over, but they argued that more needed to be done to stimulate distribution, particularly to a mass reading public, in line with Mussolini's slogan of "going to the people" (*andare verso il popolo*), and that to this end more state intervention was necessary. As Gherardo Casini, Director General for Press and Publishing of the Ministero della Cultura Popolare (MCP), summed up the debates:

After the Florence conference it became clear that the book market needed to be driven by the ministries. The circulation of books had to be facilitated with every means, from a lightening of postal tariffs to an increase in the number of lending libraries to a raising of the tone and seriousness of literary prizes, which need to be better organized. Authors, publishers and booksellers have all been mobilized to make the book an efficient instrument of culture.[22]

After the conference postal tariffs were cut and there were other forms of facilitation of book export and regulation of paper prices. A series of articles on the paper industry in the *Giornale della Libreria* in 1938–1939, in line with the Fascist government's drive toward economic autarky after the League of Nations sanctions crisis, asserted that Italy was now self-sufficient in paper production. However, what this meant was that Italy was able to produce enough finished paper, in particular at the plants in Fabriano (the main center of paper production, in the Marche region, dating back to the thirteenth century), to meet domestic demand without having to import, not that it was self-sufficient in raw materials. In fact, Italy needed to import the two raw materials needed for making paper, cellulose and wood pulp, and when supplies of these dried up, as happened during World War II, a severe paper shortage resulted.

Radio constitutes a particular case of state support for a cultural industry because of the unusual public-private status it had in Italy (see chapter 6). The government in 1931 renewed the convention giving the EIAR a monopoly (*concessione in esclusiva*) for broadcasts on national territory and extended this to include Italy's colonies. The license fee levied by the Ministry of Posts, the main source of revenue for the broadcasting industry, was an indirect form of state funding. When SIP, the major shareholder in the EIAR, was taken over in 1933 by IRI, the injection of public capital increased state control of EIAR in both financial and managerial ways.[23]

PROTECTIONISM

We saw in chapter 3 how opposition to foreign influence in the form of translated books, as well as popular imported genres like thrillers and comics, along
with calls to restrict their number, became a dominant theme of public statements from the mid-1930s by elements in the state and PNF as well as by "patriotic" publishers like Vallecchi. The case against foreign works was summed
up by Gherardo Casini in his speech of 1937 quoted above. The speech condensed the key themes of this form of Fascist nationalism: love of foreign
things (*esterofilia*) was a form of snobbery by effete intellectuals; and foreign
culture was vacuously cerebral, unlike the healthy and vigorous cultural traditions of Italy.[24] Even the young Giulio Einaudi, who had set up his firm in
1934, felt compelled to justify himself. Writing in *Il Libro Italiano* in March
1939 he said that his firm's catalogue contained forty books by Italian authors
as against twenty by foreign authors, and that the latter were all either literary
works or texts by important contemporary scientists or scholars. He took the
opportunity to dismiss translations of popular novels, popular science, and
popular history and thus to distinguish his own firm's cultural criteria from
those of other houses. "My publishing company carries out its activity, even
in the delicate field of foreign literature, in full awareness of the needs of our
[Italian] culture."[25]

Children's magazines were the object of one of the loudest calls for protectionism. At a national conference on children's literature in 1938 there were
particularly harsh criticisms of the use of the American style of comic strip
with characters' speech in "bubbles," in place of the older European-style
comic with speech or narrative placed underneath the drawing in captions
(*didascalie*), often in rhyming couplets. As Domenico Lombrassa put it, reporting on the conference in *Il Libro Italiano:* "The captions at the foot of
each drawing were replaced, under the influence of cinema, by 'speech' coming out of the characters' mouths."[26] The bubbles were known in Italian as
nuvolette (little clouds) or *fumetti* (puffs of smoke); the latter word subsequently became, by synecdoche, the standard term for this type of comic strip
as a whole. Lombrassa's argument, and that of others present at the conference, was that the predominance of image over text was diseducative. Implicit
here was the fear of a reversion to illiteracy. The reading of American-style
comics was "a purely visual exercise, a sudden rush to the head like all inges-
tions of narcotics." At the level of content, what Lombrassa found particularly offensive and galling was that, in reading these comics, Italian children
were identifying with blond, Anglo-Saxon heroes against swarthy Latin vil-
lains.[27] The objection echoed the complaints made earlier in the 1930s about
the negative stereotypes of Italians in American films.

In the film industry protectionist attitudes had been present throughout

Europe since the 1920s. They expressed a reaction against the enormous share of the film market that Hollywood had cornered after World War I. The most common responses were to impose a ceiling on film imports and to use a quota system to ensure that a minimum number of domestic films were shown in cinemas, but other protectionist methods were also used, from tariffs and visas to fees on dubbing to censorship. All of these had been adopted in Italy between 1927 and 1933. In 1935 an agreement signed by Italian Foreign Minister Galeazzo Ciano and William Hays, chairman of the U.S. film industry association MPAA, fixed a ceiling of 250 American films a year that could be imported into Italy. However, by far the most radical piece of protectionist legislation was that already mentioned in chapter 5: the Monopoly Law (Decree Law no. 1389), passed on September 4, 1938 and in force from January 1, 1939. As we saw, this gave the Italian company ENIC (Ente Nazionale Industrie Cinematografiche) a monopoly on the purchase, import, and distribution in Italy and its colonies of all foreign films, and it provided Italian producers with financial supports and guarantees and wider freedom to act. There began a new period in which U.S. competition was reduced, and this led to an expansion of Italian film production. Freddi was replaced by the ex-prefect Vezio Orazi, who in 1941 was in turn substituted by Eitel Monaco, formerly president of the FNFIS (Federazione Nazionale Fascista Industriali dello Spettacolo [National Fascist Federation of Industrialists of Entertainment]) , the precursor of ANICA, founded in July 1944 (on these organizations see chapter 4), which Monaco would also head from 1949.

The process by which Freddi was marginalized provides a good illustration of the tensions both among different parts of the state and among the different branches of the film industry. The Monopoly Law was interpreted by the four U.S. major studios (Twentieth Century Fox, Paramount, Metro-Goldwyn-Mayer, and Warner Bros.) as an attack on their commercial freedom to distribute their own films in Italy, and they responded by pulling out of the Italian market. There is still no consensus among historians of cinema on why the Monopoly Law was introduced. Freddi himself believed it to have been a power-seeking move by Giacomo Paolucci de' Calboli, the president of ENIC and the Istituto Luce. According to the Minister of Popular Culture, Dino Alfieri, however, the primary motive was financial. "We could not remain inactive," Alfieri said; "the Minister of Exchange and Currency decided in agreement with me to make a radical change to the system of film imports."[28] Pressure for the Monopoly Law does not appear to have come, as one might have expected, from Italian producers, even though they were to benefit from it. Indeed, an unpublished manuscript by Monaco, quoted by Argentieri, suggests that the FNFIS also protested against the legislation before it was implemented because they feared reprisals against exports of Italian films.[29] Whatever the facts of the case, it is clear that the Monopoly Law was not the result of coordination among the various Italian forces in play, and that on the contrary it generated conflict between different agencies (Freddi's directorate and the leadership of the Ministry of Popular Culture, for instance) as well as being bitterly opposed by Italian exhibitors, who feared a drastic drop in attendances.

From the audience's point of view, the cinema was predominantly American before 1939 and again from 1946. In between these dates, protectionism succeeded in significantly modifying the nature of the cinema in Italy for audiences. Although, as we saw in chapter 5, not all the U.S. studios withdrew from the Italian market during the intervening years (the minor ones—United Artists, Columbia, and RKO—all distributed some films in Italy during the war), and although a few films produced even by the major studios found their way into circulation, most people remember this period as one of near or total absence of U.S. films. With the return to democracy, apart from the Monopoly Law, which was abolished, most of the other forms of state regulation of the film industry either continued or were resumed after an interval. In 1949 the Andreotti law (see chapter 4) introduced new fiscal measures that increased government support for Italian film production. The law was seen, both then and subsequently, as a mixed blessing, since while it protected domestic production from the full blast of U.S. competition it also effectively tightened government control of the industry in the form of what has sometimes been referred to as "economic censorship," namely, the effective withholding of funds from nonapproved productions and the awarding of financial bonuses to already commercially successful films.

PROMOTION OF EXPORTS

Support for the export of cultural products was an important way in which the state could further the ideological goal of disseminating Italian culture abroad while furthering the commercial interests of the exporting firms. In the film industry one aim of the Fascist government, and in particular of Freddi, was to turn Italy into a world center of filmmaking and restore the international prestige that Italian cinema enjoyed before 1920. The intention was to win back technicians and directors, such as Augusto Genina, who had gone abroad, and to recruit foreign personnel who could help raise the quality of the films produced. In this way it was hoped that foreign companies would be attracted to film in Italy and that Italian films would be promoted abroad. According to Freddi, export earnings were virtually nil between 1930 and 1935.[30] They began to increase thereafter because of improved quality and better commercial organization. By 1937 approximately one-third of Italian film production was being exported to around nineteen countries. In several countries companies were formed solely to import Italian films. Freddi was understandably proud of winning back this "right of citizenship" of Italian films in the world, and one of the efforts to increase the quantity and quality of production at home. The measures adopted included the use of diplomatic bags to take films to embassies (where they were previewed for local artists, producers, and journalists), financial rewards to producers who exported, and the granting of the right to import to those who exported. Such was the success that, according to Freddi, by the end of the 1930s a balance between import costs and export profits had been achieved.[31] A combination of commercial action and official intervention achieved a presence for Italian film in Spain, France, Britain, and Germany.

Entry into the coveted North American market (see chapter 4) was more difficult. Whereas exchange agreements could be reached between Italy and the European states, no such arrangement was possible with the United States. The Americans always insisted that their market was completely open to foreign films, but while this was true in the sense that there were no special taxes or restrictions, it was exceptionally difficult in practice for foreign films to gain access to American mainstream circuits. The *Motion Picture Review Digest* published news of some thirty-six Italian-made films released in the United States between 1936 and 1940, many without subtitles (and therefore clearly destined for Italian immigrant audiences). Many were reviewed in the daily press as well as trade publications and they appear, on the whole, to have been judged to be of a good standard, although no film received universally positive reviews and several were harshly criticized. One example of the latter was *Darò un milione* (*I'll Give a Million*, 1935), a comedy starring Vittorio De Sica and Assia Noris, directed by Mario Camerini and produced by Rizzoli's Novella Film. The story, by Zavattini and Giaci Mondaini, was about a millionaire who only discovers the meaning of true friendship when he changes places with a homeless man. *Film Daily* called it "a disappointing picture . . . that on no account measures up to the higher standards of foreign production."[32] *Variety* wrote, "Production is slipshod and inept, editing is clumsy and photography uncomplimentary,"[33] but it saw possibilities for a more dynamic Hollywood remake, an idea soon followed up by Twentieth Century Fox. *I'll Give a Million*, directed by Walter Lang and starring Warner Baxter, Marjorie Cleaver, and Peter Lorre, was released in 1938. However, the reviews were poor. *Variety* complained of "the phoney accents" and felt the remake added nothing to the original.[34]

Two films released in 1935 in which Freddi invested great hopes were *Casta Diva*, about the love affair of Vincenzo Bellini and Maddalena Fumaroli (played by Martha Eggerth) in Naples in 1825, which featured numerous scenes shot in and around Naples and music by Bellini and Rossini, and *Passa-*

porto rosso (*Red Passport,* 1935), a patriotic drama directed by Guido Brignone about Italian emigration to South America in the 1890s. The former received positive reviews in the United States. For *Film Daily,* on October 8, 1937, "the film is thoroughly up-to-the-minute in general technique and boasts uncommonly fine direction by the deft Carmine Gallone. Miss Eggerth is pleasing, alluring and effective."[35] Yet, even though it was filmed in Italian and English versions, it was only the Italian version that was released in the United States, three years after completion. If *Casta Diva* was a quality production, *Passaporto rosso* had the added advantage of including elements of nationalism and propaganda. However, the reviewers found it "tedious" and "long," "a sprawling and cumbersome screen drama" with "lethargic direction."[36] Released in Italian only with English subtitles, it was seen as intended for Italian immigrants and their descendants, at whose heartstrings it would certainly pluck. Nevertheless, the *New York Times* said, "The film is exceptionally well-acted and has a beautiful and appealing heroine in Isa Miranda, who bears a striking resemblance to Marlene Dietrich and would be a sparkling addition to the Hollywood firmament."[37]

With this less than satisfactory record of export and reception of films made in Italy, all of them distributed in the United States by small companies specializing in Italian films, Italian desires to enter American mainstream circuits increased. The 1937 historical epic about the Punic Wars, *Scipione l'africano,* was designed, in part, to show that Italy, and in particular the new Italy reborn under Fascism, could produce international-level films on a grand scale capable of prominence in world markets, and especially in the United States, similar to the status of films in silent era. *Scipione* was one of a very few films financed directly by the state, to the tune of some ten million lire,[38] and it also had a clear propaganda purpose. Planned on the eve of the regime's colonial war in East Africa and alluding also to Italy's earlier colonization of Libya and desire to expand its North African presence, it was designed to show that Fascist Italy was the true heir of imperial Rome. It was a prestige production in every sense, and several prominent foreign film personalities, including Marcus Loew, George Cukor, and Alexander Korda, were invited to the set during shooting. The intention was to follow it up with other blockbusters, including films about Christopher Columbus and Michelangelo. However, after the less than triumphant reception of *Scipione,* mainly in Italy but also abroad, these other films were never made.

Scipione did in fact do reasonable box office abroad and recovered its costs, but the attempt to get MGM to buy it for U.S. distribution failed. The Italian Foreign Ministry archives reveal that negotiations went on for several months in 1937, as the film was being shot. At first they seemed to go well, with Hays taking a personal interest, despite a rather blunt approach by the

Italians. "Please explain to Mr Hays that the purchase of *Scipione* by Metro would represent an extremely important factor not only for cinema relations between the two countries but also in other fields," Alfieri told the Foreign Ministry in January.[39] In the negotiations, the Italians stressed the film's spectacular qualities and its affinities with blockbusters of the past like *Ben-Hur*. Although there was mention of the parallels between the glorious period of ancient history depicted in the film and the present, the negotiations played down the impression that it was a political film with a propagandistic intent. In May a potential distribution deal with MGM fell through when the Italians refused to accept the American company's request that they inspect the completed film before deciding whether to buy it. By August, following a derisory bid from Columbia, negotiations were in train with Monogram, but there appear to be no archival records of these. When the film eventually opened in the United States in November 1939 it was distributed by Esperia, a company that took on many Italian films. Reviews were for the most part very positive. There was praise for the grand scale of the film, its dramatic and spectacular qualities, its use of masses of extras, and the rich settings. However, there were also some limiting remarks. *Time* described it as "as magnificent a bit of Fascismo as has come out of Italy. . . . It has up-to-the-minute double meanings for ardent Fascists: (1) the Semite is still public enemy No. 1; (2) conquered Carthage stood in what is now Fascist-coveted French Tunis."[40] The film was sold to many other countries, including Britain, France, Germany, and Switzerland.

As for relations between the Italian film industry and European film industries, Freddi was afraid that the placing of restrictions on foreign film imports would have negative effects on Italian exports. Thus it was essential to get export markets if the Italian film industry was to grow and prosper. This view was shared by Eitel Monaco, head of the producers' association FNFIS.[41] There had been extensive cooperation and remakes of German films in the early 1930s and the Germans also remade some Italian films and shot some exteriors in Italy, but it was they who saw Italy as an export market rather than the other way around. Unlike the Italian market, the German one did not need many foreign films to cover the gap between supply and demand. For Freddi, the Italian industry had been little more than a satellite of the German one between 1932 and 1934.[42] Only from 1937 did Italian films reach Germany in any quantity. Yet, despite the Axis, cinematic relations with Germany were never easy, even though most important issues were discussed at the state level. The Nazis exercised tighter censorship than the Italians on politically related themes (*La corona di ferro*, *Bengasi*, and other Italian films were banned in Germany) and they did not want films in which Jewish people had been involved.[43] They also sought to establish a relationship with the Italian film in-

Figure 12. Italian poster, designed by Alfredo Capitani, for *Gilda* (Charles Vidor, United States, 1946) with Rita Hayworth in the title role. This was one of the films that hit the Italian market after the Monopoly Law was rescinded in 1945. From Raccolta di Manifesti Salce, Museo Civico L. Bailo, Treviso. By permission of Soprintendenza per i Beni Artistici e Storici del Veneto.

dustry in which they would be the dominant force. In order to prevent this unappealing prospect, Italy cultivated bilateral relations with Hungary and also with France, the second biggest exporter of films to Italy after the United States, which in turn became a big export market for Italy in 1940–1942. Companies were formed by ENIC in Hungary, Bulgaria, Romania, Croatia, and Greece that imported and distributed Italian films, showing them in cinemas acquired for the purpose. Although the quantity of Italian films in these countries never matched that of German films, they were a welcome alternative. The Italians gained business but also deluded themselves that they were in some way challenging German hegemony.[44]

The publishing industry also appealed to the state to facilitate its foreign trade. In 1929 Franco Ciarlantini argued that Italy needed a single organization to coordinate book exports. He called on the government to sign up to Article 34 of the 1924 Stockholm Convention for member states of the Postal Union, which stipulated that printed paper should be given a 50 percent discount on standard postal tariffs (Italy did eventually sign up, in July 1936, although by 1938 the discount was still not being applied) and that it should promote indirect exports in the form of translations of Italian works, where foreign publishers sold the work on their own domestic markets but the Italian publisher and author earned translation rights or royalties.[45] As we saw in chapter 3, Arnoldo Mondadori pointed out in 1938 that the number of Italian books exported had increased by 40 percent in the three-year period 1934–1937. He used the occasion to plead for more support from the state with book exports: support with customs and currency but in particular with transport costs.[46] He proposed that a single export organization be set up that all publishers could use. The state could then encourage publishers to export by awarding premiums as an incentive, as in Germany where publishers were able to sell their books abroad at the same rate as at home. As for translations abroad of Italian works, Mondadori reported that he had signed deals with a number of European publishers—Bruckmann in Munich, Albatross in Paris, Athenaum in Budapest, Kasiaznica-Athas in Warsaw—which included an agreement by these houses to translate works by authors including Bontempelli, d'Annunzio, Deledda, Pirandello, and Verga.[47]

With Italy's entry into World War II, the market for book exports shrank. It now included only Italy's allies, notably Germany, the countries it had occupied, such as Greece, where troops were stationed, or those with which it had maintained friendly diplomatic relations, like Spain. Despite this contraction, some of these markets proved to be quite lucrative and exports did relatively well. In Leipzig, where a Centro del Libro Italiano was set up in August 1942, sales over a two-week period in December reached 50,000 Reichsmarks. Magazine exports were also quite successful. Mondadori produced a

German-language edition of *Tempo* whose earnings were about 700,000 lire a month, three times as high as those in Italy of the Italian-language edition of the German magazine *Signal*. At the same time, these export activities were hampered by the long delays, often over a year, in obtaining currency returns on sales and, since the profit margins on exports were already very small, publishers were discouraged from pursuing these markets and again sought state support. The Istituto nazionale per le Relazioni Culturali con l'Estero (IRCE), whose president was the Minister of Popular Culture, Alessandro Pavolini, drew attention to the fact that in Germany the state purchased books from publishers, which it then distributed free abroad as part of its propaganda effort, whereas in Italy private publishers were left to bear these costs with minimal state support. An IRCE memorandum complained that

there has been a deplorable lag between the efforts of the publishing industry and the necessary support of the finance ministries, the result of sometimes inexplicable delays in the bureaucratic machinery, which threatens to pull down what it has taken so much effort to build up and to undermine the very existence of those national activities that have proved most eager to fight the battle of the book.[48]

The IRCE proposed that the Ministry of Exchange and Currency might intervene to alleviate the problem by making repayable credit payments to the publishers equivalent to their foreign earnings within four months of sales, or making an arrangement to this effect with a credit bank such as the Banca Nazionale del Lavoro.[49] But these proposals were not put into effect and state support for book and magazine export remained half-hearted.

Propaganda
The term "propaganda" may be taken to mean any communication designed to express the opinions, beliefs, or values of an organized collective group and to persuade others of its truth, or at least of its ideological force. Not all propaganda is state propaganda, and indeed both the Vatican and, after the fall of Fascism, the left parties had their own well-oiled propaganda apparatuses. Under the Fascists, however, there had been a progressive extension of state propaganda activity, accompanied by a reorganization of the bodies responsible for propaganda and censorship. The areas of cultural activity that the Fascist regime could most easily use for propaganda purposes were those it controlled directly; the private cultural industries generally had to be persuaded or cajoled with some kind of incentive into producing propaganda on the state's behalf. An example of the former type of activity was the Mostra della Rivoluzione Fascista, which ran in Rome's Palazzo delle Esposizioni for two years, starting in October 1932, to celebrate the tenth anniversary (Decen-

nale) of the Fascists' accession to power. In its first thirteen months alone it made a net profit of 5.6 million lire and by the time it closed in October 1934 it had been visited by nearly four million people.[50] It is interesting as a case both of the use of modern advertising and marketing methods (it was launched with 100,000 posters, 200,000 postcards, and 1.33 million signs)[51] and of modernist design. Louis Gillet, national curator of French museums, described it in the *Revue des Deux Mondes* as "all very Futurist, of an adroit and unfettered Futurism in which everything is calculated according to a unique ballistics so as to machine-gun the spectator, to increase the power to shock."[52]

The centralization of propaganda functions in a single ministry in Fascist Italy was almost certainly influenced by the creation in Nazi Germany in March 1933 of the Ministry for People's Enlightenment and Propaganda (Reichsministerium für Volksaufklärung und Propaganda) headed by Joseph Goebbels, followed in September that year by the affiliated Chamber of Culture (Reichskulturkammer). The latter was divided into seven subchambers: press, radio, film, theater, literature, music, and fine arts. Up to the early 1930s press censorship and propaganda in Italy had been overseen by Mussolini's Press Office, the Ufficio Stampa del Capo del Governo, and there were no special state bodies responsible for propaganda in other media and arts such as film, radio, theater, and literature. The expansion of the Press Office took place under Galeazzo Ciano, Mussolini's son-in-law, who became its director in 1933 and enlarged it in 1934 into an Undersecretariat of State for Press and Propaganda (Sottosegretariato di Stato per la Stampa e la Propaganda), divided into three directorates (*direzioni generali*): Italian press, foreign press, and propaganda. The directorates for cinema and tourism were added later in 1934 and the inspectorate for theater in 1935. In June 1935, still under Ciano's direction, the body became the Ministry of Press and Propaganda (Ministero della Stampa e Propaganda). Ciano left in 1935 to fight in the Ethiopian War but was only formally replaced in June 1936 when he became Foreign Minister and the post of Minister of Press and Propaganda was filled by Dino Alfieri. In 1936 the Ministry was reorganized into six directorates and in 1937 it was renamed Ministero della Cultura Popolare. Alfieri continued as minister until October 1939 when his post was taken over by Alessandro Pavolini. The MCP was suppressed in the South after the liberation of Rome in July 1944 and replaced by the Undersecretariat of State for Press and Information (Sottosegretariato di Stato per la Stampa e le Informazioni) (1944–1945). However, it remained operative in the North until the fall of the Salò Republic in 1945. It was formally suppressed in July 1945 but the Undersecretariat of State for Press, Entertainment [Theater and Cinema] and Tourism took over many of its functions. Just as the gradual enlargement, in 1934–1937, of what had originally been Mussolini's Press Office into the MCP had reflected the state's extension of vigilance and control into many other areas of mass culture, notably publishing, theater and cinema, so a significant part of Fascism's legacy to the postwar state was this grouping of cultural functions into a single body.

In publishing, if we leave aside newspaper publishing, which was fascistized by the mid-1920s, only a small part of the state's relationship with the industry may be judged to have been directly propagandist in the Fascist period. There was a state-funded publishing and printing firm, the Poligrafici dello Stato, which produced official publications. The publication of the *Libro di Stato*, the prescribed school reader, which was taken under direct state control from 1929 (to the chagrin of the publishers who thereby lost a lucrative, guaranteed market), can also be seen as propaganda activity. Beyond this there was a fairly steady production of Fascist texts—biographies of leading Fascists and books on agriculture, education, or Italy's wars—by publishers aligned with the regime. In many cases these represented a good economic proposition, but such overtly Fascist texts never dominated any one publisher's lists and taken as a whole they constituted a small proportion of all books produced during the regime.

A particular case, however, is represented by the biographies of Mussolini. The first, Antonio Beltramelli's *L'uomo nuovo* (*The New Man*), was published in 1923. It was followed in 1926 by Margherita Sarfatti's *Dux* and Giorgio Pini's *Benito Mussolini: la sua vita fino ad oggi dalla strada al potere* (*Benito Mussolini: His Life So Far from the Streets to Power*). In 1932 Emil Ludwig's *Colloqui con Mussolini* appeared: it was not a biography but a written record of a series of interviews with Mussolini in March–April 1932. All these books, except Pini's, were published in Italy by Mondadori. The good sales of these texts demonstrated that Mussolini was a profitable subject. Ordinary Italians may have found official Fascist publications boring, as the authorities sometimes privately acknowledged, but for many of them the Duce seems to have exerted an endless fascination. There was also, right from the beginning, a worldwide audience for books about Mussolini. *Dux* had first appeared in English as *The Life of Benito Mussolini* (Butterworth: London, 1925) and Ludwig's conversations came out in 1932 almost simultaneously in several languages, including English (as *Talks with Mussolini*), French, German, Dutch, and Spanish. Subsequently, various salacious and unreliable accounts of his life appeared abroad, such as *My Love Affair with Mussolini* by the French journalist Magda Fontanges, which was serialized in three issues of the American magazine *Liberty* in August 1940.

In cinema, the question of propaganda is more controversial, at any rate as regards fictional feature films—historians generally agree that the nonfiction films, newsreels, and documentaries, produced by the Istituto Luce under the Fascists and by the Settimana Incom after the war, were vehicles of governmental opinion. There is no real consensus on the question of whether feature films in the main served a propaganda purpose. On the one hand is the view, dominant in early postwar accounts of the cinema under Fascism but still with some supporters today, that all Italian fiction films were in a broad sense ideologically aligned with the regime—otherwise they would not have received funding and gotten past the censors—and that they either expressed covert propaganda for a clerico-conservative ideology (for instance, support of "traditional family values" or an ethos of thrift, hard work, and subservience to authority) or functioned propagandistically in a "negative" way by avoiding controversial issues or evading reality altogether (the argument of cinema as "escapism"). On the other hand is the view recently summed up by Peter Bondanella:

Out of the more than 700 films produced under fascism, only a handful can be called propaganda pieces. Even the use of the term "fascist cinema" is misleading, for the films actually espousing the truly original ideology of the regime (the corporate state, the glorification of conflict, imperialism, the "Roman" heritage of Fascist Italy) are conspicuous by their virtual absence. It is more accurate to speak of "film during the Fascist period," "prewar cinema" or "wartime cinema," since so few of these films espouse any kind of ideology except a traditional nationalism, a conservative morality, and a Catholic religion.[53]

What is at stake in this debate is a disagreement not over what kind of feature films were made in Italy under Fascism, since it is clear that the majority of them were not explicitly political, nor over their core values, but rather over whether or not they should be considered as expressing indirect or covert propaganda for the regime. The debate raises some difficult questions. However, we believe that the view of entertainment cinema as escapism and the equation of escapism with propaganda are both reductive and that they fail to recognize the complexity of meanings of these films, or of audiences' responses to them.[54] Ultimately, we believe that behind the "covert propaganda" thesis lies that reductive view of the state's role in relation to mass culture as instrumental, which we discussed in the first section of this chapter.

As for propagandist newsreel production and the question of continuity across our period, clearly there were important ideological differences between the Fascist newsreels of the Istituto Luce and those of the postwar years. However, there were continuities in the mode of production and exhibition—newsreels were still inserted between successive projections of features—and in certain aspects of style: duration, tone of commentary, and use of accompanying music. Between 1949 and 1956 La Settimana Incom distributed at least 150 newsreels a year, peaking in 1952 with 190, a frequency of around two a week.[55] Despite the fact that Incom was a private company, and newsreel production was contracted both to its own crews and to a number of small private documentary-producing firms, the content of the newsreels was determined by the Centro Documentazione, a body set up by Alcide De Gasperi within the Prime Minister's Office, and therefore the newsreels were still, as they had been under Fascism, an official voice of the government.[56] The main discontinuities were in the treatment of the principal themes. For example, both the Luce newsreels of the Fascist period and those of the 1950s featured the efforts of the state to build the nation through an energetic program of public works and welfare and by tackling major public health problems (such as tuberculosis in the Fascist period, deficiency diseases and malaria after the war). The Incom newsreels were more candid about Italy's poverty and social problems—understandably so, since they could present these as a bad legacy of Fascism—and thus presented the efforts to tackle these problems, as well as to provide work for the unemployed and underemployed, as part of the political reconstruction, the building of democracy. In other words, the newsreels were still propagandistic, but the propaganda was differently inflected.

The elements of continuity in the structures of propaganda, like the continuation of the structures and functions of the Fascist Ministry of Popular Culture into the postwar Undersecretariat of State for Press, Entertainment and Tourism, were an important part of the continuity of the state in the transition between regimes. In the two-year period from the first Allied landings (July 1943) to the summer after the liberation (April 1945) propaganda in Italy had reflected the complex politico-military situation. In the areas occupied by the Germans and under the political control of the RSI, German and Fascist propaganda competed with the clandestine counter-propaganda of the Resistance. In the liberated areas, all propaganda was officially under the control of the Psychological Warfare Branch (PWB), dependent on Allied Force Headquarters (AFHQ), which had a mixture of British and American personnel. As Alejandro Pizarroso Quintero argued in the first well-documented study of the PWB's activities in Italy, its role there was more complex than in other countries, in which the Allies were either an occupying or a liberating force. Italy was an "enemy ally," a former Fascist state under Allied military occupation whose press and propaganda needed to be purged and reconstructed, and the PWB consequently had two distinct functions. On the one hand its role was to oversee direct propaganda and information, disseminated through its own publications, and on the other it was to oversee and vet the Italian press, radio, publishing, and cinema and steer them in the country's transition from dictatorship to democracy, preparing for the handover to the Italian authorities.[57]

The PWB's influence on book publishing has been relatively neglected and yet it appears to have been significant, helping to reorientate Italian publishers toward American and British authors and thus to shape their postwar lists. In April 1945 Mondadori had in press 5,000 copies of a translation of Hemingway's *For Whom the Bell Tolls;* the paper to publish it was sold to the firm at a reduced price by the Publications Office of the PWB, which strictly controlled paper supply in the liberated areas of the country.[58] In July 1945 Enzo Pagliara recollected: "They themselves [the Allies] gave the authorizations to publish books and they themselves insisted on publishing those they considered propaganda."[59] In the case of radio, the PWB took control of all spoken programs—news and political commentary, drama and prose readings—but left control of music broadcasting in the hands of the existing EIAR personnel. As the "Radio Plan for Liberated Italy" (November 23, 1944) explained this decision:

PWB had retained the above responsibilities because of the potentialities of all such [spoken] programmes for propaganda purposes, and because they are relayed by shortwave to German-occupied Italy. They thus become operational and, for security as well as for psychological warfare reasons, must remain the direct responsibility of PWB.[60]

Despite this, radio was a more difficult case for PWB management. The Allies were unable to monopolize the flow of radio information in the same way as they monopolized the flow of printed paper, and the PWB-controlled stations always competed with Fascist broadcasts from the nonliberated areas. Moreover, the sharing arrangement with the EIAR personnel led to conflicts between them and the PWB over how the radio should be run after liberation. Unlike the press, publishing, and cinema, the radio had been a monopoly under Fascism and there was the question of whether reconstructing it democratically should also mean decentralizing it or whether a single, centralized broadcasting system was preferable. Franco Chiarenza has suggested that the decentralized model was more attractive to the Americans in the PWB than to the British: the former encouraged local radio because it fitted with their own experience.[61]

As for the cinema, the film industry, which in Rome had virtually ceased production when the Allies took the city in June 1944, was placed under the supervision of the PWB's Film Section that included, among its leading officials, Pilade Levi, a former Paramount executive who would later represent the company in Rome, and Stephen Pallos of Britain, a former assistant to Alexander Korda. The PWB conducted a check of all Italian films in circulation and banned all those that showed Fascist bias, that would profit Fascists, or that featured stars or directors who had shown sympathy with Nazism or Fascism. The PWB banned all films by Carmine Gallone, the director of *Scipione l'Africano,* as well as those starring, among others, the collaborators Osvaldo Valenti and Luisa Ferida (see chapter 5), and Beniamino Gigli, who was suspected of collaboration (see chapter 6). Each film shown had to have PWB approval and all Luce newsreels were prohibited. However, it was not always easy for the PWB to win control of cinemas. Every time an area was liberated, one PWB official wrote, "It is a requisitioning dogfight between the Church, Red Cross, Special Services, the Army involved and the PWB to see who is going to get what theatre. Each of these organizations have [*sic*] a different objective. The results of this competition have been far from efficient or satisfactory."[62] The PWB opened the first cinemas in Rome just six days after the liberation, using generators for power since no other electricity was available. Many Italian civilians were employed in this activity. Some newsreels, or local inserts, were made in Italy to accompany films. The choice of films was designed to win the population to the side of the Allies by revealing the evils of fascism and the merits of democracy. They were intended to show allied objectives, explain plans for Italian reconstruction, and promote peace and transmit hope. Some forty-seven films (plus shorts) had been stockpiled in Tunis prior to the Allied landing, carefully selected by film companies working with the U.S. State Department and the Commerce Department.

CENSORSHIP

In most historical situations censorship operates according to rules that are fairly transparent to all the parties involved, namely the censors themselves, the artists, or other cultural "makers" whose work is subject to censorship, and the cultural "mediators," such as publishers or film producers, who commission the works and put up the production costs. This does not mean that all these parties always agree on censorship decisions or that the cultural producers always like the rules—just that they know what they are. In Fascist Italy, prefascist norms and legislation regulating censorship of books, plays, films, and songs were initially carried over largely unaltered, although, as had occurred with the press, by the mid-1920s oppositional publishers and theater companies linked to the left either had to transform themselves or they were suppressed. With all these cultural products, by the middle period of Fascism, around the Decennale in 1932, new rules of censorship had become relatively stable and transparent to the contracting parties. In the mid-1930s, however, as the regime moved toward a more interventionist phase, the situation began to change again, and the rules governing censorship started to become opaque to the cultural makers. This period—the years that included the creation of the Ministry of Popular Culture, the racial laws (see below), and World War II up to Mussolini's removal from office—may be seen as exceptional, a time when the previously agreed-upon rules began to break down and new, nonconsensual rules emerged, producing a sense of arbitrariness, unpredictability, disorientation, and fear, though not preventing cultural industries from continuing to try and negotiate with the state. After the Resistance and Liberation a new, wider set of consensual rules of censorship were briefly introduced but again the consensus broke down in the Cold War period, 1947–1954, when arbitrariness and unilateral acts of censorship once more came into play. The pattern we propose from just before our period to the end of it is therefore, with approximate dates, consensus up to 1934–1935, collapse of consensus 1935–1945, new consensus 1945–1947, and new collapse 1947–1954.

In the phases of consensus, a large amount of censorship was in practice pre-censorship, which was carried out by those in the cultural industries who rejected projects or required changes to a given work, rather than the more visible types of censorship—demands for cuts or outright bans—exercised from outside by official censorship bodies. In cases where revision was required by the censors, it too was applied at different levels. Demands for revision might consist of the requirement to cut one or two lines; the removal of a character or scene considered defamatory toward Italy or to organs of the state, such as the armed forces; the elimination of a whole act or episode, or, more rarely, the complete prohibition of a script or a novel.[63] Cesare Zavattini described this process from a writer's point of view in 1960:

The damage done by censorship is not to be found principally in the highly visible veto or in seizures of works but in the more hidden intimidations and secret pressures to which authors are subjected . . . . We know very well that even those authors who believe themselves to be most free and in good faith are exposed to these pressures.[64]

Political censorship as narrowly conceived— censorship in accordance with government or party policy and motivated on explicitly political grounds —was only a part of the totality of censorship at any given time. This is true of the Fascist regime before what we have called the collapse of consensus (1935–1945), as well as of the period 1945–1947, when most cases of censorship were based on moral or religious grounds. Works during this time were censored because they were considered "offensive to decency" (*buon costume*) or contrary to Christian morality (such as when a character committed suicide) or liable to corrupt "susceptible" social groups: women, children, the lower classes. Even in the last period of Fascism, which encompassed the propaganda struggles against "Bolshevik atheism" in Spain (1936–1939) and in the Soviet Union (1941–1943) and against the "plutocratic democracies," Great Britain and the United States, the reasons given for many refusals of permission to publish books continued to be moral or religious. In September 1941 Mondadori's request to publish a translation of John Steinbeck's *To a God Unknown* was turned down on the grounds that the novel, "as well as ending with a suicide, seems to be pervaded by an extreme and crazed sexuality." In December 1941, Mondadori was permitted, by contrast, to publish a translation of Knut Hamsun's novel *Vagabonds* (*Landstrykere*) but on the condition that four passages were removed, in which a woman is accused of infanticide, a skeleton is exhumed to retrieve a gold ring, the use of a contraceptive by a married woman is mentioned, and a black woman is killed while being raped.[65]

Although our discussion here is concerned with state censorship it is important to remember that the Catholic Church had its own apparatuses of censorship alongside those of the state. For books there was the *Index librorum prohibitorum*, whose first edition had appeared in 1564, which proscribed a number of works that had been passed by the state censors. Among the modern Italian authors whose works were included in the *Index* were Leopardi and d'Annunzio and, among contemporary writers, Alberto Moravia, whose novels were all placed on the *Index* in the edition of 1952. The *Index* remained in force until 1966. Sexual censorship by the *Index* was directed particularly against works that represented sex in materialist terms, that severed it from the spiritual dimension and from conjugal love, and that appeared to sanction free love or divorce. For films, Catholic censorship was handled centrally by the Centro Cattolico Cinematografico (CCC), instituted in 1934, which classified films according to a system of colored discs that included the categories "excluded to all" (*escluso a tutti*) and "unadvisable for all" (*sconsigliato a tutti*). Here too conflicts and differences of judgment arose between religious and state censors.

In the period when the agreed-upon rules broke down, and particularly after Italy's entry into World War II in June 1940 and the subsequent spread of clandestine antifascism, it becomes harder to draw such a clear line between the different grounds for censorship. Let us consider two famous cases: Elio Vittorini's novel *Conversazione in Sicilia*, published in 1941, and Luchino Visconti's film *Ossessione*, released in March 1943. The official reasons for the sequestration orders on both of them were not political but moral and religious. Vittorini's novel, which had appeared originally in five installments in the magazine *Letteratura* between April 1938 and April 1939, was published twice as a book in 1941, first by the Florentine publisher Parenti in a small edition of 355 copies, together with a short story and with the overall title *Nome e lagrime*, and then by Bompiani as *Conversazione in Sicilia*. The book had received generally positive reviews in the press, including Fascist organs like *Roma Fascista* and *Il Popolo Fascista*, and the Bompiani edition had been on sale for a year and had gone through three reprints, with total sales of around 15,000 copies, when it was withdrawn in late 1942. The catalyst seems to have been an unsigned editorial entitled "Una sporca conversazione" (A dirty conversation), which had appeared on July 30, 1942 in the leading Fascist daily, *Il Popolo d'Italia* and attacked the novel for pornography.[66] The novel included various allusions, veiled in metaphor and allegory, to Fascist internal repression, militarism, and imperialism and to antifascist struggle, but it also included a son's conversations with his mother about her adulterous affair and a mention of his father's adultery, and it was the latter that were cited as the reasons for censorship. Visconti's film, an unauthorized adaptation of James M. Cain's *The Postman Always Rings Twice* (1934), which centered on a passionate adulterous affair and the murder by the lovers of the cuckolded husband, was withdrawn from cinemas in various provinces after complaints by the religious authorities had impelled the prefects to act. In Bologna the Catholic newspaper *Avvenire d'Italia* attacked the film for obscenity and immorality.[67] Renato Guttuso's painting of the Crucifixion, which won a prize at the Mostra di Bergamo in 1941, was likewise condemned by the Church, along with the exhibition that housed it. Yet in each of these cases the fact that the individuals who produced these works were known to be antifascists meant that both the censors and the defenders of the work could interpret its transgressions of moral or religious norms as also having a political character, and this interpretation did not need to invoke any political allusions of an oppositional nature in the works themselves, even when these allusions were present. Raffaele Crovi, in his biography of Vittorini, cites a recollection from 1973 by Communist Giancarlo Pajetta that *Conversazione in Sicilia* was "like a message of struggle to those hoping in exile or prison for a conspiracy [against Fascism]" and another by Alfonso Failla that it was "certainly the most widely read novel among those in *confino* [internal exile] at Ventotene."[68] Similarly, the transgression of norms of propriety in Guttuso's depiction of the crucifixion, where the breasts of the weeping Mary Magdalene are exposed, and in *Ossessione* in the sexual relationship between Gino (Massimo Girotti) and Giovanna (Clara Calamai), were seen as signs of a political transgression.[69]

The rules governing the censorship of books, plays, and films were similar to one another and they stemmed from the same generic legislation dating from just after Unification. The two most important new laws relating to censorship introduced under Fascism were the Public Security Laws (Testo Unico delle Leggi di Pubblica Sicurezza) of November 6, 1926 and the Penal Code of June 18, 1931 (Decree no. 773), which recognized the Testo Unico. The Testo Unico empowered the police and prefects to seize publications and films and prevent theatrical performances deemed to constitute an affront to decency or national dignity or a risk to public order.

The first legislation specifically regulating film censorship had been framed between 1913 and 1920 and had then been modified by a decree of September 24, 1923 signed by Mussolini in his capacity as Minister of the Interior.

By contrast with the earlier legislation, the 1923 law significantly concentrated powers of revision in the hands of the state, in that the primary censorship commission, which had the task of examining scripts as well as completed films, was composed entirely of functionaries of the Interior Ministry, and only the second-level commission had a slightly more pluralist composition: three members of the General Division of Public Security (DGPS), the branch of the ministry with responsibility for the police, plus one magistrate, one mother (*madre di famiglia*), one journalist (*pubblicista*), and one secondary-school teacher (*professore*). However, the law gave the Interior Ministry the right to replace any of the other members if they proved unsuited to the task. There were successive modifications to this law, and particularly to the composition of the censorship bodies, during the Fascist period. The most important was the law of June 18, 1931 (Law 857), which laid the basis for censorship until World War II, and by which members of the PNF were introduced into the commission alongside the representatives of the Interior Ministry, the magistrate, and the mother. However, the wording of the 1923 legislation was to remain fundamental. It was reverted to after the fall of Fascism and became the basic regulatory framework until 1962.

Luigi Freddi, whose responsibilities as Director General for the Cinema from 1934 to 1939 included overall control of state censorship of films, wrote for the most part unapologetically and defensively in his postwar memoirs about his role as censor in the Fascist regime. In the case of Italian films, he noted that when he had taken over responsibility for film censorship in 1934, preproduction censorship (*censura preventiva*) of scripts was nonexistent—producers would simply present the script together with the finished film in requesting that the film be passed, in other words given a *nulla osta* (from the Latin phrase *nihil obstat*, "nothing stands in the way")—and the essential change he had introduced was to intervene earlier, at the preproduction stage. He represented this as a means of making censorship no longer simply negative and repressive but also positive, an "enabling" activity, using the revision of scripts as a way of intervening to shape the cinema. In his initial report to Mussolini in 1934 he wrote: "Film censorship is still considered police work," and in his memoirs (1949) he added: "State intervention . . . should not be limited to restrictive action but should be geared towards developing, by every possible means, an appropriate function of inspiring and arousing."[70]

Toward foreign films, which constituted the vast majority of those that came before the censor during Freddi's tenure of office, his position was similar. In general, he admired the technical virtuosity and positive energy of American cinema and in his memoirs he contrasted American films, which he felt were generally suited to Italian tastes, with the corrupt atmosphere often found in French films. As far as he was concerned, it was sufficient to use the levers of censorship to weed out "morally and artistically damaging" foreign products.[71] Jean Gili, in his study of Fascist film censorship, claims that the "decadence" of some French films was taken by the Fascists as proving their point that the Western democracies were in decline and they passed them for this reason.[72] Others, notably Renoir's antiwar film *La Grande illusion*, provoked great ire and embarrassment. Freddi writes about it at length and refers to the steps he took to ensure that it was not awarded the major prize at the 1937 Venice Film Festival.[73]

With all the cultural industries, the formal shift from censorship handled by prefects to a centralized system came in 1937 with the setting up of the Ministry of Popular Culture. However, moves toward centralization had already begun in 1934. In April 1934 publishers received a letter from their local police headquarters (*questura*) instructing them to send three copies of all works that they proposed to publish—books, magazines, or pamphlets—to the prefecture.[74] This followed a circular of April 3, signed by Mussolini, which specified that, of these three copies, one was to be forwarded to the DGPS and another to his own Press Office, the Ufficio Stampa del Capo del Governo. Publication could only proceed if a *nulla osta* was issued.

Censorship and governmental repression intensified in the late 1930s and publishers, even those who considered themselves to be loyal fascists, were increasingly made aware of it. The stepping-up of censorship was not arbitrary but followed a number of turns in government policy in this period: the tightening alliance with Nazi Germany (Rome–Berlin Axis, October 1936; intervention of German and Italian expeditionary forces in the Spanish Civil War, November 1936; Pact of Steel, May 1939; entry into World War II, June 1940); the more aggressive and expansionist foreign policy (invasion and conquest of Abyssinia, 1935–1936; invasion of Albania 1939); antisemitism (the racial laws from September 1938); and the drive to economic autarky. The effect was a breakdown in the system of shared values and agreed-upon rules that had been negotiated with the cultural producers and the cultural industries up to the early 1930s and it produced surprise, disorientation, and sometimes fruitless attempts at bargaining.

Antisemitic censorship constitutes the most nefarious instance of breakdown of consensus. The first "laws for the defense of the race," commonly known as the "racial laws" (*leggi razziali*), were issued in September 1938, although the decisive turn toward this legislation can be dated back to "a still not yet well identified moment between the end of 1935 and the summer of 1936."[75] The announcement of the laws was preceded by a mounting wave of race propaganda in the Italian press in 1936–1938.[76] The Nuremberg laws, passed in Germany in November 1935, and the theory and practice of colonial racism in Abyssinia, conquered by the Italians in May 1936, with the subsequent campaign against interracial liaisons there, have both been seen as precedents.[77] Along with other forms of repression directed against Jews resident in Italy, the racial laws introduced a specific targeting of censorship against Jewish cultural products and producers, and may therefore be taken as a limit case by which to test the thesis of censorship as normally operating within consensual parameters. Giorgio Fabre, the author of the most fully documented account of book censorship under the racial laws, argued that it had been well-nigh erased from Italy's collective memory:

Between 1938 and 1942, the Italians, like the Germans, had carried out their book burning. But, unlike in Germany, it was done without fire. In Italy thousands of volumes, perhaps millions of tons of paper, had disappeared, had been scattered, and no one had spoken about them again.[78]

The racial laws made an immediate impact on publishing. Already in April 1938 an internal memorandum of the MCP suggested the drawing up of a list of "authors to be avoided" and ordering publishers and editors of newspapers and magazines to eliminate from circulation "Jewish and pro-Jewish writers or those of a decadent tendency."[79] A Commissione per la Bonifica del Libro (Commission for the Reclamation of the Book) was set up by the MCP and its members drew up a list of proscribed authors. The Jewish identity of an author now became a sufficient reason for the MCP to refuse to authorize publication. Mondadori's requests to publish translations of André Maurois's life of Chateaubriand (1938) and Joseph Roth's novel *Das falsche Gewicht* (1937) were refused by the MCP with the same words: "because the author is of the Jewish race."[80] As with other areas where the racial laws were applied, the policies of the Commissione per la Bonifica del Libro were given a spurious intellectual justification in the form of articles on the supposed intellectual inferiority of Jewish thought and culture. In September 1938 *Il Libro Italiano*, the periodical published by the MCP, carried an article by Riccardo Miceli entitled "Racism of the Book" (*Razzismo del libro*) which repeated the arguments of Renan, Pouchet, and others that the Jews lacked the culture of critical reflection common to the "Aryan" peoples.[81] Italy's Jewish publishers were also affected. Angelo Fortunato Formiggini, director of Edizioni dell'ICS (abbreviation of the firm's literary periodical, *L'Italia che scrive*), committed suicide in a public protest against the laws, throwing himself off the Ghirlandina, the bell tower of Modena cathedral, on the morning of November 29, 1938.[82] Publishing firms run by Jewish families had changes in ownership, shareholdings, and management imposed on them. Treves, which had been the most successful publisher in Milan until the rise of Mondadori, had its name changed to Aldo Garzanti Editore after an extraordinary general meeting of directors and shareholders on March 16, 1939. On June 39 of the same year a similar meeting in Florence of the board of Bemporad, which had merged with another Florentine firm, Barbèra, changed the new firm's name to Marzocco, a name redolent of "native" Florentine tradition, and led to the exclusion of the former director, Emilio Bemporad.[83] In literary circles the racial laws not only stirred up fear among Jewish writers but also created for the first time a whole body of officially prohibited reading. In the recollection of the poet Piero Bigongiari it was

a tragedy: it was without any doubt the point of rejection and supreme break. Many of our friends, the ones we continued seeing or we took in, we kept hidden at home. Loria, Bonsanti whose wife was Jewish . . . Montale who lived with the woman he called Mosca ["Fly"] who was Jewish. We were already in the midst of the tragedy, accepting what was happening.[84]

The antisemitic measures were stepped up during the period of RSI administration of the German-occupied areas of Italy (October 1943–April 1945), when they coincided with the systematic drive by the SS, assisted by the Fascist police, to round up and deport all Jews to concentration camps or extermination camps. On November 24, 1943 the Ministry of Popular Culture of the RSI gave publishers two weeks to withdraw all books by Jewish authors, as well as those from enemy countries, from their depositories and from all bookshops and itinerant booksellers and hand them in to their local prefecture.[85] On January 4, 1944 Mussolini signed a legislative decree declaring that Jews were no longer entitled to hold property and that all their goods were to be confiscated.[86] Article 2 required anyone with payments owing to Jews to supply the local authorities with a list of names and amounts. Publishers thus had to declare royalty earnings accruing to their Jewish authors and these were then seized by the state. On February 29, 1944 the Mondadori firm provided the RSI administration of the Province of Milan with the names of thirteen "persons of the Jewish race (Italian and foreign)" with amounts owing to each. They were Arturo Castiglioni, Laura Orvieto, Margherita Sarfatti, Alfredo Segre, René Fülöp Miller, Ernst Lothar, André Maurois, Alfred Neumann, Ludwig Toeplitz, Hedwig Toeplitz, Jacob Wassermann, Arnold Zweig, and Stefan Zweig.[87] Giorgio Fabre has estimated that the "reclamation of the book" resulted overall in the withdrawal from circulation of works by about 700 Jewish authors, Italian and foreign.[88]

Parallel points about the phasing in of censorship and the tightening of restrictions as a result of the racial laws can be made for the cinema, including film journalism, and the music business. In 1936 an article on Chaplin appeared in *Cinema*, the journal edited by Mussolini's son Vittorio. One of the authors was the Jewish critic Giacomo Debenedetti, and the article stressed positively the Jewish roots of Chaplin's humor, linking it to the work on the inferiority complex by Sigmund Freud, "an Israelite from Vienna." By 1939 Chaplin's films were banned in Italy and Debenedetti was no longer able for racial reasons to sign his film criticism.[89] In 1942, the MCP refused a *nulla osta* to Laterza to publish a book of essays in honor of Croce's seventy-fifth birthday and one of the reasons was that it included a reprint of an essay by Debenedetti, "The Style of Benedetto Croce," first published in 1922.[90]

As for the censorship of radio, clandestine listening was increasingly policed and repressed during the war (see chapter 1). Since the Spanish Civil War, when antifascist transmissions had become widespread, prefects across Italy had sent reports of intercepted broadcasts to the Minister of the Interior.[91] However, interceptions and jamming had limited success, mainly because of the ability of the transmitting stations to switch frequency and the inability of the jamming centers in Italy to keep track of them.[92] Nevertheless, the government continued to make great efforts to staunch the flow of these broadcasts. In September 1940, 60 million lire were made available to the EIAR by the MCP to set up new interception centers in Palermo, Catanzaro, Rome, and Turin. More effective as a repressive measure were the arrests, threats of arrest, and punishments of those found listening to or spreading information from antifascist broadcasts. In May 1942, three antifascists were arrested in the province of Ancona, accused of having spread news from Radio Londra; in July a group was sentenced in Naples; in September various workers were sentenced in Taranto for crimes against the state and for having listened to enemy radio stations.[93]

After the Liberation in April 1945 much of the specific legislation on censorship introduced in the Fascist period was abrogated and there was a widespread sense that a new period of freedom of expression and freedom from censorship had arrived.[94] However, this did not stop entrenched practices of regulation and censorship from continuing. This may be illustrated with the case of cinema. A Decree of October 5, 1945 (DLL no. 678) removed the requirement that scripts or treatments needed to be examined and approved by the censorship office before a film could go into production. It also repealed Law 2125 of November 30, 1939, which required prior approval of a script, known as a *nulla osta preventivo*. Nevertheless, precensorship returned in practice less than two years later when a Central Film Office (Ufficio Centrale per la Cinematografia) was set up with a censorship commission (Commissione per la Revisione Cinematografica) divided into two committees, the second for appeals against the decisions of the first. The law instituting this censorship office (no. 379 of May 16, 1947) gave a producer the *option* of submitting a script for prior approval. As Maurizio Cesari comments, the pressure to do so was high given the financial risk of the completed film later being refused a *nulla osta*.[95] The pressure increased in 1949 with the introduction of the Andreotti law (see chapter 4), which offered a premium equivalent to 10 percent of the box office gross accumulated over the first four years of the film's distribution, provided that the project had been put before the Ufficio Centrale and had obtained prior approval.[96] It thus became essential in practice for a film to get the *nulla osta preventivo* if it was to receive funding from the Banca Nazionale del Lavoro and go into production. Some indication of the restrictiveness of the postwar censorship regime can be gauged from the fact that in 1950 only 72 out of 104 Italian films submitted for examination got this prior approval.[97]

The collective perception of a new freedom of expression after the Liberation had produced, predictably, a conservative backlash. From 1946 onward a more restrictive framework was put back in place that was couched largely in moral terms. The Sottosegretariato per la Stampa, Turismo e Spettacolo (Undersecretariat for the Press, Tourism, and Entertainment) had been quick to undo the more obvious forms of Fascist political censorship, most notably the racial laws. The new consensus that emerged after 1945, acceptable to all the political forces that were to be represented in the new constitution, focused on the need for censorship on moral rather than political grounds.

In May 1947, De Gasperi, following his visit to the United States, expelled the left parties from the government coalition and the political climate changed sharply. In the new cabinet Giulio Andreotti was nominated Undersecretary for the Press, Entertainment, and Tourism, an office he would hold to the end of De Gasperi's premiership in 1953. Andreotti is often represented in histories of postwar Italian cinema as the Big Bad Wolf of film censorship but in fact his line, as Marco Barbanti has demonstrated, was essentially a moderate one.[98] His attitude toward the moral molding of the film industry, for instance, was not wholly dissimilar to that of his predecessor, Luigi Freddi, under the Fascists. Both men sought to shape the film industry ideologically by encouragement more than by repression, and to provide economic incentives to this end. Nevertheless, increasingly vociferous protests came from the left in this period about the political controls being exercised over cinema, theater, publishing, and radio. In 1948, Umberto Barbaro, who had joined the Communist Party at the end of the war, was fired from the directorship of the Centro Sperimentale di Cinematografia. In the same year thirty-five film directors signed an open letter of protest about the new censorship regime claiming that the ostensibly moral and "national" criteria invoked for censorship were merely a pretext for a directly political intervention from the center-right.[99]

There were similar complaints from the opposition parties about increasingly overt political control of radio broadcasting after the turn to the right in mid-1947. An article in the Communist daily *L'Unità* of November 23,

1947, referring to the editing out from the program *La voce dei lavoratori* (The Workers' Voice) of a sentence critical of the employers' organization Confindustria, asked, "Has the Minculpop [Ministero della Cultura Popolare] risen from the grave? So it would seem."[100] The most sustained critique of the new censorship regime was *Ritorno alla censura* (*Back to Censorship*), the pamphlet written by Vitaliano Brancati in 1952 in the wake of the refusal of permission to stage his play *La governante* (*The Governess*) on the grounds of alleged obscenity. Brancati was writing mainly about the theater but he also referred to the cinema, mentioning, for example, the instruction to blip out the soundtrack over an allegedly blasphemous line of dialogue in Visconti's *Bellissima* (1951) in which a character says, referring to a woman's body, "Who will enjoy this gift of God?" (*Chi se lo gode questo ben di Dio?*). Brancati argued that there had been not only a continuity of censorship from the MCP to the Sottosegretariato per lo Spettacolo but also a persistence of the same mentality among the officials responsible for censorship. His venom was directed as much against their servility to the diktats of their masters (and thus against the continuation of a bootlicking mentality from Fascism) as against the quality and quantity of the censorship itself.[101]

In the long period of DC-led center-right hegemony that ran from 1947 until the first center-left coalitions in 1963, Catholic control over film censorship worked both through the government bodies dominated by the DC (the Sottosegretariato per la Stampa, Spettacolo e Turismo, and more particularly the Ufficio Centrale per la Cinematografia that contained the state censorship body Commissione per la Revisione Cinematografica), which in turn had powerful Catholic lobbies behind them, and directly through the Centro Cattolico Cinematografico. Indeed, at first there was an overlap between the state and the CCC in that Monsignor Albino Galletto, the president of the latter's commission, which divided films into categories and gave them color-coded discs, was also the ecclesiastical advisor to the Ente dello Spettacolo. There were nonetheless some differences too. The CCC classed as "unadvisable for all" or "excluded to all" a number of films to which the Commissione per la Revisione Cinematografica had granted a *nulla osta* and in different provinces Fascist prefects, empowered to seize films, sometimes supported and at other times overrode local Catholic opposition to the screening of a particular film. Nevertheless the role of the CCC remained extremely important. A film that it classed as "excluded," "unadvisable," or restricted to "adults of full moral maturity" (*consigliato agli adulti di piena maturità morale*) would be unattractive to distributors and exhibitors because of the restricted audience on the commercial circuit and a complete ban on the parish circuit. The threat of this classification deterred producers at the script stage from funding any project that was likely to fall foul of the CCC.

The most notorious case of censorship in the cinema toward the end of

Figure 13. Painted poster for *Peccato che sia una canaglia* (*Too Bad She's Bad*)
(Alessandro Blasetti, 1954), depicting Sophia Loren. The poster was sent by Don
Mario Gatti, parish priest of Tomba Extra (Verona), to Giulio Andreotti, with a letter dated February 8, 1954: "EXCELLENCY, I invite you to examine this filth, which
is permitted and authorized by the organs of government. Every cinema and
every news kiosk has become a school for crime and corruption. . . . How much
longer do we have to watch, powerless, this tide of mud that is only serving to
swell the ranks of the Communists? Why aren't the real criminals in the cinema
and the press put under arrest? Why doesn't the government do something, or
why does it do so little to hold back the nefariousness of modern life?" The letter
and poster are in ACS, PCM Gab. 1951–1953, b. 3-2-6, f. 32227. By permission of
Archivio Centrale dello Stato, Rome.

our period involved neither the refusal of a *nulla osta* nor the withdrawal of a film from circulation but the arrest, trial, and imprisonment of two people. In 1953 Guido Aristarco, editor of the lefist *Cinema Nuovo*, published Renzo Renzi's sketch of a "prohibited film" to be called *L'armata s'agapò* (*The "I Love You" Army*), which was to have critically portrayed the Italian army's conduct in the Greek campaign during the World War II. Aristarco and Renzi were both arrested, tried by a military tribunal, and given prison sentences for "libelling the armed forces."[102] The opposition parties and press were outraged by a military trial of civilians and denounced it and the sentences as a further attack by the state on freedom of expression in the cinema in the supposedly free and democratic era that had begun in 1945.

Intervention in Perspective

This chapter has examined the different types of state intervention in culture from the 1930s to the mid-1950s. Our aim has been to give a more nuanced and balanced account of the state's operations in the cultural sphere than most of those currently available and to provide evidence against the argument that the state simply used mass culture instrumentally. The last forms of intervention we have dealt with—propaganda and censorship—are the most familiar because they have been the most analyzed. They are also the ones that seem to give most sustenance to the instrumentalist view. However, as we have tried to show, propaganda, for all its importance, was always a particular and circumscribed part of the totality of the state's activities in the cultural sphere and censorship, although notoriously harsh in some cases, always worked in combination with other forms of intervention such as selective economic support and protection of the home market. It is important, ultimately, to see state intervention as a whole, in all its forms, as part of the wider play of forces between cultural industries, consumer tastes, and the actions of various groups and organizations in civil society. It is to the latter that we turn in the next and final chapter.

8 Civil Society and Organized Leisure

The Fascists, the Catholics, and the Christian Democrats, and the forces of the left, led by the Communists, were all required to respond in a variety of ways to commercial leisure, new means of communication, and to the possibilities, as well as the challenges and dangers they represented. In this final chapter we explore the relationship between cultural forms delivered through the market and the cultural activities organized by the political and religious forces active in society between the 1930s and the 1950s. It is undeniable that forms of commodified leisure became more important over this period and that the patterns of social relations on which organized leisure was first developed underwent change and decline. But it would be wrong to conclude from this that the phenomenon of organized leisure, and still less the broader phenomenon of cultural interventionism, declined or became marginal between the 1930s and the 1950s. On the contrary, the desire of the Fascists to disarticulate the structures of leisure produced by the labor movement, widen support for the regime, and form the nation according to their own militaristic project meant that there was a quantitative increase in voluntary nonmarket leisure and cultural activities. This increase was also affected in the postwar years by the intense competition between Catholics and the left for the loyalty of the middle and working classes. In the Italian context, the market did not displace or erode voluntary popular cultural consumption until the late 1950s. Instead, the market stimulated political and religious forces to seek to condition it, compete with it, and develop alternatives to it.

This is not to say that political forces succeeded in dominating or controlling cultural markets, except in specific instances and over relatively short time periods. But political and religious institutions played an important role in the cultural development of the country; they were not "backward" with respect to innovations in communication and new patterns of living but rather were integral, if sometimes contradictory, facets of Italian modernization. This was so even when they quite explicitly opposed such fundamental trends as urbanization and feminine self-fashioning. Such oppositions could only arise in a context of modernization and were attempts to shape and even direct its influence.

Three questions will be addressed here. First, to what extent did the promotion of political and religious affiliations and bonds of loyalty intersect with, reinforce, or undermine collective identification with the nation? Second, how far did the various forces succeed in elaborating strategic responses to cultural innovations? Third, can common patterns be observed in the modes of intervention of all three forces? And if not, were the differences more marked between reactionary/conservative (Fascist and Catholic) and left forces, between secular (Fascist and Communist) and religious forces, or between the authoritarian context of the Fascist regime and the democratic context of the postwar period?

Fascist Social Organization

During its twenty years as Italy's ruling party (1922–1943), the Partito Nazionale Fascista (PNF) developed and put into practice a range of policies on culture and leisure. Different forms of intervention took shape in response to the different requirements at given moments and in specific spheres. In addition, there was a plurality of currents and generations within Fascism ("Fascists of the first hour," intransigents, conservatives, Fascist youth and students) and different organizations, including the Opera Nazionale Dopolavoro (OND), Opera Nazionale Balilla (ONB, containing the various youth organizations), the Opera Nazionale Combattenti (ONC, the war veterans' association, responsible among other things for land reclamation projects), and the Gruppi Universitari Fascisti (GUF). However, some common themes and directions can be seen. Culture and leisure were not peripheral for Fascists but central. Both offered scope for furthering their strategy of refounding the nation and molding the Italian people in new ways. Because Fascism enjoyed a monopoly of state power, it is not always possible to draw a distinction between party activities in civil society and the forms of state intervention we discussed in chapter 7. Often the division was blurred by the Fascists themselves. With their totalitarian aspirations, they recognized no distinction between the state and civil society, a view that was confirmed by the transformation of the PNF into a state party that imposed compulsory membership on certain categories of people and aimed to draw in and regiment virtually the whole population. Here, however, we shall consider those forms of associationist activism under Fascism that most affected the organization of society and daily life.

The Fascists deliberately made the nation ideological by identifying it strictly with their own movement. They rejected earlier identifications of the nation with liberty, humanity, and all Italians and identified it more narrowly with the state, which now had the task of refounding the nation and remaking Italians. For the Fascists, the state was a concept before it was a set of institutions and practices; it came before the nation, and both nation and state stood above mere individuals. In the 1930s the Fascists pursued a policy of "politicization from above, compulsory, pedagogical, unilateral."[1] As part of this strategy, they turned the PNF from a mass party of around one million members in 1926 into a party of 4.5 million cardholders by 1932. The aim was to draw all sectors of the population into a range of official structures related to territory, work, sex, and age. It was not just adults who were involved. The organizations for children involved obligatory membership even for infants, who were Figli della Lupa (Sons of the She-wolf) before the age of six, when they became Balilla (boys) or Piccole Italiane (girls). Further associations catered to children and adolescents aged between nine and fourteen and fourteen and eighteen. The Fascists aimed to form minds, build loyalty, and create a set of external identifications with the regime. Orderly rallies, parades, and uniforms were an integral part of their strategy of incorporation. Such events did not only occur at the national level but also became part of the structure of the life of communities in the cities.

It emerges from some of the oral testimonies we collected that uniforms were a source of irritation to some people and also of division between generations. Adults were constrained to buy a uniform and attend rallies if they wished to avoid being *segnalati*, in other words, having their names recorded by the police. In Cagliari, F. P. recalled that "Dad was pretty well forced to get a uniform, because they had started to mark him, to watch him as someone

who didn't turn up at parades" (50/51: 41). For parents, the obligation to en-
roll children in Fascist youth organizations was sometimes a source of dis-
pleasure that was further exacerbated by the cost of the uniform. Avelina G.,
in Bologna, said that her parents tried to stop her becoming a Piccola Italiana
but were forced to give in (24: 7). Adelia Q., in Rome, recalled that her father
was forced by the Fascists to buy her a uniform and a black cloak after initially
having refused (57: 3–4). There was strong peer pressure to have the uniform
and those who did not have it felt left out (41: 26). To avoid this, parents sometimes went to unusual lengths. In Cosenza, Carmela F. recalled that her indi-
gent mother, in order to provide a Balilla uniform for her son, "unstitched one
of her dresses and made him a black shirt. She made his short trousers out of
a pair of soldiers' trousers" (71/72: 8). In this case she went against the wishes
of her socialist husband. When the latter saw his son wearing a black shirt he
said, "Take that shirt off. You can wear it when your mother dies" (71/72: 9).
The boy, however, was happy.

The Fascists could sometimes drive a wedge between known antifascists
and their children. Luisanna D., born in Sardara (Cagliari) in 1928, recalled
that, despite the views of her father, who had refused to buy his daughters
uniforms, when Mussolini visited Cagliari in 1935 the teachers at her school
gave her and the other children Piccole Italiane dresses, and she was also given
flowers.

My elementary school teacher or another teacher had given me a bunch of flowers to give to the Duce, and I remember I was desperate because I lived, I had
lived an enormous contradiction. All the same, when I gave these flowers to
the Duce, the Duce took me in his arms and gave me a kiss, but I was happy,
happy about this, because I had in a way become the protagonist of the situation, maybe this counted, this prevailed over [my inner feelings] . . . and I remember I never told my father, ever. (52: 20)

For the young, there was pleasure in organized activities. "I really liked
putting on a uniform and marching; I even did a squad leader course so that I
would be more important, I didn't like just being an ordinary Piccola Italiana,"
F. P. told us (50/51: 40), while her sister E. P. remembered how "the gymnastic
performances were so beautiful" (50/51: 41). As eleven- and twelve-year-old
middle-class girls in Sardinia, they enjoyed all types of public Fascist activities "either because you went out or because you got to be with your friends"
(50/51: 41). Rita L., born in Casole (Cosenza) in 1916, remembered with fond-
ness the details of her family's uniforms and the activities they engaged in every Saturday (76/77: 14). Nicola A., born in 1931 in Gravina (Bari), spoke of
seeing the parades as a child: "I remember when the girls with their black tunics and white blouses, with Mussolini over there, and the Balilla too, pa-

raded and danced, making a square on the ground. It was a masterpiece, it was a dream, it was" (99/100: 48–49). To some extent these feelings transcended class barriers. Susanna Agnelli, a member of one of the richest families in the country, the owners of Fiat automobiles, recalled in her memoirs her delight at the uniforms, badges, medals, marching, and singing. For a child such rituals were simply fun; they implied not constriction but a measure of freedom: "Parade days are the only ones when you are allowed to walk through town on your own, ride on the tram, hang out with school friends, eat doughnuts and get home as late as you like."[2] But the introduction of regular uniformed activities in 1935 was not welcomed by everyone. Riccarda G., born in Rovereto in 1923, recalled, "We were a bit annoyed . . . we weren't antifascists, but it put us out a bit to have to go on parade on a Saturday, because Saturday afternoon at half past two there was the parade and everyone had to dress as Piccole Italiane, Giovani Italiane, it was a bit [of an imposition] . . . ." (112: 3).

The centerpiece of the choreography of the regime was the cult of the Duce. Mussolini was a constant presence, a figure whom it was impossible to ignore and who accompanied Italians in many spheres of their lives. His portrait and sayings featured in public places, his activities were reported continuously in the daily press, and he inspired imitation in speech, appearance (the jutting jaw and, latterly, shaven head), gestures, and attitude. Although Mussolini had no Goebbels to mold and promote his image, but only the much ridiculed secretary of the Fascist Party, Achille Starace, the newsreels of the Istituto Luce ensured that the Duce's every enterprise was familiar to a substantial proportion of the population. The Duce's image was multiple and varied; depending on the circumstances, it could be martial, menacing, statesmanlike, bourgeois, familiar, or athletic. There were constant reminders that he was in origin a man of the people, ready to assist where necessary—for example, bare-chested with the harvest in the "Battle for Wheat," the drive that the regime launched to increase wheat production—but there were many other instances of the exaltation of his physical and sporting activities. The Duce was not just a political leader but the best representative of the new spirit of vigor and energy that the Fascists wished to instill in Italians, and Italian men in particular.

In some ways Mussolini was also Fascism's leading film star. Gian Piero Brunetta has studied his star projection with reference to the American film *Mussolini Speaks.*[3] It may be argued that this film was not an isolated incident but was related to the personalized method of Mussolini's rule within Italy itself, where foreign coverage always had domestic ramifications. Mussolini was surrounded by a star-style apparatus that took the form of fan letters, personal appearances, film performances, non-sphere-specific projection, product endorsement (books, Perugina Baci chocolates, alcoholic drinks, and so on). The

Figure 14. Gymnastic display of physical education teachers in the presence of Mussolini, Foro Mussolini, Rome, March 1, 1939. Source: Istituto Luce. By permission of Alinari Archives, Florence.

construction and projection of the Mussolini personality occurred within a framework in which the collective consciousness had already been shaped and conditioned by certain real enterprises and by certain archetypes of popular literature and film. Forms of charismatic mass leadership had been rehearsed by d'Annunzio at Fiume, and city-dwellers had experienced similar types in silent film. In an intriguing essay, Renzo Renzi has discussed the influence of the actor Emilio Ghione (*Za la Mort*) on Mussolini's gestures and public persona.[4] Renzi also suggests that the activist, vitalistic posturing associated with the *squadristi* (members of the Fascist action squads) may have owed something to the swashbuckling adventures of Douglas Fairbanks, who often appeared on screen in dark clothing. Monica Dall'Asta has explored the contribution of the archetypal masculine hero of Italian silent cinema, the strong man or Maciste figure (Bartolomeo Pagano, Giovanni Raicevich, and so on), and this has since been taken up by Pierre Sorlin.[5]

Whatever credit is given to these accounts, in the urban centers of Italy, where cinema had already become a mass phenomenon before World War I, the impact of stars on social behavior was notable and this created a propitious terrain for the star cult of Mussolini. Moreover, at just this time Italian cinema, after its resplendent beginnings, was in decline due to a weak industrial and financial structure and the retirement and marriage of many of its early stars. As Dino Biondi has written, looking back at this period:

The grand divas of the silent era were either getting old or getting married: Francesca Bertini was about to become Countess Cartier; Lyda Borelli had just become Countess Cini. Practically the only star left was Mussolini: such that one evening at the theatre he was even introduced to the audience, much to the amazement and applause of the public up in the gods. The language the newspapers used to describe him was taken directly from the "star system."[6]

It should be noted that images of Mussolini were only a part of his personality projection. A great deal of emphasis was placed on his personal appearances. These took the form not only of the celebrated staged rallies and his set-piece speeches from the balcony of Palazzo Venezia but also of visits to the most varied localities. Mussolini was the first Italian prime minister to travel widely in the country and address the crowds in public squares. He was also in the habit of engaging in impromptu exchanges with individuals during unannounced lightning visits. These visits and the tales to which they gave rise, Biondi notes, fueled the sensation that the Duce was omnipresent.

Given all this, it is not surprising that many of our oral witnesses had vivid recollections of Mussolini. The language they used goes beyond that reserved for politicians and recalls that associated with religion and with film stars. Pietro P., born in the province of Cagliari in 1913, said: "For us Mussolini was like a god. . . . Everything he said was gospel for us, and, physically, he was a man of notable appeal, with so-called magnetic eyes and a unique, unmistakable tone of voice. He sent shivers through your veins" (48/49: 29). "Mussolini was an idol for me," said Arturo M., born in Celico in 1917 (74: 19). A striking number of interviewees recalled seeing him on his visits to Sardinia (45, 46, 48) and Cosenza (76/77, 79, 100). Gustavo V. recalled him on horseback on Rome: "He made a rather martial impression" (75: 12). Arnaldo B. said he saw him visiting Rome's San Lorenzo neighborhood after the air raid of July 1943 and shedding tears (19: 5). However, while various other anecdotal reports exist of a visit by Mussolini to San Lorenzo after the bombing, it is not certain that it actually took place and the testimony is possibly a retrospective fabrication, though not necessarily one made in bad faith. An even more striking case of the same type of evocation of Mussolini as a physical presence in memory narratives is that of Rita B. (born 1927):

We dressed as Piccole Italiane . . . we went to school, and we used to shout "Viva il Duce! Viva il Duce!" We met him, he used to come into our classes. . . . And then, when I was little . . . we always used to go to summer camp and he came together with the children. Lots of times he picked me up and threw me into the sea; he used to have fun along with the children. (11/12: 41)

Vittorio Mussolini pointed out in 1983 that his father had not been keen on sport in his youth and only became so after World War I.[7] Later he became "Italy's number one sportsman," flying, driving, playing tennis, skiing, swimming, fencing, riding, because it invigorated him but also because he wanted to offer an example, to indicate that this activity was a key to the renewal of the Italian character. Sport constituted the arena of Fascism's most significant contribution to popular culture. Stefano Jacomuzzi points out that, contrary to received opinion, the Fascists did not introduce sport in Italy, since it was already well established in the Liberal era (including the National Olympic Committee [CONI], established in 1914) but they did centralize it, sponsor it, and give it considerable importance.[8] Fascist organizations took over from earlier sports associations and in 1927 all professional and competitive activity was placed under the direction of CONI. Before World War I sport had been an elite phenomenon; it was seen as an affectation of well-to-do gentlemen. Under the regime it took on more general connotations and purposes. The roots of this shift can be traced to the decision, after the military defeat at Caporetto in 1917, to introduce sport into the army. Until then it had been seen as individualized and bad for cohesion. The shock-troops known as the Arditi, whose black dress and reckless bravery became core elements of the self-image of Fascism, had physical education as a key point of their training. For the Fascists, sport constituted not just a useful distraction from politics, and a terrain on which the nation could assert itself in peacetime, but a tool for promoting the moral and physical vigor of the people. To forge the "new man" of the Fascist era, sport was indispensable; it was a tool in the struggle against the old mentality and also a way of domesticating the *squadristi*. After the March on Rome in 1922, which accompanied Mussolini's rise to power, it was promoted systematically, not for its own sake, but in a way that emphasized its martial connections.

The intention was not to foster an ideal of sport as individual activity or as an end in itself. Rather it was to use sport to train the Italians and put them at the service of a higher ideal. New stadiums and facilities were built. From a starting point of virtually nothing, a situation was reached where it was expected that every municipality (*comune*), even the smallest, would have a sports field. By ending the distinction between body and spirit, it was hoped sport would also promote national identifications and transcend regional and class boundaries. Despite these efforts, sports facilities were not widely available for all, according to Augusto C., who was living in the province of Bologna in the 1930s. In schools there was an attempt to create the impression of mass sporting activity through the organization of gymnastic competitions (*saggi ginnici*), with a final display at the end of the year, but there was no regular school sport and only those in teams had access to facilities. "It was difficult to get in the gym, it was difficult to get on to the playing field because there was a 'watchdog' who kept the boys out because there was the team that had to practice. It's not that it was strictly out of bounds but there were lots of restrictions, so it could never be a pastime" (55: 6). At eighteen or nineteen, he applied with other young workers to go to a summer campsite (*campeggio*) as it lasted twenty days, whereas the Ducati factory where he worked closed for just twelve. The camp involved a lot of sport, which appealed to the youngsters, although access was restricted to those who were politically approved. When he returned home there were pressing invitations to join a Fascist organization (55: 5).

The subsidies that the Fascists lavished on sport were channeled toward improving the performance of the best sportsmen. The achievements of sports champions, especially on the international plane, were taken as signs of the new Italian spirit and could be offered as examples to the people. In the context of mass athleticization, this was deemed useful. The champion became a banner, a calling card for the nation abroad, and a convenient symbol for domestic use. The idea was to overcome class conflict and to unite the people in an identification with the *patria*. Sport forged bonds and elevated a common consciousness and sense of belonging. The male champion had a special role in this because he was the hero in a peacetime context in which sport took the place of war in forming men and supplying glory. In general there was more emphasis on the collectivity, the team, and the nation, than the individual, but there were some exceptions. Tazio Nuvolari in motor racing, Primo Carnera in boxing, Nedo Naldi in fencing, and Giovanni Raicevich in wrestling were individuals in non-team sports who attracted admiration. The successes of these men was harnessed by the Fascists to the glory of their regime.

However, there were problems with the way in which sport, which was considered in more or less paramilitary terms, became bound up with ideas and practices of leisure that served certain purposes under Fascism but also led in uncontrollable directions, and sometimes in directions contrary to the intended thrust of policy, at least in their longer-term effects. In the Fascist press there was dissatisfaction with the way the sort of hyperbole normally associated with genuine heroes and achievers for the *patria* was being associated in newspaper reports with mere sports champions. The periodical *Anno XIII* in particular engaged in criticism of this type. But as Paolo Facchinetti points out, the hero rhetoric and elevation of champions originated not with the press but with the regime itself.[9] Eugenio Pagnini in *Lo Sport fascista* in 1943

denounced the way the "educative aims" of sport had become corrupted and
he called for moralization. He attacked "the buying and selling of athletes,
loans, representatives who are regional only in name, payments for lost earnings, cash prizes, a star system and a cult of champions, training for competitions based not on all the available athletes but only on tried and tested
names."[10] Similarly there was suspicion of spectator sports, which were seen
as fostering passivity rather than activity.

As the Fascists saw it, sport was meant to act as an antidote to the sort of
"bourgeois mentality" that encouraged sloth and inaction. The rise of professional sports and the creation of "passive" mass audiences therefore was trou-
bling. This concern tied in with other preoccupations about the persistence
and even extension of individual and family consumerism, especially in the
middle classes. The campaign for a Fascist civilization was deeply associated
with the battle for "reform of custom," launched in the late 1930s, but it cannot be confined to that period, since the late 1930s merely witnessed the re-
assertion of antibourgeois attitudes that had marked Fascism from its origins.
One of its precursors was the Futurist cult of dynamism and speed that pre-
dated the rise of Fascism by a decade. In November 1930 Marinetti launched
a campaign against pasta, asserting that it was an unsuitable food for an alert
and warrior people as it weighed heavily on the stomach and induced "scepti-
cism, sloth and pessimism."[11]

The Fascist attitude toward family-based and individual consumption
was hostile. Attitudes of this sort reached their apotheosis in the late 1930s;
one of the Fascists' leading spokesmen was Starace, the architect of the antibourgeois campaign. He blamed the "bourgeois mentality" for the failure of
Fascism to impress itself fully on national life. He saw it as pacific and pacifist,
foreign-loving, satisfied with the already achieved and diffident toward the regime's efforts to promote national glory.[12] It was perhaps appropriate that this
campaign should have been headed by a southerner, but Mussolini, who came
from Romagna, was not slow to jump on the bandwagon. His antibourgeois
outlook derived from his early involvement in the socialist movement.

Not surprisingly, rural images were numerous and constant throughout
this period. They were a reference point in the cultural conservatism of the
regime and a sign of its determination to combat a corrupt urban culture.
The countryside, Gian Paolo Ceserani notes, was seen as being truly Fascist, and thus authentically Italian, because it was laborious, frugal, and anti-
consumerist.[13] It was also the largest part of Italy, and became the site of the
Battle for Wheat and the example to the urban population in the demographic
campaign. The countryside was also a useful symbolic counterweight to the
urban elites, who were deemed to be snobbish in their attitudes to Fascism,
and to the working class, which had never responded with enthusiasm to Fas-

cist rhetoric. To this extent, ruralism became an ideal opposite to an urban way of life that was rapidly taking shape. James Hay has examined several of the rural film comedies that were made in the 1930s and early 1940s. These show country life to be healthy and happy, though Hay notes perceptively that city and country are nearly always played off against one another within the plot and that the overall ideological message was therefore more complex than one of simple ruralist nostalgia: "These films do not insist on a return to rural lifestyles but favor the creation of a modern 'popular' society based on a conservative value system and an awareness of Italy's cultural heritage."[14] In addition, there were there many songs, like the famous "Reginella campagnola" (see chapter 6), which mined a similar ruralist vein. These were not of course authentic products of folk culture, but mythical representations produced by urban cultural industries for the consumption mainly of the populations of the northern cities. The nature of the effects they had is difficult to gauge, although Venè asserts that the urban lower middle classes were skeptical of rural populism. They did not like the exaltation of rural prolificness, which seemed to them unrefined and animal-like.[15]

Along with masculine imagery, the 1930s also saw the proliferation of images of beautiful young women in films, advertisements, magazines, and photographs. This derived largely from the commercial culture related to new beauty products and an attention to the body that was encouraged by the Fascist concern with fitness and health. Victoria de Grazia has suggested that Fascism tried to check the potentially emancipatory aspects of this trend by manipulating it to its own antifeminist ends. But the degree to which these images provoked controls (the banning of beauty contests, for example) and hostile campaigns is evidence that they could not easily be dovetailed to a conservative design.[16] Fascists attacked the new women's fashionable image spreading from Paris, Britain, and the United States—short hair, masculine appearance, skimpy clothes, thinness—which had, they claimed, culminated in the type they called the "crisis woman" (donna-crisi), a product of the crisis of World War I and its aftermath.[17] Depicted by Mino Maccari in his satirical magazine Il Selvaggio as thin, elegant, and childless, the crisis-woman gave rise to a minor moral panic. In response an alternative ideal was held up, that of the "authentic woman," who was motherly and homely. In contrast to the socially useless thinness, and apparent infertility, of the crisis-woman, Fascist rural beauties were seen as embodying all the virtues of the Italian race. Less numerous than the former type, images of this new ideal nonetheless appeared on posters, on magazine covers and in photographs, where they conveyed the implicit message that the future of the race depended on the preservation of the rural world.[18]

Although the Fascists campaigned against the effects of individual or private consumption, they aimed to win over or cater to the aspirations of a variety of social strata by offering them something practical in a collective, controllable context. In relation to the intellectual and artistic sphere, they reproduced and indeed reinforced the conventional division of high and low culture. They associated true culture with high culture and saw this as confined to the rather narrow ambit of the intellectuals. In general they dealt with intellectuals by offering them incentives, combined always with the threat of sanctions ranging from a reprimand to internal exile or imprisonment. Young intellectuals were seen by Fascists as potential allies who could most easily be brought into the fold and kept under observation by means of resources and organization. Journals, subventions, and organized forums were all provided to keep intellectuals occupied and to channel their energies. Because they came from the middle classes, which were broadly aligned with the regime, they were assumed to be relatively "safe."

In the extraordinarily valuable account first published in 1947 of the Littoriali della Cultura of 1937 and 1938, Ruggero Zangrandi showed both the extent and the limits of Fascist intervention. The regime was able to organize these national conventions, bring bright young men from all over the country to attend them, and guarantee their outward conformity by insisting that all the attendees wore a black shirt, an *orbace* (black woolen jacket), and knee-high boots. Yet the regime could not prevent some of the intellectuals from seeing these occasions as an opportunity for criticism and internal opposition at a time when there was much disquiet among students about the alliance with Nazi Germany, the race policy, and the intervention in Spain. Officials did not intervene repressively when nonconformist opinions were expressed at the Littoriali. On the contrary, they tolerated this situation, intervening only to marginalize the protagonists who expressed open dissent and criticism and to prevent them from winning any prizes. Zangrandi considered this not necessarily a result of Machiavellian calculation by the authorities or as evidence of the organizers' "ambiguity" but as the strategic acceptance of a situation that the PNF and the government were unable to change. What they could do was police the most overt forms of dissent and, more generally, try to absorb or otherwise buy off the dissident elements.[19]

The role of Fascism as a regime concerned with maintaining order and attempting to build consent rather than "reforming custom" and instilling a new spirit in Italians is also apparent in its attitude toward the urban lower classes. One of Fascism's early concerns was to undo and take over activities that had been bound up with subversive leftist and labor union organizations and had survived the outlawing of parties and unions. The Opera Nazionale Dopolavoro (OND), which, as Victoria de Grazia has shown, was an invention of Americanizing reformers who passed to Fascism in the early 1920s, was designed to replace working-class voluntary organizations.[20] It was to be non-class-specific, to keep working people away from "bad" leisure and especially from subversive politics. Fascists opposed ideas of the spreading of "culture" to all because they viewed them as democratic and leftist and therefore antithetical to their basic purposes. Yet, in order to undo previous developments in this area undertaken by socialists and labor unionists, and to fill the gap that remained, they were obliged to form their own version of "popular culture," which was mediated by provincial intellectuals and involved a celebration of national traditions, chauvinism, and the promotion of the more traditionalist and figurative aspects of modern Italian art.

In place of private consumption, the OND organized many activities that at the time were not considered to be "cultural," at least by elitists in the Giovanni Gentile mold, but which are nonetheless best considered as part of a broad-ranging popular cultural strategy. These included traveling theater, amateur theatricals, sports and film clubs, day trips to places of interest, radio listening, and the sale of some consumer goods at discounted prices. The OND was not intended as a channel of politicization in a Fascist sense; the purpose was rather to keep people occupied and happy by offering them some proof of the regime's benevolence in the form of discounts on tickets to the cinema and theater; group trips to Great War monuments, places of historic interest, and commercial exhibitions like the Milan Fair; and small consumer items like radios. Bowls, table tennis, cycle races, and children's competitions constituted further activities. De Grazia noted: "Promoted nationwide, in factories, city neighbourhoods, and villages, the nearly 20,000 after-work circles founded by the late 1930s played host to the recreational pastimes of perhaps four million Italian working people."[21]

The PNF and the state therefore organized leisure to some degree and aimed to control everyday leisure pursuits. The architects of the OND were aided by the development of mass communications technology such as radio and sound cinema and also welfare capitalist techniques pioneered in the United States that involved distributing a little largesse in order to combat unionism and absenteeism and to raise productivity. The growing importance of the OND can be seen in the way it passed from modest beginnings to a position where it was the regime's chief weapon in the battle to win the consent of the governed. Initially an auxiliary of the PNF, it was brought into the state sphere in 1937 and placed under the direct control of Mussolini. Many of its activities were geared to the male working class, as this group was perceived to be a possible source of instability. But, precisely because the aim was to divorce leisure from the workplace by attaching it to the community, the OND centers were open to people of any class and were not restricted to party members. Better equipped and more appealing than the PNF branches, they sought to harness consumption to the goals of the regime by ensuring that in a primitive form some of the benefits of technology and raised production reached the lower urban classes. The regime also extended the reach of its communications network into the countryside, but it was careful not to tempt peasants with alluring images of urban life. Traveling cinema vans, for example, showed documentaries and newsreels but not feature films.

As Arnaldo B. in Rome confirmed, the OND was successful at drawing in masses of people. Only very hardened antifascists were able to resist the offer of discounted and modest amusements (19: 14). But at the same time, the regime's need for consent contradicted the Fascist desire to found a new civilization. The idea of the Fascist revolution was counterbalanced by images of leisure and pleasure. The holiday and the beach came to be represented in magazines and in newsreels as places where there were no conflicts or social differences, where all could be reconciled and social stability was guaranteed. Pictures of leading Fascists at the seaside, including Mussolini at Riccione, showed a certain leveling, and the location of the Venice Film Festival at the Lido suggested the accessibility of what had once been a privilege of the elite. The lower classes received their first taste of holidays on day trips to the seaside or, more commonly, the mountains. Many girls experienced their first trips to the sea as Piccole Italiane (96: 10).

From the propaganda point of view, what was being offered here was an idea of a pause in the work of the revolution, a moment of recovery before surging forward anew. But in the context of a developing commercial culture, leisure also represented a different perspective on life. The emphasis on the sun, youth, and the body was as much a part of the ideology of Hollywood as, in a different inflection, it was of Fascism. The issue was complicated by the fact that certain forms of escapism were officially encouraged. By giving birth to an incipient mass tourism, as shown for example in Matarazzo's *Treno popolare* of 1933 (see chapter 2), Fascism suggested that, alongside the more dutiful and personally disinterested existence of the Fascist citizen, there was another more domestic and enjoyable sphere, that allowed for some carefully managed pleasures. Through these, Antonio Faeti has argued, quintessentially petty-bourgeois values were given public sanction and universal application.[22]

Fascist officials bemoaned the lack of political activity and propaganda in the OND. They could see that leisure was not neutral and that even sport was treated less as a proto-political activity than as a distraction from politics.[23] By the same token, there were complaints about the failure to use cinema more consistently as a propaganda weapon; the polished and stylish "white telephone" comedies were regarded with particular contempt. Ultimately, however, the strategy of using organized leisure as a safety valve and as a sort of cushion to moderate the effects of the international depression and then of the effects of League of Nations sanctions was not successful. Not only was the reform of custom a failure but so too was the attempt to maintain high levels of support for the regime.

There were several reasons for this. In the first place, the impact of the OND should not be exaggerated. While it was extensive in the North, membership was not evenly distributed and it was virtually absent in the South. Moreover, it was not as generous as it liked to appear. Bruno O. in Turin remembered that for the *treni popolari* (discount train trips) tickets were strictly limited and difficult to come by (3: 5). Although many enjoyed their first trips away from home in the 1930s, tangible material improvements were relatively few. As even these were eroded in the late 1930s, so resentment set in. Simona Colarizi suggests that workers became restless and combative in an antiregime direction as a result of rises in the cost of living and the impact of antifascist activity within the unions, the OND, and sports organizations.[24]

Disaffection spread after entry into World War II, as a result of military setbacks, the bombing of cities, and material privations. These had the effect of shaking the very concept of the nation that the Fascists had championed. Although those who voted against the Duce in the Fascist Grand Council in July 1943 hoped to save the *patria* by dissolving the union between the nation and Fascism, their action was too late to be effective.[25] Indeed, precisely the confusion of the nation with Fascism meant that the defeat of the latter resulted in the discrediting of the former. The flight from Rome of the King and Badoglio in September 1943 killed any chance of transferring support to the only remaining legitimate symbol and representative of national unity. Thus the forces that sought to assert their leadership in postwar Italy were constrained not only to take account of the masses who had been organized and integrated by the Fascists but also to elaborate their own visions of the nation.

Catholic Associationism

No less than Fascism, the Catholic world consisted of a plethora of different organizations, groups, and strands of opinion. This must be balanced against the fact that there was a clear hierarchy of authority and, in the period under consideration here, a relatively high degree of central command under the imposing figure of Eugenio Pacelli, Pope Pius XII (1939–1958). However, it should not be overlooked that different segments of the Catholic world operated according to different priorities (spiritual or terrestrial, short-term or long-term) and adopted sometimes differing attitudes first toward Fascism and subsequently toward the challenges of the postwar era.

The first issue that must be addressed is the relationship between the Catholics and Fascism. With the Lateran Pacts of 1929, longstanding problems in the relations between Church and state were resolved. Catholicism became Italy's official religion, and its access to and influence within branches of the state, including education and censorship, began. Catholic lay associations and parish activities, as well as magazines and newspapers, all existed under the regime. The point at issue concerns the extent to which the accord with Fascism was stable and organic. After the fall of the regime, there was an understandable attempt on the part of Catholic publicists to mark out the divide that separated Church associations from the regime. For example, in his slim volume *Azione cattolica e fascismo* (*Catholic Action and Fascism*, 1945), Giuseppe Della Torre, editor of *L'Osservatore Romano*, argued that there was an "irreducible incompatibility of character" between the two.[26] However, historians have subsequently tended to place the emphasis on the extent to which the Church in some or all of its ramifications shared views, concerns, and enemies with the regime. Writing in 1979, Pietro Scoppola drew attention to a letter from De Gasperi to Stefano Jacini written around 1939–1940, which stated that the leadership and personnel of Catholic Action (AC) were uniformly profascist.[27] More generally, Giovanni Miccoli argued that the alliance between Fascism and Catholicism was a fundamental one, sealed by their common social conservatism and hostility to socialism and communism.[28]

Undoubtedly there was much that the Church hierarchy and lay leaders on the one hand and the Fascist regime on the other did share. But relations between the two were by no means always easy. At certain points the differences between them were marked, notably in 1931 when there was a sharp conflict over the activities of Catholic Action and from 1938 when the regime drew closer to Nazi Germany and introduced the racial laws. In order to account both for the substantial convergence and the areas of division and disagreement, it is useful to consider the Church as a parallel organization that maintained throughout the Fascist period an agenda of its own and that, due to the Concordat (the part of the 1929 Lateran Pacts between the Italian state and the Catholic Church regulating Church–state relations in civil society), was able to pursue this agenda with relative autonomy, exercising more freedom in society than Catholics enjoyed in Nazi Germany after 1936. Catholics and Fascists were allies but they were also in some measure competitors. The 1931 conflict over AC and the Church's great influence over the education of youth was the most visible sign of this. The regime felt that AC's associations were tending toward the (re)formation of a Catholic political party and first gave license to squads to attack AC people and offices and then ordered prefects to dissolve AC's youth associations. Faced with this showdown, the Vatican stood firm and the regime opted to abandon frontal conflict and recognize AC's right to exist. According to John Pollard, the dispute resulted essentially from the different interpretations made respectively by the regime and the Church regarding how the Lateran Pacts would affect "the future balance of power between them."[29] Whereas the regime saw the Pacts as setting clear limits to Catholic influence and as a propaganda coup that boosted Mussolini's popularity at home and abroad, the Church saw them as an authorization to extend its influence in society. After the dispute, the Church operated within more delineated spaces outside its acknowledged competence in the moral field but it conserved a significant influence that tended to grow as the regime welcomed its support in its campaigns and as infrastructures expanded and communications developed. This convergence between Church and regime lasted until the next set of tensions in 1938–1939, occasioned largely by the regime's increasingly close ties with Nazi Germany.

Catholics adopted a different view of the nation from that of Fascism, even though the Church supported Mussolini's invasion of Ethiopia and Fascism's colonial activities. In contrast to the regime's emphasis on the state authority and imperial power of ancient Rome as an "animating myth" in relation to the future, Catholics regarded the Church as the source of Italian civilization; Rome was only eternal because Christianity had conferred this quality upon it.[30] It was the Church, therefore, not the regime, that was the true bearer of "Romanness" (*romanità*) insofar as Christianity was situated ideologically at the core of Italy's claim to cultural primacy. As far as Catholics were concerned, religion and the Church possessed a resonance and continuity that went far beyond Fascism's purely temporal and conjunctural significance.

By contrast with Fascism's predominant concern with the present and future, Catholics looked backward to find their concept of national identity. This meant that there was a substantial measure of accord in areas where Fascism's concept of modernity involved resistance against Americanism and preservation of what were perceived as the virtues and essential traits of Italian civilization. No less than the Fascists, the Catholics believed that the rural world was the seat of true Italian values. They also believed, like the former, in the need for organization and education, and there was awareness by Catholics (at least among some of the more advanced sections of the Catholic world) of the importance of harnessing modern means of communication to the task of protecting their followers from the harmful influences of commercial culture. In the late 1920s and 1930s, Catholics gained greater influence in the state than before, in education, in broadcasting, and in censorship commissions.

The parish was the true center of all Catholic activity. Through Catholic Action, Catholics organized men and women, young people, and university students. Activities were organized that, following the dispute of 1931, excluded sport but included theater, cinema, and organized excursions. These activities were always strongest in the most Catholic areas of the country: the Veneto, Lombardy, and Piedmont. It was here that Fascism had to accept a continuing Catholic role in associational life. There were significant levels of Catholic associational activity in other centers too, particularly cities like Bologna and Rome. Several witnesses recalled that their first experiences of film took place in parish cinemas or during religious festivals (4: 20; 75: 17). In the San Lorenzo district of Rome, the cinema of the Church of the Immacolata was popular because it provided cheap or free entertainment on Saturdays and Sundays. As was quite typical with "priests' cinemas," free tickets were distributed to those who attended Mass (22: 17). The parish also organized recreational circles that offered table tennis, billiards, and, until the Fascists set up an OND circle, some sports activities (22: 17). Typically, parish sports were simple and cheap; they usually consisted of football and basketball. Those whose interests extended to boxing and cycling were obliged, even if they were practicing Catholics, to go elsewhere (23: 9).

Under Pius XI (1922–1939) the Church had opened up somewhat to ideas of progress. There were sectors of the Catholic world that believed modern communications should be harnessed and used for good ends. From the late nineteenth century a Catholic press had flourished in the North of Italy. In 1931 Vatican Radio was founded. The Centro Cattolico Cinematografico (CCC), founded in 1934, kept a regular watch on films and advised on their morality (see chapter 7). While Catholic film production was nonexistent under the regime, and only a handful of films were made that dealt with Catholic themes, the Church had appreciated very early on the importance of cinema and in the years after World War I had set about forming a network of infrastructures with the intention of influencing production. While grassroots publications often railed against cinema as a tool of the devil, more enlightened Catholics realized that the negative influence of a medium that offered models of behavior differing widely from its own could only be combated if pressure, assisted by the existence of a network of grassroots institutions, was brought to bear to make the medium conform to its own values and world view.[31] To this end they organized, setting up in 1926 a consortium of parish cinemas and founding the *Rivista del cinematografo,* long before the regime began to intervene actively in the field. The Church's emphasis was always on moralization; it stood out against sex and violence and championed anticommunism. This action was not limited to Italy; it was developed effectively in

Figure 15. Gymnastic display by children of the Pontificia Scuola Elementare Parificata Pio X in the playing field of the Knights of Columbus, San Lorenzo, Rome, circa 1939. The Parish of the Immacolata was in this period an important social center in a working-class district of strong socialist and anarchist traditions. By permission of the Parrocchia Santa Maria Immacolata e San Giovanni Berchmans, Quartiere Tiburtino, Rome.

the United States first, where the Legion of Decency was instrumental in securing the adoption of the Hays Code by Hollywood.

The papal encyclical of 1936, *Vigilanti cura,* represented the culmination of Catholic interventions. As a complete statement of Catholic views on the cinema, it both denounced the evils caused by the medium (see chapter 2) and insisted on the need for action to protect spectators and to turn cinema toward positive, educational, and uplifting ends. Although the regular denunciation of examples of nudity, violence, and immorality in films distributed in Italy in the bulletins of the CCC might lead one to suppose otherwise, the Church built up a major influence. According to Brunetta:

The Church ... by means of the Centro, acquired effective powers of control over production, distribution and exhibition. Its influence over the auditoria of its own circuits and over those of Catholic managers in the normal exhibition sector, since they faced no antagonistic organized political forces, became an almost hegemonic force at certain levels.[32]

During World War II and the political interregnum, Catholic cultural apparatuses continued to function. Both *L'Osservatore Romano,* the Vatican newspaper founded in 1861, and Vatican Radio were important alternative sources of information at this time. The credibility that these institutions retained, and to some extent acquired, during this phase needs to be seen in relation to two quite different but not unrelated factors. First, there was the need of the Church to extricate itself from its association with Fascism and to relegitimate itself. Second, there was the greater identification with the Church that occurred in response to the crisis of values and beliefs precipitated for many people by World War II and the crisis of modernity and urbanism of which the war was seen by some Catholics as a symptom. "Modern civilization" was regarded by them as having produced, on its "dark side," both the pathological degeneration into Nazi barbarism and the military technologies that had unleashed a war of mass destruction.

After the defeat of the Fascist regime the Church managed quite rapidly and quite successfully to relegitimate itself in civil society, despite having been intertwined with the regime at various levels. One source of this relegitimation was the important welfare role it had played during the war. The grassroots activity of Catholic organizations between 1943 and 1945 "lent heavy support to the assertion that Catholicism was the backbone of Italian civilization."[33] Giovagnoli argues that a part of the popular legitimacy conferred on Pius XII by the people of Rome during the war was the result of local actions by priests, nuns, and lay Catholics that he had not himself promoted and of which he was sometimes unaware.[34] He examines the meanings of some of Pius XII's public appearances, suggesting that his visit to San

Lorenzo after the bombing of July 19, 1943 was more a protest against the dese-
cration of the holy city (the bombs, as well as destroying houses, had damaged
the Basilica of San Lorenzo and part of the adjacent Cimitero del Verano)
than an expression of solidarity with the victims. He also argues that in June
1944, after the liberation of Rome, many of the people in the crowd may have
been expressing their gratitude not to the Pope as such but for spontaneous local acts of Catholic assistance and charity. However, there are other aspects to
this question. Simona Colarizi argues that when Mussolini's popularity declined there was a deliberate attempt on the part of the religious authorities
to promote the personality cult of the Pope instead.[35] This occurred principally through the documentary film *Pastor angelicus* (1942), which was widely
shown and which even resulted, much to the chagrin of the Catholic authorities, in the Pope's photograph being published on the cover of *Cinema* and in
other film magazines. Despite this, Pius XII remained austere and aloof. He
was a towering figure of immense authority, who was a forceful presence in
Italian society up until his death in 1958. Silvio Lanaro argues that, although
Pacelli understood the importance of cinema and made frequent radio broadcasts, he came across as an austere and severe figure, not comfortably incarnated in a body.[36]

After 1945, the Church struggled to assert its particular vision of the nation against leftist alternatives that drew sustenance from the Resistance. Catholicism became the embodiment of a national unity that excluded the Communists. Oliver Logan has shown that the Church became more accepting of
the political realm, partly out of necessity.[37] As Christian Democracy became
the new establishment, and the Church reconciled itself to liberal democracy
and the West, old ghetto mentalities fell by the wayside. Mario Isnenghi notes
that between 1947 and 1949 Catholics aimed to mobilize the silent majority in
public squares and in mass rallies to prevent the left from establishing a monopoly on this terrain, which from the 1920s the Fascists had made their exclusive preserve.[38]

Sport offers another example of the way in which Catholics occupied
some of the spaces that had been dominated by the Fascists. Catholics had
been diffident toward the Fascist use of sport and they disliked competition, but it was not a sphere they could ignore totally. A few figures, including
Luigi Gedda, president of AC's youth organization GIAC (Gioventù Italiana
di Azione Cattolica) from 1934 to 1946, saw the importance of sports figures as
a potential source of positive behavioral models. According to Stefano Pivato,
Gedda was instrumental in making Pius XII aware of sport and encouraging
him to devote attention to it.[39] Between 1944 and 1950 AC, ACLI (Associazioni
Cristiane Lavoratori Italiani) and other Catholic associations founded sporting organizations and the Pope delivered a variety of speeches on sport. The

Catholic role model was the cyclist Gino Bartali. Already in the 1930s, Bartali had been held up as "a sort of counter to the human as well as the sporting models of the regime."[40] From 1936, when it first became public knowledge that he attended Mass and wore a Catholic Action lapel badge, he became the ideal Christian sportsman: honest, modest, not excessively proud of his body, and a good father. This continued and grew in the postwar years, as Bartali continued to race even in his late thirties. In September 1947, Pius held him up as an example in St. Peter's Square before 60,000 Catholic Action rank and file members. A popular figure, whose peasant extraction endeared him to Italy's lower classes, Bartali played his part to the full and offered his backing to the DC in the April 1948 election.

After the decisive victory of the Christian Democrats in 1948, a great effort was made by the Church and its allies to reestablish hegemony by seizing influence within the state and by promoting Catholic morality. Catholics were able to use their enhanced position within the state to step up their interventions in education, children's books, periodicals, and cinema. In cinema, Catholics were able to expand their influence within state organizations, with Giulio Andreotti piloting the passage of the semi-protectionist cinema legislation in 1947 and 1949 that allowed him and his successors to influence producers and to some extent determine the type of films that were made. Censorship, as we have seen in chapter 7, provided a further tool of control.

Moreover, many new parish cinemas were built, often with public monies granted for the rebuilding of churches and church property damaged in the war. By the mid-1950s, at a time of great commercial expansion of the cinema, around 5,000 cinemas, one-third of the total in Italy, belonged to the parish circuit, a huge increase in comparison with 1937, when parish cinemas had accounted for about 12 percent of all cinemas. This figure needs to be put in proportion: parish cinemas on average had smaller seating capacities than commercial ones, were open on fewer days of the year, and sold fewer tickets. Thus, in 1953, when 34 percent of all cinemas were parish cinemas, they accounted for only 20 percent of seats, 15 percent of screening days, 7 percent of tickets sold, and 5 percent of expenditure on cinema.[41] Nevertheless, parish cinemas did acquire in this period a substantial presence in the exhibition sector and a strong influence on distribution, which followed from the classifications of the CCC. However, this influence was not matched in film production. Despite the involvement of several directors in specific Catholic projects, these were few in number and sometimes produced problematic results. Lanaro describes a difficult balancing act between the essentially repressive demands of the upper clergy and attempts by the laity to work creatively within a broadly Catholic framework.[42] For example, Blasetti's *Fabìola* (1949), produced by Universalia (founded in 1946 under the presidency of Giuseppe

Della Torre), was classified "for adults" because of scenes of "nudity," which in fact consisted of a small number of slightly revealing costumes.

The campaign to extend Catholic influence in society also involved grass-roots campaigns and institutions. Touring statues of the Virgin Mary, known as the *Madonne pellegrine*, played a central role in the general ideological counteroffensive launched by the Church against secularization and the moral breakdown associated with the effects of the war. One interviewee, Mario V., a retired priest in Challand Saint Anselme (Aosta), stated that the visit of a *Madonna pellegrina* to parishes in his area in 1952 was a huge success. The Madonna spent twenty-four hours in each parish and people waited all night to see her (90: 16). The use of this tool enabled the Church to cut through ideological and political barriers. Elsewhere, the statues were taken into factories. Even if the workers did not all kneel before the Madonna pellegrina, neither did they manifest opposition or disrespect. In mainly working-class San Lorenzo in Rome, the annual Festa dell'Immacolata, with its processions, firework displays, and commercial stalls, offered something to everyone, regardless of political loyalties (21: 17). Fearful of the damage to the social and moral fabric of the country wrought by war and foreign occupation and of the threat posed by the left, the Church intervened to promote a restoration of order.

After the war the Church also carried out a significant rearguard action in sexual morality in an effort to stem the tide of secularization and moral decadence. An important instance of this was the Vatican's beatification (in 1947) and canonization (in 1950) of Maria Goretti. She was an eleven-year-old peasant girl who had been stabbed to death in 1902 in the kitchen of her house in Nettuno in the Pontine Marsh by twenty-year-old Alessandro Serenelli after she had resisted his attempts to rape her. The campaign to canonize her had begun in the 1920s, in response to a popular cult of her sanctity that had spread out from her native village of Corinaldo, in the province of Ancona, and which had subsequently benefited from the well-publicized repentance of Serenelli, who, on his release from prison after twenty-seven years, claimed that his victim had on several occasions miraculously appeared to him in his dreams. Serenelli, whom press reports at the time of the murder had called a "human beast" (*belva umana*), was subsequently reconciled with the Goretti family—he spent Christmas with them in 1934—and became a tireless advocate of Maria's canonization. A pamphlet published in 1931 by the Gioventù Femminile Cattolica Italiana described Maria Goretti as a "martyr of purity" (*martire della purità*),[43] and it was in these terms, as an emblem of a moral battle against sexual license and in defense of chastity or purity, that the Church officially co-opted her after the war. Addressing the massive crowd that assembled in St. Peter's Square on June 24, 1950, Pius XII called her "the little sweet Martyr of purity." His words were addressed not only to the young people present, who were asked whether they were prepared to resist "any assault that anyone might dare to attempt against your purity," but also to their parents. Maria's eighty-eight-year-old mother, Assunta, was present at the canonization ceremony and Pius held her up as a model of parental vigilance and education in the ways of chastity.[44]

In the promotion of Maria Goretti as martyr of purity were condensed various motifs of the Catholic campaign against sexual license and the modern world. In the first place, she was a poor peasant, from the most "humble" social stratum: the image of the simple virtue of chastity transmitted by her mother was merged with that of the good rural traditions of 1902 against the bad urban modernity of 1950, the virtues of the traditional peasant family and the "people" against the vices of "mass society." Secondly, she was a child, a girl just on the threshold of puberty, who stood for the values of candid innocence threatened by the insidious wiles of experience. Neither of these ideological meanings of the Goretti cult had much to do with the facts of her case. Her attacker was also a poor peasant who with his father had moved in with the Goretti family after the death of Assunta's husband. Alessandro's father had attempted to have sex with Assunta; Alessandro, taking advantage of Assunta's absence at work in the fields, had taken to ordering Maria about the house like a servant. Twice before the murder he had lifted her skirt and brandished his erect penis at her; on both occasions she had refused him. The third time he had a knife ready, and he stabbed her repeatedly near the vagina, rammed a handkerchief in her mouth to silence her cries for help and then slashed her in the belly, causing part of her intestine to spill out. In sanctifying Goretti and sprinkling sugary metaphors over these facts (in a book of 1947 by Padre Aurelio della Passione she became a "dove" attacked by a "serpent")[45] the Church repressed not only the violence of the episode but also other possible readings: that such acts of sexual coercion might be influenced by social conditions of extreme poverty and forced cohabitation; that Maria's refusal may have been prompted not by her religiosity but simply by fear; that acts of sexual violence such as Serenelli's were sustained by a culture of male supremacy that the Church not only did not condemn but, with its advocacy of female submissiveness and obedience and its tacit acceptance of coercive customs such as the "deflowering" of virgin brides on their wedding night, helped to sustain.

The "vigorous state of health" of the Church and its networks in the early 1950s is beyond dispute. At the parish level, there was an extension of both the quality and quantity of activities on offer.[46] Salvatore B., born in Foggia in 1936, recalled being rewarded with American cheese and chocolate for taking part in parish sports activities (94: 45). The great appeal of parish activities continued to be their cheapness. Many were able to go on their first day trips thanks to subsidized visits. "When I was young and maybe I didn't have any money, the people from the parish paid for those who couldn't go and so we went and had a good time," said Lina (68: 36). In San Lorenzo, the parish cinema cost half the price of a commercial cinema. But, by the 1950s, workers could sometimes afford on Sunday to go to a first-run cinema in the center of Rome, and one's best Sunday clothes would be worn for the occasion (17: 17). Maria P., in the province of Cosenza, said that by the 1950s parish trips to religious shrines were merely one opportunity among several to visit new places (81: 14). In this context, the trips organized as a reward for children who had attended catechism, a long tradition according to Mario V., no longer exercised the same appeal (90: 8).

For young people, restrictions and censorship often colored their experiences of parish activities. Since the early 1940s, the Church had taken a stand against the influence of film stars, who were seen as a source of mistaken ideas about personal identity and the purpose of life. The Catholic *Rivista del cinematografo* had applauded wartime restrictions on the salaries of stars and in the postwar years the Catholic press continued to regard most forms of earthly renown with skepticism. Wider ideas emanating from the cinema were also rejected. Several interviewees recalled official disapproval of romance and contact between the sexes, either as representation or reality. Tito A., who lived in the province of Bologna, recalled:

There was the parish cinema and when you got to a certain point [of a film] when, particularly for us young boys who thought we were pretty cool, there was a girl and maybe they started kissing, the priest would put his hand up and you couldn't see anything. . . . you saw he put his hand up, the moment passed and then you saw something else. (28: 13)

Enzo P. from Rovereto, born in 1935, said:

We used to go regularly to the parish cinema but then we stopped going, at any rate our group did, because there was an integralist outlook there as well that we didn't like, because we might go to the cinema with a girlfriend, without doing anything scandalous, maybe just to hold hands, but this wasn't tolerated. . . . There were even arguments with the priests. (110: 12)

Those who went dancing regularly could be barred from becoming godfathers or godmothers (90: 29) and there was great pressure to have a steady girlfriend: "I wasn't able to have a girlfriend before, before her I had a fixed girlfriend because if you were a Catholic you had to have a fixed girlfriend, otherwise there would be trouble," said Cesare B., also from Rovereto (111: 18).

According to Giuseppe A., born in Rome in 1934, very often it was the family and community context that led young people to identify with the Church. There was only a limited engagement with the Church's own program.

This relationship, this commitment to the Church wasn't taken very seriously because, let's say, sometimes you find yourself thrown into certain situations, maybe because at that time, while you were religious and took part, there wasn't a very close or fervent relationship with the [spiritual aspect] . . . for example, the sermons, this thing with the Church, I remember never taking much notice [of them], there wasn't this very strong link even though we were religious, we professed our beliefs and voted Christian Democrat, but the whole thing was lived in a rather superficial way . . .]. We cared more about dancing, having a good time and hanging out than about the anathemas and dire warnings the Church issued. None of us, at least no one in our group, ever did very much, took much notice of them. (63: 21–22)

Livio S., born in Rome in 1936, recalled that Mass could even be an important place of courtship:

the ritual to court a girl was the dance and another ritual was Sunday Mass, it was a very important meeting place. You'd say: "What time are you going to Mass?" "Midday, eleven o'clock." So we would all go at eleven. It was a way of meeting because the situations then weren't free like they are today. (17: 10)

Rather like the Fascist parades, church services provided unscripted opportunities for young people who only took part because they were obliged to do so.

One sphere where contradictory attitudes to modernization were played out was the press. In the North of Italy there was a consolidated tradition of the Catholic press. In the postwar years this underwent development as restrictions were removed and the Church struggled to widen its influence in society. Magazines tackled general themes, adopted a contemporary appearance, and made wide use of pictures. The most significant development concerned *Famiglia Cristiana*, a weekly published by the Pia Società San Paolo from 1931, which in the early 1950s evolved into an illustrated magazine of broader appeal.[47] Although it was sold entirely in churches or through subscriptions, the magazine's print run grew to 250,000 by 1954 and to one million by 1960. Well before it reached its all-time peak of 1.7 million copies in 1973, it had become the most popular weekly in Italy.[48] Directed mainly at women, but with the passing of time at other family members too, it offered an attractive mixture of human interest stories, fiction, recipes, advice columns, and news alongside religious themes. Politics had little place in the publication, but what did appear was colored by a deep anticommunism. Up until 1954, the year Don Giuseppe Zilli took over the editorship (a post he would hold until 1980), there was also a certain anti-Americanism, expressed in articles denouncing Hollywood cinema, urban civilization, beauty contests, and dancing. From 1954 this was replaced by a more positive and less fearful view of America (*Famiglia Cristiana* had its own American correspondent from 1955) as the pioneer of a model of consumerist modernity that reinforced family and spiritual values. The magazine sought to stay close to its readers as they encountered new ways of life and customs, offering constructive advice and spiritual guidance.

Although Catholics deplored the immorality of many American films and star lifestyles, they applauded the few stars who professed the Catholic faith. These included Bing Crosby, Irene Dunne, Jean Crain, and Rory Calhoun (and, following his conversion to Catholicism in the 1950s, Gary Cooper). These were all accorded ample coverage, as was the Christian Democrat leader Alcide De Gasperi. Although he was a modest, deeply reserved man, whose origins in the mountainous Trentino region seemed to be reflected in his tall, angular physique, he was the object of a minor personality cult in mainstream illustrated magazines.[49] His home and family life were often represented in photographs and his few excursions into fashionable society were described with zeal. In 1949 he appeared on the cover of the weekly *Oggi* in the company of the American actress Linda Christian, shortly before her Rome wedding to Hollywood heartthrob Tyrone Power.

Famiglia Cristiana represented a popular version of the most advanced Catholic thinking. Its publishers and editors were liberal Catholics who sought to respond without undue prejudice to the challenges of the modern world. They aimed to use modern means to adapt the Christian message to industrial society. In this they were undoubtedly successful. The magazine offered a vision of modernization that combined aspects of American-style consumerism with established customs and values. This appealed widely, especially among lower-middle-class people living outside large towns. It may be doubted however that *Famiglia Cristiana* succeeded in its aim of spreading the religious message more widely. Rather it succeeded in explaining modernization to large numbers of people who were thereby assisted in making sense of a way of life that ultimately was organized on the basis of principles and values that had little or nothing to do with Catholicism. The paradox of the Catholic forces, Angelo Ventrone has written, was that "dreaming of a Christianity that placed itself beyond both communism and capitalism, they found themselves, in reality, offering mass support to precisely the new industrial society that within a short time would undermine the very bases on which their presence in our country rested."[50]

The Communist Subculture

The Communist Party returned to national life in Italy from 1944 as a force that was in many respects different from what even its own members expected. The party leader Palmiro Togliatti renounced revolution and pursued a policy of consensus-building instead. To this end, the PCI presented itself as a potential mass party rather than as a cadre party of the conventional type. Convinced that, with the collapse of Fascism, the bourgeoisie was discredited and monopoly capitalism had reached the end of its life cycle, Togliatti opted for a long-range strategy, sure that power would soon fall into the party's hands. To prepare for the establishment of working-class hegemony, he went out of his way to build his party as a national force. At the grassroots the PCI sought to establish itself as a pole of community life. It recruited more or less without restriction or impediment and soon acquired a membership that by the end of 1945 was over 1.5 million. The majority of members were male workers and peasants living in the large cities or the central regions of Emilia-Romagna, Tuscany, and Umbria. The party grew so quickly because it played a leading role in organizing the Resistance in 1943–1945 and in promoting demands for reform and economic justice. Moreover, it operated an "open door" policy, accepting many who had been members of the PNF provided that they had not held positions of responsibility or been implicated in crimes against the people.

The left's concept of the nation was different from both that of the Fascists and that of the Catholics. Whereas both of these, in different ways, developed concepts that not only placed themselves at the heart of the national tradition but also excluded all other forces, the left, and in particular the Communists, aimed to find a way of including nearly all the people. In his speeches in 1943–1944, Togliatti branded as antinational only the Fascists and those sections of the bourgeoisie that had supported Mussolini's imperial designs. The left sought to promote a vision of the nation as more markedly democratic and popular than other versions. At the level of ideas, there was an attempt to construct a progressive tradition onto which could be grafted, by way of the work of Antonio Gramsci, the contribution of Marxism as the most advanced body of social theory. At a more popular level, the Resistance increasingly came to be seen, especially in the North, as the left's contribution to national rebirth. Popular history was shaped through commemorations, monuments, education, and so on. As the Christian Democrats in government entertained a more conservative vision, which tended to minimize the role of the Resistance, so the Communists, especially in regions like Emilia-Romagna where they had mass support, tended to accentuate the role of armed resistance, so as to stake a claim to moral leadership of the nation.[51]

At the root of the Communists' concept of the nation was the belief that the working class, as the economically most progressive class and the one that had proved itself to be the most national by its role during the period 1943–1945, had the best claim to lead the nation. The Communists assumed in 1943–1944 that the demise of Fascism also signaled the decline of monopoly capitalism, with the result that the historic moment had arrived for the working class to assert its hegemony. Like Lenin and Gramsci, the postwar leaders of the PCI believed that high culture should be appropriated by the working class. The party's role was to provide workers with ideological tools to make them worthy of their historic task. Thus education played an important part in the PCI's efforts to consolidate its large membership and make it aware of Marxism. Great stress was placed on reading both as a tool of personal emancipation and as a necessary part of political preparation. The PCI believed that the dominant classes had a vested interest in keeping the masses ignorant. Courses, party schools, promotion of the press, and books, sometimes distributed by traveling libraries, were therefore a constant of party activity. By these means, many poor people, particularly those living in rural areas or small towns in areas sympathetic to the left, were brought for the first time into contact with newspapers (29: 13). However, there were problems with this approach. It was widely assumed, in keeping with an Italian labor movement tradition, that workers had no culture of their own and therefore needed to have "culture" taken to them.[52] "Popular culture" was seen not as the sum of existing working-class values and practices but as the end product of a process of workers' education. Intellectuals inspired by their political commitment struggled to forge links with workers, but rarely were they prepared to render their speeches or writings simple and accessible. Thus the level often remained too high. As far as the party was concerned, education for its own sake was less important than ideological preparation. The exception was *Il Calendario del Popolo,* a periodical that tried to combine a left perspective and a genuine involvement with adult education. Edited by Giulio Trevisani, *Il Calendario* was attractive and quite pedagogical. For this reason it was looked down on by some intellectuals, and even Togliatti dismissed it as "encyclopedic."[53]

The PCI flattered intellectuals, courted them, and persuaded them of their vital role in national life. As a result it benefited from a vast wave of interest and sympathy that was greatly magnified by the credibility the party enjoyed as the leading force of resistance to Fascism.[54] Whereas the Fascist regime had tolerated intellectuals, humored them, corrupted them, and found outlets and apparatuses to keep them occupied, the PCI appeared to value them on their own individual merits and to regard their activities as essential to the destiny of the nation. Togliatti personally appealed to the young intellectuals who had either withdrawn from public involvement or who had participated in the regime's institutions. He established and edited the magazine *La Rinascita* (subsequently called *Rinascita*), which showed the party's interest in culture and its determination to reintroduce Marxism into intellectual debates, but without dogmatism or demands for sudden conversions.

The great success of the PCI in recruiting intellectuals was due in part to the high status it offered them with respect to Fascism and even to bourgeois society itself.[55] It did so not as a tactic but because it did not fully understand the change in the way in which hegemony was formed in Italy. Absent from Italy for nearly twenty years, Communist leaders took little account of the important new roles taken on by the state in welfare, entertainment, and recreation. They adopted a backward view that brought great success in recruitment of intellectuals but rather less in terms of wider social influence.

The labor movement played a key role in organizing working-class leisure, as it had done before Fascism. The *Case del Popolo* (literally, "Houses of the People") were important centers of class and community identity. Suppressed by the Fascists in the 1920s and turned into PNF sections or OND centers, in many cases they were seized at the end of the war. New ones were built when the DC claimed them for the state in the early 1950s and turned them over to ENAL (the postwar version of the OND) or even made them into police stations. Denied official recognition or funds, the *Case* were purely the expression of the organized working class. Sponsored by the labor unions and the parties of the left, they organized a great variety of activities including billiards, competitions, and lectures. Dances were especially popular and were a sphere in which the Catholics offered no rivalry. Although politics was still a male-dominated activity, the *Case* welcomed families. Children were invited to join the *Pionieri* (Pioneers), an organization that was modeled more on the Soviet group of the same name than its Fascist predecessors. The *Pionieri* also catered to women, adolescents, and young people. "The *Casa del Popolo* was the place you went to dance, the only place where youngsters and women could go, because at one time it was almost impossible for a woman to enter a bar. Only a 'loose woman' would go into a bar to have a coffee," said Augusto C., born in 1921, who until 1951 lived in the province of Bologna (55: 16–17) and who later became a PCI worker. This discrimination did not apply to the *Case del Popolo,* which "granted access to everyone, regardless of their social background":

The *Case del Popolo* were brave enough to have not only billiards but also dance floors. In those days there was a lot of dancing and there were even competitions. We held competitions by getting bands and organizing competitions between them. Me and my brother-in-law organized things lots of times, copying of course because it's difficult to invent . . . . It was a way of bringing people together because the *Casa del Popolo* was not profit-making, there were no bosses, only those who came, the members, and everything you earned you reinvested. . . . The Emilia region had the great merit of keeping people together with this tool. (55: 17)

Workers and their families liked the *Casa del Popolo* because it was "theirs" and it was accessible. Commercial bars and dance halls tended, by contrast, to be the preserve of specific hobby or interest groups on the one hand or of particular social strata or age groups on the other (15: 14–15; 55: 25). In some areas, there was a texture of community activity that the left could take over. The *Casa del Popolo* occupied a similar role in community life after 1945 to that of the after-work organization in urban local areas (*Dopolavoro rionale*) in the 1930s.[56] But the higher degree of spontaneous participation and the role of the parties of the left gave them a democratic flavor and antagonistic significance that was wholly at variance with the paternalism and authoritarianism of the 1930s. It must be borne in mind that the Communists, together with their allies the Socialists and unlike both the Fascists in the 1920s and 1930s and the Catholics over most of the period under examination, were not able to make use of state resources to bolster their action in civil society. Excluded from government in 1947 and heavily defeated in the 1948 election, they conserved a limited measure of power only in local government.

More numerous than the *Case*, the PCI's territorial branches (*sezioni*) were the main focus of its presence and activities. In addition, a range of associations that were initially established on an all-party basis but which, following the onset of the Cold War and the split of Christian Democrats and centrists from the left parties, became exclusively leftist, catered to specific groups such as women, peasants, young people, and ex-partisans. In working-class districts of the large cities and the heavily leftist regions of the Center, these provided a subcultural framework that sustained the PCI as a mass organization. At election time, on anniversaries, and for specific campaigns, such as that for peace in the late 1940s and early 1950s, the party's militants could readily mobilize tens of thousands of people for rallies, demonstrations, and festivals. The annual festivals of the Communist press (at first called *festival de "l'Unità"* and later *feste*) provide a good example of the way in which a ritual initially copied from the French Communist Party (*fête de "l'Humanité"*) developed from a one-day national event for militants in 1946 into a feature of the community-based mass party. Already by 1948, towns, urban districts (*quartieri* or *rioni*), and even village party branches were holding their own festivals and using them to draw in wider sections of the population.[57]

The Communists possessed a range of symbols and rituals that could be projected outward and used to attract people and cultivate a sense of belonging. The most potent of these in the 1940s were associated with the Resistance and with the Soviet Union, which were closely bound to one another through the idea of antifascism. The Communists benefited from the popularity of the U.S.S.R. and Stalin and used both extensively in their propaganda. The Resistance, however, provided a more effective way of establishing the party's national and democratic credentials and building bridges between it and other, more moderate sections of the community. Although the Resistance never became the unifying focus of a new national identity, for reasons concerning its internal politics, its having Italians among its enemies as well as the German occupiers, and its geographical concentration in the North and Center, it did enjoy semiofficial status as the founding ideology of the Republic as the latter took shape from 1946.[58]

On the left, consigned firmly to a subordinate position after 1948, the dominant figure was Stalin. "For ten years the Soviet dictator was one of the great unconscious protagonists of Italian politics," wrote Enzo Forcella in 1963. "In the eyes of several million people he appeared as the personification of greatness and power."[59] For people disappointed and disillusioned with the course taken by events after the war, he was a reference point, a source of hope and of change. Stalin personified the Soviet Union, the country of working-class power that had in February 1943 inflicted the first defeat on Hitler's armies and changed the course of the war. Such was his standing that the Communists used his name and image to integrate their party from 1947 and render it ideologically compact. His picture appeared on the walls of party branches and was placed in trees at party festivals; his texts, in particular *Questions of Leninism*, became compulsory reading. For his seventieth birthday in 1949 gifts poured in to PCI headquarters and were packed up to be sent off to the U.S.S.R. No rank-and-file Italian leftist ever saw Stalin in the flesh; even glimpses in newsreels were rare. Italian Communists had to make do with his film look-alike who appeared in *The Fall of Berlin* and other Soviet films of the period. Tales of Stalin's exploits were invented and recounted by activists who admired his brusque, direct approach and few words. For Forcella, the Stalin cult, although it was fueled by the Communist Party above all, corresponded to a psychological need, that of an oppressed proletariat in need of protection.

The second star of the left was Palmiro Togliatti. An aloof figure associated with a moderate political line that did not enjoy the full support of grassroots activists, the PCI leader was never loved. But a cult nonetheless developed following an assassination attempt on July 14, 1948. The tributes that flowed in to the hospitalized Togliatti, including a powerful endorsement from Stalin, formed the basis of the personality cult that was consolidated in successive months. The film *Togliatti è ritornato*, about the September 1948 festival that marked Togliatti's return to active politics, consecrated the PCI leader, according to Carlo Felice Casula, as "the red Pope."[60] His sixtieth birthday in 1952 was much celebrated and the cult was promoted from 1953 in order to fill the gap left by the death of Stalin. It would be wrong to suggest that his private life was turned into a spectacle in the manner of a film star, but his decision to leave his wife and live with a young Communist member of parliament, Nilde Jotti, gave rise to much comment, mostly of an adverse type.

There was also admiration for local political leaders who, within a local ambit, were perceived as charismatic. One witness in Rovereto recalled the duels between the Communist lawyer Giuseppe Ferrandi and the Catholic mayor Giuseppe Veronesi in the 1950s. Several interviewees in the province of Cosenza remembered Fausto Gullo, the Communist lawyer based in Cosenza who was Minister for Agriculture in the immediate postwar years (73: 3; 82/83/84: 24). One, whose father had been defended by Gullo when he was put on trial in the Fascist period, said

Fausto Gullo represented the popular consciousness of the peasantry, of the unemployed workers, he was their moral defender at least.... After Fascism, when he came to do his first rallies, some women went up to him as if he were a saint ... they kissed him, because he aroused these memories of suffering in them. (82/83/84: 24–25)

Like the Catholics, the left was not keen on celebrity, but it nonetheless sought to appropriate stars generated by film and sport. In the divisive climate of 1948 and after, this sort of symbolic appropriation was inevitable. In some cases there was a straightforward propaganda use of stardom; in others the relationship was more complex and indirect. The link with sport fell into the latter category. In general, the left showed little interest in sport. It was contaminated by its association with Fascism in the eyes of many politicians, some of whom recalled and perpetuated old socialist prejudices against physical exercise and the cult of the body. The body was seen as the possible terrain only of right-wing discourses, whereas socialism and communism addressed the mind. Despite this, a left sports association, UISP, was established and organized some gymnastics and athletics. Its membership was concentrated in areas where the left was strong in the North and Center. At the same time spectator sports enjoyed even greater popularity in the 1940s and 1950s than they had in previous decades. Cycling, which had attracted a widespread following in the 1930s, was especially popular; it was the sport of a rural society that admired the strength and determination of cyclists, who reflected the hopes and desires of ordinary people. Although he was not a man of the left, and indeed he even lent his name to an appeal to vote Christian Democrat in 1948, Fausto Coppi took on the role of a symbolic function for the communists in the same way that his sporting rival Bartali did for the Catholics. The two great champions of the period had been well known before the war but it was only from 1946 that they became a focus of passion and the country divided to support one or the other.

Hollywood cinema was treated in a similar way by left activists. Because the vast majority of films shown in Italy in the 1940s were American, Communists had little choice but to seek elements within them that in some way conformed to their world view. This was not an easy task, because several Hollywood stars were enrolled in the fight against Communism. Communist magazines featured pictures and cover photographs of "progressive" stars like Katharine Hepburn, Humphrey Bogart, and Lauren Bacall who took a stand against the anticommunist witch hunt of the McCarthy period. Even Rita Hayworth was felt by some to be a force for progress since she was contracted to Columbia Pictures, a small studio that according to a rather rough and ready Marxist analysis was acceptable because it was not dominated by monopoly capital. However, the fact that her photograph was affixed to the first hydrogen bomb, dropped in the test on Bikini Atoll in 1945, rendered this particular symbolic appropriation highly controversial.[61] The Communist women's organization UDI (Unione Donne Italiane) also latched on to the strong women of American cinema like Katharine Hepburn, Bette Davis, and Joan Crawford, who offered positive role models.

The main thrust of the left's activity in this area, however, was geared to the defense of Italian cinema and consequently the denunciation of Hollywood imperialism. Initially, the PCI took little interest in neorealism, but from 1948 it became involved in the efforts of film directors, actors, and workers to defend their industry against foreign competition. The party press urged support for protectionism while the Christian Democrats were denounced for seeking to use the laws passed in the late 1940s (see chapters 4 and 7) to eliminate realist impulses from cinema. In Rome and Milan the party drummed up support among its members for *Ladri di biciclette* and other films that were at risk of not receiving a proper showing. The campaign lasted the best part of ten years and ensured that there was always a close relationship between the PCI and the most artistic part of Italian cinema. However, it proved extremely difficult over the long term to sustain the interest of the grassroots in films that often lacked the pure entertainment values of American and commercial films.

Dedicated activists relied on sympathy for the U.S.S.R. to arouse interest in the Soviet, Mexican, and other films that were shown in the left film clubs (*circoli del cinema, cineclub*) that flourished at this time. But the membership was always composed more of intellectuals than workers. "It was hard for us to keep this kind of cinema going," said Augusto C., "because it was expensive and also difficult to understand, or badly understood, I mean it wasn't a cinema of stars, there was no longer any Tyrone Power or Gary Cooper or Gloria Swanson, it was a cinema of themes, it was *The Battleship Potemkin*" (55: 19–20).

Like the Catholics, the left found it difficult to understand or appreciate fashion. Female party members were not supposed to take an interest in fashion or beauty, which were seen as bourgeois. Although Togliatti urged Communist members of parliament to dress smartly, and always himself wore a double-breasted suit (the symbol of bourgeois respectability), vanity and elegance were viewed as contrary to Communist morality. Adelia Q. was a middle-class woman, born in 1924, who joined the PCI in 1945 and moved to Rome from Calabria in 1948:

I have never followed fashion because I liked being very free and very practical. And also because, at the time, the Communist Party said we shouldn't imitate bourgeois women, so the scruffier you looked, the more Communist you were. Fortunately now it's not like that, but in those days . . . I never bought a fur coat, even though I could have when I was young, because I said to myself, "I go out campaigning in the *borgate,* how can I wear a fur coat when I go and see those poor folks who live in shacks?" I could just see myself going to preach to those folk and them telling me, "Go to hell!" I didn't buy a fur coat for this reason; in part because I didn't like them and in part because I didn't think it was right for me to show off my luxuries to people who don't have the basic necessities to live on. . . . There was a time when it was fashionable to wear your hair long, in plaits: my sister did, but I didn't, always like this. . . . Politics was useful to me for this too, in that I never wore any makeup, never, at most a bit of lipstick and nothing else because I thought, "A Communist must be a strong woman, what's makeup got to do with it?" (57: 32–34)

In spite of attitudes like this and the general concern to render the party and the subculture more compact, Communists could not entirely ignore the pastimes and material aspirations that workers and their families shared. Rather like the Catholic *Famiglia Cristiana,* the left-wing weekly *Vie Nuove* tried to mediate between the ideological imperatives of the party and the changing leisure patterns of its readers.[62] After an initial period in which it differed little from *Rinascita, Vie Nuove* evolved into a popular periodical along the lines of the commercial *La Domenica del Corriere.* Although it never shed its pedagogical vocation and regularly included a large amount of material about the Soviet Union and life in the Eastern bloc, the magazine also became progressively more aware of the need to compete directly with illustrated weeklies like *Epoca* and *Oggi* in catering to the tastes of its readers. This meant that alongside articles about the living conditions of workers in Russia and Soviet achievements in the arts and sciences, there were articles about Italian politics, sport, and cinema. As the editors understood the need to reach beyond male workers to women and the family, so features were introduced about fashion and cooking. America was regularly denounced for its belligerence and material inequalities, but *Vie Nuove* was not immune to the allure of

Hollywood stars. Moreover, it adopted techniques such as cover girls, ample use of photographs, and advertisements (all of which were deplored by hard-liners); and it even ran an annual beauty contest that became the Communist equivalent of the Miss Italia pageant.

Like *Famiglia Cristiana, Vie Nuove* enjoyed much success within a sub-cultural orbit. Even though it relied for sales on subscriptions and volunteer sellers (*diffusione militante*), its print run rose from 30,000 in 1946 to 120,000 in 1948, before reaching a peak of 350,000 in 1952.[63] The periodical's subse-quent slow decline (it eventually closed in 1978) was due to the fall in po-litical commitment in the mid-1950s, difficulties in responding to innovations such as television, the rise of private transport, and the failure adequately to reflect the role of women in acting as a channel between the family and the market at a time when the first consumer goods were coming within the pur-view of the lower classes.[64] Ultimately, the magazine did not manage to con-vey a sugar-coated Communist message to the unconverted, as had been the original intention; rather it provided a means whereby elements of commer-cial mass culture were incorporated within the left subculture. That this oc-curred was a tribute to the flexibility of the mass party and its journalists and functionaries, but also proof that there were areas in which it was impossible to beat commercial culture.

Associationist Culture and Modernization

In all three of the cases we have examined—Fascist, Catholic, and Communist—cultural intervention and associationism was driven by two concerns: the de-sire to shape and mold from above, and the need to attract as many people as possible to the movement in question. Without some form of associative cul-ture, it would have been impossible for the Fascists, the Catholics, or the Com-munists to develop the sort of organizational presence that they achieved. In fact, even in the presence of a coercive regime, the network of participatory involvement did not extend very significantly beyond the areas of the country where a developed civil society had existed before the regime. All forms of or-ganized leisure appealed because, in a climate of scarcity, they offered some-thing for little or no cost. Sometimes this involved an engagement with com-mercial culture that could not be completely regulated even by the two forces that occupied the state, the Fascists and the Catholics. Nevertheless, it is clear that the Fascists were able to achieve a degree of dominance in leisure and cul-ture that neither the Catholics nor the Communists could even aspire to. The removal of the Fascists freed up a terrain that could be exploited by the two forces that would dominate Italian society after 1945 in establishing their cul-tural networks, which they did in remarkably similar ways, albeit with differ-

Figure 16. Contestant for "Miss Vie Nuove" competition, 1952. By permission of the Istituto Milanese per la Storia della Resistenza e del Movimento Operaio.

ent emphases. But they too found in the long run that the sphere of leisure was an insidious one that offered limited scope for ideological conversion.

Each of the three forces we have examined championed visions of modernization that combined political, economic, and cultural elements. The autarkic model of the Fascists, the traditional-conservative model of the Catholics, the Soviet example, and the democratic-participatory ideal associated with the Resistance were the main alternatives. These visions underpinned the views by each force of the nation and informed its attitudes toward cultural innovations and external influences. The nation figured most prominently in Fascist discourses, and the experience of the war, foreign occupation, and the fall of the regime, followed by the abolition of the monarchy, profoundly undermined its political currency. However, by the mid-1950s not only the vision of the Fascists but also that of the other forces had either been defeated, bypassed, or weakened as a practicable possibility. The model of modernization followed in Italy was not that of any of these forces. Rather it was one that combined American influences with domestic economic, political, and cultural practices. Within this were some of the paternalistic elements that were shared by both Catholics and the left, with different inflections, and the democratic values that formed the common patrimony of the forces that were responsible for shaping the Constitution of the Republic. But the subcultures themselves proved to be remarkably long-lived, in part because of their adaptability and in part because of the uneven nature of Italian economic development. Expectations were raised before they could be fulfilled, and thus there were great disjunctions between the most advanced areas and the more backward ones, as well as considerable scope for the mediating role of organized forces. These forces exercised their main role in the period that immediately preceded the development of the consumer society but continued to influence social and cultural life, and also electoral behavior, for much longer.[65]

Conclusion

We have dealt in this book with mass culture in Italy between 1936 and 1954 from the point of view of consumption, production, and distribution. We have also examined the various modes of political intervention and associationist organization. What we have not done is analyze in depth the cultural products enmeshed in these processes. This was a deliberate decision, since such an analysis would have made this into a different kind of project, one concerned with the description or interpretation of texts, rather than their production and consumption. In some of our other work we have engaged in textual analysis, but it did not seem appropriate here. In pulling together the main findings, we now want to consider three questions about the material as a whole. How is the period we have examined related to the one that followed it, in terms of the development of mass consumption? How far did the forms of mass organization change across the period? What are the wider implications of our findings and their potential applications to other times and places?

In answer to the first question we would say that the growth in the market for commercial culture between the 1930s and the 1950s laid the basis for the consumer culture associated with the economic boom of the late 1950s and early 1960s. Commercial culture, in the form of cinema, spectator sports, the press, and popular music was not regularly part of the repertoire of most Italians over this earlier period, but it was a feature of most people's lives, even if only as an occasional experience. It had the effect of separating the producers from the consumers of culture. The mass media then widened this separation and contributed to changes in the community and the family by encouraging the privatization of leisure. Although the media were more systematically present in the cities than in the countryside, among the middle classes and workers than the peasants, and in the North-West and Center than in other regions, they broadly standardized the public, constructing it as a "mass," whose only input or creative role was to be in the realm of consumption. Cinema and radio won wide audiences during this period and mass communications consequently came to occupy a more central place in national life.

The construction of consumers as a mass does not mean the suppression or negation of their individuality or agency. Even the modest forms of cultural consumption that we have identified provided opportunities for the assertion of individuality. Purchases of nonessentials, cheap luxuries, or film tickets appealed to working-class people because they allowed an escape from drabness and from humdrum living. Commercial culture was successful because cosmetics, magazines, popular music, and dance halls all focused on individuals, as we saw in chapter 2, often enabling them to incorporate and express new forms of appearance and behavior and make changes in their modes of intimacy and interpersonal relations. The ideas of the good life communicated through the media and in advertising were readily translatable into the realm of experience. A great strength of consumerism was that it met established needs. It comforted and offered dreams; it was at once mundane and exceptional. It required no radical transformation of values or customs in order to prosper. Through consumption, some individuality could be asserted and possibly some respect gained. Mass culture also permeated women's spaces— the home, the hairdresser's salon, the dressmaker's workshop—as well as creating particular immediate experiences for young people. The experience of economic hardship and social disruption during World War II and the immediate postwar period aided the triumph of consumption by undermining some of the newly acquired pleasures and stimulating expectations of their return.

It is worth stressing, in this respect, that the spread of consumer culture happened incrementally and, to a significant extent, within the grooves of existing traditions. Although foreign, and especially American, ideas, techniques, and products arrived in Italy systematically from the 1920s, and their popularity, as we have sought to demonstrate, played an important role in undermining the successive nationalistic and autarkic cultural projects of certain intellectuals and political activists, mass culture was never a purely imported phenomenon. In Italy as elsewhere, consumer practices had first developed in the late nineteenth century, and many popular commercial cultural products were manufactured domestically. Even those that were not, such as Hollywood films, were domesticated to some extent through the dubbing of dialogue, the local production of publicity materials, and the familiar contexts in which they were viewed and consumed. Consumerism in Italy adapted to preexisting customs and styles of behavior and often presented itself in ways that were familiar and reassuring. In other words, it meshed with what was already there. Our research has shown how spending and leisure was related to existing experience. Most working-class people did their shopping in neighborhood stores, went to local second-run and third-run cinemas or nearby dance halls, and listened to the radio in neighbors' homes, their own or at work. On the whole, it was not until after the war they went to the city centers, bought magazines, or attended luxurious first-run movie houses. Consumerism therefore was not a complete experience and indeed perhaps was not really perceived as a phenomenon in their lives at all until the boom years and the advent of television advertising in 1957. Its progress was gradual and, despite the efforts of political forces, it was rarely perceived by individuals as ideological.

As we saw in the last chapter, in Italy organized leisure indirectly assisted the spread of consumption. The promoters of associational activities generally had a poor understanding of the strengths of commercial and consumerist alternatives to them. Organized leisure almost always sought to uplift or mold its public; it had ulterior motives that were usually political and this led to an attitude of selection or ideological discrimination. In reality, as many of our oral witnesses highlighted, conflicts often occurred in the church or the party, as well as the family, over individual pleasures such as dancing, makeup, clothes, films, and film stars. The public culture of organized leisure also suffered from more specific defects, such as the fact that it was predominantly, and in some instances almost exclusively, masculine and was run largely by mature adults. It was poor at catering to women's needs and desires and those of adolescents. Involvement in collective activities occurred due to a mixture of constraint, opportunity, and choice. No matter how pragmatic or reluctant the engagement with organized activities may have been, there was always the sense of taking part in something whose significance went beyond the simple act of watching a film or going on a day trip, or even of attending a rally. Yet these broader projects were not without more general consequences. In the period between the mid-1930s and the mid-1950s, Italians were drawn for the first time en masse into the collective life of their nation and were attributed importance in shaping its destiny. This attribution may have been cynical, or regarded at times as false, but it reflected a situation in which the forms of mass society and a modern political system were taking shape.

This last point leads to the second question. How far did the forms of mass organization and the dynamics of collective life change over the period we have examined? In recent years several scholars have argued that there was a continuity of form and mode of associationism of the mass party between the National Fascist Party (PNF) on the one hand and the PCI (Italian Communist Party) and the DC (Christian Democrats) on the other. Silvio Lanaro has written that the mass parties of the Republic were "forced to move within the furrows cut by the Fascist Party machine, simply because it was Fascism that introduced mass politics in Italy, established several of its fixed rules and tapped much of its potential."[1] Giorgio Galli has also argued that mass politicization was part of the heritage that Fascism left to postwar democracy. In 1946 the combined membership of the three mass parties—the PCI, the PSIUP (Socialist Party), and the DC—was almost identical, at 4.5 million, to the number of members of the Fascist Party in 1943. The new parties enjoyed the same capillary presence too, Galli has argued, although they were compelled to establish and maintain their followings in a competitive rather than a monopoly environment.[2] Although some disenchanted observers after the Fascist period, like the writer Vitaliano Brancati, were critical of the role of crowds in political life ("the crowd believes and individuals doubt; the crowd shouts and individuals think," he wrote in 1946), public spaces were zealously filled by the postwar parties, which competed to demonstrate the level of their support.[3] It might also be said that the parties enjoyed the highest levels of involvement in the same areas of the Center-North as those in which Fascism had had a mass base. Moreover, although the leaders of the postwar parties were careful to adopt styles of speech, dress, and physical posture that were in no way reminiscent of those employed by Mussolini, a certain cult of the authoritative father figure continued. It is striking that recollections of the Duce far outnumbered those of any other political figure in our oral testimonies; quite evidently, his removal left a cultural gap that was not entirely or immediately closed by the passage from dictatorship to democracy.

Plausible though these arguments may at first appear, in fact the question of continuity or otherwise is more complex. Lanaro himself casts a shadow over his argument by suggesting that the rigid top-down command structure of the "Communist galaxy" was "Bolshevik rather than Fascist" in origin.[4] Moreover, all postwar parties relied not on compulsory or semicompulsory adhesion but on voluntary participation. They did not require their members to wear uniforms, nor did they demand repeated ritual displays of uncritical support. Even in regions where one party was dominant, there were always alternatives.

In assessing the issue of continuity it is useful to distinguish the structural from the conjunctural. Structural continuities included the trend toward mass, secular forms of party and associationist organization, the crystallization of political power in public spaces, the development of mass communications, including political communications, and the pattern of Italy's economic development. In all these areas there were relatively few innovations or changes of direction between the 1930s and the 1950s. Only the return of democracy altered patterns of participation. Conjunctural continuities, by contrast, included the opportunistic transfers of membership and loyalties, realignment on the basis of habit and interest without regard to ideology, and the ambiguous conversion of rituals and symbols to new purposes. Obviously, continuities of the latter type may be seen as morally questionable. However, they are also eminently practical. For those who had been accustomed to having their interests, collective or individual, taken care of by Fascism, adhesion to a new force offered a prospect of continuity of privilege. The DC, Carl Levy asserts, simply took over the Fascists' care of the needs of artisans and small traders.[5] Something similar occurred in the area of sport, while in cinema the Catholics extended an already strong presence.

An example of confusion between the two types of continuity is Galli's observation, mentioned above, on membership figures, the implication of which is that PNF members passed en bloc to the postwar mass parties. Yet this was simply not the case. The Resistance brought many into contact with politics for the first time and so did the economic conflicts of the 1940s, such as the occupations of land by poor peasants in the South. The membership of the PCI and the PSIUP was drawn predominantly from people of a lower-class origin than that of the PNF. Also, the Church encouraged the faithful, previously distant from politics, to support the DC, producing a further new wave of entry. In addition, it is safe to assume that many former Fascists simply withdrew from politics. In terms of organizational practices, the Communists may have sought to occupy the public squares left vacant by the Fascists, but of course it was the latter that twenty or so years previously had taken over spaces that were once the preserve of the left. Moreover, in many respects, leading Communists saw the Church as their model and rival. As their slogan said, "For every belltower a party branch" (*per ogni campanile una sezione*), and the comparisons grew more marked as competition between the two forces turned into conflict.

Each force possessed peculiar traits of its own that reflected its origin and ideology. Each also had a different relationship with the apparatuses of the state. Distinctions between state action and party action were obscured under Fascism and it is not possible even for the postwar period to draw a clear dividing line between state and civil society. Cultural intervention was sometimes contained within the state, as in the case of Freddi's film strategy, discussed in chapters 4 and 5. However, the organization of society became an increasingly important objective as the Fascists sought to stabilize their regime and create a civic culture that was infused with their values. The Catholics gained influence within the state after the signing of the Lateran Pacts in 1929. With the recognition of these pacts in the Constitution of the Republic (Article 7) and the victory of the DC in 1948, their influence expanded markedly. Mass associations grew in significance under Fascism, but they became a central part of Catholic activity in civil society only as the center-right's attempt to build hegemony came under threat from the left. Once the DC was firmly installed in power, the parish again replaced the public square as the primary focus of organized activity. Since the left had access neither to the resources or instruments of the state, it was bound to invest all its energies in building a solid presence in civil society. For this reason, the left subculture was the only example of pure voluntary associationism in the period. Like the Catholics, the Communists were able to rely, in the areas of their greatest strength, on community and family pressure toward participation but, unlike these, they could depend neither on the compliance of political and economic elites nor on a firm influence over rites of passage. In compensation, they were far more successful than their rivals at winning the genuine commitment of the country's artists and intellectuals.

The Fascists, the Catholics, and the Communists all aimed to proselytize and to change society. But they also all aimed to stabilize their support and extend their influence in everyday community life. These contradictory impulses were a source of conflict within each camp, and nowhere was this conflict more pronounced than in reactions and responses to commercial culture. Sport, cinema, and magazine publishing not only offered opportunities to political and religious organizations to bridge the gap between supply and demand, by making available to the masses things they would not be able normally to afford, but also were a source of competition that escaped control, and this was increasingly the case between the 1930s and the 1950s. If the Fascists were most disturbed by the commercialization of sport, it was cinema and dance that caused most anguish, respectively, to the left and the Catholics. American models and suggestions provoked fearful responses on the part of all three forces. It is possible, for example, to read the Catholic and Communist appropriation of parts of Hollywood cinema in two ways: either as proof of the strength and flexibility of the two subcultures or as a sign of their failure to insulate their populations against the influence of a powerful and attractive external medium. Both readings are valid. In Italy, subcultural appropriations of this sort showed creativity and flexibility that would aid the subcultures in enjoying a remarkably long life, but they also ultimately contributed to their decline. The Catholics and the Communists succeeded in projecting powerful, admired personalities. But, in the vast majority of cases, stars were formed outside the subcultures according to a logic and procedures over which they had no control.

Our third and last question is about the wider implications of our arguments and findings in this book. Since our focus is on a particular national case, it must be acknowledged that some of what is described, as in all country-specific studies, is unique to that case. There were, as we have noted throughout, several historical and geographical particularities that gave a distinctive shape to the development of mass culture in Italy. Uneven economic development, due to the persistence until the 1950s of traditional agriculture and industrial growth limited to specific areas of the north and center, explains many of the cultural differences between regions of Italy and between city, provincial town, and village. Similarly, the emergence of a single-party regime in the interwar years and the strong social presence of the Catholic Church and, after 1945, of the parties of the left, were also distinctive features of the Italian cultural landscape. Each of these features had analogues or counterparts in other European countries, at least for part of the twentieth century—Germany also had a one-party state, Spain a one-party state and a strong Catholic culture, France a strong Catholic presence and a Communist subculture—but they were not all replicated in the same combination at the same time anywhere else.

Despite this distinctiveness, at least three of the features we have described in the Italian case are to be found elsewhere. The first is the pattern of state–culture relations. From the mid-1920s to the mid-1970s, as we noted in chapter 7, most European states increased their involvement in cultural activities in both "positive" (enabling) and "negative" (repressive) ways. The line between these is not always easy to draw, since the same action may sometimes be seen as both repressive and enabling, depending on who is affected. For instance, the imposition of import quotas on foreign films was repressive for the foreign film companies and enabling for the domestic producers. However, one may describe as essentially enabling the use of public funds to pro-

vide recreational and leisure facilities and to subsidize arts and cultural industries and as essentially repressive the tighter regulatory controls on the press
and the more systematic censorship of all media.

The second feature that the Italian case has in common with others is the
co-presence of these state interventions with an expanding private sector of
commercially delivered mass culture. The trend we have noted toward a commercialization of culture and mass leisure could also be seen at the same time
in most other European countries. This fact is important for an understanding
of the forms of state intervention, since private cultural operators in all these
countries actively lobbied or resisted various state agencies and did not simply
"undergo" state directives. They could attempt to circumvent legal curbs or
get restrictive laws changed or prevent new ones from being introduced; they
could also ask representatives of the state to further or protect their interests.
Individuals or groups of citizens could try to produce or obtain material or
information not approved by the state, or they could attempt to get censorship
tightened or relaxed in a particular area or to obtain more public provision of
leisure and recreation. In the latter case, in Italy, as Victoria de Grazia has argued, what the Fascist Dopolavoro attempted was a variant on a wider European and North American response on the one hand to the growing power of
labor unions and on the other to the move toward rationalization (including
"scientific management" of the labor process) of the workplace and of workers' leisure time.[6] Naturally, it had a particular political inflection that was
characterized, among other things, by a higher degree of coercion (like Nazism) and a distinctive ideological packaging that distinguished it from the
liberal-democratic countries.

The third common feature is what we might call the social implications
and effects of mass culture. Mass culture and the media, as we initially argued
in the introduction and have sought to demonstrate throughout this book,
may have had some negative properties but they were not the agents of social control or leveling that certain exponents of mass society theory believed
them to be in the interwar years. They were for the most part agents of change,
channels through which a more modern society was fashioned. Mass culture
and the improvement of mass communications made society more transparent, more visible and audible to itself; opened up "national culture" to the cultures of other countries; and led to new forms of cultural behavior within
communities and families. Some of these behaviors—such as new tastes in
music or fashion—were sources of conflict within particular social groups (in
families and between generations, most notably) as well as means by which
the individual could try to shape his or her identity. The marking out of these
identities on the body was a particularly important manifestation of the new
mass culture, in areas from dress to dancing to sport.

What applies in the Italian case applies also, we believe, in other countries where mass culture takes root. In these other countries, too, mass culture plays an ambivalent role, as it did in Italy, in relation to national identity: on the one hand helping to strengthen the idea of a national community by creating—in particular through the cinema newsreel and through mass radio and television consumption—a simultaneously and homogeneously networked nation with nationally recognized stars and texts, on the other hand breaking down the nation's cultural borders, opening the floodgates to products, styles, and stars from other countries. To be sure, this twin process of reinforcing national forms of popular culture and opening out to foreign styles is not value-neutral. It may be considered to have positive social effects or negative ones, according to who judges these effects and what criteria they use to judge them. But the point is that the process happens, and the complex way in which it happens is one of the things we have sought to capture in this book.

APPENDIX 1.
THE ORAL HISTORY PROJECT

MARCELLA FILIPPA

The collection, transcription, and analysis of 117 oral testimonies comprise a major part of the research for this book. These testimonies have provided one of the most important sources on cultural consumption. The interviews were conducted between May 1991 and May 1992 by myself, David Forgacs, Stephen Gundle, and Paola Pallavicini, then a young researcher based in Turin, who carried out the largest number of interviews (nearly half the total) with great professionalism and sensitivity. We used three age bands, by year of birth: age band I, 1900–1914; age band II, 1915–1929; and age band III, 1930 and after. The oldest interviewee was born in 1904 and the youngest in 1937. Approximately half our interviewees were from the second age band. We subdivided our sample further by three sets of geographical divisions: North/Center/South and Islands (our survey included Sardinia but not Sicily); large city/provincial town/village; and town center/suburb (*periferia*). Details about the interviewees are provided in appendix 2. The interviews, in Italian, are archived with the Economic and Social Data Service, ESDS Qualidata, at the University of Essex, where they may be consulted on request.

In selecting people to interview, we kept in mind a number of variables and different types of belonging—gender, generation, level of formal education, political and union affiliation, religious belief, employment history—but we did not claim to be assembling a representative sample in a sociological sense. Instead, we followed networks of friendships and political, labor union, and professional connections, as well as the networks provided by old people's associations, and we focused on geographical areas that we considered particularly interesting for a reconstruction of cultural processes in Italy in the period under examination. We also chose places where there were mediators who could help us get accepted in the community, and in some cases help us also overcome the barrier created by the use of dialect, the most common means of communication for several of the older interviewees.

Each interview was conducted in three stages. First, the subject was asked to tell her/his life story; then s/he was asked questions based on a questionnaire (reproduced in appendix 3); finally, s/he was asked to fill in a form giving personal details. In the first stage, the subject was allowed to structure the narrative freely as s/he wished, to decide how much importance to give to the telling of the life story, and to choose what temporal order to establish in narrating the phases of her/his life. In this stage, the interviewer's interventions were kept to a minimum. S/he had to be able to listen in silence, try to understand the interviewee, and pay attention to their silences, moments of perplexity, or hesitation, in order to be able to select and target the questions in the next stage.

In the second stage, the interviewer used the questionnaire as a framework for asking questions, but here too ample space was left for the subject's answers, narrative, and recollections. We agreed, in fact, that the questionnaire should be treated largely as a checklist for the interviewer, a model on which s/he could draw, but which s/he did not have to use in all its sections. In practice we hardly ever followed all of the items on the questionnaire. Rather, we adapted it to the life experience of the subject being interviewed, who was given space to narrate, remember, and go into detail on moments or events that assumed importance in her/his individual life history. For example, interviewees from the world of entertainment and the arts—singers, musicians, actors, conductors—were almost always asked detailed questions about their profession, and relatively few questions were brought up from the questionnaire. We felt that to have insisted on other questions could have resulted in evasive, generalized, or superficial answers, given the overwhelming importance of professional experience for these subjects.

We made a choice, in other words, of finding out in detail about certain aspects of each individual's life, aware that in doing so we were leaving out others. We realized as we carried out the interviews that our interviewees, particularly those we did not know well or at all, were often prepared to give us only a limited amount of time. The possibility of narration was limited within a definite space and time, particularly when the interviewee lived in a city. It was the time of the city that determined and delimited the time of narration, but perhaps it was also anxiety about death and ending. This gives a different dimension to the time one can spend on relations with others, forcefully restructuring it. The testimonies are noticeably marked by the place in which they were collected. The city/country polarity is fundamental in differentiating the time that interviewees chose to give us.

In 1997, when I was writing up with Luisa Passerini another research project that drew on oral testimonies, those of former workers at the Fiat Mirafiori factory in Turin, we compared our findings with projects that had been carried out in the early 1980s and described what we saw as an impoverishment of the narrative function as a whole:

This impoverishment is the result, above all, of the death of the oldest witnesses, those born between the end of the nineteenth century and the first years of the twentieth, who belonged to a generation with great storytelling abilities and rich narrative languages deriving from ancient popular traditions. However, the decline in ability to tell stories is linked only in part to age. It seems to be connected also to other factors, some of which we have considered in other research projects. One is Walter Benjamin's claim that the figure of the storyteller has come to an end as the value of experience has been eclipsed in the modern world. Another is the tendency towards nuclearization of the family, which drastically reduces contact with the oldest generations. Others are the extension of compulsory school attendance and the homogenization and impoverishment of language, which is linked on the one hand to the spread of the mass media, in particular television, and on the other to the commercialization of cultural products. These processes, although fundamental in spreading and democratizing culture, have reduced people's ability to listen to one another.[1]

These ideas seemed to me to be borne out by another piece of research I did subsequently on representations of death in the twentieth century, in particular during Fascism, in which I likewise identified a growing difficulty in establishing relations between generations through the transmission of narrative, and the decline in the capacity to listen alongside that of storytelling.[2]

In the third phase, the filling in of the form, the subjects were at liberty not to answer questions they considered too personal. However, when they declined to give a direct answer to these questions, the answer had in any case sometimes already emerged indirectly from the narration, as in the case of questions about political or religious beliefs or about date of birth (three of our subjects, two of them from the world of entertainment, declined to answer the latter question on the form).

Different channels were used for finding people to interview: some individuals were known directly to the interviewer; those in the entertainment professions were mainly traced through personal contacts; most of the others were found through professional academic contacts—historians, sociologists, and anthropologists—in different parts of Italy. The mediation and guarantee provided by associations, political parties, and trade unions were particularly useful in locating people to interview and allowing us to make contact with them. Yet another type of mediation proved indispensable: the local mediator who took the interviewer to individuals whom s/he knew personally. This not only ensured that the interview could happen but also allowed others to follow on from it, according to the criterion of opening up a network. In some cases, the mediator became an active participant in the interview, helping the subject remember in difficult or problematic cases, or reconstructing together with him or her a set of reminiscences, since s/he functioned within the network as a point of reference offering knowledge, guarantees, and security to the interviewee. This happened particularly in small centers, in villages, above all in Calabria and Sardinia, where the figure of the mediator is particularly important in organizing the network of small group relations as well as those within the community. In those cases where the interviewee spoke partly in an unfamiliar dialect, or used some dialect expressions (this happened particularly with some of the oldest witnesses of peasant origin, above all in Sardinia and Calabria), the mediator also functioned as an interpreter, providing a simultaneous translation into Italian.

The importance of the mediator was pointed out in the 1970s by Nuto Revelli in his research on "the world of the defeated" ("il mondo dei vinti") in peasant communities of Piedmont, which acted as a formative influence and methodological model for many of our generation:

The organized meeting, with a "mediator" who introduces me as "a man you can trust," is also based on instinctive distrust. Distrust is always the first obstacle I face. I don't find it offensive. I justify it. It is not easy to enter a peasant's house, it is not easy to pin a peasant down to a table for hours on end. Without an efficient network of "locals," of "mediators," you can't get into peasants' homes.

The "mediator" suggests the meeting and is present at the interview: he breaks the ice, thaws the interlocutor, invites him to speak freely, as if he's "among family."[3]

The debate on the use of oral sources has been going on now for several decades. Up to the late 1980s there was a strong polarization for and against oral history, often in a rigid and a priori manner, but already when we carried out our research in the 1990s this was starting to change. Historians had largely moved beyond the view of oral sources as providing factual information or as being representative or necessarily truthful and had increasingly focused on their symbolic and narrative aspects, using them as sources of memory and self-representation.[4]

The work done in the 1970s and 1980s by the French historian Philippe Joutard provided an important theoretical model for our research. In my view it still remains a high-water mark of reflection on the use of collective and individual memory sources. Joutard's awareness of how the historian intervenes in the object of study led him to recognize the limitations of the method and of the object itself and to develop a historical critique of oral sources. In his major work *La Légende des Camisards* (1977), he emphasized not so much the quantity as the quality of oral testimonies and rejected the idea, which some other oral historians put forward at that time, that one can construct a representative sample.[5] Although Joutard insisted, as we did in our research, on certain data in constructing a group of interviewees—age, place of origin, social and cultural status, religion, sex, generation, career history, and so on— he argued that the group that thereby emerges, however complex and internally differentiated, can never be a faithful reproduction of a real population. It is a selection of narrators and life stories, one that allows the researcher to reconstruct an "inventory of collective memory," in his case that of the inhabitants of the Cévennes Mountains.[6] Joutard examined the confusions, the errors of memory, not only individual ones but also those common to the whole collectivity. In this case, he argued, "historical research cannot be separated from the examination of collective mentalities."[7] As he put it in another text, even when memory produces distortions, silences, repressions, and censorship, these are to be understood not as its weaknesses but as its points of strength:

What makes the oral testimony interesting is precisely the relationship between spontaneous recollections, those that are stimulated and exhumed in the interview, and silence. Absences are as significant as presences. Since both memorization and forgetting are active processes, it is clear that one cannot interpret forgetting as failure and memory as simple reproduction of past reality.[8]

Another influential model for us was the work of Luisa Passerini, particularly that of the early 1980s on working-class people in Turin during the Fascist period. As with Joutard, the silences of memory, the distortions and errors made in recollecting, led Passerini to some interesting interpretive hypotheses, for instance, on the role of ideas of order in the day-to-day acceptance of political power and the primacy of work in many of the testimonies. For Passerini in this context, oral sources oblige us to reconsider the notion of consent to Fascism in relation to the working classes.[9]

We applied different readings and types of interpretation to the oral testimonies we collected. At one level, we were concerned with what people said about particular events or aspects of their cultural consumption because they enabled us to amplify, correct, or corroborate other sources on the themes that interested us. At another, we were attentive to strategies of self-presentation, the perceptions subjects have of themselves and the way they present themselves to others, the values they consider it important to understand and transmit in their life story.

Only on a few occasions were we refused an interview. In many cases the people we interviewed showed an active interest in the research after our brief explanation of the project. While on the one hand our presentation of our research often made people, even those who had been initially reluctant, more willing to tell their stories and be accepted, on the other, the fact that they knew they were being interviewed for a British-based research project (or that in some cases a British interviewer was present) meant that they sometimes presented themselves to the interviewer in a stereotyped fashion, at least at the start of the interview. In such cases they might start with "textbook" images of Italy and the Italians, or by going over the general history of the period employing clichés about Italians and "Italianness" and giving their judgments on the war, the actions of the British government, and of British troops in Italy. In these cases "macrohistory" dominated and squeezed out the personal story, which the subject considered unworthy of being told because it was "too normal," too tied to everyday life, and in these cases we had to intervene to try to steer the interview in another direction. In several life stories we found what Ascanio Celestini has noted of the stories of the war he has collected recently, namely that the interviewee gives priority to "official history."[10] One of the people we interviewed in Rome, for instance, who had lived since childhood in a working-class district, gave, in a rather somber and measured tone of voice, a "history book" account of Italy at war, occupied Rome, and the "open city," which was strongly influenced on the one hand by schoolroom memories and on the other by images from the films of neorealism.

Other influences also colored some of the testimonies, in particular literature and television. One example among many is that of a woman who had lived for much of her life in San Lorenzo in Rome. Her account of the war, the bombing of July 19, 1943, and the persecutions of the Jews, of which some inhabitants of the district had direct experience, was strongly influenced by images from Elsa Morante's novel *La storia* (*History: A Novel*, 1974), which is partly set in San Lorenzo, together with a further layer of narratives that seemed to come out of the later television adaptation (directed by Luigi Comencini, transmitted on Raidue, 1987). Personal history had become entwined with those images until it had superimposed itself on them and become history itself, collective history, an indistinct chorus of voices. On these and other occasions the account of an individual's own story becomes entangled with those of other characters, real or imaginary, and is modeled on other stories, true or presumed to be so. The same phenomenon has emerged in other works using oral history, such as Alessandro Portelli's on the Nazi massacre of March 1944 at the Fosse Ardeatine and Ascanio Celestini's on memories of the war and its effects in Rome, both of which have an extraordinary ability to offer a powerful, choral representation based on a long period of collecting and elaborating individual and collective stories, and an attempt to build a bridge of narration and knowledge between generations.[11]

Accounts like these are mainly to be found in the cities, even though in a few cases one finds them also in small towns or outlying villages in the rural south, and they generally deal with major traumatic events like the war. Moreover, they seem to belong to a consolidated, collective narrative tradition in which the epic character of the story is highlighted and which is characterized by particular forms of transmission of historical memory and collective identity between generations.

Since it was our intention to work with relatively homogeneous networks, families, and kin groups, we interviewed a number of married couples. In these cases we often found a tendency on the part of the woman to defer to the man, whom she considered the depositary of "truth," better able to narrate both his own life story and hers, seen as the mirror image of his. At the same time the man tended to subsume the woman's narrative into his own, as a life lived almost always in symbiosis with his or considered of less importance and little significance. Because of this we tried to collect the two testimonies separately, but in many cases the older couples insisted on being interviewed together. In these cases, the woman's capacity to narrate was often crushed by the presence of the man judging and sanctioning her account.

There were, however, some situations in which strong female figures emerged in the narratives. This happened with a seventy-year-old woman who was present at the interview with her husband although she had refused to be interviewed herself because she considered her story to be of little relevance. For much of the time she sat in silence, but at certain points, and sometimes at her husband's request, she added precision to his story and in this respect her contribution was very important. She hardly ever figured in the narrative as an active subject but she was present as part of a couple, in an indivisible unity with her husband, who was an able narrator but imprecise in laying out events on a temporal axis. The woman's conception of time was by contrast very precise and was marked by subjective events—the birth of her children, particular anniversaries, moments connected to developments or changes related to the body—more than by the events of public history such as the fall of Fascism, the liberation, or the general election of 1948.[12] In many cases, in fact, we observed that the life story was not told in a strictly chronological order. Each story is an attempt to construct an individual's own temporal order, one that respects a personal chronological hierarchy that intersects with a hierarchy of degrees of relevance established by the narrator in relation to his or her own life.

In many cases, along with the oral testimonies we were shown visual materials by some of our interviewees, which in part reinforced the verbal testimony and added details to particular themes. Photographs documented moments of celebration, places of sociability, family celebrations, weddings, popular traditions and festivities, concerts and public demonstrations, moments of intimacy, and significant moments of everyday life, such as the purchase of a new piece of dining-room furniture, the first car or scooter, or the first suit for a girl, symbolically marking her entry into the adult world. The camera in those years forcefully entered the family and the home, documenting the lifestyles and aspirations of Italians, including those of the working classes. It would be worth making a detailed reflection on such photographic sources both for a reconstruction of everyday life and material culture and for the analysis of the collective imaginary in that period.

The testimonies drawn on in this book were collected in 1991–1992. The attempt to reflect theoretically on work done fifteen years ago inevitably poses a number of problems that need to be taken into account. The debate on the use of oral sources in Italy has proceeded apace, and it has become richer with the passing of time. It has partly shed the strongly ideological, militant, and antagonistic connotations that had characterized it for many years, when oral sources had been represented as "alternative" to the ones traditionally used in historical reconstructions. A new generation of researchers is now using oral sources with a greater self-awareness, accepting part of the suggestions that many of us developed previously, reconstructing parts of the history of Italy that had long remained in the shadows, but rarely using them as the only sources, in a totalizing way, as had often been done in prior decades. Time has also moved on for the authors of this book and for me. I no longer consider oral sources as representing the totality of available sources; they are just one of many sources I have drawn on in my work of the last ten years. Since working on the part of this research dealing with the cultural consumption of Italians from the 1930s to the early 1950s, I have not taken part in another collective project with such a large corpus of testimonies. In fact, as far as I am aware, this is, to date, one of the largest oral history samples that has ever been assembled in Italy, and one of the most ambitious in its aim of going beyond a particular locality or region and taking into consideration aspects linked to national history and to the forms of construction of identity of Italians in the passage through the war to the postwar period and the first years of the reconstruction.

APPENDIX 2.
TABLE OF INTERVIEWEES

No.	Name	Sex	Birth Year	Age Band[1]	Birthplace	Province of Birth[2]	Area of Birthplace[3]	Social Class[4]	Employment	Inter.[5]
1	Sergio P.	M	1925	II	Torino	TO	NW	III.2	skilled worker>singer>skilled worker	MF/DF
2	Mario C.	M	1934	III	Roma	RM	C	III.4>2	manual>skilled worker	MF/DF
3	Bruno O.	M	1932	III	Torino	TO	NW	IIb.3	artisan	MF/DF
4	Natalia	F	1922	II	Pontelongo	PD	NE	III.2>IIa.1	worker>employee	MF/DF
5	Gualtiero	M	1927	II	Torino	TO	NW	IIc.3	actor	MF
6	Editta L.	F	1913	I	Torino	TO	NW	IIa.3	teacher	MF
7	Roberto R	M	1935	III	Torino	TO	NW	IIb.5	traveling salesman	MF
8	Maria G.	F	1905	I	Alba	CN	NW	IIc.3	private income	MF
9	Aldo B.	M	1912	I	Torino	TO	NW	I.1	director	MF
10	Francesca C.	F	1911	I	Collio	BS	NW	IIc.3	housewife/sales assistant	MF
11	Adriana A.	F	1929	II	Boretto	RE	NE	III.1>IIb.1	agric laborer>smallholder	MF
12	Rita B.	F	1927	II	Reggio Emilia	RE	NE	III.1>IIb.1	agric laborer>smallholder	MF
13	Elsa	F	1937	III	Torino	TO	NW	IIb.4	small business	MF
14	Lidia A.	F	1906	I	Trana	TO	NW	IIc.3	private income	MF
15	Edgher A.	M	1914	I	Porto Maggiore	FE	NE	III.2>IIc.3>I.1	worker>musician>impresario	MF
16	Gino G.	M	1920	II	Roma	RM	C	III.4>2	manual>skilled worker	MF/DF
17	Livio S.	M	1936	III	Roma	RM	C	IIb.3	artisan	MF/DF

No.	Name	Sex	Year		Place	Prov.	Region	Code	Occupation	
18	Mario M.	M	1927	II	Roma	RM	C	IIc.3	cinema projectionist	DF
19	Arnaldo B.	M	1928	II	Roma	RM	C	IIb.4	barber	DF
20	Teta	F	1928	II	nd	TV	NE	IIb.4	hairdresser	MF
21	Sara C.	F	1928	II	Roma	RM	C	IIc.3	housewife	MF
22	Nello M.	M	1914	I	Roma	RM	C	III.3	building worker	DF
23	Giuseppe C.	M	1910	I	Roma	RM	C	IIb.3	tailor	DF
24	Avelina G.	F	1919	II	Molinella	BO	NE	III.2>4	worker>shop assistant	SG
25	Angela C.	F	1919	II	Sasso Marconi	BO	NE	III.2	worker	SG
26	Loris C.	M	1925	II	San Giovanni in Persiceto	BO	NE	IIa.2	station master	SG
27	Alberto L.	M	1923	II	nd	nd	NE	IIb.3	artisan	SG
28	Tito A.	M	1932	III	San Cesario	MO	NE	III.3	worker	SG
29	Bernardina A.	F	1931	III	Sasso Marconi	BO	NE	IIb.1>3	peasant>dress-maker	SG
30	Rosalia A.	F	1913	I	Bisceglie	BA	S	IIb.3	artisan	SG
31	Psyche M.	F	1919	II	Napoli	NA	S	IIa.3	teacher	SG
32	Lisa G.	F	1921	II	Torino	TO	NW	III.2	worker	MF
33	Dina F.	F	nd	nd	Torino	TO	NW	IIc.3	singer	MF
34	Delfina F.	F	nd	nd	Torino	TO	NW	IIc.3	singer	MF
35	Zia P.	F	1906	I	Teulada	CA	I	III.1/6	domestic servant	PP
36	Zio A.	M	1921	II	Teulada	CA	I	IIb.1	peasant	PP
37	Paolo M.	M	1909	I	Teulada	CA	I	I.2	doctor	PP
38	Iole G.	F	1920	II	Cagliari	CA	I	IIa.3	teacher	PP
39	Emilio C.	M	1927	II	Burcei	CA	I	IIc.1>III.5	soldier>worker	PP
40	Mariella S.	F	1937	III	Villaverde	OR	I	IIc.3	housewife	PP
41	Mariarita P.	F	1933	III	San Nicolò Gerrei	CA	I	IIb.1	peasant	PP

Continued on the next page

Table of Interviewees. *Continued*

No.	Name	Sex	Birth Year	Age Band[1]	Birthplace	Province of Birth[2]	Area of Birthplace[3]	Social Class[4]	Employment	Inter.[5]
42	Desiderio P.	M	1926	II	Burcei	CA	I	IIb.1>a.1	peasant>white-collar worker	PP
43	Igino Q.	M	1929	II	Burcei	CA	I	IIb.4>1	tradesperson> peasant	PP
44	Anna A.	F	1919	II	Burcei	CA	I	IIb.1	peasant	PP
45	Michele Z.	M	1922	II	Burcei	CA	I	III.5	unskilled worker> transport worker	PP
46	Lina C.	F	1919	II	Cagliari	CA	I	III.5	nurse	PP
47	Olga C.	F	1928	II	Cagliari	CA	I	III.5	shop assistant	PP
48	Elisa A.	F	1923	II	Sant'Antioco	CA	I	IIc.3	private income	PP
49	Pietro P.	M	1913	I	Carloforte	CA	I	I.2	magistrate	PP
50	E. P.	F	1930	III	Cagliari	CA	I	I.2	doctor	PP
51	F. P.	F	1935	III	Cagliari	CA	I	I.1	administrator	PP
52	Luisanna D.	F	1928	II	Sardara	CA	I	IIa.3	teacher	PP
53	Giuseppe M.	M	1914	I	nd	PD	NE	IIb.4	barber	MF
54	Severino M.	M	1936	III	Aosta	AO	NW	III.2	skilled worker	PP
55	Augusto C.	M	1921	II	Medicina	BO	NE	IIa.1	employee	DF
56	Fulvio M.	M	1927	II	Roma	RM	C	III.3>5	worker	MF/DF
57	Adelia Q.	F	1924	II	Napoli	NA	S	IIa.3	teacher	MF
58	Mimmo V.	M	1930	III	Minturno	LT	C	III.4	unskilled worker	MF
59	Mena V.	F	1935	III	Minturno	LT	C	IIb.3	dressmaker	MF
60	Mario S.	M	1927	II	Roma	RM	C	III.3	construction worker	DF

	Name	Sex	Year		Place				Occupation	
61	Marisa A.	F	1932	III	Roma	RM	C	IIb.3	dressmaker	DF
62	Augusto M.	M	1922	II	Roma	RM	C	IIa.2	employee	MF
63	Giuseppe A.	M	1934	III	Roma	RM	C	III.2>5	worker	MF
64	Felice	M	1924	II	Roma	RM	C	III.4>5	unskilled worker	MF
65	Vita R.	F	1915	II	Roma	RM	C	IIa.1	employee	DF
66	Clorinda	F	1923	II	Providence, R.I.	abr	C	III.2>6	worker>domestic servant	DF
67	Agnese S.	F	1920	II	nd	SA	S	IIa.1	employee	DF
68	Lina A.	F	1935	III	Cadelbosco di Sopra	RE	NE	III.1>2	maid>rice worker>worker	MF
69	Ottavio F.	M	1909	I	Spresiano	TV	NE	III.2>IIc.3	skilled worker>painter	MF
70	Maria I.	F	1932	III	Celico	CS	S	IIb.1>4	peasant> tradesperson	PP
71	Carmela F.	F	1912	I	Celico	CS	S	IIb.1>4	peasant>tradesperson	PP
72	Pietro I.	M	1928	II	Celico	CS	S	III.5>3	carter>builder	PP
73	Leandro N.	M	1929	III	Spezzano	CS	S	IIa.3	teacher	PP
74	Arturo M.	M	1917	II	Celico	CS	S	IIb.3>4	carpenter>trades-person	PP
75	Gustavo V.	M	1910	I	Celico	CS	S	IIc.3	private income: scholar/writer	PP
76	Rita L.	F	1916	II	Casole	CS	S	IIc.3	housewife	PP
77	Teresina L.	F	1934	III	Casole	CS	S	IIc.3	housewife	PP
78	Giuseppe G.	M	1935	III	Cosenza	CS	S	I.1	director	PP
79	Giuseppina A.	F	1910	I	Palmi	RC	S	IIc.3	private income	PP
80	Rosina I.	F	1906	I	Rogliano	CS	S	IIb.2	tenant farmer	PP

Continued on the next page

Table of Interviewees. *Continued*

No.	Name	Sex	Birth Year	Age Band[1]	Birthplace	Province of Birth[2]	Area of Birthplace[3]	Social Class[4]	Employment	Inter.[5]
81	Maria P.	F	1935	III	Rogliano	CS	S	III.2	worker>housewife>cook	PP
82	Francesco C.	M	1923	II	Spezzano	CS	S	III.1>2	unskilled worker	PP
83	Giuseppe V.	M	1922	II	Spezzano	CS	S	IIa.3	teacher	PP
84	Silvio L.	M	1924	II	Spezzano	CS	S	III.1>IIa.2	unskilled worker>employee	PP
85	Antonio F.	M	1926	II	San Giovanni in Fiore	CS	S	III.4>IIb.4	barman>tradesperson	PP
86	Francesco F.	M	1934	III	San Giovanni in Fiore	CS	S	III.2	stonecutter>skilled worker	PP
87	Rosario B.	M	1930	III	San Giovanni in Fiore	CS	S	IIb.2>5	smallholder>forest ranger	PP
88	Antonio C.	M	1929	II	San Giovanni in Fiore	CS	S	IIb.3	tailor	PP
89	Cesare G.	M	1904	I	Savigliano	CN	NW	IIc.3	orchestra conductor	MF
90	Mario V.	M	1916	II	Fontainemore	AO	NW	IIc.2	priest	MF
91	Giovanni B.	M	1917	II	Challand St Anselme	AO	NW	IIc.1	soldier	PP
92	Augusta R.	F	1935	III	Challand St Anselme	AO	NW	IIc.3	hotel worker/shop assistant	MF
93	Barbara T.	F	1907	I	Challand St Anselme	AO	NW	IIb.1>c.3	peasant>housewife	PP

#	Name	Sex	Year	Class	Place	Prov.	Region	Mobility	Occupation	Type
94	Salvatore B.	M	1936	III	Foggia	FO	S	III.4>2	shopworker>worker	PP
95	Augusto C.	M	1919	II	Savona	SV	NW	IIc.1>b.4	soldier>tradesperson	MF
96	Delfina D.	F	1920	II	Pont Saint Martin	AO	NW	IIb.4	tradesperson	PP
97	Amerigo T.	M	1930	III	Pont Saint Martin	AO	NW	I.2	lawyer	MF
98	Paolina G.	F	1908	I	Pont Saint Martin	AO	NW	IIc.3	housewife	PP
99	Teresa C.	F	1935	III	Gravina	BA	S	IIb.2>III.1	peasant/embroidery>worker	PP
100	Nicola A.	M	1931	III	Gravina	BA	S	IIb.1>III.2	cobbler>transport>electrician	PP
101	Laura S.	F	1930	III	Torino	TO	NW	I.2	architect	DF
102	Pupa	F	nd	nd	Roma	RM	C	IIa.2>c.3	employee>housewife	MF
103	Bianca G.	F	1908	I	Pergine Valsugana	TN	NE	IIb.4>c.3	tradesperson>housewife	PP
104	Germinia Z.	F	1917	II	Pescantina	VR	NE	IIa.2>c.3	employee>housewife	PP
105	Livia T.	F	1928	II	Rovereto	TN	NE	IIa.1	employee>housewife	PP
106	Giuseppe P.	M	1926	II	Cles	TN	NE	IIa.1>I.1	employee>director	PP
107	Sergio M.	M	1930	III	Trento	TN	NE	III.5>IIb.4	worker>tradesperson	PP
108	Ermanno	M	1915	II	Salzburg	abr		IIb.4	tradesperson	PP
109	Lidia B.	F	1924	II	Tunis	abr		IIb.4/c.4	tradesperson>housewife	PP
110	Enzo P.	M	1935	III	Cles	TN	NE	IIc.3	casual student work>teacher	PP
111	Cesare B.	M	1932	III	Mantova	MN	NW	IIa.1	employee	PP
112	Riccarda G.	F	1923	II	Rovereto	TN	NE	IIa.2	employee	PP
113	Franca	F	1918	II	Sclemo di Stenico	TN	NE	III.6>IIb.4	domestic servant>tradesperson	PP

Continued on the next page

Table of Interviewees. *Continued*

No.	Name	Sex	Birth Year	Age Band[1]	Birthplace	Province of Birth[2]	Area of Birthplace[3]	Social Class[4]	Employment	Inter.[5]
114	Guido	M	1906	I	Rovereto	TN	NE	IIb.2>4	gardener> tradesperson	PP
115	Aldo G.	M	1920	II	Predosa	AL	NW	IIc.3	accordion player	MF
116	Carlo A.	M	1921	II	Palermo	PA	I	IIb.3	woodworker> stage designer	PP
117	Carlo G.	M	1908	I	Rivarolo Canavese	TO	NW	IIb.4	tradesperson	PP

Key to Table

nd   not declared
>   change of occupation/class category

1. Age Band

I 1900–1914; II 1915–1929; III 1930 and after

2. Province of Birth

AL	Alessandria
AO	Aosta
BA	Bari
BO	Bologna
BS	Brescia
CA	Cagliari
CN	Cuneo
CS	Cosenza
FE	Ferrara
FO	Foggia
LT	Latina
MN	Mantova
MO	Modena
NA	Napoli
OR	Oristano
PA	Palermo
PD	Padova
RC	Reggio Calabria
RE	Reggio Emilia
RM	Roma
SA	Salerno
SV	Savona
TN	Trento
TO	Torino
TV	Treviso
VR	Verona
abr	abroad

3. Area of Birthplace

Istat   Macroareas of the Twenty Administrative Regions:

NW   North-West (Piedmont, Valle d'Aosta, Lombardy, Liguria)

NE   North-East (Trentino Alto Adige, Veneto, Friuli Venezia Giulia, Emilia
      Romagna)
C   Center (Tuscany, Umbria, Marche, Lazio)
S   South (Abruzzo, Molise, Campania, Puglia, Basilicata, Calabria)
I   Islands (Sicily, Sardinia)

4. Social Class

The categories used are those proposed by Paolo Sylos Labini, *Saggio sulle classi sociali* (Bari: Laterza, 1974). Like all class categorizations they have limitations, as we have noted in chapter 2, and they occasioned some controversy when Sylos Labini's book was published (for instance, in several of the contributions to *La sociologia della classi sociali*, ed. Gerardo Ragone and Cecilia Scrocca [Naples: Liguori, 1978]). However they are well known to historians and sociologists working in or on Italy and they have been widely adopted. Partly for this reason we consider them useful for a provisional classification of people to classes.

I   Bourgeoisie
      1. Owners, entrepreneurs, company directors
      2. Professionals

II   Middle class

IIa   White-collar petty bourgeoisie
      1. Private employees
      2. Public employees
      3. Teachers

IIb   Relatively autonomous petty bourgeoisie
      1. Farmers
      2. Peasant smallholders
      3. Artisans
      4. Tradespeople
      5. Transport and service employees

IIc   Special categories
      1. Armed forces
      2. Merchants/other tradespeople
      3. Others

III   Working class
      1. Agricultural wage laborers
      2. Industrial workers

3. Construction workers
4. Commercial workers
5. Waged transport and service workers
6. House cleaners/domestics

5. Interviewers

MF = Marcella Filippa; DF = David Forgacs; SG = Stephen Gundle; PP = Paola Pallavicini

Radio

1. Did you listen to the radio? How often? (a) once a week (b) more often (specify when, also in relation to life cycle).

2. At what time/s did you listen? (a) 7A.M.–9P.M. (b) 12 noon–2P.M. (c) 8P.M.–10P.M. (d) other times.

3. Who did you listen with? (a) alone (b) same-sex friend/s (c) other-sex friend/s (d) relatives (specify) (e) others.

4. Where did you listen? (a) home (b) relatives' or friends' home (c) public place (specify which).

5. When did your family buy their first radio? Where was it located in the home? Who chose the programs, the volume? Were there disagreements over which programs to listen to?

6. What were your favorite kinds of programs? (a) light music (b) classical music (c) sport (which) (d) news (e) variety/revues (f) Dopolavoro, Ente Radio Rurale, etc. (g) others (which).

7. Were there programs you didn't like? Why? When you were looking for a station were there programs you discarded immediately?

8. Which personalities did you like most (performers, presenters)?

9. Did you notice changes in radio programming over time?

Music, Dance

10. Did you often listen to music?

11. Did you play an instrument? (which, with whom, where, type of music).

12. Where and how (by what means) did you listen? (a) live (indicate type and places, e.g., dance band, orchestra, etc.) (b) radio at home (c) record player at home (d) radio in relatives' or friends' house (e) radio in public place (specify) (f) record player in public place.

13. Who did you listen with? (a) alone (b) same-sex friend/s (c) other-sex friend/s (d) relatives (specify) (e) others.

14. Who bought the records you listened to?

15. If you bought them, approximately how many did you buy a year and how? What format? (date changes 78, 33, 45 rpm).

16. What type of music did you like listening to? (a) Italian dance tunes (b) foreign dance tunes (c) jazz (d) opera or operetta (e) classical (f) traditional popular/folk (g) other.

17. Were there types of music you hardly ever or never listened to?

18. What did your parents/husband/wife think of your musical tastes? (a) shared them (b) approved (c) did not approve.

19. Which singers did you like most and why? Have you kept records, newspapers/magazines, or cuttings about these singers?

20. Did you like dancing? If so, what type of dance did you like? Where and when did you like to dance (e.g., at home, since what age, outside, with whom, how often).

Cinema

21. Did you often go to see films? (a) less than once a month (b) less than once a week (c) once a week (d) more than once a week (specify how often). At what time and on what days did you prefer to go?

22. Where did you see films most often? (a) commercial cinema (b) parish cinema (c) cine club (d) at home (e) outdoors (where) (f) other (specify whether first-, second-, or third-run cinemas).

23. Who did you go with usually? (a) alone (b) same-sex friend/s (c) other-sex friend/s (d) relatives (specify) (e) others (specify).

24. Where did you prefer to sit in the cinema? (a) near the screen (b) middle of stalls (c) back rows (d) circle (e) no fixed place.

25. Did you take anything into the cinemas with you, such as drinks, ice cream, sandwiches, a cushion, or a blanket?

26. What kinds of films did you like most? (a) drama (b) adventure (c) comedy (d) horror (e) Westerns (f) love stories (g) thrillers (h) other (specify, e.g., musicals, costume dramas, mythological films, political films, etc.).

27. Were there films you saw more than once? Which, how many times, why?

28. Were there types of film you didn't like and/or tended to avoid?

29. Did you see Italian films (which, specify period) or mainly foreign ones? If mainly foreign, whether American, British, German, or other,

30. What did you think of Italian films compared with foreign ones?

31. What determined your choice of film? (a) on at nearest cinema (b) newspaper (c) recommended by friends (d) actor's name (e) poster (f) other.

32. Do you remember a film or a scene that struck you particularly?

33. What was the first color film you saw?

34. Talk about a film that you liked particularly. Have you seen it rerun recently at the cinema or on TV?

35. Which actors/actresses did you like most? Have you kept photographs, newspaper/magazine cuttings, or other memorabilia about these actors/actresses?

36. What did your parents/husband/wife think of your film tastes? (a) shared them (b) approved (c) did not approve.

Theater, Variety, Live Entertainment, Amusements

37. Did you often go to the theater? (a) less than once a week (b) if more, how often.

38. Did you perform? If so, where did you perform (home, parish, professional, political party, amateur theatrical society)? What kind of performance did you give?

39. What type of theater did you go to? (a) spoken plays (b) opera (c) variety (d) puppets (e) other.

40. What type of performance did you prefer? (a) serious drama (b) opera (c) musical (d) mixed (e) magicians, illusionists, hypnotists (f) comedians (g) other.

41. Were there kinds of performance you didn't like or tended to avoid?

42. Who did you go with usually? (a) alone (b) same-sex friend/s (c) other-sex friend/s (d) relatives (specify)

43. If you went to spoken plays, did you prefer Italian or foreign plays?

44. What plays or performances do you remember?

45. Did you go to amusement parks, the circus, rides, or take part in local festivals (e.g., patron saint) or village festivals?

46. What did your parents/husband/wife think of your tastes in live performances? (a) shared them (b) approved (c) did not approve.

Print

47. What printed materials passed through your hands? (ask for title/s) (a) weekly magazines (b) photoromances (c) comics (d) parish bulletins or party/union newsletters (e) sports newspapers (f) party newspapers (g) non-party newspapers (h) books (specify) (i) school textbooks (l) others.

48. Which materials did you buy yourself, which were bought/loaned by others? By whom?

49. Where did you see these materials? (a) home (b) relatives' or friends' homes (c) public place (specify) (d) school (e) library (specify whether public, party, parish) (f) elsewhere.

50. How often did you see these materials? (a) less than once a week (b) if more often, specify.

51. What did you prefer to look at or read?

52. How did you look at it? (a) leafing through (b) looking mainly at the pictures (c) reading the words too.

Sport

53. Which sports did you follow?

54. Were you a spectator, fan, or did you take an active part? Where? (associations, dopolavoro, etc.)

55. How and with what means did you follow sport? (a) attendance at event (b) radio (c) newspapers/magazine (d) other.

56. Do you remember any particularly significant sporting events (football matches, championships, motor races, bicycle races, etc.).

57. Did you have favorite sports personalities? What did they represent for you and your generation?

58. Were they Italian or foreign? Why?

59. Did your parents/husband/wife share you sporting tastes?

Clothes, Personal Appearance, Consumer Products

60. When did you begin to be aware of fashion and start to follow it?

61. When did you start choosing your own clothes? (attention to hair, stockings, makeup, trousers, long/short trousers) Who made your clothes?

62. What models did you follow? (e.g., magazines, cinema)

63. Did your parents agree with your choices?

64. When did you first use: chewing gum, canned tomatoes, canned meat, powdered milk, condensed milk, instant coffee, prepackaged ice cream, cookbooks, refrigerator, gas stove, gramophone?

Advertising

65. What advertisements do you remember as particularly significant? (type, place, medium)

66. What is the first advertisement you remember?

67. Do you think you were influenced by advertising campaigns or particular products? How, why did you choose them?

Places and Forms of Sociability

68. Did you like walking? Did you go to cafés, inns (*osterie*)? Did you hang out in the square?

69. When did you take your first summer holidays and where? How did you travel?

70. When did you spend your first weekends out of town? Where and how did you travel?

71. Did your habits and tastes change (a) before and after the war (b) at the end of the war and start of television?

72. How and when did your tastes and preferences change?

73. What caused the changes?

74. With your parents/husband/wife did you speak mainly about (a) films (b) radio (c) sport (d) music (e) other?

75. Which of these did you never talk about?

76. Which activities did you like most of all?

77. When did the idea of free time become significant for you?

78. What were the most significant events/moments? (identify breaks: when, how)

79. In your opinion are songs, films, radio programs linked to political interests? Did you think this then, or do you think it now?

NOTES

Introduction

1. For these concepts see respectively Emilio Gentile, *The Sacralization of Politics in Fascist Italy,* trans. Keith Botsford (Cambridge, Mass.: Harvard University Press, 1996), 13 and passim; and Mario Isnenghi, *L'Italia in piazza. I luoghi della vita pubblica dal 1848 ai giorni nostri,* 2d ed. (Bologna: Il Mulino, 2004), 356.

2. *Lo spettacolo in Italia nel 1951* (Rome: SIAE, 1952), 96.

3. Joshua Meyrowitz, *No Sense of Place: The Impact of Electronic Media on Social Behavior* (New York: Oxford University Press, 1985).

4. See Anna Treves, *Le migrazioni interne nell'Italia fascista. Politica e realtà demografica* (Turin: Einaudi, 1976).

5. John B. Thompson, *The Media and Modernity: A Social Theory of the Media* (Cambridge, UK: Polity Press, 1995), 134.

6. Italo Insolera, *Roma moderna. Un secolo di storia urbanistica* (Turin: Einaudi, 1972), 73–83; Marcello Pazzaglini, *San Lorenzo 1881–1981. Storia urbana di un quartiere popolare a Roma* (Roma: Officina Edizioni, 1984), 33; Mario Sanfilippo, *San Lorenzo 1870–1945. Storia e "storie" di un quartiere popolare urbano* (Rome: Edilazio, 2003), 19–21.

7. Lidia Piccioni, *San Lorenzo. Un quartiere romano durante il fascismo* (Rome: Edizioni di Storia e Letteratura, 1984), 16.

8. This and all subsequent references to the oral history interviews provide the interview number and the page number(s) of the transcription, separated by a colon. Where two people were interviewed together their interview numbers are combined, e.g. 11/12, since they share a single transcription. For information and data on all the interviews and the location of the interview archive, see the appendices on pp. 281–305.

9. Piccioni, *San Lorenzo,* 139; Sanfilippo, *San Lorenzo 1870–1945,* 93.

10. Vasco Pratolini, *Il Quartiere* (Milan: Mondadori, 1979), 17, 20.

11. Anna Anfossi, Magda Talamo, and Francesco Indovina, *Ragusa. Comunità in transizione. Saggio sociologico* (Turin: Taylor, 1959), 164–65. On changes in intimacy marked by the use of pronouns of address see below, chapter 2.

12. Emilio Colombo, "Ciclismo," in *Enciclopedia italiana di scienze, lettere ed arti* X (Rome: Istituto Giovanni Treccani, 1931), 208.

13. Quoted in Giuseppe Vota, *I sessant'anni del Touring Club Italiano, 1894–1954* (Milan: Touring Club Italiano, 1954), 29.

14. Filippo Tommaso Marinetti, "The Foundation and Manifesto of Futurism," in *F. T. Marinetti: Critical Writings,* ed. Günter Berghaus, trans. Doug Thompson, new ed. (New York: Farrar, Straus and Giroux, 2006), 12–13 (originally published in *Poesia* 5, nos. 1–2 [February–March 1909]).

15. Stefano Pivato, *La bicicletta e il Sol dell'avvenire. Sport e tempo libero nel socialismo della Belle époque* (Florence: Ponte alle Grazie, 1992).

16. *Automobili in cifre 1956* (Turin: Associazione Nazionale fra Industrie Automobilistiche e Affini, 1956), 27.

17. Daniele Marchesini, *L'Italia del Giro d'Italia* (Bologna: Il Mulino, 1996), 197–99.

18. Quoted in ibid., 199.

19. Maurizio Gribaudi, *Mondo operaio e mito operaio. Spazi e percorsi sociali a Torino nel primo Novecento* (Turin: Einaudi, 1987), 124.

20. Anna Maria Ortese, "Giro d'Italia," in *La lente scura. Scritti di viaggio* (Milan: Marcos y Marcos, 1991), 213 (originally published as "Una scrittrice al Giro d'Italia," *L'Europeo*, May 29–June 12, 1955).

21. Franco Cordelli, *L'Italia di mattina* (Milan: Leonardo, 1990), 55.

22. For the role of the latter in nation-building during the nineteenth century see Silvana Patriarca, *Numbers and Nationhood: Writing Statistics in Nineteenth-Century Italy* (Cambridge: Cambridge University Press, 1996).

23. Tullio De Mauro, *Storia linguistica dell'Italia unita* (Bari: Laterza, 1963), 123–26.

24. Paola Filippucci, "Landscape, Locality and Nation: The case of Bassano," *Paragraph* 20, no. 1 (1997): 51–52.

25. W. W. Rostow, *The Stages of Economic Growth: A Non-Communist Manifesto* (Cambridge, UK: Cambridge University Press, 1960).

26. See Paul A. Baran and E. J. Hobsbawm, "The Stages of Economic Growth," *Kyklos: International Review for Social Sciences* 14, no. 2 (1961): 234–42; and André Gunder Frank, *Sociology of Development and Underdevelopment of Sociology* (London: Pluto, 1971), 18–27.

27. Gareth Stedman Jones, "Class Expression versus Social Control? A Critique of Recent Trends in the History of 'Leisure,'" in *Languages of Class: Studies in English Working-Class History 1832–1982* (Cambridge, UK: Cambridge University Press, 1983), 85 (originally in *History Workshop* 4 [autumn 1977]).

28. Jürgen Habermas, *The Structural Transformation of the Public Sphere*, trans. Thomas Burger and Frederick Lawrence (Cambridge, UK: Polity Press, 1989), 57–79.

29. Benedict Anderson, *Imagined Communities: Reflections on the Origin and Spread of Nationalism* (London: Verso, 1983).

30. Habermas, *The Structural Transformation of the Public Sphere*, 202–207; 217–21.

31. Thompson, *The Media and Modernity*, 75.

32. Ibid., 63.

33. Ibid., 63.

34. Silvio Lanaro, *Storia della Repubblica italiana. Dalla fine della guerra agli anni novanta* (Venice: Marsilio, 1992), 18.

1. Patterns of Consumption

1. Silvio Lanaro, *Storia della Repubblica italiana. Dalla fine della guerra agli anni novanta* (Venice: Marsilio, 1992), 221.

2. *Impiego del tempo libero in Calabria. Indagine statistica campionaria* (Rome: SIAE, 1960). The survey was carried out between November 10 and 20, 1958 when the SIAE was doing a preliminary study for a regional office in Calabria (inaugurated in Catanzaro in November 1959). The total regional population according to the 1951 census was 2,148,160. The survey was based on interviews with 5,157 people aged 15 and upward (i.e., 0.24% of the regional total, or roughly 1 in every 400 people) from 117 *comuni* (out of a total of 417 in the region): 40 in the Province of Catanzaro, 42 in the Province of Cosenza, and 35 in the Province of Reggio Calabria. The interviews were conducted in all *comuni* with a population over 13,000 (there were 23 of these) and in 94 of the 394 *comuni* with a population below 13,000. Of the interviews, 5,023 replies

were used, from people distributed thus: males 2,583, females 2,440; ages 16–25 1,039; ages 26–45 2,079; ages over 46 1,905; unmarried 1,373; married, widowed, and separated 3,650; without formal education 1,614; elementary education 2,682; postelementary education 684; level of education unknown 43.

3. Ibid., ix.

4. Ibid., ix and xi.

5. Nuto Revelli, *Il mondo dei vinti. Testimonianze di vita contadina. La pianura. La collina. La montagna. Le Langhe* (Turin: Einaudi, 1977).

6. Valerio Castronovo, *Il Piemonte* (Turin: Einaudi, 1977) (part of the series *Storia delle Regioni italiane dall'Unità a oggi*), 619–29.

7. Revelli, *Il mondo dei vinti*, 87.

8. Ibid., 93.

9. Ibid., xcv.

10. Ibid., lxxviii.

11. For a contemporary account of the conditions of these migrant workers see Castronovo, *Il Piemonte*, 388, n. 22.

12. Pierpaolo Luzzatto Fegiz, *Il volto sconosciuto dell'Italia. Dieci anni di sondaggi Doxa* (Milan: Giuffrè, 1956), 866–67.

13. Antonio Gramsci, *Quaderni del carcere*, ed. Valentino Gerratana, 4 vols. (Turin: Einaudi, 1975), 1890.

14. Domenico Lombrassa, "La difesa del ragazzo italiano," *Il Libro Italiano* 2, no. 11 (1938): 460.

15. Leonardo Becciu, *Il fumetto in Italia* (Florence: Sansoni, 1971), 138.

16. Simonetta Piccone Stella and Annabella Rossi, *La fatica di leggere* (Rome: Editori Riuniti, 1964), 166, 104.

17. On these precursors see the interesting study by Raffaele De Berti, *Dallo schermo alla carta. Romanzi, fotoromanzi, rotocalchi cinematografici: il film e i suoi paratesti* (Milan: Vita e Pensiero, 2000).

18. Alberto Abruzzese, "Fotoromanzo," in *Letteratura italiana. Storia e geografia*, vol. 3 of *L'età contemporanea*, ed. Alberto Asor Rosa (Turin: Einaudi, 1989), 1269.

19. *I lettori di otto periodici italiani: Epoca, Grazia, Arianna, Confidenza, Bolero Film, Storia Illustrata, Il Giallo Mondadori, Topolino. Studio Statistico sulle caratteristiche demografiche, economiche, sociali e culturali* (Rome: Istituto Doxa, 1963), 20, 25, 59, 21.

20. The remark is reproduced in Gian Piero Brunetta, *Buio in sala. Cent'anni di passioni dello spettatore cinematografico* (Venice: Marsilio, 1989), 248.

21. Gian Franco Venè, *Mille lire al mese. La vita quotidiana della famiglia nell'Italia fascista* (Milan: Mondadori, 1988), 283.

22. Piero Santi, *Ombre rosse* (Florence: Vallecchi, 1954), 95, 96, 97, 100–101.

23. Ibid., 102.

24. Alessandro Portelli, *Biografia di una città. Storia e racconto: Terni 1830–1985* (Turin: Einaudi, 1985), 171. *Purosangue* was the Italian title of *Sporting Blood*, of which there were two sound versions: one in 1931 with Clark Gable and Madge Evans and one in 1940 with Robert Young and Maureen O'Sullivan.

25. Goffredo Fofi, "Cinema 'basso' e cinema 'alto'" (1978), in *I limiti della scena. Spettacolo e pubblico nell'Italia contemporanea (1945–1991)* (Milan: Linea d'Ombra Edizioni, 1992), 70.

26. Ibid., 70.

27. The same notion reemerges in Fofi's essay of 1980, "Storia del teatro minore," also reproduced in *I limiti della scena*.

28. Francesco Savio, *Cinecittà anni trenta*, 3 vols. (Rome: Bulzoni, 1979), 1: 84.

29. Italo Calvino, "Autobiografia di uno spettatore," preface to Federico Fellini, *Quattro film* (Turin: Einaudi, 1974), xiv.

30. Savio, *Cinecittà anni trenta*, 3: 1138.

31. Vittorio Spinazzola, *Cinema e pubblico. Lo spettacolo filmico in Italia 1945–1965*, 2d ed. (Rome: Bulzoni, 1985), 115.

32. Ibid., 116.

33. Venè, *Mille lire al mese*, 282.

34. Ibid., 283.

35. "Rosamunda," recorded by Dea Garbaccio in 1942, was the Italian version of the song known in German as "Rosamunde" and in English as "Roll Out the Barrel" or "The Beer Barrel Polka." The tune was originally written in 1927 by Czech songwriter Jaromír Vejvoda.

36. Alberto Monticone, *Il fascismo al microfono* (Rome: Studium, 1978), 67.

37. Gianni Isola, *Abbassa la tua radio, per favore . . . Storia dell'ascolto radiofonico nell'Italia fascista* (Florence: La Nuova Italia, 1990).

38. Ibid., 85.

39. Antonio Papa, *Storia politica della radio in Italia*, vol. 2: *Dalla guerra d'Etiopia al crollo del fascismo 1935–1943* (Naples: Guida, 1978), 80.

40. Ibid., 80–81.

41. The figures are reproduced in a table in ibid., 82.

42. Anna Lucia Natale, "Cultura di massa e fascismo. Il referendum radiofonico 1940," in *Problemi dell'informazione* 6 (1981), no. 2: 243–67; subsequently adapted in her book *Gli anni della radio (1924–1954). Contributo ad una storia sociale dei media in Italia* (Naples: Liguori, 1990), 75–100. The stratification model is in Paolo Sylos Labini, *Saggio sulle classi sociali* (Bari: Laterza, 1974).

43. See the table reproduced in Isola, *Abbassa la tua radio, per favore,* 95.

44. Quoted in Natale, *Gli anni della radio,* 76.

45. Papa, *Storia della politica della radio,* 79; Natale, *Gli anni della radio,* 75; Isola, *Abbassa la tua radio,* 97.

46. Isola, *Abbassa la tua radio,* 97.

47. The negative votes are tabulated in Natale, *Gli anni della radio,* 94–95.

48. Ibid., 95.

49. Isola, *Abbassa la tua radio,* 223.

50. Simona Colarizi, *L'opinione degli italiani sotto il regime, 1929–1943* (Rome and Bari: Laterza, 1991), 233.

2. Practices of the Self

1. Mary Douglas and Baron Isherwood, *The World of Goods: Towards an Anthropology of Consumption* (London: Allen Lane, 1979), 59.

2. For this concept see the section "Morale et pratique de soi" in Michel Foucault, *L'usage des plaisirs,* vol. 2 of *Histoire de la sexualité,* (Paris: Gallimard, 1984) 36–45; also *Le Souci de soi,* vol. 3 of *Histoire de la sexualité* (Paris: Gallimard, 1984); and the series of lectures from 1982 collected as *L'Herméneutique du sujet* (Paris: Gallimard, 2001).

3. Maria Occhipinti, *Una donna di Ragusa* (Palermo: Sellerio, 1993), 29 (originally published Florence: Landi, 1957; republished Milan: Feltrinelli, 1976).

4. The testimony is in the documentary *Scene per una storia dei consumi* (1989, 25 minutes), directed by Luisa Cigognetti, produced by Archivio Storico della Coop Emilia-Veneto and the Istituto Regionale per la Storia della Resistenza in Emilia-

Romagna in collaboration with Laboratorio Nazionale per la Didattica della Storia, distributed on VHS.

5. Chiara Saraceno, "La famiglia: i paradossi della costruzione del privato," in *La vita privata. Il Novecento,* ed. Philippe Ariès and Georges Duby (Rome and Bari: Laterza, 1988), 58.

6. Cecilia Dau Novelli, *Famiglia e modernizzazione in Italia tra le due guerre* (Rome: Studium, 1994), 254.

7. Victoria de Grazia, *How Fascism Ruled Women* (Berkeley and Los Angeles: University of California Press, 1992).

8. Victoria de Grazia, "Nationalizing Women: The Competition between Fascist and Commercial Cultural Models in Mussolini's Italy," in *The Sex of Things: Gender and Consumption in Historical Perspective,* ed. Victoria de Grazia (Berkeley and Los Angeles: University of California Press, 1996).

9. Bruno P. F. Wanrooij, *Storia del pudore. La questione sessuale in Italia, 1860–1940* (Venice: Marsilio, 1990), 215; de Grazia, *How Fascism Ruled Women,* 119–20.

10. Marzio Barbagli, *Sotto lo stesso tetto. Mutamenti della famiglia in Italia dal XV al XX secolo* (Bologna: Il Mulino, 1984).

11. The national statistics agency Istat groups the twenty regions of Italy in various ways, according to the different levels of detail employed in its analyses. In the text we use Istat's three-part classification, which groups the regions into the macro-regions North, Center, South. In Appendix 1 we use their five-part classification: North-West, North-East, Center, South, and Islands (Sardinia and Sicily).

12. Barbagli, *Sotto lo stesso tetto,* 491.

13. Ibid., 487, 490.

14. Saraceno, "La famiglia," 36.

15. Pier Paolo Pasolini, *Una vita violenta,* in *Romanzi e racconti,* ed. Walter Siti and Silvia De Laude (Milan: Mondadori, 1998), 917–23.

16. Saraceno, "La famiglia," 54.

17. Giovanni Agnese, *Con quale mezzo vedo possibile il risanamento dei costumi e il progresso morale di una moderna nazione. Proposta di un codice dei costumi* (Turin: Botta, 1929), 6–7, quoted in Wanrooij, *Storia del pudore,* 124 (we are indebted to Wanrooij's work for directing us to this pamphlet).

18. Agnese, *Con quale mezzo,* 13–16.

19. Quoted in Dau Novelli, *Famiglia e modernizzazione,* 94.

20. Quoted in Giovanni De Luna, *Donne in oggetto. L'antifascismo nella società italiana, 1922–1939* (Turin: Bollati Boringhieri, 1995), 200.

21. "Encyclical Letter (Vigilanti Cura) Of His Holiness Pius XI, By Divine Providence Pope, To Our Venerable Brethren the Archbishops and Bishops of the United States of America and to the Other Ordinaries Enjoying Peace and Communion with the Apostolic See, On the Motion Pictures," 1936, in *Twelve Encyclicals of Pope Pius XI* (London: Catholic Truth Society, n.d.), 13.

22. Brunetta, *Buio in sala,* 230.

23. *Amado mio,* in Pasolini, *Romanzi e racconti,* vol. 1, 262–63. This short novel was written 1947–1950 but not published until 1982, after Pasolini's death. A short story by Pasolini on the same theme as this episode, "La nebulosa del cinema di Caorle," was published in *Il Mattino del Popolo* on December 11, 1947.

24. Irene Brin, "La moda nel cinema," 1943, in *La moda e il costume nel film,* ed. Mario Verdone (Rome: Bianco e Nero, 1950), 57.

25. Jackie Stacey, *Star Gazing: Hollywood Cinema and Female Spectatorship* (London: Routledge, 1993).

26. *La Domenica del Corriere,* November 18, 1945, 3; December 16, 1945, 6.

27. Giovanna Grignaffini, "Female Identity and Italian Cinema of the 1950s," in *Offscreen: Women and Film in Italy,* ed. Giuliana Bruno and Maria Nadotti (London: Routledge, 1988), 123.

28. The term originated as a wordplay of dubious taste in the 1952 film comedy *Altri tempi,* directed by Alessandro Blasetti. It was coined in a courtroom scene to contrast with *minorati psichici* ("mentally disadvantaged").

29. Rosella Isidori Frasca, "L'educazione fisica e sportiva e la 'preparazione materna,'" in *La corporazione delle donne. Ricerche e studi sui modelli femminili nel ventennio,* ed. Marina Addis Saba (Florence: Vallecchi, 1988).

30. Quoted in ibid., 287.

31. Quoted in ibid., 292, 287–88.

32. Quoted in Miriam Mafai, *Pane nero. Donne e vita quotidiana nella Seconda guerra mondiale* (Milan: Mondadori, 1987), 111–12.

33. "Puritane in pantaloni," unsigned, *Tempo* 3, series 2, no. 7 (1939): 24.

34. Ibid., 25.

35. Quoted in Mafai, *Pane nero,* 110.

36. Quoted in Gian Piero Brunetta, "La censura ecclesiastica," in *Cinema italiano tra le due guerre. Fascismo e politica cinematografica* (Milan: Mursia 1975), 64.

37. Quoted in Mafai, *Pane nero,* 110, 111.

38. Ibid., 111.

39. Ibid., 111.

40. Giorgio Triani, *Pelle di luna, pelle di sole. Nascita e storia della civiltà balneare 1700–1946* (Venice: Marsilio, 1988), 170.

41. Agnese, *Con quale mezzo vedo possibile il risanamento dei costumi,* 26.

42. ACS PCM Gabinetto 1951–1954 b. 3–2–6, f. 32227, sf. 1. All quotations in this paragraph are from this file (fasicolo).

43. Wanrooj, *Storia del pudore,* 125–26.

44. De Grazia, *How Fascism Ruled Women,* 121–2; de Grazia, *Le donne del regime fascista* (Venice: Marsilio, 1993), 171.

45. Testimony in *Scene per una storia dei consumi* (see above, n. 4 to this chapter).

46. See Reka Buckley, "The Female Film Star in Postwar Italy, 1948–1960," University of London, Ph.D. thesis, 2002; and, also by Buckley, "National Body: Gina Lollobrigida and the Cult of the Star in the 1950s," *Historical Journal of Film, Radio and Television* 20, no. 4 (2000): 527–47.

3. Publishing

1. See David Forgacs, "Americanization: The Italian Case, 1938–1954," in *Americanization and the Transformation of World Cultures,* ed. P. H. Melling and D. J. Roper (Edward Mellen: London, 1996), 81–96.

2. Anna Lisa Carlotti, "Editori e giornali a Milano: continuità e cambiamento," in *Libri giornali e riviste a Milano. Storia delle innovazioni nell'editoria milanese dall'ottocento ad oggi,* ed. Fausto Colombo (Milan: AIM–Abitare Segesta, 1998), 184.

3. Franco Ciarlantini, *Vicende di libri e di autori* (Milan: Ceschina, 1931), 41.

4. Ibid., 54–55.

5. Giovanni Ragone, "Editoria, letteratura e comunicazione," in *Letteratura italiana, Storia e geografia,* vol. 3, ed. Alberto Asor Rosa (Turin: Einaudi, 1989), 1076.

6. According to former Mondadori employee, Orlando Bernardi, interviewed by David Forgacs and Gianluigi Mariani in Milan on May 15, 1991, it was not Rusca but another employee of Rizzoli, Paolo Lecaldano, who devised the BUR. An unpublished transcript of the interview is kept at the Fondazione Arnoldo e Alberto Mondadori.

7. Maria Iolanda Palazzolo, "L'editoria verso un pubblico di massa," in *Una società di massa*, vol. 2 of *Fare gli italiani. Scuola e cultura nell'Italia contemporanea*, ed. Simonetta Soldani and Gabriele Turi (Bologna: Il Mulino, 1993), 299–301.

8. Enrico Decleva, *Arnoldo Mondadori* (Turin: UTET, 1993), 383–85; Mimma Mondadori, *Una tipografia in paradiso* (Milan: Mondadori, 1985), 115–16.

9. Rizzoli had been, in 1924, one of the first Italian publishers to import, from Germany, a rotogravure press. De Agostini in Novara, a publisher specializing in colored maps and atlases, installed one in 1927.

10. Cesare Zavattini, *Uno, cento, mille lettere*, ed. Silvana Cirillo (Milan: Bompiani, 1988), 39; also in Valentino Bompiani and Cesare Zavattini, *Cinquant'anni e più. . . . Lettere 1933–1989*, ed. Valentina Fortichiari (Milan: Bompiani, 1995), 13.

11. *Ottobre*, March 14, 1934, n.p. The periodical's title alludes to the start of the "Fascist revolution," the March on Rome of October 28, 1922.

12. On the early *rotocalco* see Ermanno Paccagnini, "Il giornalismo dal 1860 al 1960," in Giuseppe Farinelli et al., *Storia del giornalismo italiano. Dalle origini ai giorni nostri* (Turin: UTET, 1997), 293–95. The Interior Ministry ordered the suppression of *Omnibus* ostensibly because of accusations against the Prefect of Naples in a satirical piece by Alberto Savinio but probably because the magazine had become an irritant to the regime with its openness to foreign influence and Longanesi's rebarbative behavior as editor. Alberto Asor Rosa has attributed Longanesi's politically chameleonic character to an underlying conservatism: "The conformism of the regime releases the corrosive acids of this intelligence, which is critical under Fascism but then philo-fascist or nostalgic under antifascism." Alberto Asor Rosa, "Il giornalista: appunti sulla fisiologia di un mestiere difficile," in *Storia d'Italia. Annali, 4, Intellettuali e potere*, ed. Corrado Vivanti (Turin: Einaudi, 1981), 1246.

13. Decleva, *Arnoldo Mondadori*, 240–43.

14. Enrico Piceni, interview with Gianluigi Mariani and Mauro Zerbini, Milan, June 28, 1985. Unpublished transcript at the Fondazione Arnoldo e Alberto Mondadori.

15. The main letters are reproduced in *Caro Bompiani. Lettere con l'editore*, ed. Gabriella D'Ina and Giuseppe Zaccaria (Milan: Bompiani, 1988), 39–46.

16. Letter (in English) of October 5, 1945, in D'Ina and Zaccaria, *Caro Bompiani*, 51.

17. Giovanni Papini, letter of July 12, 1937 in Giovanni Papini-Attilio Vallecchi, *Carteggio (1914–1941)*, ed. Mario Gozzini (Florence: Vallecchi, 1984), 267.

18. Arnoldo Mondadori, "Il libro italiano all'estero," *Il Libro Italiano* 2, no. 5 (1938): 240, 245.

19. Ibid., 241.

20. Giulio Einaudi to Pavese and Balbo, May 16, 1945, in Archivio Einaudi, incartamento Pavese; quoted in Luisa Mangoni, *Pensare i libri. La casa editrice Einaudi dagli anni trenta agli anni sessanta* (Turin: Bollati Boringhieri, 1999), 209.

21. Ibid., 209, 211.

22. Ibid., 222.

23. Crocenzi's "photographic short stories" (*racconti fotografici*) included "Italia senza tempo," in *Il Politecnico*, no. 28 (April 6, 1946): 2; "Occhio su Milano," in *Il Politecnico*, no. 29 (May 1, 1946): 13–15; and "Andiamo in processione," in *Il Politecnico*, no. 35 (January–March 1947): 54–59. On *Il Politecnico* generally see Raffaele Crovi, *Vittorini. Una biografia critica* (Venice: Marsilio, 1998); Anna Panicali, *Elio Vittorini. La narrativa, la saggistica, le traduzioni, le riviste, l'attività editoriale* (Milan: Mursia, 1994), 204–208; and Marina Zancan, *Il progetto 'Politecnico.' Cronaca e struttura di una rivista* (Venice: Marsilio, 1984), 233–70.

24. The correspondence between Giulio Einaudi with the PCI about the Gramsci

editions is largely in AE, incartamento Platone (Felice Platone was responsible within the PCI leadership for the first editions of Gramsci's prison writings).

25. Palazzolo, "L'editoria," 302.

26. Carlo Feltrinelli, *Senior Service* (Milan: Feltrinelli, 1999), 80–83.

27. The main letters are reproduced in Alberto Mondadori, *Lettere di una vita, 1922–1975,* ed. Gian Carlo Ferretti, (Milan: Mondadori, 1996), 88–116.

28. Mondadori, *Una tipografia in paradiso,* 117–18.

29. *Epoca* 1, no. 1 (October 14, 1950): 13.

30. See Pierpaolo Luzzatto Fegiz, "Political Opinion Polling in Italy," in *Political Opinion Polling: An International Review,* ed. Robert M. Worcester (Basingstoke and London: Macmillan, 1983), 133–51; and Sandro Rinauro, "Il sondaggio d'opinione arriva in Italia (1936–1946)," *Passato e presente* 52, no. 19 (2001): 41–66.

31. Silvana Cirillo, "Cronologia," in Cesare Zavattini, *Opere. 1931–1986,* ed. Silvana Cirillo (Milan: Bompiani, 1991), xxxii.

32. Carlotti, "Editori e giornali a Milano," 184.

33. Paolo Murialdi, *Storia del giornalismo italiano* (Bologna: Il Mulino, 1996), 213.

34. Giambattista Vicari, *Editoria e pubblica opinione* (Rome: Cinque Lune, 1957), 37.

35. Ragone, "Editoria, letteratura e comunicazione," 1117.

36. The trial was mentioned to David Forgacs in an interview in Florence on June 10, 1991 with Enrico Vallecchi's widow, Maria Luigia Guaita, herself a former partisan, although we have found no mention of it in the published sources on Vallecchi.

37. Geno Pampaloni, interview with David Forgacs, Florence, June 13, 1991.

38. Franco Fossati, "Disney Made in Italy," *IF,* 1–2 (1982): 45–46; and Franco Fossati, *Topolino: Storia del topo più famoso del mondo* (Milan: Gammalibri, 1986), 77–85; and Leonardo Gori, "I Disney di casa nostra," *LG Argomenti* 23, nos. 1–2 (1987): 53–54.

39. The contracts between Creazioni Walt Disney and Mondadori, together with other legal documents including the convention with King Features Syndicate, are conserved in two boxes in Mondadori's commercial offices at the firm's headquarters in Segrate, Milan, and are cited hereinafter as "D-M Contracts."

40. D-M Contracts: "S.A.I. Creazioni Walt Disney, Licenza n. 177/G, 17.5.39, art. 7." Italy was the first nation to create long stories about Donald Duck (known there at first as Paolino Paperino, then simply as Paperino). Before Carl Barks created his Donald Duck strips in America two long stories, written and drawn by Federico Pedrocchi, had appeared in Mondadori's *Paperino:* see Gori, "I Disney di casa nostra," 55–56; Fossati, "Disney Made in Italy," 68; and Mario Gentilini, *Io Paperino* (Milan: Mondadori, 1971).

41. Archivio della Fondazione Arnoldo e Alberto Mondadori (hereinafter AFM), Fondo Arnoldo Mondadori (F. Arn.), scatola [box] (sc.) 38: "Disney, Walt," Mondadori to the Ministry of Popular Culture, March 18, 1941.

42. AFM, F. Arn., sc. 38, Mondadori to Pavolini, December 11, 1941.

43. Fossati, "Disney Made in Italy," 88; Gori, "I Disney di casa nostra," 57.

44. AFM, F. Arn., sc. 30: "Consigli di gestione e commissione straordinaria," Promemoria del Commissario Straordinario Corrado Marchi, 24.9.44.

45. Domenico Porzio, "Arnoldo Mondadori," *Panorama* (June 24, 1971): 5; quoted in Claudia Patuzzi, *Mondadori* (Naples: Liguori, 1978), 65.

46. Replies from E. J. Davis and Roy O. Disney, dated respectively March 3, 1945 and May 8, 1945, are in AFM, F. Arn., sc. 38.

47. Claudia Patuzzi, *Mondadori,* 65.

48. AFM, F. Arn., sc. 30: "Verbale seduta consiglio di gestione del 20 giugno 1945," 4.

49. AFM, F. Arn., sc. 38, Arnoldo Mondadori to Roy Disney, May 23, 1946; Arnoldo Mondadori to E. J. Davis, June 8, 1946.

50. AFM, F. Arn., sc. 38, Arnoldo Mondadori to Walter Feignoux, September 10, 1946.

51. D-M Contracts: *Topolino* contract, June 30, 1946.

52. D-M Contracts: appendix to *Topolino* contract, October 31, 1949.

53. D-M Contracts: Memorandum of agreement November 6, 1947 between Kay Kamen International Corporation, New York, and Helicon S.A., Lugano, Switzerland; art. 1.

54. Documentation of this episode includes AFM, F. Arn., sc. 38, Arnoldo Mondadori to Walter Feignoux, September 10, 1946; G. Cortese to Arnoldo Mondadori, September 21, 1946; G. Cortese to Mondadori, January 24, 1947.

55. AFM, F. Arn., sc. 38, Arnoldo Mondadori to Armand Bigle, September 23, 1949.

56. AFM, F. Arn., sc. 38, Oliver B. Johnston to Arnoldo Mondadori, August 14, 1962.

57. AFM, F. Arn., sc. 38, Jack Holmes to Arnoldo Mondadori, December 5, 1950.

58. Richard Schickel, *The Disney Version: The Life, Times, Art and Commerce of Walt Disney,* 2d ed. (London: Pavilion, 1986), 157–261.

59. AFM, F. Arn., "Life," Arnoldo Mondadori to Henry R. Luce, April 12, 1955.

60. Decleva, *Arnoldo Mondadori,* 397–99.

61. Quoted in ibid., 399.

62. "'Doves of Peace" compete,'" *The Reader's Digest International Editions Newsletter,* June 9, 1953, 4.

63. Cesare Pavese, *Saggi letterari (Opere di Cesare Pavese),* vol. 12 (Turin: Einaudi, 1968), 257.

64. Chiara Campo, "L'America in salotto: il *Reader's Digest* in Italia," in *Nemici per la pelle. Sogno americano e mito sovietico nell'Italia contemporanea,* ed. Pier Paolo D'Attorre (Milan: Franco Angeli, 1991), 420.

65. *Ritratto della famiglia dei lettori di Selezione* (Milan: Selezione dal Reader's Digest, Ufficio Pubblicità, 1962), 20, 26, 70, 82.

66. Campo, "L'America in salotto," 418–19.

4. Film Production

1. Franca Faldini and Goffredo Fofi, eds., *L'avventurosa storia del cinema italiano raccontato dai suoi protagonisti, 1935–59* (Milan: Mondadori, 1979), 158–96.

2. Mino Argentieri, "La Titanus e il mercato," in *Dietro lo schermo: ragionamenti sui modi di produzione cinematografici in Italia,* ed. Vito Zagarrio (Venice: Marsilio, 1988), 15–34.

3. Alberto Farassino, "Il costo dei panni sporchi: note sul 'modo di produzione' neorealista," in *Dietro lo schermo: ragionamenti sui modi di produzione cinematografici in Italia,* ed. Vito Zagarrio (Venice: Marsilio, 1988), 139.

4. See Libero Bizzarri and Libero Solaroli, *L'industria cinematografica italiana* (Florence: Parenti, 1958); Lorenzo Quaglietti, *Storia economico-politica del cinema italiano 1945–1980* (Rome: Riuniti, 1980); and, from a liberal standpoint, Ernesto Rossi, *Lo Stato cinematografaro* (Florence: Parenti, 1959).

5. Barbara Corsi, *Con qualche dollaro in più. Storia economica del cinema italiano* (Rome: Riuniti, 2001), 10.

6. Ibid., 39–41.

7. Ibid., 53.

8. Gian Piero Brunetta, *Cent'anni di cinema italiano* (Rome and Bari: Laterza, 1991), 16.

9. Ibid., 169–70.

10. Ibid., 165–66.

11. Ibid., 177.

12. Corsi, *Con qualche dollaro in più*, 25; Quaglietti, *Storia economico-politica*, 23.

13. Brunetta, *Cent'anni*, 274.

14. Farassino, "Il costo dei panni sporchi," 138–40.

15. Ibid., 137–38.

16. Corsi, *Con qualche dollaro in più*, 49–50.

17. Untitled news item, *Intermezzo*, May 31, 1948, 2.

18. Corsi, *Con qualche dollaro in più*, 51.

19. Quaglietti, *Storia economico-politica*, 52–73.

20. Otello Angeli, "Strutture produttive, contratti, organizzazione," in *La città del cinema: produzione e lavoro nel cinema italiano 1930–1970*, ed. Massimiliano Fasoli et al.(Rome: Napoleone, 1979), 50; Mario Monicelli, untitled testimony in ibid., 217; Farassino, "Il costo dei panni sporchi," 141.

21. Argentieri, "La Titanus e il mercato," 19–20.

22. Angeli, "Strutture produttive," 50.

23. Charles Higham, *Merchant of Dreams: Louis B. Mayer and the Secret Hollywood* (London: Pan, 1994; first published 1993), 76–103.

24. NA, RG 151, 281 Italy Transfer file 1049-, 1929–31. Memorandum North to Canty, January 17, 1929.

25. See WSHS, Papers of Walter Wanger, b. 48, f. 20 Società Anonima Italiana Cinematografica (SAIC).

26. WSHS, Papers of Walter Wanger, b. 48, f. 20 SAIC Correspondence. Luporini to A. H. Giannini of the Bank of America, June 25, 1936.

27. WSHS, Papers of Walter Wanger, b. 48, f. 20 SAIC Correspondence. Luporini to Wanger, June 13, 1938.

28. WSHS, Papers of Walter Wanger, SAIC. b. 48, f. 21. Note dictated by Wanger, May 21, 1964 to Miss Fitch, Samuel Goldwyn Studios. Wanger retrospectively explained that he had decided to support Mussolini after receiving assurances on the race issue: "I even got into the question of racism and he [Mussolini] assured me, as was confirmed in the telegram that I have framed in my office from the Minister of Foreign affairs, that he was not going to agree to Hitler's projects. . . . That's the reason that I was trying to help him, which I was not able to do."

29. Luigi Freddi, vol. 1 of *Il cinema* (Rome: L'Arnia, 1949), 299.

30. The document is reproduced in ibid., 311–21.

31. Ibid., 319.

32. Ibid., 318–19.

33. A report from the Italian Embassy in Washington was quite candid about the protests but sought to minimize their significance: "There was an occasional discordant note, but it did not amount to much." MAE b. 43, f. 2 Cinematografia (1936–37), sf. 26, Vittorio Mussolini in America. Ambasciata d'Italia, Washington DC a MAE "Viaggio di Vittorio Musolini," October 15, 1937.

34. Quaglietti, *Storia economico-politica*, 37–38.

35. Gian Piero Brunetta, "La lunga marcia del cinema americano in Italia tra fascismo e guerra fredda," in *Hollywood in Europa: industria, politica, pubblico del cinema 1945–1960*, ed. David W. Ellwood and Gian Piero Brunetta (Florence: Ponte alle Grazie, 1991), 80.

36. NA, RG 331, Allied Control Commission—Italy, HQ Pub. Rels., Film Board Aug 44–July 45. Notes for Chief Commissioner of Film Board, March 21, 11.00 hours.

37. NA, RG 331, Allied Control Commission—Italy, HQ Pub. Rels., Film Board

Aug 44–July 45. Temporary Film Board, sub-committee for the revision of Fascist legislation, March 27, 1945.

38. Ennio Di Nolfo, "La diplomazia del cinema americano in Europa nel secondo dopoguerra," in *Hollywood in Europa: industria, politica, pubblico del cinema 1945–1960,* ed. David W. Ellwood and Gian Piero Brunetta (Florence: Ponte alle Grazie, 1991), 35.

39. Paul Swann, "Il 'Piccolo Dipartimento di Stato': Hollywood e il Dipartimento di Stato nell'Europa del dopoguerra," in *Hollywood in Europa: industria, politica, pubblico del cinema 1945–1960,* ed. David W. Ellwood and Gian Piero Brunetta (Florence: Ponte alle Grazie, 1991).

40. NA, RG 59, 865.452/7–1350. State Department, Italy 1950–54. Report from Rome Embassy on Motion Pictures—Theatre Equipment, July 13, 1950. The vast bulk of the refugees who had been temporarily lodged there had been removed from Cinecittà by July 1947, although a few were apparently still there in April 1950. ACS, Presidenza del Consiglio dei Ministri. 10474, f. 1.1.2, s.f. 12, Roma: centro raccolta profughi di Cinecittà (1948–50).

41. Higham, *Merchant of Dreams,* 398–99.

42. NA, RG 59, 865.452/7–1350. State Department, Italy 1950–54. Report from Rome Embassy on Motion Pictures—Theatre Equipment, July 13, 1950.

43. HRHRC, Selznick Coll., Selznick admin. corres. 1940–50: De Sica, b. 543, f. 7. Memo from Reissar to O'Shea, October 13, 1947.

44. HRHRC, Selznick Coll., Selznick admin. corres. 1940–50: De Sica, b. 543, f. 7. Cable from Selznick to Reissar, October 25, 1947.

45. HRHRC, Selznick Coll., Selznick admin. corres. 1940–50: De Sica, b. 543, f. 7. Selznick cable, November 14, 1947.

46. HRHRC, Selznick Coll., Selznick admin. corres. 1940–50: De Sica, b. 543, f. 8. Cable from Selznick to Reissar, January 5, 1948.

47. HRHRC Selznick Coll., Selznick London: production files 1946–57: *Stazione Termini.* B. 670, f. 6, Selznick memo, May 28, 1952.

48. Ibid.

49. Selznick's biographer, David Thomson, argues "Coproduction requires self-deception on all sides." The film rested on the assumption that the contradiction could be reconciled between the Italians who wanted "American money, big stars and a chance of getting to Hollywood" and Selznick, who wanted "art, prestige, continental sophistication." See *Showman: the Life of David O. Selznick* (New York: Knopf, 1992), 582.

50. See Ottavio Oppo, untitled testimony in Fasoli, *La città del cinema,* 219–22; Clemente Fracassi, untitled testimony in ibid., 168.

51. Bizzarri and Solaroli, *L'industria cinematografica;* Corsi, *Con qualche dollaro in più,* 67–68.

52. Corsi, *Con qualche dollaro in più,* 68.

53. Documentation concerning the making of *Ulysses,* including daily reports from the set, written by production assistant Anne Budyens (Douglas's future wife), is contained in WSHS, Papers of Kirk Douglas, b.13, f. 26 *Ulysses:* Correspondence, June 1953–September 1956.

54. Tullio Kezich and Alessandra Levatesi, *Dino. De Laurentiis, la vita e i film* (Milan, Feltrinelli, 2001), 88–89, 97.

55. Ibid., 99.

56. Corsi, *Con qualche dollaro in più,* 92–98, 99.

57. Thomas H. Guback, *The International Film Industry: Western Europe and America since 1945* (Bloomington: Indiana University Press, 1969), 191.

58. Christopher Wagstaff, "Il cinema italiano nel mercato internazionale," in *Identità italiana e identità europea nel cinema italiano dal 1945 al miracolo economico,* ed. Gian Piero Brunetta (Turin: Edizioni Fondazione Agnelli, 1996), 152

59. Ibid., 159.

60. NA, RG 59, 865.452/12–1250 Italy 1950–54. Report on the hostile Italian reaction to the censorship of *Ladri di biciclette* dated February 5, 1950.

61. AAMPAS, MPAA PCA Files, *Bicycle Thief.*

62. AAMPAS, MPAA PCA Files, *Bitter Rice,* Joseph Breen memo to Gordon White.

63. AAMPAS, MPAA PCA Files, *Bitter Rice,* Gordon White office report.

64. AAMPAS, MPAA PCA Files, *Bitter Rice,* press cutting.

65. AAMPAS, MPAA PCA Files, *Boy on a Dolphin,* press cutting. See also file on *Woman of the River.*

5. The Film Market

1. Lorenzo Quaglietti, *Storia economico-politica del cinema italiano 1945–1980* (Rome: Riuniti, 1980); and Ernesto Rossi, *Lo Stato cinematografaro* (Florence: Parenti, 1959), 28.

2. Barbara Corsi, *Con qualche dollaro in più. Storia economica del cinema italiano* (Rome: Riuniti, 2001), 125.

3. Kristin Thompson, *Exporting Entertainment: America in the World Film Market, 1907–34* (London: BFI Publishing, 1985), 131.

4. Ian Jarvie, *Hollywood's Overseas Campaign: The North Atlantic Movie Trade* (Cambridge, UK: Cambridge University Press, 1992), 180.

5. Ibid., 5.

6. The papers are held at the Wisconsin State Historical Society (WSHS), University of Wisconsin at Madison.

7. Tino Balio, *United Artists: The Company Built by the Stars* (Madison: University of Wisconsin Press, 1976).

8. The history of the company is summarized in WSHS, UA Collection, For. Corres.—Italy; f. 18.3 1944–46 Artisti Associati, memo from Walter Gould, December 15, 44.

9. WSHS, UA Collection, Black books—foreign statistics; Italy—box office values, as of May 1934.

10. WSHS, UA Collection, For. Corres.—Italy, f. 18.1, 1933–38.

11. ACS, Ente Nazionale Acquisti Importazioni Pellicole Estere (ENAIPE), f. 826 Infrazioni—film americani.

12. Viniccio Marinucci, "Cinema proibito," *Star,* August 1944, page unnumbered.

13. Gian Piero Brunetta, *Storia del cinema italiano dal 1945 agli anni ottanta* (Rome: Editori Riuniti, 1982), 229.

14. Lorenzo Quaglietti, "Cinema americano, vecchio amore," in *Schermi di guerra: cinema italiano 1939–1945,* ed. Mino Argentieri (Rome: Bulzoni, 1995), 314.

15. Gian Piero Brunetta, "La lunga marcia del cinema americano in Italia tra fascismo e guerra fredda," in *Hollywood in Europa: industria, politica, pubblico del cinema 1945–1960,* ed. David W. Ellwood and Gian Piero Brunetta (Florence: Ponte alle Grazie, 1991), 80.

16. See David W. Ellwood, *Rebuilding Europe: Western Europe, American and Postwar Reconstruction* (London: Longman, 1992), chap. 12.

17. Vittorio Spinazzola, *Cinema e pubblico. Lo spettacolo filmico in Italia, 1945–65* (Milan: Bompiani, 1985, first published 1974), 9, 19.

18. *Cinestar,* July 3, 1948, 6.

19. NA, RG 84, Rome Embassy and Consulate, 840.6 motion pictures, confidential telegram of December 3, 1948, received from the Secretary of State.

20. NA, RG 59 865.452/11–250 State Department, Italy 1950–54, memo of November 2, 1950 refers to MPAA representatives describing these delays as "calculated obstruction."

21. Quaglietti, *Storia economico-politica,* 48.

22. See, e.g., *Araldo dello spettacolo,* November 6, 1948. American government reports noted the building up of the campaign against alleged dumping: NA, RG59, Italy 1950–54, 865.452/12—1250. Report dated February 5, 1950.

23. Libero Bizzarri, "L'economia cinematografica," in *La città del cinema: produzione e lavoro nel cinema italiano 1930–1970,* ed. M. Fasoli et al. (Rome: Napoleone, 1979), 42.

24. Paolo Bafile, "Il 'dumping' cinematografico in Italia," in *Sull'industria cinematografica italiana,* ed. Enrico Magrelli (Venice: Marsilio, 1986), 81.

25. NA, RG 59, 865.452/11–2450 State Department: Italy 1950–54, Rome Embassy dispatch November 24, 1950.

26. WSHS, UA Collection, Motion Picture Export Association 1946–58, minutes of special meeting of Board of Directors, New York, December 9, 1948. "The board was . . . informed that a possibility of transferring funds from Italy had arisen through the North American College, a Roman Catholic institution, for which money was at present being collected here and for which a committee was endeavouring to buy lira at a rate more favorable than the official rate and then giving a donation, so as to adjust the rate as desired." Warner Brothers, it transpires from the minutes, had already begun negotiations of this type and was benefiting from the assistance of a priest working in the office of Cardinal Spellman of New York.

27. "Vatican Aiding Coin Thaw," *Hollywood Reporter,* March 9, 1949, 1.

28. NA, RG 286, Records of Agency of International Development, mission to Italy, office of director, subject files, 1948–57, pr—press, box 50. Rome Embassy to State Department September 23, 1955.

29. For a fuller discussion of stardom in Italy in the 1930s and 1940s, see Stephen Gundle, "Film Stars and Society in Fascist Italy," in *Reviewing Fascism: Italian Cinema, 1922–1943,* ed. Jacqueline Reich and Piero Garofalo (Bloomington and Indianapolis: Indiana University Press, 2002), 315–39; Stephen Gundle, "Divismo," in *Dizionario del fascismo,* ed. Victoria de Grazia and Sergio Luzzatto (Turin: Einaudi, 2003); and, for Italian stars only, Gian Piero Brunetta, *Buio in sala. Cent'anni di passioni dello spettatore cinematografico* (Venice: Marsilio, 1989), chap. 13.

30. See Paola Valentini, "Modelli, forme e fenomeni di divismo: il caso Vittorio De Sica," in Mariagrazia Fanchi and Elena Mosconi, eds., *Spettatori. Forme di consumo e pubblici del cinema 1930–1960* (Rome: Fondazione Scuola Nazionale di Cinema, 2002).

31. See Guido Aristarco, *Miti e realtà nel cinema italiano* (Milan: Il Saggiatore, 1961).

32. G. V. Samperi, "Divismo," *Lo Schermo* (1939): 18–20.

33. Francesco Savio, *Cinecittà anni trenta,* 3 vols. (Rome: Bulzoni 1979).

34. See Francesco Alberoni, *L'elite senza potere* (Bologna: Il Mulino, 1963).

35. Savio, *Cinecittà anni trenta,* 468.

36. Bort, "Alida Valli trova un personaggio," *Film,* April 19, 1941, 5.

37. Alessandro Ferraù, "Lettere d'amore a Roberto Villa," *Film,* February 27, 1941, 11.

38. Alessandro Ferraù, "Lettere d'amore," *Film,* April 5, 1941, 8.

39. For a general analysis of glamour and its cinematic applications, see Stephen Gundle and Clino T. Castelli, *The Glamour System* (London: Palgrave Macmillan, 2006).

40. The polyvalent appeal of Rita Hayworth was apparent in the Max Factor advertisements in which she often appeared. See, e.g., *Hollywood,* October 18, 1948, 14.

41. Pier Giorgio Amerio, "Ty, a Torino," *Hollywood,* November 8, 1947, 5.

42. For a close examination of this see Stephen Gundle, "Memory and Identity: Popular Culture in Postwar Italy," in *Italy Since 1945,* ed. Patrick McCarthy (Oxford: Oxford University Press, 2000), 183–87.

43. See Graham McCann, *Rebel Males: Clift, Brando, and Dean* (Cambridge: Polity, 1993).

44. Giulio Cesare Castello, *Il divismo. Mitologia del cinema* (Turin: ERI, 1957), 408.

45. Anon., "I film italiani nel mercato interno," *Cinespettacolo,* February 14, 1953, 5–8; and Anon., "I film italiani che sono andati male nel mercato interno," *Cinespettacolo,* March 7–14, 1953, 6.

46. E. O., "Le grandi città e i grandi divi," *Cinespettacolo,* March 15–30, 1956, 7; see also, Anon., "Il patrimonio attori," *Cinespettacolo,* January–February 1957, 4–5.

6. Radio and Recorded Music

1. Franco Monteleone, *Storia della radio e della televisione in Italia. Società, politica, strategie, programmi 1922–1992* (Venice: Marsilio, 1992), 56.

2. Gianni Isola, *Abbassa la tua radio, per favore . . . Storia dell'ascolto radiofonico nell'Italia fascista* (Florence: La Nuova Italia, 1990), 23, 25.

3. Ibid., 23.

4. Quoted in Isola, *Abbassa la tua radio,* 12.

5. Peppino Ortoleva, "Linguaggi culturali via etere," in *Fare gli italiani. Scuola e cultura nell'Italia contemporanea,* vol. 2, *Una società di massa,* ed. Simonetta Soldani and Gabriele Turi (Bologna: Il Mulino, 1993), 449; see also Alberto Monticone, *Il fascismo al microfono* (Rome: Studium, 1978), 67.

6. Monteleone, *Storia della radio,* 51.

7. Quoted in Isola, *Abbassa la tua radio,* 24.

8. Ibid., xix.

9. Ibid., 180.

10. Pekka Gronow and Ilpo Saunio, *An International History of the Recording Industry* (London: Cassell, 1998), 114.

11. Giuseppe Richeri, "Italian Broadcasting and Fascism 1924–1937," *Media, Culture and Society* 2, no. 1 (January 1980): 50, n. 4.

12. Gronow and Saunio, *An International History,* 39.

13. The interview was recorded in Milan on September 20, 1993.

14. Mario De Luigi, *L'industria discografica in Italia* (Rome: Lato Side, 1982), 12.

15. Ibid., 13.

16. Baldi, Giulia. "L'industria fonografica in Italia fino al 1970. Mercato e società," Tesi di Laurea, Università degli Studi di Roma "La Sapienza," Facoltà di Lettere e Filosofia, 2000, 145.

17. De Luigi, *L'industria discografica,* 16.

18. Baldi, *L'industria fonografica,* 144–46.

19. Ibid., 144–47.

20. Interview with Marcella Filippa, September 20, 1993. *Limelight* had opened in New York in October 1952. The dancer, Terry, was played by Claire Bloom (see chap. 1) and the tune written by Chaplin was called "Eternally" in English.

21. Anna Lucia Natale, *Gli anni della radio. 1924–1954* (Naples: Liguori, 1990), 96–97.

22. Isola, *Abbassa la tua radio,* 91.

23. Ibid., 146–50.

24. Ibid., 147–48.

25. Ibid., 200–202.

26. S. Valeri, "Ernesto Bonino," *Il Canzoniere della radio,* October 1, 1941, 3–4.

27. Gianni Borgna, *Storia della canzone italiana* (Milan: Mondadori, 1992), 145.

28. Ibid., 132–33.

29. Gianfranco Baldazzi, *La canzone italiana del Novecento* (Rome: Newton Compton, 1989), 48.

30. The controversy over Gigli is explored in Fiorenza Fiorentino, *La Roma di Charles Poletti (giugno 1944–aprile 1945)* (Rome: Bonacci, 1986), 39–40.

31. Beniamino Gigli, *Memorie* (Milan: Mondadori, 1957), 331.

32. Gianni Isola, *Cari amici vicini e lontani. Storia dell'ascolto radiofonico nel primo decennio repubblicano* (Florence: La Nuova Italia, 1995), 233.

33. Ibid., 242–43.

34. Borgna, *Storia della canzone,* 192, 210–13.

35. Baldazzi, *La canzone italiana,* 77.

36. Borgna, *Storia della canzone,* 213.

37. The main reason for this was her irritation at the moralism of RAI functionaries, who objected to her as a separated woman who had had liaisons with colleagues. Interview with Stephen Gundle, November 3, 1982.

38. Gigli, *Memorie,* 292.

39. Ibid.

40. At the end of 1954 an "agony column" (*Moira risponde*) was created to deal with personal questions from readers who evidently—and not implausibly, given the nature of many popular songs—regarded the singers as experts on love.

41. Borgna, *Storia della canzone,* 201.

42. Claudio Villa, *Una vita stupenda* (Milan: Mondadori, 1987), 69.

43. "Firmamento," unsigned, *Sorrisi e canzoni,* August 23, 1953, 4.

44. Ibid., 4.

45. Villa, *Una vita stupenda,* 82.

46. Borgna, *Storia della canzone,* 202; Villa, *Una vita stupenda,* 94.

47. Piero Palumbo, "Una tessera contro la noia," *Lo Specchio,* December 28, 1958, 12. The other installment of the inquiry was published on December 21.

48. Baldazzi, *La canzone italiana,* 83.

49. Ibid., 96; Isola, *Cari amici,* 334.

50. Marcella Filippa, "Fred Buscaglione: un mito degli anni Cinquanta," in *Il Piemonte vivo* 2 (1990): 44–51.

51. Vera Zamagni, *The Economic History of Italy 1860–1990: Recovery after Decline* (Oxford: Clarendon Press, 1993), 308.

52. Ibid., 314.

53. Monteleone, *Storia della radio e della televisione in Italia,* 272–75.

7. State Intervention in Cultural Activity

1. Claudio Pavone, "La continuità dello Stato. Istituzioni e uomini," in Enzo Piscitelli et al., *Italia 1945–48. Le origini della Repubblica* (Turin: Giappichelli, 1974), 137–289. This and other essays were subsequently collected in Claudio Pavone, *Alle origini della Repubblica. Scritti sul fascismo, antifascismo e continuità dello Stato* (Turin: Bollati Boringhieri, 1995). See also Guido Quazza, *Resistenza e storia d'Italia* (Milan: Feltrinelli, 1976); and his "Passato e presente nelle interpretazioni della Resistenza," in *Pas-*

sato e presente della Resistenza (Rome: Presidenza del Consiglio dei ministri, n.d. [but 1993]).

2. Adrian Lyttelton contrasts totalitarian and authoritarian regimes on two grounds: that the former are characterized by the supremacy of the party (the party either dominates the state or pervades the state machinery with its values) whereas the latter are characterized by the limitation of the party's role, its subordination to the state; and that in totalitarian regimes, citizenship is active, with coerced participation, whereas in authoritarian regimes the citizen is passive and obedient. *The Seizure of Power: Fascism in Italy 1919–1929*, 2d ed. (London: Weidenfeld and Nicolson, 1987), 149–50.

3. Mariuccia Salvati, *Il regime e gli impiegati. La nazionalizzazione piccolo-borghese nel ventennio fascista* (Rome and Bari: Laterza, 1992).

4. Alberto Aquarone, *L'organizzazione dello Stato totalitario* (Turin: Einaudi, 1965), 293–301 (301 quoted).

5. Philip V. Cannistraro, *La fabbrica del consenso. Fascismo e mass media* (Rome and Bari: Laterza, 1975). Along similar lines is Maria Malatesta, "Campo dei media, campo di potere," *Italia Contemporanea*, nos. 146–47 (1982): 15–33. The phrase "the manufacture of consent" was used by Walter Lippmann in *Public Opinion* (New York: Harcourt, Brace, 1922), 248, and the idea was adapted to public relations in *The Engineering of Consent*, ed. Edward Bernays (Norman: University of Oklahoma Press, 1955). The metaphor has since reappeared in Edward S. Herman and Noam Chomsky, *Manufacturing Consent: The Political Economy of the Mass Media* (New York: Pantheon, 1988).

6. Ibid., 3.

7. This criticism of Cannistraro's book was made by Silvio Lanaro in his review, "Il casco di sughero," *Belfagor* 32, no. 2 (1977): 219–28.

8. For the critique of the "mass consent" thesis see Gianpasquale Santomassimo, "Antifascismo popolare," *Italia Contemporanea* 32, no. 140 (1980): 39–69; Luisa Passerini, *Torino operaia e fascismo. Una storia orale* (Rome and Bari: Laterza, 1984); and Luisa Passerini, "Oral Memory of Fascism," in *Rethinking Italian Fascism: Capitalism, Populism and Culture*, ed. David Forgacs (London: Lawrence and Wishart, 1986); Nicola Tranfaglia, *La prima guerra mondiale e il fascismo*, vol. 22 of *Storia d'Italia*, ed. Giuseppe Galasso (Turin: UTET, 1995). The terms "political theatre" and "collective performance" (*recitazione collettiva*) are used by Mario Isnenghi, "Al teatro dell'Italia nuova. Fascismo e cultura di massa," in Mino Argentieri et al., *Fascismo e antifascismo negli anni della Repubblica, Problemi del socialismo*, vol. 7 (Milan: Franco Angeli, 1986). The terms "lay religion" and "secularization of politics" are used by Emilio Gentile (see following note).

9. Emilio Gentile, "Fascism as political religion," *Journal of Contemporary History* 25 (1990): 229–51; *Il culto del Littorio: la via italiana al totalitarismo. Il Partito e lo Stato nel regime fascista* (Rome: La Nuova Italia Scientifica, 1995).

10. Jeffrey T. Schnapp, "Epic Demonstrations: Fascist Modernity and the 1932 Exhibition of the Fascist Revolution," in *Fascism, Aesthetics and Culture*, ed. Richard J. Golsan (Hanover, N.H.: University Press of New England, 1992).

11. Simonetta Falasca-Zamponi, *Fascist Spectacle: The Aesthetics of Power in Mussolini's Italy*, (Berkeley and Los Angeles: University of California Press, 1997). Benjamin's remarks about Fascism "making politics aesthetic" were made not about Fascism in general but about its cult of war, with specific reference to the glorification of technologized warfare by the Futurist-Fascist Marinetti. The remarks drew on the Marxist analyses of fascism in circulation in the 1930s. Since fascism (Benjamin meant both the German and Italian varieties) sought to involve the proletariat in mass poli-

tics without changing capitalist property relations it had to give them "an expression while preserving property," and the ultimate expression it gave them was the celebration of war, since only war "can set a goal for mass movements of the largest scale while respecting the traditional property system." Imperialistic war makes use of the technology and means of industrial production that necessarily remain underutilized when fettered by capitalism. The text Benjamin then quotes is Marinetti's manifesto on the Ethiopian war, which sees the beauty of war in the expression it gives to military technology: machine guns, tanks, flamethrowers. Benjamin comments: "The horrible features of imperialistic warfare are attributable to the discrepancy between the tremendous means of production and their inadequate utilization in the process of production—in other words, to unemployment and the lack of markets." Fascism, Benjamin concludes, "expects war to supply the artistic gratification of a sense perception that has been changed by technology." Walter Benjamin, "The Work of Art in the Age of Mechanical Reproduction" (1936), in *Illuminations*, ed. Hannah Arendt, trans. Harry Zohn (Glasgow: Fontana, 1973), 243. For a criticism of reductive applications of Benjamin's dictum to Nazi Germany see Lutz P. Koepnick, *Walter Benjamin and the Aesthetics of Power* (Lincoln: University of Nebraska Press, 1999).

12. Falasca-Zamponi, *Fascist Spectacle*, 190–91.

13. Steven Lukes, "Political Ritual and Social Integration," *Sociology* 9, no. 2 (1975): 298–301.

14. The quotation is from James C. Scott, *Domination and the Arts of Resistance: Hidden Transcripts* (New Haven, Conn., and London: Yale University Press, 1990), x; see also 70–107; and his *Weapons of the Weak: Everyday Forms of Peasant Resistance* (New Haven, Conn.: Yale University Press, 1985), 314–50.

15. Scott, *Weapons of the Weak*, 287; *Domination and the Arts of Resistance*, x–xii.

16. Michel de Certeau, *L'invention du quotidien*, vol. 1, *Arts de faire* (Paris: Gallimard 1990) (first published 1980), xiii.

17. Ibid., 145–46.

18. Ernesto Ragionieri, *La storia politica e sociale*, tomo 3 of *Storia d'Italia*, vol. 4: *Dall'Unità a oggi* (Turin: Einaudi, 1976), 1687.

19. Luigi Freddi, *Il cinema*, 2 vols. (Rome L'Arnia, 1949), 285.

20. See Giulia Barone and Armando Petrucci, *Primo: non leggere. Biblioteche e pubblica lettura in Italia dal 1861 ai nostri giorni* (Milan: Mazzotta. 1976), 84–90; and Vera Zamagni, *The Economic History of Italy 1860–1990: Recovery after Decline* (Oxford: Clarendon Press, 1993), 307.

21. Pasquale Saraceno, *L'Istituto per la ricostruzione industriale*, vol. 3, *Origini, ordinamenti e attività svolta* (Turin: UTET, 1956), 343, as reported in Giorgio Fabre, *L'elenco. Censura fascista, editoria e autori ebrei* (Turin: Zamorani, 1998), 11–12, n. 4.

22. Gherardo Casini, "Il libro e la cultura italiana," *Il Libro Italiano* 2, no. 2 (1938): 52.

23. See Antonio Papa, *Storia politica della radio in Italia*, 2 vols. (Naples: Guida, 1978), 2:106.

24. Casini, "Il libro e la cultura italiana," 54.

25. Giulio Einaudi, "Esperienze di un editore giovane," *Il Libro Italiano* 3, no. 3 (1939): 172.

26. Domenico Lombrassa, "La difesa del ragazzo italiano," *Il libro italiano* 2, no. 11 (1938): 459–60.

27. Ibid., 462, 460.

28. Quoted in Mino Argentieri, *L'asse cinematografico Roma-Berlino* (Naples: Sapere, 1986), 13.

29. Ibid., 13.

30. Freddi, *Il cinema,* 2:58.

31. Ibid., 2:61.

32. *Film Daily,* April 8, 1937, 11, in *Motion Picture Review Digest* (MPRD), June 28, 1937, 19.

33. *Variety,* April 7, 1937, 29, in MPRD, June 28, 1937, 19.

34. *Variety,* July 13, 1938, 15, in MPRD, September 26, 1938, 37.

35. *Film Daily,* August 10, 1937, 13, MPRD December 12, 1938.

36. The reviews listed are from *Variety,* September 9, 1936, 17 and *The New York Times,* September 2, 1936, 18, in MPRD, September 28, 1936, 78.

37. *The New York Times,* September 2, 1936, 18, in MPRD, September 28, 1936, 78.

38. Freddi, *Il cinema,* 1:327.

39. MAE, Serie affari politici 1931–45, USA, b.52 (1938), f.7 Cinematografia, s.f. 2: Trattative film "Scipione l'Africano," Alfieri a MAE, January 6, 1937.

40. *Time,* November 27, 1939, 83 in MPRD, December 25, 1939, 96.

41. Argentieri, *L'asse cinematografico,* 13.

42. Ibid., 112.

43. Freddi, *Il cinema,* 2:101.

44. Argentieri, *L'asse cinematografico,* 129.

45. Franco Ciarlantini, *Vicende di libri e di autori* (Milan: Ceschina, 1931), 220–22.

46. Mondadori, "Il libro italiano all'estero," 241–43.

47. Ibid., 244–5.

48. IRCE, "Memorandum," undated (but 1942), in ACS, MCP, b. 245, f. 179, 2.

49. Ibid., 6–7.

50. Schnapp, "Epic Demonstrations," 18.

51. Ibid., 15.

52. Quoted in ibid., 22.

53. Peter Bondanella, "The Making of *Roma città aperta:* The Legacy of Fascism and the Birth of Neorealism," in *Roberto Rossellini's "Rome Open City,"* ed. Sidney Gottlieb (Cambridge, UK: Cambridge University Press, 2004), 44–45.

54. For a more detailed discussion of this point see David Forgacs, "Sex in the Cinema: Regulation and Transgression in Italian Films, 1930–1943," in *Re-viewing Fascism: Italian Cinema 1922–1943,* ed. Jacqueline Reich and Piero Garofalo (Bloomington and Indianapolis: Indiana University Press, 2002).

55. Augusto Sainati, *La Settimana Incom. Cinegiornali e informazione negli anni '50* (Turin: Lindau, 2001), 28.

56. See Maria Adelaide Frabotta, "Government Propaganda: Official Newsreels and Documentaries in the 1950s," in *The Art of Persuasion: Political Communication in Italy from 1945 to the 1990s,* ed. Luciano Cheles and Lucio Sponza (Manchester: Manchester University Press 2001), 50.

57. Alejandro Pizarroso Quintero, *Stampa, radio e propaganda. Gli alleati in Italia 1943–1946* (Milan: Franco Angeli, 1989) (a selection of key PWB documents is reproduced in English in an appendix).

58. Luigi Rusca to Arnoldo Mondadori, Rome, April 24, 1945, in AFM, Fondo Miscellanea Arnoldo Mondadori, b. 13, f. 6 (Sede Roma. 1943–1948 e s.d.), s.f. 3 (Sede Roma, copie corrispondenza di Arnoldo e Alberto Mondadori, Enzo Pagliara, Luigi Rusca e Ufficio Stampa ed informazioni britannico, July 28, 1943–October 10, 1946).

59. Enzo Pagliara to Arnoldo Mondadori, July 8, 45, in ibid.

60. Allied Force Headquarters, Psychological Warfare Subcommittee, "Radio Plan for Liberated Italy" (November 23, 1944), in NA, RG 331. Allied Control Commission, Italy, HQ Chief Commissioner, 10000/136/502, Italian Radio Station EIAR.

61. Franco Chiarenza, *Il cavallo morente. Storia della RAI,* 2d ed., enlarged (1st ed. 1978), (Milan: Franco Angeli, 2002), 26.

62. NA, RG 208. Records of the Office of War Information; PWB films, Jackson to McChrystal, November 23, 1943.

63. See Pasquale Iaccio, *La scena negata. Il teatro censurato durante la guerra fascista 1940–1943* (Rome: Bulzoni, 1995), 11.

64. The statement is from an interview with Zavattini by Tommaso Chiaretti in *Mondo Nuovo*, December 11, 1960, quoted in Domenico Tarantini, *Processo allo spettacolo* (Milan: Comunità, 1961), 214.

65. Archivio di Stato di Milano (ASM), Prefettura-Gabinetto, Versamento 1989, 044 Case editrici, Cartella 155 (L-R), 1940, 1941, Mondadori; ACP MCP DGSI to R. Prefettura di Milano, September 26, 1941 and December 15, 1941.

66. See Guido Bonsaver, *Elio Vittorini: The Writer and the Written* (Leeds: Northern Universities Press, 2000), 83.

67. See the articles reproduced in Mario Quargnolo, *La censura ieri e oggi nel cinema e nel teatro*, no. 123 of *Il timone* (Milan: Pan, 1982), 185–88. There is a larger selection of press cuttings in the files on *Ossessione* in the Fondo Luchino Visconti at the Fondazione Istituto Gramsci, Rome.

68. Raffaele Crovi, *Vittorini: una biografia critica* (Venice: Marsilio, 1998), 188.

69. There is an interesting early post-liberation account in these terms of the censorship of Visconti's film by Gino Avorio, "Schedario segreto," *Star* 1, no. 5 (September 9, 1944): 10 (*Star* was published in Rome, liberated on June 4, 1944).

70. Freddi, *Il cinema*, 1:46.

71. Ibid., 159.

72. Jean A. Gili, *Stato fascista e cinematografia. Repressione e promozione* (Rome: Bulzoni, 1981), 43–44.

73. Freddi, *Il cinema*, 1:160–69, 443–44.

74. See, e.g., Vito Laterza, *Quale editore. Note di lavoro* (Rome and Bari: Laterza, 2002), 18–19.

75. Michele Sarfatti, "Gli ebrei negli anni del fascismo: vicende, identità, persecuzione," in tomo II, *Dall'emancipazione a oggi* in *Gli ebrei in Italia*, vol. 11 of *Storia d'Italia, Annali*, ed. Corrado Vivanti (Turin: Einaudi, 1997), 1668.

76. Nicola Caracciolo, *Gli ebrei e l'Italia durante la guerra, 1940–45* (Rome: Bonacci, 1986), 25; Dan Vittorio Segre, *Memoirs of a Fortunate Jew: An Italian story* (London: Paladin, 1988), 77 (original edition *Storia di un ebreo fortunato*, Milan: Bompiani, 1985); Michele Sarfatti, *Gli ebrei nell'Italia fascista. Vicende, identità, persecuzione* (Turin: Einaudi, 2000), 126–32 (this book is an amplification of Sarfatti's 1997 essay "Gli ebrei negli anni del fascismo").

77. Sarfatti, *Gli ebrei nell'Italia fascista*, 108; Tranfaglia, *La prima guerra mondiale e il fascismo*, 597.

78. Giorgio Fabre, *L'elenco. Censura fascista, editoria e autori ebrei* (Turin: Zamorani, 1998), 7.

79. Memo from DGSI to Alfieri, April 8, 1938, quoted in Alberto Cavaglion and Gian Paolo Romagnani, *Le interdizioni del Duce. A cinquant'anni dalle leggi razziali in Italia (1939–1988)* (Turin: Meynier, 1988), 33.

80. Dino Alfieri, MCP, to Prefetto di Milano, December 23, 1938 and July 5, 1939. ASM, Prefettura-Gabinetto, versamento 1989, 044 Case editrici (L-R), 155: 1940, 1941: Mondadori.

81. Riccardo Miceli, "Razzismo del libro," *Il Libro Italiano* 2, no. 9 (1938): 380–81.

82. On Formiggini's suicide see Gabriele Turi, *Il fascismo e il consenso degli intellettuali* (Bologna: Il Mulino, 1980), 151–52.

83. The minutes of the extraordinary meeting of the board of Treves are in Camera del Commercio, Milan, Cancelleria delle società commerciali, Milano, Treves-Garzanti, n. soc. 5817, vol. 213, fascicolo 871. The minutes of the Bemporad meeting are

in ASG, Fondo Bemporad, *Libro verbali assemblee dal 1907 al 1937*. Renato Giunti took over Marzocco in 1956 and subsequently merged it with another firm, Parenti, into the publishing house that bears his name. It is worth recalling that Bemporad, as well as being an important literary publisher in the 1930s, had also been aligned with the regime and had published various texts by Fascist authors.

84. Piero Bigongiari, interview with David Forgacs, Florence, June 12, 1992.

85. Prot. n.1103, Ministro della Cultura Popolare ai Capi delle Provincie, carbon copy, dated November 24, 1943, in AFM, Fondo Sede Verona, b.2, f.16, "Volumi bloccati per la censura," s.f.a, "Circolari 24.4.43–19.12.44."

86. The decree is reproduced in Alberto Cavaglion and Gian Paolo Romagnani, *Le interdizioni del duce: le leggi raziali in Italia* (Turin: Claudiana, 2002).

87. AFM, Fondo Arnoldo Mondadori, b. 36, "Denuncia beni ebraici," Casa Ed. A. Mondadori to Capo della Provincia di Milano, carbon copy, February 29, 1944. A letter in the same file, dated April 26, 1945, from the Credito Fondiario della Cassa di Risparmio delle Provincie Lombarde (Milan) mentions a decree of the Capo della Provincia di Milano dated July 15, 1944, which confiscates in the state's favor the amounts owing to Jewish authors.

88. Fabre, *L'elenco*, 433.

89. See Sergio Amidei's testimony in Francesco Savio, *Cinecittà anni trenta*, 3 vols. (Rome: Bulzoni, 1979), 1:62.

90. ASL, Registri copialettere, b. 71 (5/11/41–21/1/43), Giovanni Laterza to Alessandro Pavolini, 5/2/42.

91. Franco Monteleone, *La radio italiana nel periodo fascista. Studio e documenti: 1922–1945* (Venice: Marsilio, 1976), 173.

92. Ibid., 178.

93. Ibid., 186, nn. 59 and 185; n. 58.

94. See for instance Mino Argentieri, *La censura nel cinema italiano* (Rome: Riuniti. 1974).

95. Maurizio Cesari, *La censura in Italia oggi (1944–1980)* (Naples: Liguori, 1982), 82–83.

96. Ibid., 83.

97. Luca Pes, "Cronologia 1945–1991," in Silvio Lanaro, *Storia della Repubblica italiana. Dalla fine della guerra agli anni novanta* (Venice: Marsilio, 1992), 469.

98. See Marco Barbanti, "La classe dirigente cattolica e la 'battaglia per la moralità' 1948–1960. Appunti sul 'regime clericale,'" *Italia Contemporanea*, no. 189 (1992): 606–34.

99. The letter is quoted in Argentieri, *La censura nel cinema italiano*, 71.

100. Quoted in Maurizio Cesari, *La censura nel periodo fascista* (Naples: Liguori, 1977), 70–71.

101. See Vitaliano Brancati, *La governante, con la nota dell'autore "Ritorno alla censura"* (Milan: Bompiani, 1974), 39. *Ritorno alla censura* was originally published in a separate volume (Bari: Laterza, 1952) with the text of *La governante* in an appendix.

102. Renzi's article, "L'armata s'agapò," was published in *Cinema Nuovo* II, no. 4, February 1, 1953, and is reprinted in Renzo Renzi, *La bella stagione. Scontri e incontri negli anni d'oro del cinema italiano* (Rome: Bulzoni, 2001) along with his interesting autobiographical open letter, written after the trial to an army general, "Rapporto di un ex-balilla," originally published in 1954.

8. Civil Society and Organized Leisure

1. Giorgio Galli, "Masse e politica: 1920–1960," in Giorgio Rumi, ed., *Vita civile degli italiani. Società, economia, cultura materiale*, vol. 6: *Trasformazioni economiche, mutamenti sociali e nuovi miti collettivi 1920–1960* (Milan: Electa, 1991), 193.

2. Susanna Agnelli, *Vestivamo alla marinara* (Milan: Mondadori, 1975), 27.

3. Gian Piero Brunetta, "Il sogno a stelle e strisce di Mussolini," in Maurizio Vaudagna, ed., *L'estetica della politica in Europa e America negli anni trenta* (Bari: Laterza, 1989), 161–76.

4. Renzo Renzi, "Il Duce, ultimo divo," in *Sperduti nel buio: il cinema muto italiano e il suo tempo (1905–34)*, ed. Renzo Renzi (Bologna: Cappelli, 1991).

5. Monica Dall'Asta, *Le cinéma musclé* (Lausanne: Editions Yellow Now, 1992); Pierre Sorlin, *Italian National Cinema 1896–1996* (London: Routledge 1996), 48–49.

6. Dino Biondi, *La fabbrica del Duce* (Florence: Valecchi, 1973), 88–89.

7. Vittorio Mussolini, interview in Renzo Renzi, ed., *Il cinema dei dittatori: Mussolini, Stalin, Hitler* (Bologna: Grafis, 1992).

8. Stefano Jacomuzzi, "Gli sport," in *Storia d'Italia V: I documenti*, I (Turin: Einaudi, 1973).

9. Paolo Facchinetti, *La stampa sportiva in Italia* (Bologna: Alfa, 1966), 66–7.

10. Quoted in Renato Bianda et al., *Atleti in camicia nera. Lo sport nell'Italia di Mussolini* (Rome: Volpe, 1983), 43.

11. Quoted in Elizabeth David, *Italian Food* (Harmondsworth: Penguin, 1963; first published 1954), 93.

12. On Starace see Antonio Spinosa, *Starace* (Milan: Rizzoli, 1981).

13. Gian Paolo Ceserani, *Storia della pubblicità in Italia* (Rome and Bari: Laterza, 1988), 102.

14. James Hay, *Popular Film Culture in Fascist Italy: The Passing of the Rex* (Bloomington and Indianapolis: Indiana University Press, 1987), 149.

15. Gian Franco Venè, *Mille lire al mese. La vita quotidiana della famiglia nell'Italia fascista* (Milan: Mondadori, 1988), 167.

16. Victoria de Grazia, *How Fascism Ruled Women: Italy 1922–1945* (Berkeley and Los Angeles: University of California Press, 1992), 212–13.

17. Giovanna Dompé, "Moda," *Enciclopedia italiana di scienze, lettere ed arti*, vol. 23 (Rome: Istituto della Enciclopedia Italiana, 1934), 508.

18. See, e.g., O. Cerquiglini, "Fiori dei campi, fiori della razza," *La Domenica del Corriere*, September 3, 1939, 8–9.

19. Ruggero Zangrandi, *Il lungo viaggio attraverso il fascismo. Contributo alla storia di una generazione* (Milan: Mursia, 1988; original version Turin, Einaudi 1947; expanded edition Milan, Feltrinelli 1962), 125.

20. Victoria de Grazia, *The Culture of Consent: Mass Organization of Leisure in Fascist Italy* (Cambridge, UK: Cambridge University Press, 1981), 207.

21. Ibid.

22. See Antonio Faeti, *Boccasile* (Milan: Longanesi, 1981), Introduction.

23. John Wilson, *Politics and Leisure* (London: Unwin Hyman, 1988), 147.

24. Colarizi, *L'opinione degli italiani sotto il regime*, 211–19.

25. Emilio Gentile, *La grande Italia. Ascesa e declino del mito della nazione nel ventesimo secolo* (Milan: Mondadori, 1997), 218.

26. Giuseppe Della Torre, *Azione cattolica e fascismo. Il conflitto del 1931* (Rome: Editrice A.V.E., 1945), 7.

27. Pietro Scoppola, "I cattolici tra fascismo e democrazia," in *Introduzione alla storia del movimento cattolico*, ed. Bartolo Gariglio and Ettore Passerin d'Entrèves (Bologna: Il Mulino, 1979), 401.

28. Giovanni Miccoli, "La Chiesa e il fascismo," in Gariglio and Passerin d'Entreves, *Introduzione alla storia* (originally published in Guido Quazza, ed., (ed), *Fascismo e società italiana*, Turin: Einaudi, 1973), 386.

29. John Pollard, *The Vatican and Italian Fascism* (Cambridge, UK: Cambridge University Press, 1986), 167.

30. Oliver Logan, "Italian Identity: Catholic Responses to Secularist Definitions, c. 1910–1948," *Modern Italy* 11 (1997): 57.

31. Gian Piero Brunetta, *Storia del cinema italiano 1895–1945* (Rome: Editori Riuniti, 1979), 322–23.

32. Ibid., 339.

33. Logan, "Italian identity," 62.

34. Agostino Giovagnoli, "Chiesa, assistenza e società a Roma tra il 1943 e il 1945," in Nicola Gallerano, ed., *L'altro dopoguerra. Roma e il Sud 1943–1945* (Milan: Franco Angeli, 1985), 214.

35. Simona Colarizi, *L'opinione degli italiani sotto il regime, 1929–1943* (Rome and Bari: Laterza, 1991), 309–311, 359–63.

36. Silvio Lanaro, *Storia della Repubblica italiana. Dalla fine della guerra agli anni novanta* (Venice: Marsilio, 1992), 368.

37. Logan, "Italian Identity," 62.

38. Mario Isnenghi, *L'Italia in piazza. I luoghi della vita pubblica dal 1848 ai giorni nostri*, 2d ed. (Bologna: Il Mulino, 2004), 422–28.

39. Stefano Pivato, *Sia lodato Bartali: ideologia, cultura e miti dello sport cattolico (1936–1948)* (Rome: Edizioni Lavoro, 1985), 18, 32.

40. Ibid., 15.

41. *Lo spettacolo in Italia nel 1953* (Rome: SIAE, 1954), 98; *Rilevazione dei teatri e dei cinematografi esistenti in Italia al 30 giugno 1953*, vol. 2, *Locali per genere di spettacolo, numero dei posti, prezzo medio ed anno di aperture* (Rome: SIAE, 1956), 4–5.

42. Lanaro, *Storia della Repubblica italiana*, 194.

43. Bruno P. F. Wanrooij, *Storia del pudore. La questione sessuale in Italia, 1860–1940* (Venice: Marsilio, 1990), 118.

44. Pio XII, "Nella esaltazione alla gloria dei Santi di Maria Goretti," in *Discorsi e radiomessaggi di Sua Santità Pio XII* (Rome: Tipografia Poliglotta Vaticana, s.d. [but 1951], vol. 12, *Duodecimo anno di Pontificato, 2 marzo 1950–1 marzo 1951*, 122.

45. Quoted in Nadia Tarantini, *Maria Goretti. Un delitto che parla ancora* (Rome: Editrice l'Unità, 1994), 45.

46. Paul Ginsborg, *A History of Contemporary Italy: Society and Politics, 1943–88* (Harmondsworth: Penguin, 1990), 168–69.

47. See Mario Marazziti, "Cultura di massa e valori cattolici: il modello di 'Famiglia Cristiana,'" in *Pio XII*, ed. Angelo Lombardi (Rome and Bari: Laterza, 1984); and Stephen Gundle, "Cultura di massa e modernizzazione: *Vie Nuove* e *Famiglia Cristiana* dalla guerra fredda alla società dei consumi," in Pier Paolo D'Attorre, ed., *Nemici per la pelle. Sogno americano e mito sovietico nell'Italia contemporanea* (Milan: Franco Angeli, 1991).

48. *Famiglia Cristiana. Nozze d'oro di un rotocalco* (brochure published by Società San Paolo, Milan, 1981), pages unnumbered; print runs of other illustrated weeklies are given in Nello Ajello, *Lezioni di giornalismo* (Milan: Garzanti, 1985), 89.

49. See Marzia Marsili, "De Gasperi and Togliatti: Political Leadership and Personality Cults in Postwar Italy," *Modern Italy* 3, no. 2 (1998): 250–53.

50. Angelo Ventrone, "L'avventura americana della classe dirigente cattolica," in D'Attorre, *Nemici per la pelle*, 155.

51. Stephen Gundle, "La 'religione civile' della resistenza: cultura di massa e identità politica nell'Italia del dopoguerra," in Luisa Cigognetti, Lorenza Servetti, and Pierre Sorlin, eds., *L'immagine della resistenza nell'Europa del dopoguerra* (Bologna: Il Nove, 1996). Modified English version: "The 'Civic Religion' of the Resistance in Postwar Italy," *Modern Italy* 5, no. 2 (2000): 113–32.

52. David Forgacs, *Italian Culture in the Industrial Era, 1880–1980: Cultural Industries, Politics and the Public* (Manchester and New York: Manchester University Press, 1990), 99–100.

53. For a detailed discussion see Stephen Gundle, *Between Hollywood and Moscow: The Italian Communists and the Challenge of Mass Culture, 1943–1991* (Durham, N.C.: Duke University Press, 2000), 35–41.

54. Nello Ajello, *Intellettuali e PCI 1944–1958* (Rome and Bari: Laterza, 1979), chaps. 1–3.

55. Gundle, *Between Hollywood and Moscow,* 17–23.

56. Orlando Pezzoli, *È storia: Casa del Popolo Nerio Nannetti-Santa Viola, Bologna* (Bologna: PCI Zona Santa Viola, 1981).

57. Pietro Ingrao, "Le feste dell'Unità," *Rinascita* 5, nos. 9–10 (1948): 372; more broadly on the *feste de L'Unità* see Eva Paola Amendola and Marcella Ferrara, eds., *È la festa: quarant'anni con L'Unità* (Rome: Editori Riuniti, 1984).

58. See Pietro Scoppola, *25 aprile: liberazione* (Turin: Einaudi, 1995); Gian Enrico Rusconi, *Resistenza e postfascismo* (Bologna: Il Mulino, 1995); Simone Neri Serneri, "A Past to Throw Away? Politics and History in the Italian Resistance," *Contemporary European History* 4, no. 3 (1995): 367–81; Gundle, "La 'religione civile' della resistenza."

59. Enzo Forcella, "Politica e immagine," in Sergio Morandi (ed.), *Almanacco letterario Bompiani 1963* (Milan: Bompiani, 1962), 88.

60. Carlo Felice Casula, "I comunisti e la comunicazione," in *Il 1948 in Italia. La storia e i film,* ed. Nicola Tranfaglia (Florence: La Nuova Italia, 1991), 134.

61. For a more detailed discussion see Stephen Gundle, "Il PCI e la campagna contro Hollywood, 1948–58," in *Hollywood in Europa: industria, politica, pubblico del cinema 1945–1960,* ed. David W. Ellwood and Gian Piero Brunetta (Florence: Ponte alle Grazie, 1991), 113–132.

62. Gundle, "Cultura di massa e modernizzazione," 237–44.

63. See Luigi Longo, "*Vie Nuove:* 4 anni di lotte e di successi," *Vie Nuove,* September 24. 1950; and the announcements about rising print runs published in the editions of April 15, 1951, February 3, 1952, and September 12, 1954.

64. Gundle, "Cultura di massa e modernizzazione," 251–56.

65. On the persistence of political subcultures, see Renato Mannheimer and Giacomo Sani, "Electoral Trends and Political Subcultures," in *Italian Politics,* vol. 1, ed. Robert Leonardi and Raffaella Y. Nanetti (London: Pinter, 1986).

Conclusion

1. Silvio Lanaro, *Storia della Repubblica italiana. Dalla fine della guerra agli anni novanta* (Venice: Marsilio, 1992), 48.

2. Giorgio Galli, "Masse e politica: 1920–1960," in Giorgio Rumi, ed., *Vita civile degli italiani. Società, economia, cultura materiale,* vol. 6: *Trasformazioni economiche, mutamenti sociali e nuovi miti collettivi 1920–1960* (Milan: Electa, 1991), 198.

3. "Le bocche spalancate non fanno la storia," in Vitaliano Brancati, *Il borghese e l'immensità. Scritti 1930–1954* (Milan: Bompiani, 1973), 177 (originally published in *Il Tempo,* December 19, 1946).

4. Lanaro, *Storia della Repubblica italiana,* 47.

5. Carl Levy, "From Fascism to 'Post-Fascists': Italian Roads to Modernity" in Richard Bessell, ed., *Fascist Italy and Nazi Germany: Comparisons and Contrasts* (Cambridge, UK: Cambridge University Press, 1996), 179–82.

6. Victoria de Grazia, *The Culture of Consent: Mass Organization of Leisure in Fascist Italy* (Cambridge: Cambridge University Press, 1981), 237–41.

Appendix 1

1. Luisa Passerini and Marcella Filippa, "Memorie di Mirafiori," in *Mirafiori. 1936–1962*, ed. Carlo Olmo (Turin: Allemandi, 1997), 352. For Walter Benjamin's observations see his essay of 1936 "The Storyteller: Reflections on the Works of Nicolai Leskov," in *Illuminations*, ed. Hannah Arendt, trans. Harry Zohn (Glasgow: Fontana/Collins, 1973), 83.

2. Marcella Filippa, *La morte contesa. Cremazione e riti funebri nell'Italia fascista* (Turin: Paravia Scriptorium, 2001), 177–78.

3. Revelli, *Il mondo dei vinti*, xxx.

4. For a detailed history of the debate, particularly in Italy, see Cesare Bermani, ed., *Introduzione alla storia orale*, 2 vols. (Rome: Odradek, 2001).

5. See, e.g., Paul Thompson, *The Edwardians: The Remaking of British Society* (London: Weidenfeld and Nicolson, 1975), 7.

6. Philippe Joutard, *La légende des Camisards: une sensibilité au passé* (Paris: Gallimard, 1977), 293.

7. Ibid., 356.

8. See Philippe Joutard, *Ces voix qui nous viennent du passé* (Paris: Hachette, 1983), 220. See also the two discussions by Luisa Passerini of the use of oral sources at an international level: *Le testimonianze orali*, in *Introduzione alla storia contemporanea*, ed. Giovanni De Luna et al. (Florence: La Nuova Italia, 1984) and *Storia e soggettività. Le fonti orali, la memoria* (Florence: La Nuova Italia, 1988).

9. Luisa Passerini, *Torino operaia e fascismo. Una storia orale* (Rome and Bari: Laterza, 1984), English translation: *Fascism in Popular Memory: The Cultural Experience of the Turin Working Class*, trans. Robert Lumley and Jude Bloomfield (Cambridge, UK: Cambridge University Press, 1987), in particular chaps. 1 and 2.

10. Ascanio Celestini, *Storie di uno scemo di guerra. Roma, 4 giugno 1944* (Turin: Einaudi, 2005).

11. Alessandro Portelli, *L'ordine è già stato eseguito. Roma, le Fosse Ardeatine, la memoria* (Rome: Donzelli, 1999). English translation: *The Order Has Been Carried Out: History, Memory and Meaning of a Nazi Massacre in Rome* (New York: Palgrave Macmillan, 2004).

12. Similar observations have been made by Alessandro Portelli in "L'uccisione di Luigi Trastulli. Terni 17 marzo 1949. La memoria e l'evento," *Segno Critico*, no. 4 (1980); reprinted in Bermani, *Introduzione alla storia orale*, 61–94. English translation in Alessandro Portelli, *The Death of Luigi Trastulli and Other Stories: Form and Meaning in Oral History* (Albany: State University of New York Press, 1991).

BIBLIOGRAPHY

Archival Sources Cited

AAMPAS   American Academy of Motion Picture Arts and Sciences, Beverly Hills, California (Production Code Administration files, Italian Film Export).

ACS   Archivio Centrale dello Stato, Rome (DGSI: Direzione Generale Stampa Italiana; ENAIPE: Ente Nazionale Acquisti Importazioni Pellicole; MAE: Ministero degli Affari Esteri; MCP: Ministero della Cultura Popolare; SPD: Segreteria Particolare del Duce; PCM: Presidenza del Consiglio dei Ministri; Gab.[inetto] 1951–1954).

AE   Archivio Einaudi, Giulio Einaudi editore, Turin.

AFM   Archivio della Fondazione Arnoldo e Alberto Mondadori, Milan (F. Arn.: Fondo Arnoldo Mondadori).

ASD   Archivio Storico Diplomatico, Rome (Serie affari politici 1931–1945, 1946–1950, 1950–1957).

ASG   Archivio Storico Giunti, Florence (Fondo Bemporad).

ASL   Archivio Storico Laterza, in Archivio di Stato di Bari (Registri copia-lettere).

CCM   Camera del Commercio, Milan (Cancelleria delle società commerciali).

HRHRC   Harry Ransom Humanities Research Center, University of Texas at Austin (Papers of David O. Selznick).

NA   National Archives, Washington D.C. (RG = Record Groups 59, 84, 151, 208, 286, 331).

WSHS   Wisconsin State Historical Society, University of Wisconsin, Madison (United Artists Collection, Papers of Walter Wanger, Papers of Kirk Douglas).

b. busta/box
f. fascicolo/folder
s.f. sottofascicolo
sc. scatola

Press Sources

Araldo dello Spettacolo
Cinema
Cinema Illustrazione
Cinespettacolo
Cinestar
Epoca
Famiglia Cristiana
Festival
Hollywood

Novella
Ottobre
Primi Piani
Schermo, Lo
Sorrisi e canzoni
Specchio, Lo
Star
Tempo
Vie Nuove

Untitled or Unsigned Articles
Cinestar, July 3, 1948.
La Domenica del Corriere, November 18, 1945, 3; December 16, 1945, 6.
"'Doves of Peace' compete." *The Reader's Digest International Editions Newsletter*, June 9, 1953, 4.
Famiglia Cristiana. Nozze d'oro di un rotocalco (brochure published by Società San Paolo, Milan, 1981), pages unnumbered.
"I film italiani che sono andati male nel mercato interno." *Cinespettacolo*, March 7–14, 1953, 6.
"I film italiani nel mercato interno." *Cinespettacolo*, February 14, 1953, 5–8.
"Firmamento." *Sorrisi e canzoni*, August 23, 1953, 4.
"Il patrimonio attori." *Cinespettacolo*, January–February 1957, 4–5.
Intermezzo, May 31, 1948, 2.
"Liliana, ragazza italiana." *Epoca* 1, no. 1, October 14, 1950, 13.
"Puritane in pantaloni." *Tempo* 3, series 2, no. 7, 1939, 24.
"Vatican Aiding Coin Thaw." *Hollywood Reporter*, March 9, 1949, 1.

Books and Articles
Abbonamenti alle radiodiffusioni nel 1981, Gli. Rome: Rai Radiotelevisione italiana, 1982.
Abruzzese, Alberto. "Fotoromanzo." In *Letteratura italiana. Storia e geografia*.Vol. 3 of *L'età contemporanea*, ed. Alberto Asor Rosa, 1269–87. Turin: Einaudi, 1989.
Agnelli, Susanna. *Vestivamo alla marinara*. Milan: Mondadori, 1975.
Agnese, Giovanni. *Con quale mezzo vedo possibile il risanamento dei costumi e il progresso morale di una moderna nazione. Proposta di un codice dei costumi*. Turin: Botta, 1929.
Ajello, Nello. *Intellettuali e PCI 1944–1958*. Rome and Bari: Laterza, 1979.
———. *Lezioni di giornalismo*. Milan: Garzanti, 1985.
Alberoni, Francesco. *L'elite senza potere*. Bologna: Il Mulino, 1963.
Amendola, Eva Paola, and Marcella Ferrara. *È la festa: quarant'anni con L'Unità*. Rome: Editori Riuniti, 1984.
Amerio, Pier Giorgio. "Ty, a Torino." *Hollywood*, November 8, 1947, 5.
Anderson, Benedict. *Imagined Communities: Reflections on the Origin and Spread of Nationalism*. London: Verso, 1983.
Anfossi, Anna, Magda Talamo, and Francesco Indovina. *Ragusa. Comunità in transizione. Saggio sociologico*. Turin: Taylor, 1959.
Angeli, Otello. "Strutture produttive, contratti, organizzazione." In *La città del cinema: produzione e lavoro nel cinema italiano 1930–1970*, ed. Massimiliano Fasoli et al. Rome: Napoleone, 1979.
Aquarone, Alberto. *L'organizzazione dello Stato totalitario*. Turin: Einaudi, 1965.
Argentieri, Mino. *La censura nel cinema italiano*. Rome: Editori Riuniti. 1974.
———. *L'asse cinematografico Roma-Berlino*. Naples: Sapere, 1986.

——. "La Titanus e il mercato." In *Dietro lo schermo: ragionamenti sui modi di produzione cinematografici in Italia*, ed. Vito Zagarrio, 15–34. Venice: Marsilio, 1988.

Aristarco, Guido. *Miti e realtà nel cinema italiano*. Milan: Il Saggiatore, 1961.

Asor Rosa, Alberto. "Il giornalista: appunti sulla fisiologia di un mestiere difficile." In *Storia d'Italia. Annali, 4, Intellettuali e potere*, ed. Corrado Vivanti, 1227–57. Turin: Einaudi, 1981.

Automobili in cifre 1956. Turin: Associazione Nazionale fra Industrie Automobilistiche e Affini, 1956.

Avorio, Gino. "Schedario segreto." *Star* 1, no. 5 (September 9, 1944): 10.

Bafile, Paolo. "Il 'dumping' cinematografico in Italia." In *Sull'industria cinematografica italiana*, ed. Enrico Magrelli. Venice: Marsilio, 1986.

Baldazzi, Gianfranco. *La canzone italiana del Novecento*. Rome: Newton Compton, 1989.

Baldi, Giulia. "L'industria fonografica in Italia fino al 1970. Mercato e società." Tesi di Laurea, Università degli Studi di Roma "La Sapienza," Facoltà di Lettere e Filosofia, 2000.

Balio, Tino. *United Artists: The Company Built by the Stars*. Madison: University of Wisconsin Press, 1976.

Baran, Paul A., and E. J. Hobsbawm. "The Stages of Economic Growth," *Kyklos: International Review for Social Sciences* 14, no. 2 (1961): 234–42.

Barbagli, Marzio. *Sotto lo stesso tetto. Mutamenti della famiglia in Italia dal XV al XX secolo*. Bologna: Il Mulino, 1984.

Barbanti, Marco. "La classe dirigente cattolica e la 'battaglia per la moralità' 1948–1960. Appunti sul 'regime clericale.'" *Italia Contemporanea*, no. 189 (1992): 606–34.

Barone, Giulia, and Armando Petrucci. *Primo: non leggere. Biblioteche e pubblica lettura in Italia dal 1861 ai nostri giorni*. Milan: Mazzotta. 1976.

Becciu, Leonardo. *Il fumetto in Italia*. Florence: Sansoni, 1971.

Benjamin, Walter. "The Storyteller: Reflections on the Works of Nicolai Leskov" (1936). In *Illuminations*, ed. Hannah Arendt, trans. Harry Zohn, 83–109. Glasgow: Fontana, 1973.

——. "The Work of Art in the Age of Mechanical Reproduction" (1936). In *Illuminations*, ed. Hannah Arendt, trans. Harry Zohn, 219–53. Glasgow: Fontana, 1973.

Bermani, Cesare, ed. *Introduzione alla storia orale*. 2 vols. Rome: Odradek, 2001.

Bernays, Edward, ed. *The Engineering of Consent*. Norman: University of Oklahoma Press, 1955.

Bianda, Renato, et al. *Atleti in camicia nera. Lo sport nell'Italia di Mussolini*. Rome: Volpe, 1983.

Biondi, Dino. *La fabbrica del Duce*. Florence: Valecchi, 1973.

Bizzarri, Libero. "L'economia cinematografica." In *La città del cinema: produzione e lavoro nel cinema italiano 1930–1970*, ed. Massimiliano Fasoli et al. Rome: Napoleone, 1979.

Bizzarri, Libero, and Libero Solaroli. *L'industria cinematografica italiana*. Florence: Parenti, 1958.

Bompiani, Valentini. *Caro Bompiani. Lettere con l'editore*, ed. Gabriella D'Ina and Giuseppe Zaccaria. Milan: Bompiani, 1988.

Bompiani, Valentino, and Cesare Zavattini. *Cinquant'anni e più. . . . Lettere 1933–1989*, ed. Valentina Fortichiari. Milan: Bompiani, 1995.

Bondanella, Peter. "The Making of *Roma città aperta:* The Legacy of Fascism and the Birth of Neorealism." In *Roberto Rossellini's "Rome Open City,"* ed. Sidney Gottlieb, 43–66. New York: Cambridge University Press, 2004.

Bonsaver, Guido. *Elio Vittorini: The Writer and the Written*. Leeds: Northern Universities Press, 2000.

Borgna, Gianni. *Storia della canzone italiana*. Milan: Mondadori, 1992.

Bort. "Alida Valli trova un personaggio." *Film*, April 19, 1941, 5.

Brancati, Vitaliano. *Il borghese e l'immensità. Scritti 1930–1954*. Milan: Bompiani, 1973.

———. *La governante, con la nota dell'autore "Ritorno alla censura."* Milan: Bompiani, 1974. (*Ritorno alla censura* was originally published in a separate volume with the text of *La governante* in an appendix, Bari: Laterza, 1952.)

Brin, Irene. "La moda nel cinema" (1943). In *La moda e il costume nel film*, ed. Mario Verdone. Rome: Bianco e Nero, 1950.

Brunetta, Gian Piero. *Cinema italiano tra le due guerre. Fascismo e politica cinematografica*. Milan: Mursia 1975.

———. *Storia del cinema italiano, 1895–1945*. Rome: Editori Riuniti, 1979.

———. *Storia del cinema italiano dal 1945 agli anni ottanta*. Rome: Editori Riuniti, 1982.

———. *Buio in sala. Cent'anni di passioni dello spettatore cinematografico*. Venice: Marsilio, 1989.

———. "Il sogno a stelle e strisce di Mussolini." In *L'estetica della politica in Europa e America negli anni trenta*, ed. Maurizio Vaudagna, 161–76. Bari: Laterza, 1989.

———. *Cent'anni di cinema italiano*. Rome and Bari: Laterza, 1991.

———. "La lunga marcia del cinema americano in Italia tra fascismo e guerra fredda." In *Hollywood in Europa: industria, politica, pubblico del cinema 1945–1960*, ed. David W. Ellwood and Gian Piero Brunetta, 75–87. Florence: Ponte alle Grazie, 1991.

Buckley, Reka. "National Body: Gina Lollobrigida and the Cult of the Star in the 1950s." *Historical Journal of Film, Radio and Television* 20, no. 4 (2000): 527–47.

———. "The Female Film Star In Postwar Italy, 1948–1960." Ph.D. diss., University of London, 2002.

Calvino, Italo. "Autobiografia di uno spettatore." Preface to Federico Fellini, *Quattro film*. Turin: Einaudi, 1974.

Campo, Chiara. "L'America in salotto: il *Reader's Digest* in Italia." In *Nemici per la pelle. Sogno americano e mito sovietico nell'Italia contemporanea*, ed. Pier Paolo D'Attorre, 417–28. Milan: Franco Angeli, 1991.

Cannistraro, Philip V. *La fabbrica del consenso. Fascismo e mass media*. Rome and Bari: Laterza, 1975.

Caracciolo, Nicola. *Gli ebrei e l'Italia durante la guerra, 1940–45*. Rome: Bonacci, 1986.

Carfagna, Elisabetta, and Pierfrancesco Attanasio. "Fonti statistiche per la storia dell'editoria libraria in Italia." In *Fonti e studi di storia dell'editoria*, ed. Gianfranco Tortorelli. Edizioni Baiesi, n.p., n.d., 137–62.

Carlotti, Anna Lisa. "Editori e giornali a Milano: continuità e cambiamento." In *Libri giornali e riviste a Milano. Storia delle innovazioni nell'editoria milanese dall'ottocento ad oggi*, ed. Fausto Colombo. Milan: AIM-Abitare Segesta, 1998.

Casini, Gherardo. "Il libro e la cultura italiana." *Il Libro Italiano* II, no. 2 (1938): 51–54.

Castello, Giulio Cesare. *Il divismo. Mitologia del cinema*. Turin: ERI, 1957.

Castronovo, Valerio. *Il Piemonte*. Turin: Einaudi, 1977. Part of the series *Storia delle Regioni italiane dall'Unità a oggi*. Turin: Einaudi, 1977.

Casula, Carlo Felice. "I comunisti e la comunicazione." In *Il 1948 in Italia. La storia e i film*, ed. Nicola Tranfaglia, 129–36. Florence: La Nuova Italia, 1991.

Cavaglion, Alberto and Gian Paolo Romagnani. *Le interdizioni del duce. Le leggi razziali in Italia*. Turin: Claudiana, 2002.

Celestini, Ascanio. *Storie di uno scemo di guerra. Roma, 4 giugno 1944*. Turin: Einaudi, 2005.

Cerquiglini, O. "Fiori dei campi, fiori della razza." *La Domenica del Corriere*, September 3, 1939, 8–9.

Certeau, Michel de. *L'invention du quotidien*. 2 vols. Vol. 1, *Arts de faire*. Paris: Gallimard, 1990.

Cesari, Maurizio. *La censura nel periodo fascista*. Naples: Liguori, 1977.

———. *La censura in Italia oggi (1944–1980)*. Naples: Liguori, 1982.

Ceserani, Gian Paolo. *Storia della pubblicità in Italia*. Rome and Bari: Laterza, 1988.

Chiarenza, Franco. *Il cavallo morente. Storia della RAI*. 2d ed., enlarged (1st ed., 1978). Milan: Franco Angeli, 2002.

Ciarlantini, Franco. *Vicende di libri e di autori*. Milan: Ceschina, 1931.

Cirillo, Silvana. "Cronologia." In Cesare Zavattini, *Opere. 1931–1986*, ed. Silvana Cirillo. Milan: Bompiani, 1991.

Colarizi, Simona. *L'opinione degli italiani sotto il regime, 1929–1943*. Rome and Bari: Laterza, 1991.

Colombo, Emilio. "Ciclismo." In *Enciclopedia italiana di scienze, lettere ed arti*. Vol. 10. Rome: Istituto Giovanni Treccani, 1931, 208–11.

Cordelli, Franco. *L'Italia di mattina*. Milan: Leonardo, 1990.

Corsi, Barbara. *Con qualche dollaro in più. Storia economica del cinema italiano*. Rome: Editori Riuniti, 2001.

Crocenzi, Luigi. "Italia senza tempo." *Il Politecnico*, no. 28 (April 6, 1946): 2.

———. "Occhio su Milano." *Il Politecnico*, no. 29 (May 1, 1946): 13–15.

———. "Andiamo in processione." *Il Politecnico*, no. 35 (January–March 1947): 54–59.

Crovi, Raffaele. *Vittorini. Una biografia critica*. Venice: Marsilio, 1998.

Dall'Asta, Monica. *Le cinéma musclé*. Lausanne: Editions Yellow Now, 1992.

Dau Novelli, Cecilia. *Famiglia e modernizzazione in Italia tra le due guerre*. Rome: Studium, 1994.

David, Elizabeth. *Italian Food*. Harmondsworth: Penguin, 1963. First published 1954.

De Berti, Raffaele. *Dallo schermo alla carta. Romanzi, fotoromanzi, rotocalchi cinematografici: il film e i suoi paratesti*. Milan: Vita e Pensiero, 2000.

de Grazia, Victoria. *The Culture of Consent: Mass Organization of Leisure in Fascist Italy*. Cambridge, UK: Cambridge University Press, 1981.

———. *How Fascism Ruled Women: Italy 1922–1945*. Berkeley and Los Angeles: University of California Press, 1992.

de Grazia, Victoria. *Le donne del regime fascista*. Venice: Marsilio, 1993.

———. "Nationalizing Women: The Competition between Fascist and Commercial Cultural Models in Mussolini's Italy." In *The Sex of Things: Gender and Consumption in Historical Perspective*, ed. Victoria de Grazia, 337–58. Berkeley and Los Angeles: University of California Press, 1996.

De Luigi, Mario. *L'industria discografica in Italia*. Rome: Lato Side, 1982.

De Luna, Giovanni. *Donne in oggetto. L'antifascismo nella società italiana, 1922–1939*. Turin: Bollati Boringhieri, 1995.

De Mauro, Tullio. *Storia linguistica dell'Italia unita*. Bari: Laterza, 1963.

Decleva, Enrico. *Arnoldo Mondadori*. Turin: UTET, 1993.

Della Torre, Giuseppe. *Azione cattolica e fascismo: il conflitto del 1931*. Rome: Editrice A.V.E., 1945.

Di Nolfo, Ennio. "La diplomazia del cinema americano in Europa nel secondo dopoguerra." In *Hollywood in Europa: industria, politica, pubblico del cinema 1945–1960*, ed. David W. Ellwood and Gian Piero Brunetta, 29–39. Florence: Ponte alle Grazie, 1991.

Dompé, Giovanna. "Moda." *Enciclopedia italiana di scienze, lettere ed arti*. Vol. 23. Rome: Istituto della Enciclopedia Italiana, 1934. 503–509.

Douglas, Mary, and Baron Isherwood. *The World of Goods: Towards an Anthropology of Consumption*. London: Allen Lane, 1979.

E. O. "Le grandi città e i grandi divi." *Cinespettacolo*, March 15–30, 1956, 7.

Einaudi, Giulio. "Esperienze di un editore giovane." *Il Libro Italiano* 3, no. 3 (1939): 170–72.

Ellwood, David W. *Rebuilding Europe: Western Europe, American and Postwar Reconstruction*. London: Longman, 1992.

Fabre, Giorgio. *L'elenco. Censura fascista, editoria e autori ebrei*. Turin: Zamorani, 1998.

Facchinetti, Paolo. *La stampa sportiva in Italia*. Bologna: Alfa, 1966.

Faeti, Antonio. *Boccasile*. Milan: Longanesi, 1981.

Falasca-Zamponi, Simonetta. *Fascist Spectacle: The Aesthetics of Power in Mussolini's Italy*. Berkeley and Los Angeles: University of California Press, 1997.

Faldini, Franca, and Goffredo Fofi, eds. *Storia del cinema italiano raccontato dai suoi protagonisti, 1935–59*. Milan: Mondadori, 1979.

Farassino, Alberto. "Il costo dei panni sporchi: note sul 'modo di produzione' neorealista." In *Dietro lo schermo: ragionamenti sui modi di produzione cinematografici in Italia*, ed. Vito Zagarrio. Venice: Marsilio, 1988.

Feltrinelli, Carlo. *Senior Service*. Milan: Feltrinelli, 1999.

Ferraù, Alessandro. "Lettere d'amore a Roberto Villa." *Film*, February 27, 1941.

Filippa, Marcella. "Fred Buscaglione: un mito degli anni Cinquanta." *Il Piemonte vivo* 2 (1990): 44–51.

———. *La morte contesa. Cremazione e riti funebri nell'Italia fascista*. Turin: Paravia Scriptorium, 2001.

Filippucci, Paola. "Landscape, Locality and Nation: The case of Bassano." *Paragraph* 20, no. 1 (1997): 42–58.

Fiorentino, Fiorenza. *La Roma di Charles Poletti (giugno 1944–aprile 1945)*. Rome: Bonacci, 1986.

Fofi, Goffredo. "Cinema 'basso' e cinema 'alto'" (1978). In *I limiti della scena. Spettacolo e pubblico nell'Italia contemporanea. 1945–1991*. Milan: Linea d'Ombra Edizioni, 1992.

———. "Storia del teatro minore" (1980). In *I limiti della scena. Spettacolo e pubblico nell'Italia contemporanea. 1945–1991*. Milan: Linea d'Ombra·Edizioni, 1992.

Forcella, Enzo. "Politica e immagine." In *Almanacco letterario Bompiani 1963*, ed. Sergio Morandi. Milan: Bompiani, 1962.

Forgacs, David. *Italian Culture in the Industrial Era, 1880–1980: Cultural Industries, Politics and the Public*. Manchester and New York: Manchester University Press, 1990.

———. "Americanization: The Italian Case, 1938–1954." In *Americanization and the Transformation of World Cultures*, ed. P. H. Melling and D. J. Roper, 81–96. London: Edward Mellen, 1996.

———. "Sex in the Cinema: Regulation and Transgression in Italian Films, 1930–1943." In *Re-viewing Fascism: Italian Cinema 1922–1943*, ed. Jacqueline Reich and Piero Garofalo, 141–71. Bloomington: Indiana University Press, 2002.

Fossati, Franco. "Disney Made in Italy." *IF*, 1–2 (1982): 45–46.

———. *Topolino: Storia del topo più famoso del mondo*. Milan: Gammalibri, 1986.

Foucault, Michel. *Histoire de la sexualité*. Vol. 2: *L'usage des plaisirs*. Paris: Gallimard, 1984.

———. *Histoire de la sexualité*. Vol. 3: *Le Souci de soi*. Paris: Gallimard, 1984.

———. *L'Herméneutique du sujet*. Paris: Gallimard, 2001.

Frabotta, Maria Adelaide. "Government Propaganda: Official Newsreels and Documentaries in the 1950s." In *The Art of Persuasion: Political Communication in Italy from 1945 to the 1990s*, ed. Luciano Cheles and Lucio Sponza. Manchester: Manchester University Press, 2001.

Freddi, Luigi. *Il cinema.* 2 vols. Rome: L'Arnia, 1949.

Galli, Giorgio. "Masse e politica: 1920–1960." In *Vita civile degli italiani. Società, èconomia, cultura materiale,* ed. Giorgio Rumi, 190–203. Vol. 6, *Trasformazioni economiche, mutamenti sociali e nuovi miti collettivi 1920–1960.* Milan: Electa, 1991.

Gentile, Emilio. "Fascism as Political Religion." *Journal of Contemporary History* 25 (1990): 229–51.

——. *Il culto del Littorio: la via italiana al totalitarismo. Il Partito e lo Stato nel regime fascista.* Rome: La Nuova Italia Scientifica, 1995.

——. *The Sacralization of Politics in Fascist Italy.* Trans. Keith Botsford. Cambridge, Mass.: Harvard University Press, 1996.

——. *La grande Italia. Ascesa e declino del mito della nazione nel ventesimo secolo.* Milan: Mondadori, 1997.

Gigli, Beniamino. *Memorie.* Milan: Mondadori, 1957.

Gili, Jean A. *Stato fascista e cinematografia. Repressione e promozione.* Rome: Bulzoni, 1981.

Ginsborg, Paul. *A History of Contemporary Italy: Society and Politics, 1943–88.* Harmondsworth: Penguin, 1990.

Giovagnoli, Agostino. "Chiesa, assistenza e società a Roma tra il 1943 e il 1945." In *L'altro dopoguerra. Roma e il Sud 1943–1945,* ed. Nicola Gallerano. Milan: Franco Angeli, 1985.

Golini, Antonio. *Distribuzione della popolazione, migrazioni interne e urbanizzazione in Italia.* Rome: Università di Roma, Istituto di Demografia, 1974.

Gori, Leonardo. "I Disney di casa nostra." *LG Argomenti* 23, nos.1–2 (1987): 53–54.

Gozzini, Mario, ed. *Giovanni Papini–Attilio Vallecchi, Carteggio. 1914–1941.* Florence: Vallecchi, 1984.

Gramsci, Antonio. *Quaderni del carcere,* ed. Valentino Gerratana. 4 vols. Turin: Einaudi, 1975.

Gribaudi, Maurizio. *Mondo operaio e mito operaio. Spazi e percorsi sociali a Torino nel primo Novecento.* Turin: Einaudi, 1987.

Grignaffini, Giovanna. "Female Identity and Italian Cinema of the 1950s." In *Offscreen: Women and Film in Italy,* ed. Giuliana Bruno and Maria Nadotti. London: Routledge, 1988.

Gronow, Pekka, and Ilpo Saunio. *An International History of the Recording Industry.* London: Cassell, 1998.

Guback, Thomas H. *The International Film Industry: Western Europe and America since 1945.* Bloomington: Indiana University Press, 1969.

Gunder Frank, André. *Sociology of Development and Underdevelopment of Sociology.* London: Pluto, 1971.

Gundle, Stephen. "Cultura di massa e modernizzazione: *Vie Nuove* e *Famiglia Cristiana* dalla guerra fredda alla società dei consumi." In *Nemici per la pelle. Sogno americano e mito sovietico nell'Italia contemporanea,* ed. Pier Paolo D'Attorre, 235–68. Milan: Franco Angeli, 1991.

——. "Il PCI e la campagna contro Hollywood, 1948–58." In *Hollywood in Europa: industria, politica, pubblico del cinema 1945–1960,* ed. David W. Ellwood and Gian Piero Brunetta, 113–32. Florence: Ponte alle Grazie, 1991.

——. *Between Hollywood and Moscow: The Italian Communists and the Challenge of Mass Culture, 1943–1991.* Durham, N.C.: Duke University Press, 2000.

——. "Memory and Identity: Popular Culture in Postwar Italy." In *Italy Since 1945,* ed. Patrick McCarthy. Oxford: Oxford University Press, 2000.

——. "La 'religione civile' della resistenza: cultura di massa e identità politica nell'Italia del dopoguerra." In *L'immagine della resistenza nell'Europa del dopoguerra,* ed.

Luisa Cigognetti, Lorenza Servetti, and Pierre Sorlin. Bologna: Il Nove, 1996. Modified English version: "The 'Civic Religion' of the Resistance in Postwar Italy." *Modern Italy* 5 (2000), no. 2: 113–32.

———. "Film Stars and Society in Fascist Italy." In *Reviewing Fascism: Italian Cinema, 1922–1943*, ed. Jacqueline Reich and Piero Garofalo, 315–39. Bloomington and Indianapolis: Indiana University Press, 2002.

———. "Divismo." In *Dizionario del fascismo*, ed. Victoria de Grazia and Sergio Luzzatto. Vol. 1, 439–42. Turin: Einaudi, 2003.

Gundle, Stephen, and Clino T. Castelli. *The Glamour System*. London: Palgrave Macmillan, 2006.

Habermas, Jürgen. *The Structural Transformation of the Public Sphere*. Trans. Thomas Burger and Frederick Lawrence. Cambridge, UK: Polity Press, 1989.

Hay, James. *Popular Film Culture in Fascist Italy: The Passing of the Rex*. Bloomington and Indianapolis: Indiana University Press, 1987.

Herman, Edward S., and Noam Chomsky. *Manufacturing Consent: The Political Economy of the Mass Media*. New York: Pantheon, 1988.

Higham, Charles. *Merchant of Dreams: Louis B. Mayer and the Secret Hollywood*. London: Pan, 1994. First published 1993.

Iaccio, Pasquale. *La scena negata. Il teatro censurato durante la guerra fascista 1940–1943*. Rome: Bulzoni, 1995.

Impiego del tempo libero in Calabria. Indagine statistica campionaria. Rome: SIAE, 1960.

Ingrao, Pietro. "Le feste dell'Unità." *Rinascita* 5, nos. 9–10 (1948).

Insolera, Italo. *Roma moderna. Un secolo di storia urbanistica*. Turin: Einaudi, 1972.

Isidori Frasca, Rosella. "L'educazione fisica e sportiva e la 'preparazione materna.'" In *La corporazione delle donne. Ricerche e studi sui modelli femminili nel ventennio*, ed. Marina Addis Saba. Florence: Vallecchi, 1988.

Isnenghi, Mario. "Al teatro dell'Italia nuova. Fascismo e cultura di massa." In Mino Argentieri et al., *Fascismo e antifascismo negli anni della Repubblica, Problemi del socialismo*. Vol. 7. Milan: Franco Angeli, 1986.

———. *L'Italia in piazza. I luoghi della vita pubblica dal 1848 ai giorni nostri*, 2d ed. Bologna: Il Mulino, 2004.

Isola, Gianni. *Abbassa la tua radio, per favore . . . Storia dell'ascolto radiofonico nell'Italia fascista*. Florence: La Nuova Italia, 1990.

———. *Cari amici vicini e lontani. Storia dell'ascolto radiofonico nel primo decennio repubblicano*. Florence: La Nuova Italia, 1995.

Jacomuzzi, Stefano. "Gli sport." In *Storia d'Italia*. Vol. 5, tomo 1, *documenti*, 911–35. Turin: Einaudi, 1973.

Jarvie, Ian. *Hollywood's Overseas Campaign: The North Atlantic Movie Trade*. Cambridge, UK: Cambridge University Press, 1992.

Joutard, Philippe. *La légende des Camisards: une sensibilité au passé*. Paris: Gallimard, 1977.

———. *Ces voix qui nous viennent du passé*. Paris: Hachette, 1983.

Kezich, Tullio, and Alessandra Levatesi. *Dino. De Laurentiis, la vita e i film*. Milan: Feltrinelli, 2001.

Koepnick, Lutz P. *Walter Benjamin and the Aesthetics of Power*. Lincoln: University of Nebraska Press, 1999.

Lanaro, Silvio. "Il casco di sughero." *Belfagor* 32, no. 2 (1977): 219–28.

———. *Storia della Repubblica italiana. Dalla fine della guerra agli anni novanta*. Venice: Marsilio, 1992.

Laterza, Vito. *Quale editore. Note di lavoro*. Rome and Bari: Laterza, 2002.

I lettori di otto periodici italiani: Epoca, Grazia, Arianna, Confidenza, Bolero Film, Storia Illustrata, Il Giallo Mondadori, Topolin. Studio Statistico sulle caratteristiche demografiche, economiche, sociali e culturali. Rome: Istituto Doxa, 1963.

Levy, Carl. "From Fascism to 'Post-Fascists': Italian Roads to Modernity." In *Fascist Italy and Nazi Germany: Comparisons and Contrasts,* ed. Richard Bessell. Cambridge, UK: Cambridge University Press, 1996.

Lippmann, Walter. *Public Opinion.* New York: Harcourt, Brace, 1922.

Logan, Oliver. "Italian Identity: Catholic Responses to Secularist Definitions, c.1910–1948." *Modern Italy* 2, nos. 1/2 (1997): 52–71.

Lombrassa, Domenico. "La difesa del ragazzo italiano," *Il Libro Italiano* 2, no. 11 (1938): 459–62.

Luigi Longo, " *Vie Nuove:* 4 anni di lotte e di successi." *Vie Nuove,* September 24, 1950.

Lukes, Steven. "Political Ritual and Social Integration." *Sociology* 9, no. 2 (1975): 298–301.

Luzzatto Fegiz, Pierpaolo. *Il volto sconosciuto dell'Italia. Dieci anni di sondaggi Doxa.* Milan: Giuffrè, 1956.

———. "Political Opinion Polling in Italy." In *Political Opinion Polling: An International Review,* ed. Robert M. Worcester, 133–51. Basingstoke and London: Macmillan, 1983.

Lyttelton, Adrian. *The Seizure of Power: Fascism in Italy 1919–1929.* 2d ed. London: Weidenfeld and Nicolson, 1987.

Mafai, Miriam. *Pane nero. Donne e vita quotidiana nella Seconda guerra mondiale.* Milan: Mondadori, 1987.

Malatesta, Maria. "Campo dei media, campo di potere." *Italia Contemporanea,* nos. 146–47 (1982): 15–33.

Mangoni, Luisa. *Pensare i libri. La casa editrice Einaudi dagli anni trenta agli anni sessanta.* Turin: Bollati Boringhieri, 1999.

Mannheimer, Renato, and Giacomo Sani. "Electoral Trends and Political Subcultures." In *Italian Politics,* ed. Robert Leonardi and Raffaella Y. Nanetti. Vol. 1. London: Pinter, 1986.

Marazziti, Mario. "Cultura di massa e valori cattolici: il modello di 'Famiglia Cristiana.' " In *Pio XII,* ed. Angelo Lombardi. Rome and Bari: Laterza, 1984.

Marinetti, Filippo Tommaso. "The Foundation and Manifesto of Futurism." In *F. T. Marinetti: Critical Writings,* ed. Günter Berghaus, trans. Doug Thompson. New ed. New York: Farrar, Straus and Giroux, 2006, 11–17. Originally published in *Poesia* 5, nos. 1–2 (February–March 1909).

Marchesini, Daniele. *L'Italia del Giro d'Italia.* Bologna: Il Mulino, 1996.

Marinucci, Viniccio. "Cinema proibito." *Star,* August 1944, page unnumbered.

Marsili, Marzia. "De Gasperi and Togliatti: Political Leadership and Personality Cults in Postwar Italy." *Modern Italy* 3, no. 2 (1998): 249–61.

Masi, Stefano and Enrico Lancia. *Stelle d'Italia. Piccole e grandi dive del cinema italiano dal 1945 al 1968.* Rome: Gremese, 1989.

———. *Stelle d'Italia. Piccole e grandi dive del cinema italiano dal 1930 al 1945.* Rome: Gremese, 1994.

McCann, Graham. *Rebel Males: Clift, Brando and Dean.* Cambridge, UK: Polity, 1993.

Meyrowitz, Joshua. *No Sense of Place: The Impact of Electronic Media on Social Behaviour.* New York: Oxford University Press, 1985.

Miccoli, Giovanni. "La Chiesa e il fascismo." In *Introduzione alla storia del movimento cattolico,* ed. Bartolo Gariglio and Ettore Passerin d'Entrèves. Bologna: Il Mulino, 1979. Originally published in *Fascismo e società italiana,* ed. Guido Quazza, 183–208. Turin: Einaudi, 1973.

Miceli, Riccardo. "Razzismo del libro." *Il Libro Italiano* 2, no. 9 (1938): 380–81.

Moggi Rebulla, Patrizia, and Mauro Zerbini. *Catalogo storico Arnoldo Mondadori Editore, 1912–1983.* Vol. 5, *La Cronologia.* Milan: Fondazione Arnoldo e Alberto Mondadori, 1985.

Mondadori, Arnoldo. "Il libro italiano all'estero." *Il Libro Italiano* 2, no. 5 (1938): 239–45.

———. *Lettere di una vita, 1922–1975,* ed. Gian Carlo Ferretti. Milan: Mondadori, 1996.

Mondadori, Mimma. *Una tipografia in paradiso.* Milan: Mondadori, 1985.

Monteleone, Franco. *La radio italiana nel periodo fascista. Studio e documenti: 1922–1945.* Venice: Marsilio, 1976.

———. *Storia della radio e della televisione in Italia. Società, politica, strategie, programmi 1922–1992.* Venice: Marsilio, 1992.

Monticone, Alberto. *Il fascismo al microfono.* Rome: Studium, 1978.

Murialdi, Paolo. *Storia del giornalismo italiano.* Bologna: Il Mulino, 1996.

Natale, Anna Lucia. "Cultura di massa e fascismo. Il referendum radiofonico 1940." In *Problemi dell'informazione* 6, no. 2 (1981): 243–67.

———. *Gli anni della radio. 1924–1954. Contributo ad una storia sociale dei media in Italia.* Naples: Liguori, 1990.

Neri Serneri, Simone. "A Past to Throw Away? Politics and History in the Italian Resistance." *Contemporary European History* 4, no. 3 (1995): 367–81.

Occhipinti, Maria. *Una donna di Ragusa.* Palermo: Sellerio, 1993. Originally published Florence: Landi, 1957; republished Milan: Feltrinelli, 1976.

Ortese, Anna Maria. "Giro d'Italia." In *La lente scura. Scritti di viaggio.* Milan: Marcos y Marcos, 1991, 213. Originally published as "Una scrittrice al Giro d'Italia," *L'Europeo,* May 29–June 12, 1955.

Ortoleva, Peppino. "Linguaggi culturali via etere." In *Fare gli italiani. Scuola e cultura nell'Italia contemporanea,* ed. Simonetta Soldani and Gabriele Turi. Vol. 2: *Una società di massa,* 441–88. Bologna: Il Mulino, 1993.

Paccagnini, Ermanno. "Il giornalismo dal 1860 al 1960." In Giuseppe Farinelli et al., *Storia del giornalismo italiano. Dalle origini ai giorni nostri.* Turin: UTET, 1997.

Palazzolo, Maria Iolanda. "L'editoria verso un pubblico di massa." In *Fare gli italiani. Scuola e cultura nell'Italia contemporanea,* ed. Simonetta Soldani and Gabriele Turi. Vol. 2: *Una società di massa,* 287–317. Bologna: Il Mulino, 1993.

Palumbo, Piero. "Una tessera contro la noia." *Lo Specchio,* December 28, 1958, 12.

Panicali, Anna. *Elio Vittorini. La narrativa, la saggistica, le traduzioni, le riviste, l'attività editoriale.* Milan: Mursia, 1994.

Papa, Antonio, ed. *Storia politica della radio in Italia,* 2 vols. Vol. 2, *Dalla guerra d'Etiopia al crollo del fascismo 1935–1943.* Naples: Guida, 1978.

Pasolini, Pier Paolo. *Romanzi e racconti,* ed. Walter Siti and Silvia De Laude. Milan: Mondadori, 1998.

Passerini, Luisa. *Le testimonianze orali.* In *Introduzione alla storia contemporanea,* ed. Giovanni De Luna et al. Florence: La Nuova Italia, 1984.

———. *Torino operaia e fascismo. Una storia orale.* Rome and Bari: Laterza, 1984. English translation: *Fascism in Popular Memory: The Cultural Experience of the Turin Working Class,* trans. Robert Lumley and Jude Bloomfield. Cambridge, UK: Cambridge University Press, 1987.

———. "Oral Memory of Fascism." In *Rethinking Italian Fascism: Capitalism, Populism and Culture,* ed. David Forgacs, 185–96. London: Lawrence and Wishart, 1986.

———. *Storia e soggettività. Le fonti orali, la memoria.* Florence: La Nuova Italia, 1988.

Passerini, Luisa, and Marcella Filippa. "Memorie di Mirafiori." In *Mirafiori. 1936–1962,* ed. Carlo Olmo. Turin: Allemandi, 1997.

Patriarca, Silvana. *Numbers and Nationhood: Writing Statistics in Nineteenth-Century Italy.* Cambridge, UK: Cambridge University Press, 1996.

Patuzzi, Claudia. *Mondadori.* Naples: Liguori, 1978.

Pavese, Cesare. *Saggi letterari. Opere di Cesare Pavese.* Vol. 12. Turin: Einaudi, 1968.

Pavone, Claudio. "La continuità dello Stato. Istituzioni e uomini." In Enzo Piscitelli et al., *Italia 1945–48. Le origini della Repubblica.* Turin: Giappichelli, 1974, 137–89.

——. *Alle origini della Repubblica. Scritti sul fascismo, antifascismo e continuità dello Stato.* Turin: Bollati Boringhieri, 1995.

Pazzaglini, Marcello. *San Lorenzo 1881–1981. Storia urbana di un quartiere popolare a Roma.* Roma: Officina Edizioni, 1984.

Pes, Luca. "Cronologia 1945–1991." In Silvio Lanaro, *Storia della Repubblica italiana. Dalla fine della guerra agli anni novanta,* 457–551. Venice: Marsilio, 1992.

Pezzoli, Orlando. *È storia: Casa del Popolo Nerio Nannetti -Santa Viola, Bologna.* Bologna: PCI Zona Santa Viola, 1981.

Piccioni, Lidia. *San Lorenzo. Un quartiere romano durante il fascismo.* Rome: Edizioni di Storia e Letteratura, 1984.

Piccone Stella, Simonetta, and Annabella Rossi. *La fatica di leggere.* Rome: Editori Riuniti, 1964.

Pio XII. "Nella esaltazione alla gloria dei Santi di Maria Goretti." In *Discorsi e radiomessaggi di Sua Santità Pio XII.* Vol. 12, *Duodecimo anno di Pontificato, 2 marzo 1950–1 marzo 1951.* Rome: Tipografia Poliglotta Vaticana, n.d. [but 1951].

Pius XI. "Encyclical Letter Vigilanti Cura of His Holiness Pius XI, by Divine Providence Pope, to Our Venerable Brethren the Archbishops and Bishops of the United States of America and to the Other Ordinaries Enjoying Peace and Communion with the Apostolic See, On the Motion Pictures, 1936." In *Twelve Encyclicals of Pope Pius XI.* London: Catholic Truth Society, n.d.

Pivato, Stefano. *Sia lodato Bartali: ideologia, cultura e miti dello sport cattolico (1936–1948).* Rome: Edizioni Lavoro, 1985.

——. *La bicicletta e il Sol dell'avvenire. Sport e tempo libero nel socialismo della Belle époque.* Florence: Ponte alle Grazie, 1992.

Pizarroso Quintero, Alejandro. *Stampa, radio e propaganda. Gli alleati in Italia 1943–1946.* Milan: Franco Angeli, 1989.

Pollard, John. *The Vatican and Italian Fascism.* Cambridge, UK: Cambridge University Press, 1986.

Portelli, Alessandro. "L'uccisione di Luigi Trastulli. Terni 17 marzo 1949. La memoria e l'evento." *Segno Critico,* no. 4, 1980. English translation in Alessandro Portelli, *The Death of Luigi Trastulli and Other Stories: Form and Meaning in Oral History.* Albany: State University of New York Press, 1991.

——. *Biografia di una città. Storia e racconto: Terni 1830–1985.* Turin: Einaudi, 1985.

——. *L'ordine è già stato eseguito. Roma, le Fosse Ardeatine, la memoria.* Rome: Donzelli, 1999. English translation: *The Order Has Been Carried Out: History, Memory and Meaning of a Nazi Massacre in Rome.* New York: Palgrave Macmillan, 2004.

Pratolini, Vasco. *Il Quartiere.* Milan: Mondadori, 1979.

Quaglietti, Lorenzo. *Storia economico-politica del cinema italiano 1945–1980.* Rome: Editori Riuniti, 1980.

——. "Cinema americano, vecchio amore." In *Schermi di guerra: cinema italiano 1939–1945,* ed. Mino Argentieri, 307–27. Rome: Bulzoni, 1995.

Quargnolo, Mario. *La censura ieri e oggi nel cinema e nel teatro,* no. 123 of *Il timone.* Milan: Pan, 1982.

Quazza, Guido. *Resistenza e storia d'Italia.* Milan: Feltrinelli, 1976.

———. "Passato e presente nelle interpretazioni della Resistenza." In *Passato e presente della Resistenza*. Rome: Presidenza del Consiglio dei ministri, s.d. (but 1993).

Ragionieri, Ernesto. *La storia politica e sociale.* Tomo 3 of *Storia d'Italia.* Vol. 4: *Dall'Unità a oggi.* Turin: Einaudi, 1976.

Ragone, Giovanni. "Editoria, letteratura e comunicazione." In *Letteratura italiana. Storia e geografia.* ed. Alberto Asor Rosa, 1047–1167. Vol. 3. Turin: Einaudi, 1989.

Renzi, Renzo. "Il Duce, ultimo divo." In *Sperduti nel buio: il cinema muto italiano e il suo tempo (1905–34),* ed. Renzo Renzi. Bologna: Cappelli, 1991.

———. *La bella stagione. Scontri e incontri negli anni d'oro del cinema italiano.* Rome: Bulzoni, 2001.

Renzi, Renzo, ed. *Il cinema dei dittatori: Mussolini, Stalin, Hitler.* Bologna: Grafis, 1992.

Revelli, Nuto. *Il mondo dei vinti. Testimonianze di vita contadina. La pianura. La collina. La montagna. Le Langhe.* Turin: Einaudi, 1977.

Richeri, Giuseppe. "Italian Broadcasting and Fascism 1924–1937." *Media, Culture and Society* 2, no. 1 (January 1980): 49–56.

Rilevazione dei teatri e dei cinematografi esistenti in Italia al 30 giugno 1953. Vol 2: Locali per genere di spettacolo, numero dei posti, prezzo medio ed anno di aperture. Rome: SIAE, 1956.

Rinauro, Sandro. "Il sondaggio d'opinione arriva in Italia. 1936–1946." *Passato e presente* 52, no. 19 (2001): 41–66.

Rossi, Ernesto. *Lo Stato cinematografaro.* Florence: Parenti, 1959.

Rostow, W. W. *The Stages of Economic Growth: A Non-Communist Manifesto.* Cambridge, UK: Cambridge University Press, 1960.

Rusconi, Gian Enrico. *Resistenza e postfascismo.* Bologna: Il Mulino, 1995.

Sainati, Augusto. *La Settimana Incom. Cinegiornali e informazione negli anni '50.* Turin: Lindau, 2001.

Salvati, Mariuccia. *Il regime e gli impiegati. La nazionalizzazione piccolo-borghese nel ventennio fascista.* Rome and Bari: Laterza, 1992.

Samperi, G. V. "Divismo." *Lo Schermo* (1939): 18–20.

Sanfilippo, Mario. *San Lorenzo 1870–1945. Storia e "storie" di un quartiere popolare urbano.* Rome: Edilazio, 2003.

Santi, Piero. *Ombre rosse.* Florence: Vallecchi, 1954.

Santomassimo, Gianpasquale. "Antifascismo popolare." *Italia Contemporanea* 32, no. 140 (1980): 39–69.

Saraceno, Chiara. "La famiglia: i paradossi della costruzione del privato." In *La vita privata. Il Novecento,* ed. Philippe Ariès and Georges Duby, 33–78. Rome and Bari: Laterza, 1988.

Saraceno, Pasquale. *L'Istituto per la ricostruzione industriale.* Vol. 3, *Origini, ordinamenti e attività svolta.* Turin: UTET, 1956.

Sarfatti, Michele. "Gli ebrei negli anni del fascismo: vicende, identità, persecuzione." *Storia d'Italia, Annali.* Vol. 11, *Gli ebrei in Italia,* tomo 2, *Dall'emancipazione a oggi,* ed. Corrado Vivanti, 1623–1764. Turin: Einaudi, 1997.

———. *Gli ebrei nell'Italia fascista. Vicende, identità, persecuzione.* Turin: Einaudi, 2000. Amplification of Sarfatti's 1997 essay, "Gli ebrei negli anni del fascismo."

Savio, Francesco. *Cinecittà anni trenta.* 3 vols. Rome: Bulzoni, 1979.

Schickel, Richard. *The Disney Version: The Life, Times, Art and Commerce of Walt Disney.* 2d ed. London: Pavilion, 1986.

Schnapp, Jeffrey T. "Epic Demonstrations: Fascist Modernity and the 1932 Exhibition of the Fascist Revolution." In *Fascism, Aesthetics and Culture,* ed. Richard J. Golsan. Hanover, N.H.: University Press of New England, 1992.

Scoppola, Pietro. "I cattolici tra fascismo e democrazia." In *Introduzione alla storia del movimento cattolico*, ed. Bartolo Gariglio and Ettore Passerin d'Entrèves. Bologna: Il Mulino, 1979.

———. *25 aprile: Liberazione.* Turin: Einaudi, 1995.

Scott, James C. *Weapons of the Weak: Everyday Forms of Peasant Resistance.* New Haven, Conn.: Yale University Press, 1985.

———. *Domination and the Arts of Resistance: Hidden Transcripts.* New Haven, Conn. and London: Yale University Press, 1990.

Segre, Dan Vittorio. *Memoirs of a Fortunate Jew: An Italian story.* London: Paladin, 1988. Translation of Dan Vittorio Segre. *Storia di un ebreo fortunato.* Milan: Bompiani, 1985.

Sommario di statistiche storiche 1926–1985. Rome: Istat 1986.

Sorlin, Pierre. *Italian National Cinema 1896–1996.* London: Routledge 1996.

Spettacolo in Italia nel 1953, Lo. Rome: SIAE, 1954.

Spinazzola, Vittorio. *Cinema e pubblico. Lo spettacolo filmico in Italia 1945–1965.* 2d ed. Rome: Bulzoni, 1985. First published 1974.

Spinosa, Antonio. *Starace.* Milan: Rizzoli, 1981.

Stacey, Jackie. *Star Gazing: Hollywood Cinema and Female Spectatorship.* London: Routledge, 1993.

Statistica delle pubblicazioni italiane ricevute per diritto di stampa. Firenze, Biblioteca Nazionale Centrale. Appendix to *Bollettino delle pubblicazioni italiane ricevute per diritto di stampa,* various years, 1936–1954.

Stedman Jones, Gareth. "Class Expression versus Social Control? A Critique of Recent Trends in the History of 'Leisure.'" In *Languages of Class: Studies in English Working-Class History 1832–1982.* Cambridge, UK: Cambridge University Press, 1983. Originally in *History Workshop* 4 (autumn 1977).

Swann, Paul. "Il 'Piccolo Dipartimento di Stato': Hollywood e il Dipartimento di Stato nell'Europa del dopoguerra." In *Hollywood in Europa: industria, politica, publico del cinema 1945–1960,* ed. David W. Ellwood and Gian Piero Brunetta, 40–55. Florence: Ponte alle Grazie, 1991.

Sylos Labini, Paolo. *Saggio sulle classi sociali.* Bari: Laterza, 1974.

Tarantini, Domenico. *Processo allo spettacolo.* Milan: Comunità, 1961.

Tarantini, Nadia. *Maria Goretti. Un delitto che parla ancora.* Rome: Editrice l'Unità, 1994.

Thompson, John B. *The Media and Modernity: A Social Theory of the Media.* Cambridge, UK: Polity Press, 1995.

Thompson, Kristin. *Exporting Entertainment: America in the World Film Market, 1907–34.* London: BFI, 1985.

Thomson, David. *Showman: The Life of David O. Selznick.* New York: Knopf, 1992.

Tranfaglia, Nicola. *La prima guerra mondiale e il fascismo.* Vol. 22 of *Storia d'Italia,* ed. Giuseppe Galasso. Turin: UTET, 1995.

Treves, Anna. *Le migrazioni interne nell'Italia fascista. Politica e realtà demografica.* Turin: Einaudi, 1976.

Triani, Giorgio. *Pelle di luna, pelle di sole. Nascita e storia della civiltà balneare 1700–1946.* Venice: Marsilio, 1988.

Turi, Gabriele. *Il fascismo e il consenso degli intellettuali.* Bologna: Il Mulino, 1980.

Valentini, Paola. "Modelli, forme e fenomeni di divismo: il caso Vittorio De Sica." In *Spettatori. Forme di consumo e pubblici del cinema, 1930–1960,* ed. Mariagrazia Fanchi and Elena Mosconi. Rome: Fondazione Scuola Nazionale di Cinema, 2002.

Valeri, S. "Ernesto Bonino." *Il Canzoniere della radio* (October 1, 1941): 3–4.

Venè, Gian Franco. *Mille lire al mese. La vita quotidiana della famiglia nell'Italia fascista.* Milan: Mondadori, 1988.

Ventrone, Angelo. "L'avventura americana della classe dirigente cattolica." In *Nemici per la pelle. Sogno americano e mito sovietico nell'Italia contemporanea,* ed. Pier Paolo D'Attorre, 142–60. Milan: Franco Angeli, 1991.

Vicari, Giambattista. *Editoria e pubblica opinione.* Rome: Cinque Lune, 1957.

Villa, Claudio. *Una vita stupenda.* Milan: Mondadori, 1987.

Vota, Giuseppe. *I sessant'anni del Touring Club Italiano, 1894–1954.* Milan: Touring Club Italiano, 1954.

Wagstaff, Christopher. "Il cinema italiano nel mercato internazionale." In *Identità italiana e identità europea nel cinema italiano dal 1945 al miracolo economico,* ed. Gian Piero Brunetta. Turin: Edizioni Fondazione Agnelli, 1996.

Wanrooij, Bruno P. F. *Storia del pudore. La questione sessuale in Italia, 1860–1940.* Venice: Marsilio, 1990.

Wilson, John. *Politics and Leisure.* London: Unwin Hyman, 1988.

Zamagni, Vera. *The Economic History of Italy 1860–1990: Recovery after Decline.* Oxford: Clarendon Press, 1993.

Zancan, Marina. *Il progetto "Politecnico." Cronaca e struttura di una rivista.* Venice: Marsilio, 1984.

Zangrandi, Ruggero. *Il lungo viaggio attraverso il fascismo: contributo alla storia di una generazione.* Milan: Mursia, 1988. Original version Turin: Einaudi 1947; expanded edition Milan: Feltrinelli 1962.

Zavattini, Cesare. *Uno, cento, mille lettere,* ed. Silvana Cirillo. Milan: Bompiani, 1988.

INDEX

Film and book titles are listed under name of director and author respectively. Italicized page numbers represent illustrations.

David Forgacs is Professor of Italian at University College London. His research interests are in the cultural history of modern Italy and history of the media. He is author of *Rome Open City* and *L'industrializzazione della cultura italiana (1800–2000)* and editor with Robert Lumley of *Italian Cultural Studies: An Introduction* and with Sarah Lutton and Geoffrey Nowell-Smith of *Roberto Rossellini: Magician of the Real.* He is currently Research Professor at the British School at Rome working on a three-year project (2006–2009) on language, space, and power in Italy since Unification.

Stephen Gundle is Professor of Film and Television Studies at Warwick University. His research interests are in modern Italian cultural and political history. He is author of *Between Hollywood and Moscow: The Italian Communists and the Challenge of Mass Culture, 1943–1991* and *Bellissima: Feminine Beauty and the Idea of Italy,* and editor with Simon Parker of *The New Italian Republic* and, with Lucia Rinaldi, of *Assassinations and Murder in Modern Italy.* He is currently directing a large-scale collaborative project on "The Cult of the Duce: Mussolini and the Italians, 1918–2005."